Repossessing Shanland

REPOSSESSING SHANLAND

*Myanmar, Thailand, and a
Nation-State Deferred*

Jane M. Ferguson

THE UNIVERSITY OF WISCONSIN PRESS

The University of Wisconsin Press
728 State Street, Suite 443
Madison, Wisconsin 53706
uwpress.wisc.edu

Gray's Inn House, 127 Clerkenwell Road
London ECIR 5DB, United Kingdom
eurospanbookstore.com

Printed in the United States of America
This book may be available in a digital edition.

Library of Congress Cataloging-in-Publication Data

Names: Ferguson, Jane M. (Jane Martin), author.
Title: Repossessing Shanland : Myanmar, Thailand, and a nation-state
deferred / Jane M. Ferguson.
Other titles: New perspectives in Southeast Asian studies.
Description: Madison, Wisconsin : The University of Wisconsin Press, [2021] |
Series: New perspectives in Southeast Asian studies |
Includes bibliographical references and index.
Identifiers: LCCN 2020047942 | ISBN 9780299333003 (hardcover)
Subjects: LCSH: Shan (Asian people)—History. | Shan (Asian people)—Burma. |
Shan (Asian people)—Thailand.
Classification: LCC DS528.2.S5 F47 2021 | DDC 959.1/00495919—dc23
LC record available at https://lccn.loc.gov/2020047942

ISBN 9780299333041 (paperback)

CONTENTS

ILLUSTRATIONS

ACKNOWLEDGMENTS

This project would never have been possible without generous support, guidance, and challenges from many. The very possibility of my studying Shanland as a nation-state in repossession began in 2000 on a trek to the Shan State Army–South capital of Loi Taileng. I was part of Images Asia, a Chiang Mai–based independent media production company that did news and documentary work about Myanmar and the borderlands for more than two decades. The education I received from this beautifully eclectic group of comrades and extended family is woven into every page of this book.

At Cornell University, Andrew Willford provided excellent guidance, inspiration, and input for the vital transformation of this work from the unreal to the real. He is a true planetary citizen. Jakob Rigi challenged me to work harder on the theoretical underpinnings of this research. Eric Tagliacozzo's enthusiasm for the details of history and old school puzzles is infectious. I thank Thak Chaloemtiarana for challenges and assistance over the years, including the social experience of SEAP, especially for joining on guitar with In Search of Southeast Asia: The Band. Tamara Loos offered sage advice, input, and cherished camaraderie at many important times.

I benefited incalculably from the expertise of members of the scholarly community at Cornell. I thank Benedict Anderson, Anne Blackburn, Sherman Cochran, Abby Cohn, Shelley Feldman, Marty Hatch, Maria-Cristina Garcia, Bernd Lambert, Kaja McGowan, Hirokazu Miyazaki, James Siegel, and David Wyatt. My formal training in Burmese, Shan, and Thai languages—foundational to this research—comes from the excellent instruction of San San Hnin Tun, U Saw Tun, Renu Wichasin, Kyaw Myint, Hseng Harn, and Ngampit Jagacinski. All translations are mine unless otherwise indicated.

A brave band affectionately known as the Kahin Center Cadre provided important intellectual and social sustenance: Chiranan Pitpreecha, Claudine Ang, Likhit Chua, Alex Denes, Daena Funahashi, Tyrell Haberkorn, Erik Harms, Nina Hien, Deborah Homsher, Drew Johnson, Doreen Lee, Christian Lentz, Samson Lim, Monkey Man, Tom Patton, Pong Tantinipankul, Rick Ruth, Erick White, and Benny Widyono.

A number of individuals were vital to this field research across three national horizons: Aung Aung, Aung Tun, Hseng Harn, Hseng Muay, Hseng Noung, Jaeng, Jai Jai, Kong Sai, Kyaw Myint, Lung Sai, Lyndal Barry, Moe Nguen Horm, P'Mya, Sai Aun, Sai Kham, Sai Laeng, Sai Nor, Sai Sai, Shin Pyan, Amporn Jirattikorn, Naoko Kumada, Mon Mon Myat, Min Htin Ko Ko Gyi, Nance Cunningham, and Thin Thin Kyaing.

Various phases of fieldwork, writing, revising, and repeat were supported by a number of organizations. The National Research Council of Thailand assisted me in acquiring a research visa. I was later supported by the Fulbright Thai–United States Educational Foundation (TUSEF). Trips to Myanmar and Shan State were supported by the Social Science Research Council's International Dissertation Research Fellowship (SSRC-IDRF). Foreign Language and Area Studies (FLAS) grants supported my coursework and a summer language course. The Cornell Southeast Asia Program provided assistance for preliminary visits as well as crucial support in the last months of writing the original draft. As part of a Social Science Research Council Book Fellowship, I had the pleasure of attending a two-day workshop with authors and developmental editors. Throughout the event and after, Peter Dimock offered sound advice on authorship alchemy. He is such a cool guy.

After I moved to Canberra, the Australian National University Faculty of Asian Studies, later the School of Culture History and Languages, and colleagues and friends there have offered superb assistance. Thanks to Kent Anderson, Meera Ashar, Sally Brockwell, Nick Cheesman, Robert Cribb, Assi Doron, Ken George, Patrick Guinness, Edna Hutchcroft, Paul Hutchcroft, Robin Jeffrey, Margaret Jolly, Mary Kilcline Cody, Gaik Cheng Khoo, Ann Kumar, Francesca Merlan, Marcus Mietzner, Sango Mahanty, Kirin Narayan, Eva Nisa, Alan Rumsey, Andrew McWilliam, Craig Reynolds, Kathy Robinson, Yuri Takahashi, and Philip Taylor.

Part of the ongoing fieldwork and research for this book was enabled by the generous support of a Sydney University Presidential Fellowship. At Sydney University Anthropology Department, Linda Connor was a delightful mentor and a terrific friend. I gained tremendously from conversations with Luis Angosto Ferrández, Holly High, Philip Hirsch, and Robbie Peters.

For the past six years, I have been an itinerant Affiliated Researcher with the Regional Center for Social Science and Sustainable Development at Chiang Mai University. The fascinating seminars, workshops, and library access have been integral to my ongoing education. Thanks to Chayan Vaddhanaphuti and the CMU team for your kind assistance and welcome.

For six months, I found a wonderful home at Kyoto University Center for Southeast Asian Studies. I am grateful for the friendships and inspiring conversations with Carol Hau, Yoko Hayami, Tatsuki Kataoka, François Molle, Yoshihiro Nakanishi, Ringo, Decha Tangseefa, and Julio Teehankee.

While I have thus far structured my thanks according to institutional association, beyond these, over the years I have had the pleasure of interacting with and learning from an amazing, dynamic group of friends, colleagues, and mentors. Whether working together on panels, papers, or other projects, conversations at meals, chats over coffee or other forms of adult beverage, your ideas have expanded my horizons. Thanks to Jojo Abinales, Barbara Andaya, Maitrii Aung-Thwin, Maureen Aung-Thwin, Michael Aung-Thwin, Katherine Bowie, Erik Braun, John Buchanan, Carolyn Cartier, Wen-Chin Chang, Simon Creak, Ana Dragojlovic, Prasenjit Duara, Nancy Eberhardt, Howard Gelman, Michael Herzfeld, Tammy Ho, Masako Ikeda, Leif Jonsson, Khin Zaw Win, Tasaw Lu, Ken MacLean, Jonathan Padwe, Oona Paredes, Jane Park, Mark Ritchie, Christina Schwenkel, James Scott, Dina Siddiqi, Nikki Tannenbaum, Jean Gelman Taylor, Jayde Roberts, Marvin Sterling, Ardeth Thawnghmung, Michele Thompson, Ric Trimillos, Alicia Turner, Toshiya Ueno, Krisna Uk, Deborah Wong, Chosein Yamahata, and Christine Yano.

Catherine Raymond, my partner in crime and laughter at the Center for Burma Studies, has offered incredible insight and encouragement beyond the sea. In addition to navigating coffee circles and issuing necessary instructions, Mary Callahan is an exemplary scholar and a friend. Thank you for sharing your keen knowledge of Myanmar's history and politics, asking tough questions, and encouraging me to make my work better. Thanks also to Ardeth Maung Thawnghmung for your thorough, useful, and inspiring suggestions for this project and terrific camaraderie beyond.

For a previous incarnation of this manuscript, Trasvin Jittidecharak generously recruited an excellent reviewer whose feedback was extremely useful and constructive. Gwen Walker at the University of Wisconsin Press provided initial guidance and support for this manuscript, and Nathan MacBrien saw the project through to completion, offering useful insight along the way. I am also most grateful for the thorough, constructive, and critical feedback I received from the reviewers for the University of Wisconsin Press. Alfred McCoy, at one of the revision stages, offered generous advice and crucial suggestions about my framing of the book and discussion of content for one of the chapters.

During the preparation of the final revision of this book, Khuensai Jaiyen, director of Pyidaungsu Institute, generously read and commented on the entire manuscript, offering constructive feedback and mercurial insight regarding the political history of Shanland, a topic in which he is an authoritative scholar and advocate. Above and beyond, he kindly gave suggestions for correcting or improving my translations. I am indebted to him for this integral help.

And where would I be without family and friends? Indra Leyva, Mary Stanley Reichman, and Wendy Shintani Yoshikawa, how time flies: your transcontinental friendship over the years has been such a joy. From bringing me into the world in a concrete cloverleaf building at Prentice Women's Hospital, my mother, Eileen Martin Ferguson, raised me in a house with cats and interesting books and by example taught me to appreciate the ways of quietly knowing and meaningful subversion. From my father, John Ferguson, I inherited a loud laugh, an affection for things that can be disassembled, and a propensity for finding strange fun in the everyday. I also thank Janet Ferguson for her support. Eric Martinusen and Ellen Martinusen, I am grateful for decades of your inspiration, care, and laughter; a fondness more wonderful than conventional kinship would ever deem possible. I am immensely thankful for the kindness of Arratee Ayuttacorn. She is the best *nangfaa*, with astonishing creative energy and spark.

Finally, I dedicate this book to the memory of one journalist, teacher, documentarian, and comrade extraordinaire: Sitthipong "Sam" Kalayanee (1960–2010). His empathy and fierce solidarity with the struggling peoples of the borderlands are incredible and unmatched. In fact, his sense of humor is utterly bizarre to boot. This little one is for you, P'Sam. Thank you and good-bye.

Repossessing Shanland

PROLOGUE

The Tale of the Great Tiger King

THE ANCIENT CAPITAL of Möng Mao is located on the Nam Mao River (the Shweli River on Burmese maps) in what is now the border area between Northern Shan State, Myanmar, and the southwest of Yunnan Province of China. For Shan people today, the empire of Möng Mao Long (Great Mao Kingdom) is their classical state par excellence. It is classical not for what it was at the time but rather for what it has come to represent to modern Shan patriots: the historical apex of Shan political and cultural authority in the region.

The UNESCO World Heritage sites, the archaeological remains of the cities of Bagan, Sukhotai, and Angkor—as they are projected by their denizens in Myanmar, Thailand, and Cambodia, respectively—have continuity with their supposed descendants today in language, religion, political ideals, and cultures (Aung-Thwin 2011, 31). Contemporary patriots take pride in these states as examples of the achievements of their purported ancestors, "their people." Though the latter comprise examples of classical states that have fully recognized nation-states today, can Möng Mao's "classical-ness" withstand a similar litmus test?

First, it is ancient. Möng Mao allegedly dates back to AD 568. Its founding legend tells of the descent from heaven on a golden ladder by Khun Lu and Khun Lai to establish a kingdom in the valley of the Shweli River, Nam Mao in Shan. Khun Lu and Khun Lai brought with them a minister from the sun, another from the moon, and a full royal entourage to populate their new court on earth.

Second, the resplendent Möng Mao suffered a period of decline but was later rescued by a virtuous hero who would become the leader of the greatest Shan empire in history: the warrior King Suerkhan Fa (r. 1152–1205 or r. 1336–64).[1] Under his charismatic command, Möng Mao flourished. Suerkhan Fa has been called "the first . . . Shan monarch to dream of an empire" (Gogoi 1968, 156). But he was no mere dreamer. Suerkhan Fa led armies to conquer numerous surrounding states, including those of the Burmese, Siamese, Lao, Yunnanese, and Assamese. At its height, Möng Mao's territories spanned the massif from what is now Yunnan all the way down the Irrawaddy River, west to Manipur, east to Siam, and as far south

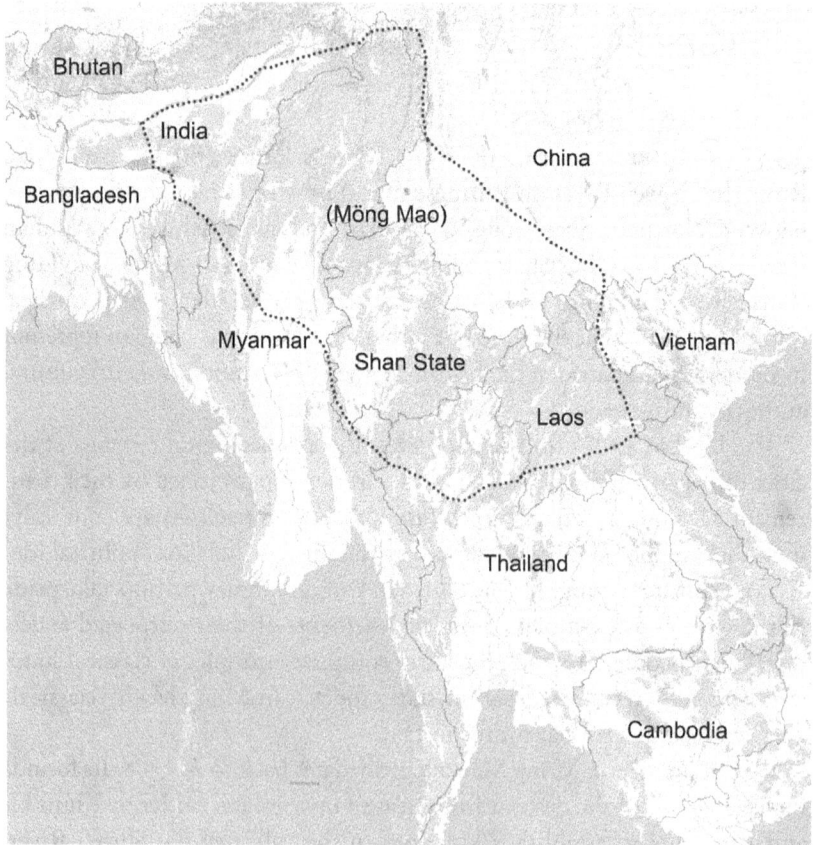

Map of the kingdom of Möng Mao under King Suerkhan Fa. Today's political boundaries, including those of Shan State, are shown for reference. (Map by the author)

as Mawlamyane. This vast territory is estimated have included some 403 smaller principalities (Sai Aung Tun 2009, 15; Möng Kham Hkö Hsang မိုင်းခမ်းခိုးသၢင် 2011, 18, 30).

The Great Mao Kingdom has also been referred to by the Buddhist term Kawsampi (also a state in ancient India). The use of the name Kawsampi for the area is argued to have predated the Burmese name, Ko Shan Pyi, meaning "nine Shan territories."[2] The actual configuration (and constituent states) of these nine—known in Shan as Kao Hai Haw—is unclear; one scholar has noted that across different records there are five different constituent lists of these nine Shan territories (Takatani 2007, 184).

Important to the arc of the legendary empire is the biography of Suerkhan Fa himself. One cannot have a proper classical state without a great warrior king: an exemplary hero to his people. Suerkhan Fa is a man of auspicious birth, who overcomes adversity and rallies the troops to reclaim territories once lost to other kingdoms, ousting unjust enemy sovereigns to build a resplendent empire. Suerkhan Fa's battlefield prowess and symbolic allure exemplified the glories of the land. He is a bona fide hero, and his image graces many Shan history books, patriotic posters, and souvenir T-shirts today. Shan schoolbooks invariably include his story as required reading. Advocates for Shan autonomy, history and culture aficionados alike, extol the virtues of their patron king Suerkhan Fa. His legend is retold in the paragraphs that follow.

The Mao Kingdom's power in the uplands had been waning. Territories that had once been vassal states to Möng Mao became tributaries to other more powerful kingdoms. Despite the empire having been "downsized," the Möng Mao *sao haw kham* ("Lord of the Golden Pavilion" or king) maintained an opulent palace with multiple queens and consorts, symbolic of kingly prowess and part of political relations of the day.

One day, an auspicious event took place in the palace of Wieng Wai, capital of Möng Mao, then ruled by Sao Khan Pharngkham. Princess Sao Nang Awn—a consort of Sao Khan Pharngkham's—gave birth to triplet boys. These new royal babies were named Khun Ai Ngam Möng, Khun Yi Khang Kham, and Khun Sam Long Fa. Where special events such as multiple royal births bring honor and represent merit for some, they steal the thunder of others. The Möng Mao palace was no exception; other royal women were jealous of Princess Sao Nang Awn, a familiar trope in the soap dramas of palace polygamy. Because of this resentment, the women started to spread vicious rumors about the princess. As the canards argued, Sao

Nang Awn had been unfaithful to the king, and her triplet boys were in fact the children of another lover. The rumor mongers asserted that Sao Nang Awn had these children under the claim of their auspiciousness as a strategy to advance her own status in the royal hierarchy. To prevent such usurpation of power, one of the malicious rivals ordered Princess Sao Nang Awn and her three boys to be banished from the palace.

The young princess and her baby sons sought refuge in the home of another princess, Ei Khamliang. However, not long after, one of the jealous women at the palace learned that Sao Nang Awn and her three boys were still alive, and she dispatched assassins to kill the little family. Learning of the plans in advance, Sao Nang Awn stole away into the forest. The first-born boy, Khun Ai Ngam Möng, accidentally became separated from the others. According to legend, a monk found the child and took him to be raised at a monastery. Coming of age in the refuge of the Buddha, Khun Ai Ngam Möng would later ordain as a monk, thus earning merit for his mother.

Back in the forest flight, and still in possession of the other two boys, Princess Sao Nang Awn got in touch with a sympathetic villager in a nearby town, who may have been a cousin of hers. This person had contact with the *sao hpa* of another Shan principality, Möng Gawng. The princess entrusted this individual with the life of her third-born child, Khun Sam Long Fa. The boy was given a royal upbringing in the court at Möng Gawng.

Now only the second-born child, Khun Yi Kang Kham, remained with his mother. Princess Sao Nang Awn was especially reluctant to part with this boy because he was sick; she was concerned he would not adjust well to new circumstances.

Trekking through the forest with her son on her hip, Princess Sao Nang Awn sought shelter in a cave. However, the woman and her child were not alone. The cave was the home to a family of great white tigers: mother, father, and cubs (Khur Hsen ခိုးသိုၵ်ႈ 1999, 31). The magnificent albino tiger father, himself auspicious, intuitively knew the genuine nobility of the human princess and her little prince. And as a result, the great cat willingly came to their aid. When the palace-hired assassins later arrived at the cave entrance, the giant tiger, claws extended, bore his fangs, growled, and pounced at the men. The men fled; in all likelihood, they surmised this savage tiger had devoured the princess and her children as a mere appetizer.

With the assassins gone, the tiger family nurtured the Shan prince and raised him as one of their own. The boy's childhood playmates and fictive kin were tiger cubs. They tumbled and wrestled together. During one of these playful tussles, one of the tiger cubs leaped at the boy, grabbing onto him with claws extended. As the boy pulled away and the feline fell downward, the cat's claws pierced the boy's skin and scratched the length of the young boy's back, from his shoulder blades down to his waist. The cuts were deep enough in his flesh to leave permanent scars, effectively striping his torso (Chaofa Saenwi เจ้าฟ้าแสนหวี 2001, 2). It is because of these distinct scars and the mythical story behind them that Khun Yi Khang Kham earned the nom de guerre Suer (tiger) khan (scratch) Fa (heavenly): Suerkhan Fa.

When Suerkhan Fa was twenty, having come of age with his blended family of humans and tigers, he learned that the Möng Mao throne was vacant, and the kingdom lacked a clear sovereign successor. Confident in his royal heritage, Suerkhan Fa returned to the capital to prove his worth and leadership ability. As with glorious legends, the tasks he was assigned were much more exciting than a state department foreign service officer written test. Suerkhan Fa was required to kill a wild bear (barehanded) and to tame a tiger. For the latter task, undoubtedly his tiger upbringing added big cat negotiating strategies to his portfolio of diplomatic skills. He triumphed in both of these endeavors. As Suerkhan Fa's accolades became known throughout the land, his long-lost brother Khun Sam Long Fa, the boy who had been spirited away to the palace of Möng Gawng, vouched for him. Soon, the Shan privy council was fully convinced that Suerkhan Fa was a worthy successor to the throne at Möng Mao, the epicenter of the Shan universe. From the age of twenty, Suerkhan Fa would go on to rule the Möng Mao empire for approximately five decades.

Suerkhan Fa has gone down in history as the first great Shan nation-builder, the first hero to unite the Tai states (Lung Kaet လုင်းၵဵတ်ႇ, 1987, 15). He has even been called a Shan Ghenghis Khan (Khuensai Jaiyen ၶုၼ်းသႂ် 1999, 37). But let's not take greatness for granted. It is important to consider the ways in which Suerkhan Fa's sovereignty is evaluated by Shan history books and patriotic narratives, and what lessons of the past are used for didactic purposes in the present.

Suerkhan Fa's legendary reign coincided with a degree of political instability in China. Because of that, he was able to bring more Tai principalities into his domain. In some history books, Suerkhan Fa's empire was due to his efforts to "recover" Tai territories that had been "lost" to other empires (Sai Aung Tun 2009, 17). As mentioned earlier, the total empire attributed to Suerkhan Fa includes what is now Assam in northeast India,

most of Burma, southeastern Yunnan, western Laos, and Northern Thailand. Many of these cities were conquered through force (Chaofa Saenwi
เจ้าฟ้าแสนหวี 2001, 7–10). However, Suerkhan Fa has the historical reputation of having *united* the Shan (even if it was against their will).

The glories of the Great Möng Mao were not just in military empire-
building: its accolades included civilizational achievements. The character
of a flourishing Shan empire follows the Theravadin ideal: the auspicious
leader is a conqueror of many kingdoms but also a sponsor of the religion
and a cultural patron. Suerkhan Fa's regime encouraged scholarly activities
and propagated the Shan written language. Temples across the reign received
Shan monks ordained in Möng Mao monasteries. Vassal states and villages
looked toward the Shan capital as the cosmopolitan center for spiritual
prestige and merit. Suerkhan Fa is remembered for emphasizing the important role of women in Shan society, "Men are handsome because of
their bravery. Women are beautiful because of their literacy. Women who
are skillful in martial arts win wars. Shan women engage in affairs of state,
their glory shall fill Heaven" (Khuensai Jaiyen ၶုၼ်းသႃႇၸၢႆး 1999, 39).

Shan nationalist histories laud Suerkhan Fa's ability to unite Tai-speaking
principalities (again, the key term being "unite," not "subsume"). Tai-ness
hardly formed the basis for Suerkhan Fa's empire, although this is presumed
by ethnicist arguments. A British colonial source even describes him as the
"only Shan that ever united these squabbling states into one solid kingdom" (Cochrane 1915, 46). The "Shan unity" he inspired during his reign
has repeatedly been mobilized for Shan nationalist movements since the
twentieth century.

Recounting the legend of Suerkhan Fa preempts several recurrent thematic patterns in the Shan political project: (1) Shan principalities should
be united because they are kith and kin; (2) disunity among the Shan
States results in their fragmentation and subordination to other powers;
and (3) through the work of a charismatic Shan hero, Shan States can be
repossessed from enemy occupiers, and a united empire can flourish. Drawing upon the legend, the albino tiger has become the symbol for the Shan
nation for more than seven decades, and its fierce independence is also
seen as a model archetype of the Shan character. Who will be the next
reincarnation of Suerkhan Fa?

INTRODUCTION

As part of their Shan National Day events on 7 February 2011, hundreds of Shan State Army uniformed soldiers march in military file. They are assembling on the parade grounds of their mountaintop base of Loi Tai-leng, located in a tiny pocket of liberated Shanland at the Thai–Myanmar border. With rhythmic military drum accompaniment, the tight formation of troops marches to receive a douse of holy water splashed by the saffron-robed Buddhist monk standing atop a platform at one end of the ocher grounds. The groups of soldiers continue in their column formations, finally lining up in orderly rows and presenting themselves in front of a stage. At center stage is a podium with a public address system and behemoth speakers looming on either side. Seated beside the podium, facing the military parade, are a dozen VIPs: respected Shan elders and scholars, and veteran leaders of Chin, Kayah, Kayin, and Mon political parties, some in Western-style suits and ties, others in military garb, and a few brightly dressed in their respective national costumes.

The soldiers stand at attention, ready to receive the words of their leader: Sao Yawd Serk, commander-in-chief of the Shan State Army (SSA). As part of his speech in the Shan language, Sao Yawd Serk—dressed in traditional Shan costume—implores his audience to feel the gravity and urgency of their liberation project: "We need to understand that today is our Shan National Day. This national day is for all the ethnicities within Shanland be they Akha, Lahu, Wa, Palaung or Pa-o. Everyone is included. . . . We have territory, we have people, we have language, we have religion, we have history; these are great things which we have had for a long time. . . . We have endured Burmese domination of our land for 64 years. Don't let it become 100 years!"

The Shan State Army represents one of the latest incarnations of a military struggle for national independence, which has been on slow burn in northeastern Myanmar since 1958. From Sao Yawd Serk's words, we glean certain key tropes: the Shan have pride in their land and their culture, they are one among many diverse groups in the area, and they have been denied their national self-determination for more than a half century.

While Sao Yawd Serk urges his audience to reclaim Shanland for the future generations, this book retraces the cultural roots and ongoing dynamic relationship between the people of Shanland, its citizens, its advocates and enemies, through the transitions of colonialism, the Cold War, heroin wars, and finally to the neoliberal economies of displacement and undocumented labor. The fight to repossess Shanland is both a military battle and a cultural war that spans three national horizons: Myanmar, Thailand, and Shanland. But unlike Myanmar and Thailand, Shanland never became a full-fledged nation-state on the world stage. Why not?

Sao Yawd Serk's speech includes the key criteria for nation-state legitimacy and self-determination; the points are akin to those of the League of Nations and later the United Nations during the post–World War II decolonization of Africa and Asia. The criteria serve as a useful guide to start looking at Shanland's claims to sovereignty in the uplands of Southeast Asia.

SAO YAWD SERK'S CRITERIA FOR NATION-STATE LEGITIMACY AND SELF-DETERMINATION
"We Have Territory . . ."

Today, Shan State is a mapped territory within the Republic of the Union of Myanmar. It comprises the largest administrative division of the country, covering 60,614 square miles (155,800 km²). The Shan State is approximately the size of England and Wales and is characterized by steep hills interspersed with flat valleys. Wet rice cultivation has sustained lowland principalities over hundreds of years. Other agricultural products include beans, vegetables, fruits, tea, coffee, and opium. Shan State is famous for its biodiversity and natural resources, which include teak forests, valuable mineral mines of tin, and precious gemstones. The Salween River—the mightiest free-flowing river in Southeast Asia—cuts off the eastern third of

Approximate timeline of armies in Shan State mentioned in *Repossessing Shanland*

Years Active	Name	Leaders / other details
1919 (1949–84 in the region)	Kuomintang (KMT)	Chiang Kai-shek, then Li and Tuan in Shan State / Thai border area
1939–89	Communist Party of Burma (CPB)	Aung San, Than Tun
1945–64	Kokang Defense Force / with SSA	Jimmy Yang; later merged
1954–64	Loi Maw Militia	Khun Sa; later becoming SUA
1956–58	Shan State Communist Party	Kawn Söng
1958–60	Num Serk Han "Brave Young Warriors"	Saw Yanta / Sao Noi
1960–64	Shan State Independence Army (SSIA)	Break-off from Num Serk Harn
1961–64	Shan National United Front (SNUF)	Kawn Söng and Khun Kya Nu
1964	Shan State Army / Shan State Progress Party	Merging of the SSIA, SNUF, and Kokang Resistance Force
1964–85	Shan United Army (SUA)	Khun Sa (rebranding of Loi Maw Militia from 1960)
1966–85	Shan United Revolutionary Army (SURA)	Kawn Söng
1976–80	Shan State Revolutionary Army (SSRA)	Lo Hsing-minh
1978	Tai Independence Army (TIA)	Priwat Kasemsri
1984–85	Tai Revolutionary Council / Tai Revolutionary Army	Kawn Söng, Khun Sa; merger of SURA and SUA
1985–95	Möng Tai Army / Shan State Restoration Council	Kawn Söng, Khun Sa; renaming of TRC/TRA
1989–	United Wa State Army (UWSA)	Bao Youxiang, Wei Hsueh-kang; splinter of CPB
1989–	National Democratic Alliance Army–Eastern Shan State (NDAA–ESS)	Phueng Kya Shin; splinter of CPB
1998–	Shan State Army–South (SSA) / Restoration Council of Shan State (RCSS)	Yawd Serk's; revitalization of SURA following Khun Sa's surrender of MTA

Sources: Sao Khwan Möng ဝင်းရှာခံမိုင်း 1986; Lintner 1994; M. Smith 1999.

Shan State, its massive gorge effectively separating the numerous historic principalities: the cis-Salween states to the west, and the trans-Salween states to the east. For years the mighty river gorge provided a natural boundary dividing the territories of the Burmese state from those of insurgent Shanland. Despite the Shan State's present geopolitical borderlines only having being confirmed in the 1960s, the Shan State map is used as an icon for Shanland, gracing Shan history books and decorating patriotic merchandise such as posters, stickers, and T-shirts.

"We Have People . . ."

The Shan State was named after the ethnic majority group it contains: the Shan people, who call themselves Tai.[1] More broadly speaking, Tai is an umbrella term for all those who speak a language within the Kra-Dai family. Tai therefore includes speakers of Thai, Lao, Tai Khün, Tai Lü, and Lanna (northern Thai) languages. Shan hereditary princes, or *sao hpa*—meaning "Lord of the Heaven"—were the political rulers of the area for centuries, although there are numerous subcategories within the term "Shan." These groups have diversity in expressive culture, including forms of music, dress, and unique artistic styles documented by archaeologists and art historians. There are significant populations of non-Tai groups in Shan State, and these include Akha, Lahu, Wa, Ta-ang/Palaung, Pa-o, as well as Burman and Chinese. Of the Shan State's total population of 5.8 million, it is

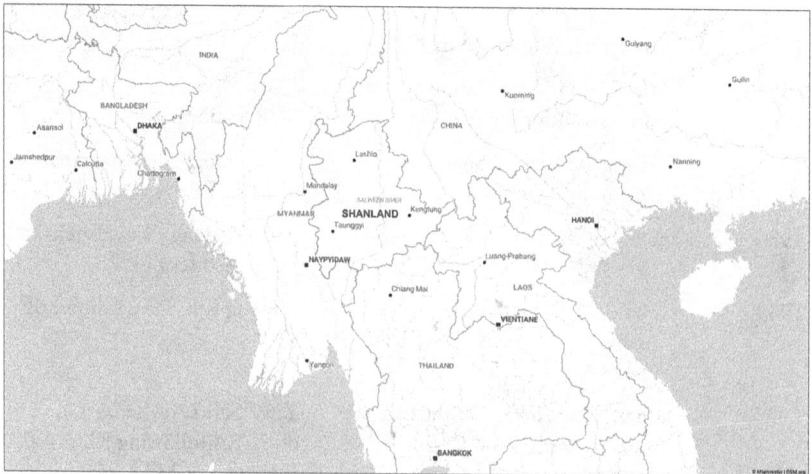

Map of Shanland and its neighbors in Mainland Southeast Asia.

estimated that one-half to two-thirds are Tai.[2] Beyond the borders of Shan State, Shan people live in other regions in Myanmar, though there are larger populations in Yunnan Province of China as well as in Northern Thailand. The ongoing war in Shan State and economic disadvantages have pushed hundreds of thousands of Shan people across the eastern border into Thailand. However, Thai law recognizes Shan people fleeing war in Shan State to enter Thailand not as legal refugees but as noncitizen subjects. Today, hundreds of thousands of Shan laborers struggle to survive in Thailand, many sending remittances to their families in the borderlands and Shan State.

"We Have Language . . ."

Sao Yawd Serk's speech is in Tai Long, a Shan language predominantly spoken in central and southern Shan State.[3] There are hundreds of years of Shan written tradition, though with cellular and disparate principalities, the production of the written language was neither centralized nor standardized. Around the time of World War II, a group of Shan literary scholars modified and established the southern Shan script as the bureaucratic print language for the Shan nation. While Tai Long is in the same language family and therefore has rudimentary similarities with Thai, a different written script is a key distinguishing factor. Shan written language was not only adopted as the bureaucratic print language for the Shan insurgencies but also taught in a standard curriculum in the two-hundred-plus elementary schools in liberated Shanland at the height of the insurgency project in the 1980s and 1990s. Today, the same written language is taught more openly in Myanmar, though the government authorities are still cautious about its subversive potential. For those Shan now residing in Northern Thailand, Shan temples and independent teachers offer classes to keep Shan literacy alive for migrants and their children.

"We Have Religion . . ."

The Shan State Army is an overt sponsor of Theravada Buddhism, and every army base will have its own Buddhist temple and school. Various Shan state-building regimes have all been sponsors of the religion and Shan armies, and political leaders have built pagodas and supported monasteries. Members of the Shan political movement, as well as the majority of Shan people, are devout Buddhists, although there is a significant Christian minority. Having religion has not only been a measure of civilization

over the centuries in Southeast Asia—the distinguishing feature of the
lowlands paddy agriculture-based states—but Sao Yawd Serk's statement
resonates with the conceptual patriotic triad of Thailand: nation-religion-
monarchy, which, in turn, is an appropriation of the British motto "For
God, King and Country."

"We Have History . . ."

Shan patriots and cultural enthusiasts proudly espouse a centuries-long history of Shan presence in upland Southeast Asia. For Shan nation-builders
today, the Shan classical state par excellence is the ancient kingdom of
Möng Mao.[4] During its golden age that started the twelfth or thirteenth
century (this is disputed), the great warrior king Suerkhan Fa united the
formerly squabbling Tai fiefdoms and built the first Shan empire.[5] Surrounding groups, including Northern Thai (Lanna), Lao, and even Burmese
principalities were vassal states to Suerkhan Fa's Shanland. The legendary
warrior king was a religious and cultural sponsor, building pagodas and
holding great festivals on holy days. Shan literary practices date back hundreds of years, and though manuscripts older than three hundred years no
longer remain, there is archaeological evidence of Shan Theravāda Buddhist
practices, cultural traditions of Shan literature and poetry, and towns organized around wet-rice agriculture. The presence of Shan principalities in
the region is acknowledged in Burmese, Chinese, and Northern Thai historical records.

Sao Yawd Serk stresses the tangible reasons for the Shan State Army to
continue its fight into the twenty-first century. There is a dynamic relationship of history, culture, and social identity that has also evolved across
these mountainous uplands. For many, this offers ideological fuel to the
ongoing project for Shan independence. At the same time, Burmese and
Thai nationalist histories may incorporate or suppress that project.

There was a watershed moment in February 1947. At the brink of Burma's
colonial independence from the British, a council of Shan chiefs signed a
formal agreement in the southern Shan town of Panglong and agreed for
their territories to join the Union of Burma. The Shan leaders did so because
they were given an important legislated caveat: following ten years' initial
membership in the new Union, the Shan State would have the right to
secede and establish an independent nation-state provided that separation
was the will of its citizens. Such a plebiscite never occurred. Successive conflict and military governments stymied the possibility of Shan independence

through bureaucratic means. Since 1958, various Shan armies have waged war against the Burmese government: their goal is to repossess Shanland.

In a State of Repossession

Repossession (or the common vernacular term, "repo") is a process through which the party that has right of ownership to a property takes said property back from the party that is currently holding it. Everyday instances of repossession consist of homeowners evicting negligent renters or car dealers taking back vehicles from buyers who are irretrievably behind on their payments; valuable items used as loan collateral can become objects for repossession. Importantly, repo often occurs without court procedure and is usually a last resort when other means to achieve compliance have failed. In the most dramatic cases of car repossession, the driver will wake up in the morning, step out of their home, keys in hand and preparing to drive to work, only to discover the vehicle missing and a repo notice in the mailbox.

A protracted struggle to establish an independent, sovereign nation-state may appear to have very little in common with a tow truck operator surreptitiously grabbing a poor cash-strapped soul's car in the middle of the night. However, the two scenarios share a key conceptual basis: they represent tactics of rightful owners to take back properties currently held by others. What comprises "rightful ownership" is frequently contested, as endless court dockets and multitudes of gainfully employed lawyers can confirm (for a fee). Furthermore, in order to *re*possess, one intrinsically has to have held the property before.

The ongoing, dynamic project of repossessing Shanland embodies changing discourses of political power and authority across multiple horizons in Mainland Southeast Asia. As forms of sovereignty change, so do ideas of political rightful ownership and cultural belonging. Varied mechanisms of power, including ritual languages, grammars of statecraft, ethnic identity and authenticity, and access to neoliberal labor markets, have—in their respective historical contexts—crucially framed the movement to repossess Shanland. Even the object of repossession, Shanland, has been reconstituted along the way.

While the Shan State Army continues the struggle today, one of its predecessor organizations—a previous incarnation in the fight to take back Shanland—is the Shan United Revolutionary Army (SURA). Led by a devout Buddhist, Kawn Söng (aka Mo Heng), in 1969, SURA established its revolutionary capital city, Bang Mai Sung (Prosperity Town), at the Shan State border with the Thai province of Chiang Mai. Kawn Söng and the SURA created both a soldier town and an embryo Shanland, founding a Buddhist temple and supporting its monastery, commanding an army, operating a Shan print shop and schools, and running a hospital.

Today, numerous SURA veterans and their families, many born in Shan State, younger generations born in Thailand, continue to live in these soldier towns, though SURA is no more. Some support the Shan State Army, organized by a SURA veteran and populated by many sons and daughters of SURA soldiers. The contemporary reality and social lives of these SURA veteran soldiers, their relatives, and their affiliates present an incisive angle to understanding the decades-long fight to repossess Shanland. They are direct participants in the Shan political and military movement, but they have their own personal histories as subjects or citizens of multiple nation-states. They were born in Shan State as citizens of Burma, became educated in Burmese schools (even Burmese universities), entered a revolutionary Shan movement, and now are subjects—but not citizens—of Thailand. The project to repossess Shanland has tangled roots spanning these three nation-states' horizons. As actively engaged in these national projects, SURA veterans' cultural lives are also intertwined with these multiple places, ideologies, and cultures.

Between 2004 and 2007, I spent two years living with a community of former SURA soldiers and their families in one of these military towns at the Thai–Shan State border. I use the name Wan Kan Hai as a pseudonym for the village. I stayed in the household of an extended family that includes one veteran SURA soldier, her father, her current husband (whose great-uncle was a SURA officer in the 1970s), their young children, and the young daughter of a cousin. Part of the town was once a SURA administrative center and is now at the foot of one of the five Shan State Army bases. Visible from the main road are hilltop encampments for the Shan State Army and the United Wa State Army, and adjacent is a small camp for the Myanmar Tatmadaw, with the Thai Army not far from the border. Although the political history of the town and the ongoing insurgency do create a unique social geography to this place, for many, daily life goes on as people struggle to get by in the political and economic context of the Thai state, a country that is ideologically warm to Shan people as a fellow ethnic Tai group yet creates endless bureaucratic and cultural hurdles for Shan migrants nonetheless.

Wan Kan Hai village. (Photo by Sai Leng Learn Kham)

The majority of the population of Wan Kan Hai is Shan. There is a significant Yunnanese Chinese community as well; the town was once one of the strategic bases of the Kuomintang.[6] Of the Yunnanese population— called *hke'* (ၕၖ) in Shan—the majority of people over fifty years old previously lived in Burma, and for them, their lingua franca with older Shan people is Burmese. On the east side of the main hill is a small tract of Lahu homes, and there is a Lahu village a forty-minute drive away. There is a Thai government elementary and high school, so some Central and Northern Thai teachers and school administrators also reside in Wan Kan Hai.

Most of the shops in town, the one restaurant, and a couple of noodle or lunch shops are owned and run by Yunnanese, with the exception of a cake shop operated by a Burmese woman (married to a Yunnanese man), a hairdresser who is Shan, and the fresh market, where Shan, Yunnanese, Lahu, and Northern Thai vendors sell vegetables, tofu, fermented beans, fresh meat, and other sundry items. Items for sale in the market reflect local tastes: *hke'p hto nao* (ၐၖႏၥၖ,ၗၖ), the flat disks of dried, fermented beans (a staple of Shan cuisine), or packets of ready-made Burmese fermented tea leaf salad. The larger *kat nat* "weekend market" sets up itinerant stalls on the school soccer field.

Most of the working population of Wan Kan Hai engages in farming or cash-in-hand daily work as laborers on others' land. The nearby environs have rice paddies as well as fruit and vegetable gardens. Many households have kitchen gardens and raise chickens or pigs for their own consumption. Extended families maintain connections with relatives in Shan State, often accommodating recent migrants, friends, and relatives, however distantly related. To supplement the modest means of the local economy, the majority of households are partially supported by remittances from family members working elsewhere in Thailand, mostly in Chiang Mai and environs, some in Bangkok. These jobs include construction, domestic, sex, garment, clerical, and restaurant work.

During my years of residence in Wan Kan Hai, participant observation included daily meals and conversations with members of the household, helping with various chores, visits to homes of family friends and neighbors, sitting with the guys at the motorbike taxi stand (sometimes playing dominoes, but not gambling), and visiting the two monasteries and an orphanage run by a Shan catholic nun. Important social events included town hall meetings, weddings and funerals, and Buddhist holiday meals and rituals. For events at the temple, working with the women in the temple kitchen to prepare massive feasts (and cleanup) was a tremendously generative social experience.

In terms of strategic fieldwork regarding political history and language acquisition, I hired two of the teachers who taught in schools for the SURA and the Möng Tai Army to give me daily lessons in the Shan written language using the Shan curriculum from the insurgency and migrant schools. Through their tutelage, I completed the curriculum up to fifth grade. In addition to fieldwork and Shan school, another regular methodology included playing bass or guitar with a neighborhood pickup band, organized by some SURA veterans.

Work in Wan Kan Hai was complemented by occasional trips to Chiang Mai in the public buses and, on several occasions, in pickup trucks with local families. In the second year of my research, I made a ten-week trip to Myanmar to gather more data about Burmese popular culture as well as to visit the Shan print shop and cultural association in Taunggyi, Shan State.

Since 2008, twice a year, I have returned to Myanmar or Thailand, with month-long stays in each country, sometimes longer. Repeat visits to Wan Kan Hai focused on updating the situation of the Shan interlocutors with whom I lived from 2004 to 2007. Although the experience of SURA veterans and their families informs the ethnographic component of repossession of Shanland as a political and cultural process, research in Myanmar and Thailand has been crucial to situate Shan people's experiences as minority citizens or subjects in two larger nation-states. To understand the minority, it is necessary to interrogate the two majorities who have pushed the Shan to their territorial or cultural margins.

SHAN I AM: WHAT'S IN A NAME?

The term "Shan" is an adaptation of the Burmese spelling and pronunciation of "Siam" and in British colonial records areas became written as such.[7] As mentioned earlier, in Shan languages, people refer to themselves as Tai (ဝၢ်း). Across Myanmar's eastern border, Thais call Shan people *Tai-yai* "great Tai," reflecting an ethnolinguistic affinity, which later has come to infer purported historic closeness and shared heritage, even blood.[8] Similarities in language are rarely sufficient basis for political solidarity (Leach 2004, 48; Wolters 2008, 59), despite a great deal of patriotic discourse in Southeast Asia insisting otherwise. Hundreds of years ago, subjects of a principality were not strictly categorized—let alone mapped or conferred citizenship—based on the languages that they spoke or their supposed race or ethnic identity. People were certainly aware of cultural difference, but those differences did not relate to political power in the same way that they do today.

Checking our contemporary nation-state and ethno-racial baggage at the door (if we can), cultural ecology offers a useful lens through which to examine difference in Southeast Asia. Different nations in the region today (Tai, Burmese, Mon, Khmer, etc.) locate their ancestral roots in wet-rice-fed kingdoms that had Hindu/Theravādin cosmological understandings of culture and social hierarchy, combined with localized spirit beliefs. These forms of civilization and high culture as practiced in these ancient Tai, Burmese, and Mon kingdoms have quite a lot in common with each other, and these political and cultural similarities comprise a shared ritual language (Leach 2004). However, it was later discourses of nation-building that have tended to look back in history through their ethnic lenses, using the past to claim a cultural continuity to argue for a political sovereignty in the present.

Without the modern concept of ethnic nation, the main distinction was not between these polities as different ethnic groups and peoples per se but rather the differences in "civilizational attainment" that juxtaposed the lowland paddy agricultural Tai states (*möng* "towns") that had feudal hierarchies and text-based religions with their "uncivilized" counterparts, the Kha, outside of the city, in the forest, or engaging in swidden production in the hills (or the *tön / pa* "forest" or "wilderness") (Ling 1979, 2; Renard 2000, 66; Toyota 2005, 111, 115; Niti นิติ 2015, 20). In 1962, for example, the Thai Department of Public Welfare claimed that hill peoples "without any exception have *not yet advanced* to stabilized farming" (Department of Public Welfare 1962, 17, qtd. in Jonsson 2006, 55). While city-dwelling snobs might think of the uplanders as unrefined barbarians, another perspective argues that uplands livelihoods, social organization, and oral cultures were not characteristics of societies uninitiated to the trappings (or blessings) of city life but rather were "strategic positionings designed to keep the state at arm's length" (Scott 2009, x).

However instructive the model of cultural ecology might be to look at as an archetype—lowlands paddy cities versus uplands swidden communities—we should not underestimate the level of mobility people had, plus their flexibility to move between these archetypes. Cultures change, identities can be multiple, and boundaries can be transgressed. Edmund Leach's now-classic 1954 anthropological study, *Political Systems of Highland Burma: A Study of Kachin Social Structure* (2004), offers evidence that people are able to transform aspects of identity depending on their circumstances and their goals. Leach observed that individuals can change the language they speak, organize themselves according to new systems of social hierarchy, and adopt new modes of production; in fact, Jinghpaw Kachin (thought of as an uplands swidden group) even have an expression, *sam Tai*, "to become Shan."[9]

Leach's demonstration that ethnicities are socially constructed, not fixed by label (or map), levied an important critique against British anthropometry, which had been actively carrying out censuses and mapping people according to race or tribe, where identity was considered innate, exclusive, and even biological. But in changing political economies of nation-states and subjects or citizens, one cannot simply take on the social identity that one feels like. In addition to material constraints and local cultural mores, new ideologies of territorial power and nationality increasingly limit one's options. As such, one dimension of ethnic flexibility that Leach neglected to acknowledge was the positive role that the modern boundary plays as a creator of nationhood (Thongchai 1994, 17). Territorial sovereignty continues to comprise the fundamental political and juridical rationale for the nation-state system, and states play a key role in the creation of naturalized links between places and peoples (Gupta and Ferguson 1992, 12; Appadurai 2019, 559). The power of states is made visible via "officializing" procedures and their capacity to bound and mark space; these codifications finally emerged as a "natural embodiment of history, territory and society" (Cohn and Dirks 1988, 224).

It is the very fact that cultural attributes are often taken for granted and perceived as natural or innate that it is necessary to understand their productive context (Munasinghe 2009, 140). Where borders are drawn and IDs issued by political and bureaucratic fiat, both lands and people are delimited. These processes have material implications and can set into motion the emergence of new cultural forms and differences. For example, there are communities of Shan people in Mae Hong Son Province, in Northwest Thailand, who have lived in the area for generations. As they were there, on what *became* the Thai side when borders were drawn, their descendants have Thai citizenship. These Thai-citizen Shans have the full set of privileges such citizenship entails: they attend Thai government schools and therefore speak and read central Thai, they can freely travel throughout the country without special permission, and they can access Thai labor markets and social services. These Mae Hong Son Shan people have grown up immersed in Thai-sanctioned narratives of history and the daily rituals of honoring the Thai national anthem and the Thai monarchy. When they move to Bangkok, they might not reveal their Shan heritage to Thai friends as they are often compelled to assimilate to mainstream Thai culture as much as possible.

Because of this, some Mae Hong Son Shans have come to see themselves as more civilized than their counterparts in Shan State, whom they refer to as "Burma-side" Shan (Niti นิติ 2004, 2; Tannenbaum 2009, 173). In other respects, Mae Hong Son Shans might see their "Thai-ization" as a force that has pulled them away from their cultural roots. For temple festivals, they will bring in "Burma-side" singers whose Shan traditional performance styles they see as more "authentic" (Kaise 1999, 83). I would add an important caveat: this discussion of cultural change and "Thai-ization" of Mae Hong Son Shans and how they differentiate themselves with Shan people in the Shan State is a projection; Shans over the border have experienced cultural change as well; they are not trapped in time or somehow more authentic for their lack of direct engagement with Thai forms of capitalist modernity.

Territorialization—control of people and markets through geopolitical boundaries and land laws—represents one major component of the modern state's power portfolio. Sovereignty over individual subjects through citizenship laws and categories of belonging represents another. Discourses of power, of which race (or ethnicity) is a part, are endlessly reconceived, redefined, and reconstrued (Shanklin 1998, 675). So, too, are the various social movements in conversation with those discourses of power. In her detailed ethnography of the Ainu in Japan, Katarina Sjöberg (1993) tracks how political movements among the Ainu have changed. Japan's nationalist ethnos had regarded the Ainu people as backward savages, and therefore they were heavily discriminated against. This historically pushed many Ainu people to assimilate as best they could into Japanese society, a society that has a strong nationalist image of racial homogeneity. Full assimilation was nearly impossible; Ainu people were treated as lesser versions of Japanese: second-class citizens, as it were. However, as Sjöberg noted in the 1990s, there has been greater resistance to assimilationism, and more Ainu people have rallied for cultural recognition and autonomy as Ainu, not as Japanese (Sjöberg 1993, 5, 119).

Myanmar, Thailand, and Shanland offer challenging testing grounds to compare the emergence of state-sanctioned discourses regarding race and ethnicity. All three countries are named after their respective majority group, though each modern nation has taken a different trajectory in relation to its cultural diversity and recognition of difference within its borders, including the deferred nation of Shanland.

Following independence in 1948, the Union of Burma established its national image as one of ethnic pluralism. Citizenship documents and national census categories acknowledge diverse groups, and territorially today there are seven states named for non-Bamar groups: Chin, Kachin, Kayah, Kayin, Mon, Rakhine, and Shan. Those seven named groups, plus the Bamar, comprise the official eight *lumyo* (လူမျိုး, meaning "type of person") "race/ethnicity" groups in Myanmar. Within the eight *lumyo* groups is a list of 135 *taingyintha* (တိုင်းရင်းသား, literally "son of the territory") "indigenous races" subgroups. The list has changed over the years, and it has been hotly contested for its inconsistencies as well as its controversial exclusion of groups such as the Rohingya, Panthay, and Anglo-Burmese (Ferguson 2015).

However, as members of an official listed *lumyo*, Shan people are recognized and entitled to bona fide full citizenship in Myanmar. Even so, decades of war, experiences of ethnic chauvinism, and violence have continued to stoke the fires for some Shan groups to fight for self-determination and separation.

Unlike Burma, and despite a history of comparable demographics, cultural diversity and ecologies of lowland paddy agriculture and uplands swidden communities, as well as a prior shared ritual language, neighboring Thailand has presented itself as an ethnically homogenous nation. In sum, to be a citizen is to be Thai. State programs to amalgamate diversity and flatten difference include the 1899 replacement of regional ethnonyms with Thai, and later the ushering of resident Chinese into mainstream Thai society and citizenship (Peleggi 2007, 36; Skinner 1957, 244; Draper and Selway 2019, 280). At the same time, some groups were actively excluded from Thai-ness: highland peoples were referred to as *Khon Pa* "forest people," and by the mid-twentieth century, *Chao Kao* "hill people" were viewed as the civilizational opposites and even biologically different kinds of humans, despite the groups having lived in the same territory for hundreds of years (Jonsson 2006, 45; Toyota 2005, 111, 115).

The Shan in Thailand offer a compelling case study for this scheme, as they are another Theravadin lowlands Buddhist Tai group (like the Thais), so they are not considered culturally as distant as the so-called hill tribes. Thai patriotic rhetoric acknowledges the Shan as ethno-linguistic "brethren" as they share an ethnic origin myth. But despite this perception of similarity, the Thai government denies Shan people fleeing war in Shan State, Myanmar, the possibility of seeking legal refuge in Thailand in an officially designated refugee camp. As a result, and unlike their Kayah, Mon, Burman, or Kayin counterparts also fleeing war, Shan people have no access to possible third-country resettlement via the United Nations High Commission on Refugees (UNHCR). One reason given is that Shan peoples' linguistic closeness and cultural familiarity with Thais makes assimilation easier for them than others fleeing Burma (who have been able to get UNHCR assistance). An odd twist on ideas of cultural intimacy forces Shan people into the lower echelons of the Thai economy; they remain subjects, but not citizens, of the Thai state. Their lack of full citizenship is a cause of constant anguish and considerable expense for already impoverished Shan migrants in Thailand, further compounded by the discrimination and everyday bigotry they receive from unsympathetic Thais.

I Am Shan: What's in a Name, Too?

At the local level, ethnicity is considered a cultural interpretation of descent; it is used to understand the way a group defines itself historically, and in relation to others (Keyes 1981, 5–6; Chit Hlaing 2007, 109). Although it had been a common approach to understand groups according to their cultural "contents," as it were, it is also instructive to examine the ways that various groups differentiate and the boundaries that they establish between themselves and other groups (Barth 1969, 15). As a component of culture, ethnicity is learned by individuals as participants in society, but for many groups in Southeast Asia, there is often a perception of biological immutability to ethnic categories: one simply *is* Thai or Burmese.

Acknowledging the constructed nature of ethnicity offers segue to examining the history of how particular national identities came into being, and thus Benedict Anderson's 1983 pathbreaking theory regarding the relationship between print capitalism, or the ideological role of novels and newspapers, in creating the infrastructure for the emergence of what he influentially termed imagined communities. It was print capitalism, industrially produced novels and newspapers, that "made it possible for rapidly growing numbers of people to think about themselves and relate themselves to others, in profoundly new ways" (Anderson 1991, 36).

The Karen (or Kayin) in Southeast Asia are similar to the Shan in that they comprise an ethnic community in both Myanmar and Thailand. Karen political and armed movements have fought for autonomy from Burma. Anthropologist Ananda Rajah studied Karen ethno-nationalism as a "Nation of Intent" that "conceives of new forms of social groups which *transcend* the empirically grounded, locale-specific ways by which communities in pre-modern societies identify themselves" (Rajah 2002, 520). In this sense, the sparks of Karen ethnic identity were located in an elite movement that organized and communicated ideas about Karen kin and history, which fostered Karen ethnic consciousness, combining numerous formerly disparate groups into a pan-Karen identity (Renard 1980, 41; Cheesman 2002; Kuroiwa and Verkuyten 2008, 400). For example, scholarly analysis of *sgaw* Karen books notes the recent coinage of a term for nation in that language as well. *Dawkalu*, etymologically meaning "the whole of a kind," appears to have emerged only in the 1880s and coincides with the formation of the Karen National Association, a group that formed with the idea that claiming nationhood would help advance their opportunities for recognition from the British (Fujimura 2020).

Whereas the *nation of intent* looks at the formation of an elite project and its communication to form a broader political movement, participation and later the effects of war create new forms of social identity. Work on refugees has examined the ways in which the socio-spatial organization of camps creates distinct subjectivities. For example, Liisa Malkki argues that the construction of a camp for Hutu refugees following the 1972 genocide in Burundi enabled transformations that resulted in "a collective, categorical Hutu-ness as a moral and essential opposite to Tutsi-ness" (Malkki 2002, 358). Jennifer Byrne observed among Liberian refugees in Ghana that the camp produced experiences that allowed people to express shared memories and collective nostalgia for Liberia (Byrne 2016, 775). Similarly, there has been a stronger tendency among Karen refugees in refugee camps to view their ethnic identity as a blood inheritance as opposed to their Karen counterparts living with the general public in towns to see their ethnicity as more fluid (Zeus 2008, 15).

Even though territorialization, displacement, and community building are powerful engines of and for different kinds of social identity, they do not instantly transform people on one side of a borderline into nation A, and those on the other side into nation B. People do not automatically incorporate national identities as part of their psyche unless there are cultural and ideological means and incentives through which they can learn and internalize these ideologies; further, there are other forms of competing identities, social distance and cynicism notwithstanding. While national identities—by definition—are expected to transcend local identities and other sociological categories, including class, gender, and age, there will be variation in how people understand and what they do with their national identity as they make their way through their lives. Individuals have the capacity to hold several identities at once, but what is expressed can be context dependent, what Jonathan Y. Okamura (1981) has aptly termed "situational ethnicity." Depending on the situation, people can have limited agency to present to others different types of social selves.

Repo on Repeat:
The Ethnic Authentic on the Move

Whereas powers of the state and political economy frame categories and demarcate boundaries, because of class position, cultural hegemony is always partial (Bowie 1997, 11). However, people do not derive their identity solely from their mode of production (Scott 1985, 43). Culture will change organically in response to those state powers or in entirely different trajectories than are anticipated, let alone named, by state bureaucracies. Thus, understanding the power dynamic does not tackle the experiential or active dimension of people's perspectives, how they work, and what they do; in short, naming a category does not make a group (Brubaker 2004, 169).[10]

With those qualifiers in mind, by focusing on an ethno-nationalist movement, there is often a tendency to overdetermine the role that ethnicity plays in participation. This is especially the case if we take the words of ethnic politicians at face value. Similar to aspects of culture such as gender identity, there is the problem that the very act of doing research about ethnicity can elicit an "ethnic" response; the ontological pitfall of finding (or creating) a topic (Eriksen 2010, 21). For example, in comparing ethno-nationalist movements in Spain, Basque separatist politics are often equated with the violence of the armed group Euskadi Ta Askatasuna (ETA) while Catalan nationalism, in contrast, is seen as more moderate. This difference, however, tends to be explained in "ethnic" terms rather than considering the varied structural, historical circumstances of identity formation between the two groups (Douglass 1998, 71, 76).

This kind of approach can create a trap for the socially marginalized: their minority identity is already "tagged" and therefore is seen by outsiders as having an overdetermined role in their lives. The challenge to the researcher on ethnicity, in particular, is to be wary of the a priori assumption that ethnicity is of primary importance to people, including among those who have been involved in a war for ethno-national liberation for more than six decades. As has been pointed out in relation to ethnic politics in Myanmar, it is important not to underestimate the existential and emotional dimension of ethnicity, but at the same time it is not ethnicity in itself that generates violence (Gravers 2007, 6).

Therefore, rather than looking inward for an essential "Shan-ness," analyzing the decades-long project to take back Shanland explores this military battle and cultural war in its ongoing relationship with Shans' principal interlocutors: Burmese and Thais. A changing political context sparks the actualization of this repossession project. While the Shan United Revolutionary Army was ideologically grounded in ideas of Theravada statecraft, it became manifest in a perfect storm of postcolonial and Cold War geopolitics and nation-building; a potent cocktail of cultural struggles, black market economies, counterinsurgencies, and a narcotics trade.

Despite changing regional politics, and the tactical surrender of some Shan armies, the Shanland repossession project continues. It is a tactic in the present, whether as a cultural movement to resist assimilation in Thailand by reminding Shan youth of their history, but also as a military war against an enemy occupant: the Myanmar military. Therefore, repossession is motivated by the plans for and anticipation of a better use of that homeland. It is the promise of returning a Shan homeland to the Shan people, and the vision for a happier place, one that is peaceful and modern, that keeps the hope alive that Shanland is worth fighting for. If it is not realized in this lifetime, it will be achieved in a future incarnation.

I

Passport to Ancient Shanland

SHAN POLITICIANS, history books, and cultural enthusiasts alike are adamant in their argument for a primordial origin of the Tai people and the presence of classical Tai states in the uplands of Mainland Southeast Asia. There are centuries of evidence of state-building across the area, holy cities built of brick with towering pagodas, all fed by paddy agriculture. As contemporary Shan activists insist, the deceptive machinations of the Burmese military government and its attendant cultural chauvinism ultimately denied the Shan people their nation-state, their Shanland. While the Burmese military is frequently seen as the main enemy, an important contributing factor to the sad situation of today is the Shan people's lack of a united front to counter the Burmese. Further, there are instances where Shan political leaders sold off their own claims to sovereignty, throwing the dreams of the Shan nation under the bus for their own financial gain. Such instances are pointed to with great frustration and sorrow.

While Shanland is a nation-state deferred, other nearby countries in Mainland Southeast Asia—Myanmar, Thailand, Laos, and Cambodia—are all modern nation-states, each internationally recognized with a sovereign government and a seat at the United Nations as well as the Association for Southeast Asian Nations (ASEAN) membership. Each of these countries is named after its dominant ethnic group that claims continuity with an ancient kingdom—a classical state—and cultural heritage and affinity with Theravadin and Hindu systems of rule (to varying degrees) despite being ruled by military regimes or elected governments. Political regimes are historically legitimated by social hierarchy; leaders present themselves as sponsors of the religion, and their status and ritual practices combine political and spiritual authority. Thus there has historically been a shared grammar for both political relations and legitimation across the region.

To a committed Shan politician such as Sao Yawd Serk at the Shan State Army rally, who will have knowledge about millennia of Shan history, will read and write in the Shan script, and might have once donned the Shan State Army uniform (only to change into a Shan traditional costume called *hko Tai* [ၵုၼ်းၶူဝ်း]—Shan clothing—for special occasions such as religious festivals, weddings, and funerals), the Shan nation is as deserving of a place at the UN as are Myanmar, Thai, Lao, and Cambodian regimes. Shan nationalists locate feelings of patriotism in history by pointing to Shan historical accomplishments in concert with their principal political interlocutors, the Burmese, asserting aspects of Tai ethno-history, all the while selectively resisting subordination to Thai nationalist history that seeks to absorb the Shan as an ethnic sibling. As argued by Partha Chatterjee, the project for the historians of oppressed groups in their effort to prove national legitimacy is not only to find their existence in histories written by others but also to have the power to write their own account of the past. This power is a fundamental sign of nationalist consciousness (1993, 77). In this sense, the Shan patriot's goal is to rescue the nation from other people's history.

How have Shan historians been emplaced to write their history? While Burmese, Shan, and Thai histories of empire in Southeast Asia have the shared state-building characteristics of paddy agriculture, Theravadin religious foundations and philosophies of politics, and comparable demographics and political ecologies, there are key historical differences worth considering across the Burmese, Thai, and Shan nations in the nineteenth and twentieth centuries:

1. Modern Burmese nationalism developed as an anticolonial project: a foreign power (the British) ousted the Konbaung king and replaced his authority with a secular government.
2. Modern Siamese/Thai nationalism was not anti-colonial but rather was imperial in its aspiration. Siam maintained its political authority and legitimation via the historic connection of the elite monarchy and religious authority. The Siamese regime united a growing national territory around ideas of Thai blood and nation. It sought to expand and consolidate its

power through erasing difference and incorporating more territories as T(h)ai.

3. From the end of the nineteenth century through World War II, Shan *sao hpa* retained their roles as semiautonomous rulers over smaller statelets across the uplands plateau as well as their connections as sponsors of Shan-style Buddhism. Colonialism drew together Shan elites, and post-colonial state-building mapped the Shan State as part of the Union of Burma while the Siamese sought to incorporate the Shan as part of their racial past and imperial future.

It was during the nineteenth century that European colonialism, as well as regional state-building, created a paradigm shift toward the so-called Westphalian notion of territorial sovereignty. In this model, a domain is mapped with discrete boundaries, subjects are counted, and citizenship is conferred through the state's definition of eligibility; finally that particular sovereign state has the exclusive right to rule over its domestic affairs and to police its lands. The governing structures of colonialism, with the Shan States ruled separately from "Burma Proper," brought *sao hpa* together as Shan, while at the same time allowed the Shan leaders to maintain certain aspects of their local cultural authority and autonomy over their subjects.

At Burmese colonial independence in 1948, Shan leaders fully anticipated there would be an independent Shanland in ten years. They had already begun building the foundation for their Shan home. Through what historian Prasenjit Duara has aptly termed the "symbolic regime of authenticity," Shan elites gave meaning to, and asserted their rightful connection with, the historic idea of Shanland. For there to be an authentic nation, there must be a people, a territory, and a history (2003, 27). How these three components came to be Shan and came together as a Shan nation-state by the end of World War II—however incomplete—is the task of this chapter. With special emphasis on the mutually understood, but fundamentally changing, grammar of sovereignty in the region, this chapter tracks the emergence of the idea of a united Shanland across congeries of statelets in the nineteenth century to the formation of an elite ethno-nation at the brink of colonial independence.

To situate Shan historiography in that combined trajectory, I first consider how ancient Shan history has been presented, both in concert with Thai/Tai origin myths and in political relationships with its Burmese counterparts but also as groups of "squabbling states" on the Shan plateau.

From there, attention turns to the political developments of the nineteenth century: colonial processes overthrew the Burmese regime, drew up boundaries, and territorialized and amalgamated approximately four dozen statelets into a single discrete set of Shan States.

Colonial mapping, state-building, and ethnology institutionalized new ideas regarding geography and political personhood. In addition to mapping the Shan States as a group, the British physically gathered together Shan elite people in their foundation of the Shan Chiefs' School in Taunggyi. By living and learning the ways of the colonial bureaucracy, Shan elites emerged (quite literally) as a new kind of class.

It is during this period that being Tai ceases to merely be a subject of a lowland paddy agriculture statelet and instead conceptually takes on the baggage of being a race or tribe in the cultural and even the biological sense. This notion of bios is mobilized at the local level, offering continuity with the imagined past, but also is mapped to a territorial homeland. This process was incorporated by Siamese (Thai) elites not only to consolidate their own political sovereignty domestically but also to justify an imperial project and ethnic Anschluss of other Tai groups, including the Shan. Twentieth-century nationalism and World War II stoked the ambitions of patriotic Southeast Asians that they would emerge as the leaders of independent, modern nations, Burmese, Thai, and Shan elites included.

As demonstrated by the personal stories and experiences of Shan people in the later ethnographic chapters, Shan peoples' lives comprise an ongoing interplay of military battles and cultural wars, fielded across multiple horizons. The ways in which Shan elites were in conversation with British, Thai, and Burmese nation-builders would crucially frame how history of Shanland is understood today. This chapter, therefore, plays on an anachronism, as stated in the title: Passport to Ancient Shanland. The passport is a technology of the modern nation-state that connects it with its eligible citizens. The state bureaucracy creates the parameters for acquiring the passport, and citizens must perform their eligibility in order to access the privileges that it encodes. The characteristics of an ideal future homeland, of a prosperous, united, independent Shanland, is projected onto the past. To Shan politicians, to repossess a Shanland, there must be evidence not only that there is such a place but also that they are its rightful owners. This chapter tracks the establishment of an ancient united Shanland, the homeland that the Shans once owned, and how the elites poised themselves to repossess it at the end of World War II.

Tracing the Shan Veins and the
Tais That Bind: A People

Like the Burmans, Thais, and the Khmer, Shan trace centuries of political history in Mainland Southeast Asia. Shan ruling classes, traders, and monastic orders maintained contact with their Burmese counterparts for centuries, in addition to relations with Chinese, Lanna, Lao, and Siamese peers, among others. There are several conflicting narratives concerning the historical beginnings of the Tai people, and it is dubious that there was a single discrete origin or migration at all. One explanation has gained a great deal of political momentum. Thai and Shan nationalists alike have latched onto the story that Terrien de Lacouperie (1844–94) advanced in his 1885 book, *The Cradle of the Shan Race*. De Lacouperie's hypothesis was iterated by the American missionary William Clifton Dodd in his 1909 book, *The Tai Race: The Elder Brother of the Chinese*.

As the story goes, seven thousand years ago, Tai peoples lived near the Altai Mountains in what is now central Mongolia. From there, they moved their towns and people southward, eventually settling in what is now southwestern Yunnan Province of China. There, they founded the Nanchao Kingdom and for centuries enjoyed independence from China. After a Mongol attack, Tai people were dispersed southward, settling in what is now the Shan States, Laos, and Northern Thailand (Suerkhan Fa would return some of these conquered areas to Tai sovereignty decades later[1]). With this southerly migration, Tai culture—particularly their wet-rice agriculture methods—spread to northeastern Myanmar, Thailand, Laos, and Vietnam. They would establish Sukhothai, the empire that Thai nationalists proudly present as their great classical state.

The Altai–Nanchao–Southeast Asia migration story has been refuted many times over the years by scholars who have argued that the Tai were not in Altai, nor was Nanchao dominated by Tais, and the story was invented by an Englishman (Terwiel 1978, 239, 240; Winai Pongsripian 1983, 414; Sujit 1984, 163, cited in Thak Chaloemtiarana 2007, 247). However, despite its uncertainty, the story has been embraced by Thai patriots, and through repetition it has become politically powerful not just in Thailand but in Laos as well (Evans 2014, 221). Various history books by Shan authors writing in Shan, English, and Burmese recapitulate this same narrative of a common Tai origin (Sao Kyan Möng ဝင်းၶျၢၼ်ႇရိင်း 1986; Khur Hsen ၶိုၼ်းသိၶႆ 1996; Sai Aung Tun 2009, 7–12; Möng Kham Hkö Hsang မိူင်းၶမ်းၶိုဝ်ႉသၢင် 2011; Sao Sanda 2008, 15; Ashin Thukameinda အရှင်သုခမိၼ 2008, 38).

For a Shan nationalist politician or a Shan freedom fighter, whose authority intrinsically depends upon these categories of ethnicity, the myth offers a common history, a connection to a civilized past, and a continuity of culture. These elements form part of the foundation for political identity and solidarity. Despite the fact that the Shan *sao hpa* with their kingdoms on the west side of the Salween River had greater political and historical connection with their Burmese neighbors than with their Siamese supposed kin to the southeast, the notion that their racial "stock" is one and the same with the Siamese would prove to be an enduring political discourse well through the twentieth and twenty-first centuries.

POLITICAL POWER AND THE THERAVADA ECUMENE: A LAND

During the centuries prior to European colonialism, Southeast Asia was sparsely populated, compared with China, India, and Europe.[2] In addition to this, there was a very different conception of sovereignty than that of the territorial nation-state we know today (Thongchai Winichakul 1994, 20, 74). Two-dimensional maps with their depictions of monochrome territories abutting discrete borderlines do very little to describe how cultural alliances or political power operate in the hills of upland Southeast Asia.

Unlike a patchwork quilt of multiple clear domains, in the Southeast Asian highlands there were cellular polities, sometimes overlapping sovereignties, with varying degrees of contact with and affinities for other principalities; who might be more powerful could be a matter of perception and speculation. Sovereignty in the Shan plateau could be akin to a complex coral reef at a gigantic scale, with holes and pockets separated by serious, but sometimes surmountable, divisions such as vast river gorges or dense forests, and varying forms of cultivation: lowland valleys with their wet-rice (paddy) agriculture, and swidden agriculturalists in the hills.[3] In addition to those who survived through fishing, hunting, and agricultural practices and a varying blend of survival strategies, from the sixteenth century on Han and Muslim Yunnanese traders crisscrossed the region (Chang 2013, 295). The Shan plateau is situated at the cultural, logistical, and ecological intersection of Southeast Asia, India, and China, still in conversation with other regions while maintaining its own degrees of autonomy and relevant local cultural dynamics of prestige and hierarchy. Although Thai and Burmese histories locate their respective classical civilization cores in their lowland kingdoms, the Shan plateau is more than a continental transit hub between these other places: it is diverse, complex, and culturally generative in its own right and through contact with migrants near and far.

Lowland towns with their paddy agriculture could accumulate surplus, attract long-distance traders, build Buddhist architecture and monuments, establish political institutions, sponsor religious orders, and host cultural events and celebrations. As such, they were often both the political and spiritual centers for the area. To have a resplendent city—with hundreds, if not thousands, of monks, gorgeous religious art, architecture, and gigantic festivals on holy days—was an important mark of civilization; it signified cosmopolitan sophistication (and probably hubris too). The city in Southeast Asian vernacular is *möng* in Shan (*myo* in Burmese; *mueang* in Thai). Other less powerful surrounding kingdoms would send tribute to these centers, in the form of symbolic gifts as well as material taxes and labor. The more power ruler would return a gift and a parchment that contained a title conferment at the initial ritual event (Thongchai Winichakul 1994, 83). In exchange for tribute and deference, more powerful patrons would be expected to reciprocate by protecting the safety and interest of their subjects.

In this system of political organization, there were not precisely defined boundaries but rather spheres of influence; sovereign power was exercised through people, not through land laws. At the district level in Shan cities of empire, a *kin möng* (town-eater, *myo sa* in Burmese) was responsible for collecting taxes and in-kind contributions from the local population. The *kin möng* would then remit these on up to the lord, or *sao hpa*, who controlled a given valley or kingdom. The *sao hpa*, in turn, may have sent tribute to other the more powerful *sao hpa*, or *sao haw kham* ("Lord of the Golden Pavilion" or most powerful king; elder Shan royalty also attracted the moniker "Khun"). These remittances were ritualized and usually took place according to the seasons and Buddhist holy days. The subordinate would present valuable gifts at the palace of his superior at the beginning of Buddhist New Year and at the end of rainy season (or Buddhist lent) to demonstrate loyalty both symbolically and materially (Asa Kumpha อาสา คำภา 2006, 93).

During the centuries under this political model, there were seldom wars of attrition; such battles would deplete future income and labor potential in an area already with a surplus of land and a relative shortage of people. Invasions and conquests resulted in war captives, which would be brought back to the capital city. Or battles might be fought to try to bring one chief to acknowledge the superior power of another and then start to remit slaves, valuables, soldiers, and royal tribute (Sompong สมพงศ์ 2001, 313). In cases of conquered cities, it was common practice to allow the conquered king to keep his throne and become a vassal state to the victor; only through this sort of arrangement could a king become a *maharaja* or king of kings (Tambiah 1976, 46).

Occasionally, rebellions were spurred by the imposition of excessive tax. To some extent, the greater king of kings had to be wary of overtaxing his vassal states and, if he did so, had to realize how to manage the unrest; in many cases, local states sought the protection of other patrons. Furthermore, the sparsely populated, complicatedly cellular kingdoms of the uplands coral reef presented a challenge to direct rule. Through experience, the Burmese developed a dictum, "Attacking the Shan seldom succeeds because it is hard to find enough Shan to attack. But one Shan can usually be neutralized through the opposition of another" (Cowell 2005, 5).

In his analysis of the relationship between Buddhism and state-building in Thailand, Stanley J. Tambiah (1976) proposed that the sum of these relationships could be understood as "Galactic Polities." The most powerful kingdom would be headed by a *cakravartin* (the Sanskit concept denoting the mover of the wheel), a divine monarch who conquered other kingdoms. But conquered kings would be left to manage their local kingdoms, so long as they sent tribute to their conqueror. Importantly as well, and in order for the king to be a true divine king of kings, his key activities included sponsoring the maintenance of the religious order, including the *sangha* (the Buddhist institution) and the construction of pagodas and supporting monasteries. The idea was mutually constitutive: an ideal king would sponsor a resplendent city where Buddhism could thrive, and in turn, the religion would reinforce the symbolic allure and power of the city and therefore its king. In this sense, a flourishing religion and merit-making economies would create a channel toward prosperity and, in a religious system predicated on cycles of rebirth, a propitious future reincarnation, assuming the system is working at its ideal.

Weaker states were not necessarily attracted to the cultural prestige of the powerful centers but sought to maintain their relative autonomy by affiliating themselves with one patron or by balancing multiple patrons against each other, hence the idea of overlapping sovereignty. The metaphor for this kind of relationship was that of a "two-headed bird" looking in multiple directions for patronage, with each patron legitimately claiming that smaller polity on their ledger as a vassal state (Owen 2005, 122).

With the Shan States located at the trade crossroads between China and Southeast Asia, there are abundant examples of Shan *sao hpa* paying tribute to multiple lords. For example, Chiang Khaeng, among others in the Upper Mekong valley, became known as a *mueang sam fai fa* "principality under three overlords" for being subordinate to three states at once (Grabowsky and Renoo Wichasin 2008, 1). The Shan state of Laikha bears that name because of this historical relationship; *lai kha* means "slaves of many masters." Shan *sao hpa* frequently paid tribute to Burmese, Chinese, Lanna (Northern Thai), and Siamese kingdoms, while at the same time collecting tribute from local towns.

This political relationship has been described by Oliver Wolters in terms of the Mandala state. According to this model, a powerful center state, with a regime identified with universal authority, would be surrounded by smaller states seeking security through affiliation with more powerful neighbors (1999, 27). As a rebuttal to this, in her book about Kachin history and politics, Mandy Sadan observes that the notion of the Mandala state tends "to be used as if it were a description rather than a paradigm." As she continues, the Mandala states as "cosmological constructs shift the emphasis towards the gravitational pull of the centers rather than the retrogression of their power outwards" (2013, 23).[4] Similarly, this dynamic has led to the notion of a physical and cultural ecology that intrinsically resists state-building projects, an area referred to as "shatter zones." The mountainous area across upland South and Southeast Asia comprises one such area that Willem van Schendel (2002) and James Scott (2009) have referred to as Zomia. For Scott, the concept of Zomia marks a new way to approach "area" studies because it is not based on an idea of bounded nation-states and instead looks to ecological characteristics, webs of interconnection, and cultures that do not lend themselves to the sovereign confines of the state (2009, 26).

While the "push" and "pull" of state power between a "core" and "periphery" makes for an instructive metaphor, it does fall short in that it fails to acknowledge the heterogeneity of spaces and groups and the dynamic ways in which multiple alliances and cultural exchanges interacted across this complex, dynamic region. Wolters's model of the Mandala state asserts that these relationships would expand and contract in "concertina-like" fashion (1999, 141). But the webs of power and patronage across this vast Shan plateau were so diverse that not every power boom would reverberate across the hills and valleys in the same way.

POLITICAL ECOLOGIES AND
CULTURAL DIFFERENCE: A STATE

Shan kingdoms—along with their Burmese, Siamese, and Lanna (Northern Thai) counterparts—are considered peer states in that they were based on paddy agriculture and followed a similar grammar of state-building and legitimation, or ritual language. While Tai principalities were located in the valley areas with their core wealth derived from paddy agriculture, other communities further up in the hills engaged in swidden (slash and burn) cultivation methods. While the latter was less labor intensive, it was also less productive and required relocation and clearing of new fields as the soil would become exhausted of its nutrients.

Even though the categories ascribed to named groups were relatively flexible at the individual level, the valley/highland division forms a fundamental cultural difference in the region. For the Shan *sao hpa*, their close interlocutors on the Shan plateau are the Kachin (which is a mass name for several groups, within which the Jinghpaw are politically dominant) and the Wa (known in Thailand as Lawa), along with numerous other groups, namely the Kayah, Pa-O, Akha, Kokang, and Ta-ang/Palaung.[5]

Shan chronicles from the thirteenth century mention sporadic confrontations of Tai kingdoms such as Kengtung and Chiang Mai with the "Lawa," later known as Wa (Fiskesjö 2013, 13). The Wa are historically prevalent in Northern Shan State, with significant populations in Yunnan Province as well. The Wa language is in the Mon-Khmer family of languages, and like the Ta-ang (Palaung), the Wa are thought to predate the arrival of Tai in the region. In the past six hundred years, the principal lowland interlocutors of the Wa have been the Shan. The Wa often maintained their autonomy by balancing the powers of their Shan lowland neighbors against those of the more distant Burmese and Chinese (Fiskesjö 2013, 6). The so-called wild Wa purportedly embrace a form of anarchic primitivism and actively eschew state-building and state-subordinating practices (Sadan 2013, 17).

In addition to varying ideas regarding political geography and sovereignty, locals in Southeast Asia subscribed to a very different concept of race or ethnicity than did the Europeans who would show up in later centuries (Gravers 2007, 13; Lee 2009, 37). Rulers of kingdoms at Ava, Ayutthaya, Bago, and Chiang Mai made reference to the peoples of other areas using terms that would foreshadow—but are not equivalent to—the names of modern nations and ethnic groups (Keyes 2002, 1173). When cultural behavior in the past is labeled as "Thai" (or any other label that has endured

over the centuries), we have to be wary of ascribing to it the same characteristics we associate with "Thai-ness" today (Wyatt 2001, 3).

Back in these precolonial Southeast Asian kingdoms, to be Tai did not
signify a common race in terms of a shared heritage, language, kinship, or
expressive culture; Tai-ness was not thought of as a biologically immutable
condition but rather as something that could be socially achieved. Up until
the nineteenth century, being Tai meant being a subject in one of these
lowland paddy-agriculture states, the *möng*, and being hierarchically organized surrounding a central ruler, *sao hpa*, and the temples that he sponsored. The counterpart, noncity-dwelling *kha* would be the people in the
forest (*ba* or *tuen*), or the highlands, engaged in slash and burn agriculture
or other forms of subsistence (Niti นิติ 2015, 20; Renard 2000, 66; Leach
1960, 53). Cultural prestige continues to coincide with political power, an
enduring theme for centuries to come.

BORDERLESS EMPIRE-BUILDING IN SOUTHEAST ASIA

Within this dynamic ethnographic terrain of upland Southeast Asia, larger
empires were in the process of consolidating their power over the smaller
ones; technologies of warfare and more efficient transportation increasingly drew the formerly isolated, independent areas into tributary relationships with fewer and fewer major states. Noting a trend across the longue
durée, historian Victor B. Lieberman observes that in 1320 there were twelve
independent empires in what is now Mainland Southeast Asia; two hundred
years later, there were eight, and by 1810, the number had shrunk to only
three: those of Burma, Siam, and Vietnam (Lieberman 1987, 187). Most
polities throughout the region, Shan principalities included, were paying
tribute to one of these big three, either directly or by proxy.

As these three major empires were the most powerful, they also became
centers of cultural prestige; the Burmese and Siamese regimes exemplified
the Brahmanic theater states in ritual and support for the Theravada Buddhism blended with Hinduism. Using these Indian symbolic models for
statecraft made sense given the dispersed demographics of the area (Lehman
2003, 17). The royal chronicles emphasized the prestigious and meritorious
accomplishments of the various regimes, ripe for later nationalist plucking,
while the actual extent of their contemporary prestige among their subjects, let alone those of their vassal states, is subject to speculation.

Shan *sao hpa* in vassal relations with Burmese regimes would demonstrate their affinity with the Burmese as the center of religious prestige by

practicing Buddhism in markedly Burmese ways, and in turn Burmese centers would dispatch monks to Shan monasteries. With the expansion of the Konbaung Dynasty in the eighteenth century in relation to the Shan, Tai elites were incorporating more aspects of dress, architecture, and religious practices from the Burmese (Lieberman 2003, 38). Conversely, there was an increased tendency to view Shan-tagged cultural practices as less modern (Khur Hsen ခွန်းသစ်ဆင် 1996, 252). Shan elites took on Burmese high culture, as a way to present themselves as worldly and cosmopolitan to their Burmese counterparts but also as a cultural strategy to differentiate themselves from their own commoner subjects.

One relevant geographic feature that does demarcate Shan political and cultural allegiance—to an extent—is the Salween River and its massive gorge that bisects today's Shan State. The Salween River Gorge, as a formidable physical boundary, has also been used to demarcate the difference in historic transfusion of Indianization through Southeast Asia over the centuries; this Indianization includes high culture and Hindu and Buddhist systems of rule. The Salween River has long formed a divide for Shan principalities' allegiance, with those on the west (from the Burmese side) called the cis-Salween states, as they tend to be subordinate to Burmese courts and therefore adopting more aspects of Burmese-tagged high culture, including Burmese Buddhist practices.[6] The throne room in the Hsipaw Palace, for example, was modeled after that of King Mindon's in Mandalay. Conversely, Shan principalities on the east side of the Salween River, the trans-Salween states, as well as the ones closer to Möng Mao and the Chinese emperor, were regarded by the Burmese as the more "savage" Shans (Sompong สมพงศ์ 2001, 205; Asa Kumpha อาสา คำภา 2006, 86). On the other hand, the trans-Salween states had their own relationships with different powerful centers of political and cultural prestige, including those in China, Lanna, Lancang (Lao), and Siam. For them, Burmese culture would not have carried the same cachet that it had for the cis-Salween Shan states. In sum, the cis-Salween Shan polities received their Indianization via the Burmese, whereas the Lao, Siamese, and Khuen (Tai of trans-Salween areas) would have acquired this high culture via Cambodian traditions (Terwiel 2003, 11).[7]

Sophistication and cosmopolitan-ness comprise an ever-shifting discourse of symbolic prestige regarding political authority, economic richness, and a positioning of up-to-date glamour, as it were. Despite there being linguistic similarity across groups as Tai, there were fundamental cultural differences based on centuries of political and cultural contact and change and, again, no specific mechanism that would draw these cellular Tai groups together; ideas of race or Tai-ness were not the existential glue that they would become in later years.

Colonial Categories, Colonial Consequences: Making the Territory

Although European traders, missionaries, and advisers had been present in the area since the sixteenth century, British annexation and colonization of what is now the Republic of the Union of Myanmar did not begin in earnest until the nineteenth century. Through a series of three Anglo-Burmese wars, 1824–26, 1852–53, and 1885–86, the area was incrementally incorporated into the British Empire.

In the middle of the nineteenth century, as the British expanded further into Burmese territory, the Konbaung King Mindon (r. 1853–78) increased the kingdom's control over the Shan principalities by dividing the area into four territories or *wun*: Möng Nai, Möng Yawnghwe, Möng Hsipaw, and Möng Hsenwi, with each of these sending scheduled taxes to the Burmese authorities in Mandalay (Renu เรณู 1998, 268). The Thathameda (tax) was first collected in 1868 in Möng Nai at the rate of 5 rupees per house, though the actual numbers did not correspond to the ledger (Saimong 1965, 103). In villages where there was a standard tax, often it was left up to the village headman how much to tax each household; the rich contributed a larger share in order to remit the appropriate sum to the government official.

During the three-week course of the third Anglo-Burmese War in November 1885, British gunboats moved up the Irrawaddy River, and troops surrounded Mandalay Palace. British soldiers removed King Thibaw (r. 1878–85), the last king of the Konbaung Dynasty, ushering him and his family to a secluded estate in Ratanakiri on the west coast of India. The Kingdom of Burma was presented to Queen Victoria as a birthday gift on 1 January 1886. However, Burma was not ruled as a colony on its own. Instead, it was annexed as a Province of British India, meaning it would be ruled via British Calcutta.

After their takeover of Mandalay, the British declared that all territories that had been vassal states to the Konbaung king (at the time of his removal) would now belong to the British Empire. Easier said than done. In the 1880s, there were approximately forty-three Shan principalities in the south and five in the north, though the territories were neither discrete nor exclusive to the various seats of power distributed across the complex coral reef of the uplands. As columns of British soldiers and bureaucrats ventured further into Shan states, they started to appreciate (or, more accurately, be bewildered by) the diversity of cultures and political allegiances they found in places that were uniformly labeled "Shan" in the Konbaung record books (Khur Hsen ခိုးသိးခင် 1999, 147).

Some Shan *sao hpa* were eager to collaborate with the British, others seemed indifferent to the idea, and no small number were downright belligerent to the prospect of joining the British Empire. For those happy to collaborate, the Shan *sao hpa* found their former enemy (the Burmese king Thibaw) had been neutralized and saw an opportunity to solidify their standing in relation to their peers. The Hsipaw *sao hpa* was especially keen to work with the British. His relationship with the Mandalay court had soured since the regime change from that of King Mindon to King Thibaw (with no irony lost on the fact that the king was part Shan and even named after the place—the names Thibaw and Hsipaw are cognates). With a new regime in Mandalay, the Hsipaw *sao hpa* sent a letter to the British representative saying that it would be "beneficial to the Shans to have their country welded into congeries of independent states like Germany" (Saimong 1965, 111).

While the Hsipaw *sao hpa* proposed a political model, the *sao hpa* of the Southern Shan State of Möng Nai assured the British that he was the leader and could speak on behalf of the *sao hpa* of the trans-Salween states. He also requested permission, as confirmation of his allegiance, to fly the Union Jack in the center of town. Permission was granted, and on 12 May 1887, in the presence of fifty Sikh colonial soldiers and a gathering of townspeople, the British flag was hoisted on a flagpole in the center of Möng Nai, to the ceremonial accompaniment of Shan drums and gongs (Saimong 1965, 144, 145).

For the British, the process of acquiring consent from dozens of other Shan states to join the empire was an expensive, laborious, and protracted endeavor. The *sao hpa* of Lawksawk was one of the Shan leaders who was hostile to the idea. A number of *sao hpa* who had already been organizing against the regime of King Thibaw to install a new monarch were unwilling to throw in their lot with yet another conqueror. In the 1890s, four of the Shan states had sought protection from the King of Siam (Sai Aung Tun 2009, 152). Between 1887 and 1895, the various Shan polities eventually were brought under the flag of the British Empire.

However, just because the Union Jack was flying on the flagpole at Möng Nai does not mean that the British ruled the area as they did in Mandalay.

Rather than replace all existing political and state structures at the local level, the British decided to designate the Shan states (as well as those controlled by Kachin *duwas* and some of the Chin areas) as Frontier Areas—as opposed to Burma Proper, or Ministerial Burma. In the Frontier (or Scheduled) Areas, Shan *sao hpa* maintained their local authority so long as they recognized ultimate allegiance to the British Crown (Department of Information 1986, 23). Although some of the *sao hpa* found this new arrangement curtailed their autonomy, others were granted greater power over their local subjects given the institutionalized status they wielded as part of the British Empire. Some of the especially profitable or desirable areas formerly under *sao hpa* control were annexed into Burma Proper: the gem mines at Mogok and the hill station of Maymyo (Pyin Oo Lwin).

The division of Colonial Burma into Burma Proper and the Frontier Areas was only one aspect of the new regime's territorial policies. After toppling the Konbaung Regime, the British replaced former local authorities with the British system of a village grid, with taxes collected according to a territorial ward system (Callahan 2003, 23). The main driver behind cooperating with the Shan *sao hpa* to annex the Shan states as a Frontier Territory was economic: it was simply cheaper to allow the Shan *sao hpa* to carry on ruling their domains than to replace their entire authority and systems with British institutions. However, the British colonial authorities did want the Shan states' bureaucracies to operate in ways that were compatible with their system. So, they opened an institution to allow Shan elites to become schooled in the ways of British Empire and English gentlemen.

SHAN CHIEFS SCHOOL AND ELITE LEARNING: A CLASS

Charles Crosthwaite, the chief commissioner of Burma (1887–90), noted in his first conference with the *sao hpa* that many of the Shan chiefs appeared not to have met each other before; as he later wrote about the occasion, he saw the British administration as a step toward creating a unified Shan country (Sao Sanda 2008, 32). In 1902 the British administration inaugurated the School for the Sons of Shan Chiefs in Taunggyi (aka the Shan Chiefs School, later to be renamed Kambawza College). The Shan Chiefs School was established with the intention of educating Shan elites in the English language and to give them a foundation in Western education so that they would be effective in their future roles as statesmen and leaders in

Shan states. It was also hoped that by training Shan leaders in the ways of British bureaucracy, the territory would become more profitable for the empire. Members of the Shan elites who attended Shan Chiefs School received bilingual education: English and Burmese, with the former thus preparing these young men for higher education in England or the United States. Some went to Oxford or Cambridge. The prince of Hsipaw in the 1950s, for example, would attend the Colorado School of Mines.

Like a British boarding school, strict discipline was enforced, and organized sports were part of the program to build esprit de corps (Simms 2017, 48). However, only the wealthier of the *sao hpa* sent their sons to study at the school. Importantly as well, the Shan Chiefs School created an institution through which the sons of elite Shans would get together, form networks, and think of themselves as Shan; while exile is the incubator of nationalism, the school took these boys away from their families and put them all together, encouraging a form of "old boys" network of class but also encouraging them to think of themselves as Shan Chiefs and, with that very notion, increasingly to have something in common with each other *as* Shan. And through their collective identity as Shan Chiefs, also thinking of their non-elite people in their home states as Shan subjects, including those of the various ethnic groups in the Shan highlands.

Ethnic Statistics and Categorical Genesis

As discussed earlier, Southeast Asians in the eighteenth and nineteenth centuries subscribed to a very different understanding of culture and ethnicity than did their European counterparts. According to colonial rhetoric, making maps of the area and studying the land, the resources, and its people would allow the British the authority to govern according to a legitimating rhetoric of being rational, scientific, and modern (Banerjee-Dube 2008, xxxvii). These endeavors included carrying out colonial censuses. The colonial census operations, by making use of notions of "race" and "tribe," constitute colonial forms of knowing about a place. By collating data, the census gives a statistical fix—a bureaucratic solidity—to certain social groups (Peabody 2001, 821; Kumar 2006, 378). All in the name of science, and empiricism in service of the colonial economy and domination.

Enter Sir Herbert Hope Risley, British ethnographer and colonial administrator. Risley was an exemplar of the fusion between administrator and anthropologist in the emergent ethnographic state (Srivatsan 2005, 1987).

In earnest enthusiasm for Victorian-era empiricism, Risley came to the field, as it were, with the belief that the previous shortcomings of ethnographic works could be corrected by "systematic original research" (Risley 1891, 236).

In 1873, as a result of his extensive work in anthropology, linguistics, and sociology of India, Risley attained the position of assistant director of statistics (Risley 1915, xxii). His project, the Ethnographic Survey of Bengal, resulted in the four-volume set, *Tribes and Castes of Bengal*. Risley's work categorized people according to caste, or their location within a hierarchical social system based on occupation and prestige and related to ideas about social boundaries and pollution. This was a master trope in the framing of the imperial census and had gained considerable traction in how colonial officials understood human variation in British India (Kumar 2006, 387). Although named hierarchies and social identities existed in Asia before Risley, the colonial act of putting together a list, another framework, and then surveying people according to that framework created a new lens through which political and social reality can be viewed, coded, understood, and managed. There was an assumption that with a scientifically accurate census, basic sociological facts about the place could be presented. At the same time, the project objectified social, cultural, and linguistic differences (Cohn 1996, 8).

Since the annexation of Upper Burma to British India took place in 1886, the next decennial census would extend to the peoples of these new colonial dominions, including the frontier areas. In 1899 Risley was appointed census commissioner, and the caste schematic that he developed in Bengal would be applied to the census in Burma, falling under the domain of C. C. Lewis, commissioner for the 1901 census.

However, as census enumerators would soon discover, those caste categories were largely inapplicable in Burma. Although the Burmese vernacular did have the idea of *jati* (derived from Sanskrit for [re]birth, but later understood in India as caste), in Burmese the cognate *zat* was understood as birth without the same occupational affiliation or pollution taboos ascribed to caste (*jati*) in India. With the exception of the royal lineage, there was a great deal more social flexibility in Burmese society than in India. For the Burmese, although *zat* was not as widely understood as a social category, the notion of *lumyo* ("type of person" in Burmese) was salient, at least at the administrative level. But an important caveat: *lumyo* was concurrent with social status or class distinction, not some notion of language, race, or tribe (Ikeya 2011, 25). It was during the colonial years that the meaning of the word *lumyo* would be fundamentally changed.

In their enumerations in Burma, census officials (unsurprisingly) encountered difficulty in trying to assess people's caste. Enumerators discovered they could not elicit a response for many. Imagine asking a Buddhist, "What is your birth?" One could think of the various abodes of existence. A great number responded to the question not with a "caste" category but rather by saying *thaman lu* or "commoner." As C. C. Lowis observed, "The Burman has, save with very rare exceptions, no idea whatever of the precise meaning of the word "caste." He is . . . so absolutely enamored of freedom that he cannot abide the bonds that caste demands" (1902, 107).

Lowis later observed that his enumerators were able to make more traction with the concept of *amyo* (as the "type" part of *lumyo*); however, in order to categorize according to the European expectation that there must be named races and tribes of people, the decision was made to name groups according to the name of the language that they spoke. As Lowis explained, "Where caste is unknown and religion indicates but little, it [language] is the most obvious and surest criterion of difference" (1902, 112). In addition to the problem of identifying people in Burma according to caste or religion, the schema they developed for physical differences had also proved difficult to apply in Bengal. In the end, rather than abandon their task to label the race of each subject of the empire in Burma, the British authorities decided to make the name of one's language contiguous with that of their race.[8]

Where notions of ethnicity coincided with ideas of prior sovereignty and contemporary expressive culture, the foment for colonial resistance would later become channeled along these very categories. While forms of political rule will symbolically privilege one group over the other, hence the creation of elites and their cultural prestige, the idea of "ethnos" as both socially constructed but increasingly considered biologically immutable is a product of European enlightenment ideas and scientific racism. The bureaucratic momentum enabled by the equation of language with ethnicity (or race or tribe) is still felt to this day, where one's *lumyo* (formerly social status, now "race") or *taingyintha* (indigenous race) is often assumed coterminous with language, despite the everyday reality of multilingualism throughout the region, especially among marginalized groups.

Siam to Thai and the Rebirth of a Nation

Siam is unique among Southeast Asian countries for having managed to avoid direct European colonization. Thai patriotic discourse frequently attributes this anomaly in Southeast Asian history to the clever diplomacy of enlightened Siamese monarchs. Furthermore, the country's noncoloniality has been treated in nationalist history as an "unqualified blessing" (Anderson 1978, 197).

Aside from Siamese diplomatic adroitness, it may have been just as well for the Europeans not to colonize Siam for two foundational reasons: there was utility in having a buffer state between British Burma and French Indochina; and the British were able to acquire special trade privileges via the signing of the Bowring Treaty in 1855. Given the fact that the Shan states were already ruled as a Frontier Area, and the British had gone to considerable effort to acquire these territories as such, the prospect of toppling and colonizing yet another Southeast Asian polity could rightly have been seen as too expensive and laborious.

It was during this period of intense Western colonial interest in Mainland Southeast Asia that the Siamese regime, through bureaucratic changes, stepped up to the world stage and sought to present itself as a unified and civilized nation-state. Again, like the Shan *sao hpa* in the cis-Salween states took on Burmese-Indic cultural forms to present themselves as cosmopolitan and sophisticated (not just to the Burmese but also to their subjects), the Siamese began to look to Europe as the center of power and of cultural prestige. The Siamese elites were very much concerned with being seen on par with the West, in terms of dress, deportment, and sovereignty (Reynolds 1991, 8). One discourse they forged was that of *siwilai*, a Thai cognate of the English word "civilize" but an ideology for a transculturation process to incorporate European ideas and practices—especially those having to do with progress and sophistication—into Siam. This was not just a response to a European imposition; it was also a strategy to assert Siamese dominance as an imperial power (Thongchai Winichakul 2000, 529). This latter assertion would have direct effects on the Shan states and how they would soon be objectified not only as former vassal states "lost" to Britain but also, later, as ethnic kin united by a common blood.

Whereas the reign of Rama V, King Chulalongkorn (r. 1868–1910), is characterized as a period of broad economic and political transformations, Siamese adoption of European ideas of race and ethnicity had massive effects (Streckfuss 1993, 125). In the centuries prior, Siam was demographically and culturally very much like Konbaung Burma; the basis for comparison is substantial. Siam and Burma were fed through wet-rice agriculture; they were ideologically and existentially nourished through Theravada Buddhist and Hindu hierarchies and connections to the cosmos; and finally, their shared vassal states and long histories of interconnection made them peer kingdoms. In addition to this, like their Burmese counterparts, Siamese peasants did not have a notion of biologically immutable race or tribe. And as with Burmese semantics, the Thai cognate for *jati* (*chat*) meant rebirth, not caste. Siamese politics would soon resignify this term, but rather than a paradigm shift coming in because of a European colonial imposition, the new Thai concept of race would be imposed by an internal elite.

During the late nineteenth and early twentieth centuries, in Siam the meaning of *chat* would start to take on the symbolic baggage that it carries today: citizenship, race or ethnicity, and nation. In his book *Siam Mapped*, historian Thongchai Winichakul details the shift in the meaning and use of *chat*: through their emphasis on aesthetic nationalism and authentic racial heritage, Siamese elites added *khwamphenthai* "Thainess" to the idea of *chat*. In addition to being born a human, people would be of the same *chat* by being subjects of the same regime and by sharing culture. Through the combination with notions of sovereign territoriality, the Siamese state fused the idea that the mapped place coincided with its racial subjects, or what Thongchai terms the geo-body (Thongchai 1994, 134–35).

For Siamese elites, formation of *chat* as nation meant collapsing regional difference, absorbing ethnic heterogeneity, and making all citizens inside the nation's borders Thai. A rebirth now meant belonging to a particular nation-state. Regional ethnonyms were erased and replaced with Thai in 1899. Regional histories were overwritten as Thai, making those areas— and those people—more Thai in the present (Niti นิติ 2004, 2; Peleggi 2007, 36). Cultural nationalism in the first half of the twentieth century in Siam/Thailand had strong economic undertones. The slogan "Thailand for the Thai" was a jab not just at European capitalists but also at the significant populations of Chinese living in the country (Wyatt 1984, 254). The name change of the country from Siam to Thailand was a chauvinistic move placing greater importance on the Thai ethnic groups, not only for Thais within the country but also claiming Tai groups beyond the borders of Siam/ Thailand (Evans 1999, 17, 5). As mentioned earlier, the Thai appropriation of *siwilai* being on par with the Europeans also meant being imperial. But where could the Siamese reasonably carry out their imperial ambitions?

Logically, such an imperial project would start with repossession of formerly owned territories (albeit anachronistically). Former vassal states to the Siamese (even though they were also vassal states to others as well) or areas deemed to be inhabited by Tai peoples were all included in a new pantheon of "lost territories."[9] Especially for areas inhabited by Tai speakers, the new discourses of race offered a powerful link to these territories through a perception of a shared ancestry.

With British imperialism throwing the status of the Shan states into question, these cultural—or even ancestral—ideologies started to test their wings. As mentioned earlier, after the fall of Mandalay in 1885 and the British troop movements to secure cooperation with the various *sao hpa*, some of the Shan states had sought protection from the Siamese regime. In a conversation with the British regarding the status of these principalities, King Rama V responded, "The Thai (Siamese), the Lao, and the Shan all consider themselves peoples of the same race (*chat*). They all respect Us as their supreme sovereign, the protector of their well-being" (Winai Pongsripian 1983, 392). Those states in question would become part of the Frontier Areas to British Burma/India. The British having the upper hand in delineating the border between Siam and Shan states has since fed into the discourse that the Shan states were "lost territories" (Onanong Thippimol et al. อรอนงค์ 2011, 110).

In addition to both uniting Tai people around *chat* and using the term to define a territorial nation, Siamese nationalism made use of a symbolic Other, an enemy to unite against. One cannot have inclusion without exclusion. Instead of predicating their Siamese identity against a European colonizer (after which they hoped to model themselves), Siamese nation-builders of the 1930s made use of the figure of a Burmese "evil enemy." Such discourse argued that the Burmese was not just a threat to the integrity of the Siamese nation but also a kind of historical colonial power over Siam (Sunait Chutintaranond 1992, 94; Reynolds 2003, 15). And this figure would be deployed in Thai school history textbooks, novels, plays, songs, and films starting in the 1930s. These texts and performances depicted the Burmese as evil incarnate, cutting off the heads of Buddha images and killing monks in meditation. These popular media had thinly veiled goals of national unity and stability through rituals of aesthetic nationalism (Jiraporn Witayasakpan 1992, 333; Charnvit ชาญวิทย์ 2001, v; Lysa 2003, 61). Conveniently for the Siamese, the Burmese had since been conquered by the British, so for the time being, the historical projection of the evil Burmese did not provoke any retaliation on the part of their historic enemy.

The crucial paradigm shift in Burma and Thai cosmologies and understandings of identity and subjectivity toward ideas of a biologically immutable idea of race had taken place in a similar way. But there were key differences. In Burma, although the British census commissioners had hoped to survey the population and categorize it according to caste, or its cognate *zat*, they were frustrated because the concept did not carry the kind of racial or tribal differentiation that fit their expectation of ethnic difference or boundary. So by shifting their queries to language and equating that with race or tribe, they eventually changed the meaning of *lumyo*. Instead of *lumyo* representing social class, it started to mean race. The Siamese elites, having a very similar concept of *chat* and being the ruling class—at the top of the order for human beings—justified their rule by drawing upon the Buddhist conception of rebirth but using it to connect not only to a territorial state but also to an anticipated empire of Tais beyond the country's present borders.[10] However, unlike the Thai use of *chat*, the Burmese term *lumyo* would never signify the territorial nation; instead, it would only be applied to "races" of people.

SHAN NATIONALISM IN THE 1930S

Shan people—as fellow Tai brethren—were included in Thai nation-building concepts of race and T(h)ai-ness. Despite the appropriations of *lumyo* in Burmese and *chat* in Thai, the equivalent of race or ethnicity in Shan is *hkö* (ၶိူဝ်း), which means lineage. *Hkö* is also used for plant vines. It denotes connection and ancestry, emphasizing the historical connection to Tai *sao hpa* as hereditary rulers. The term *hkö* is often used in conjunction with *möng*, the idea of city or civilization.[11] For example, one of the Shan history books used as a key reference in my discussion is *Pün Hkö Tai Lae Pün Möng Tai* (History of the Shan race and history of Shan civilization). For the Shan nationalists, the use of the cognate *jati* (*sat* [ၸၢတ်ႈ] in Shan) to signify race and nation-state would only gain currency in the Shan resistance movements in the late 1950s.

During the decades under British colonialism, the political structure of plural Shan states, as enforced through the colonial bureaucracy, served to preclude elites in the Shan states from completely amalgamating or uniting as Shan (or more accurately, from one Shan subsuming the others). Various *sao hpa* had argued for what would be a federation at colonialism and preferred to look after their own fiefdoms. When Maurice Collis interviewed the Tawngpeng prince in regard to the possibility of a Shan president of the Shan Chiefs Council in 1936, he was met with the response, "We Sawbwas are too jealous of each other. A Shan president of the Federation would lack support and authority" (Collis 1938, 212).[12]

Whereas the Konbaung Dynasty was toppled and replaced by the British colonial regime, in contrast, Shan elites in the Frontier Areas were largely left to their own devices (Yawnghwe 1987, 13). Some members of the Shan ruling classes would later look back on the period of semi-autonomous rule under British colonialism as a "golden age" for the Shan states. The Shan *sao hpa* no longer had to worry about their former enemies; the Burmese kings were gone, and the Chiang Mai royalty in what is now Northern Thailand was being subsumed by Bangkok authorities. *Sao hpa* had legal jurisdiction over civil cases, controlled their own military forces, and in the event of serious challenges could call upon the reinforcements of the colonial army.

The former system of the Shan rulers paying tribute to the Burmese monarch obviously was gone, as were many of the political patron-client relationships between them. Whereas Shan elites had once considered the Indian, Burmese, Siamese, and Vietnamese royalty their peers, European colonialism was a game changer. Rather than send young princes and princesses to join the courts of their Southeast Asian peers as they had done in centuries past, Shan *sao hpa* first sent their kids to Shan Chiefs School and later sent them overseas to get a Western-style education (although some of the teenage children of Shan elites did become students at the University of Rangoon).

However, one dimension of this administration that Shan politicians and members of the elite classes would later lament is the fact that the British did not dedicate significant resources to either the integration of the Shan areas with the international economy or to the broader education of the youth in that area. Economic integration could be a double-edged sword, as the Burmese lowlanders became increasingly dependent on the ups and downs of the international market, but at the same time, some Shan elites began to feel that their areas were "backward" compared with those of their Burman counterparts. Ordinary Shan people received little benefit from British colonial modernity (Adams 2000, 113).

Some of the peasantry resented that some *sao hpa* appeared to be getting wealthy at their expense (a point that was also latched onto by the budding anti-colonial nationalist movement in Rangoon). As one of my fieldwork interlocutors, Sai Lek from Möng Nai, explained: "The sao hpa did not want the rest of us to be educated. That's why they didn't teach us to read. They knew that if the villagers all could read, they would start to have more power—they would start to want to change things." This incorporation of the Shan principalities as part of the Frontier Areas made for a political distinction that led some Burman nationalists to believe that it gave the

Shan elites a greater sense of importance and political entitlement (Simms 2017, 44).

In 1922 the colonial government instituted the Federated Shan States. Under this new system, the Shan *sao hpa* would be responsible for law and order, maintaining criminal and civil courts, appointing officials, and controlling subjects, though all "under the advice of superintendents" (Shan States Manual 1933, iii). Although it may have been motivated by a desire to make the Shan States self-supporting, many saw this as a stripping away of the *sao hpa*'s powers (Maule 1993, xx; Elliott 2006, 61). Joining the federation meant that the Shan elites lost some of the previous control they had over their schools and police forces. The main reason the Shan *sao hpa* bought into the new federation scheme was they thought they might have lost their hereditary rights entirely if they were integrated into Burma Proper (Gravers 1999, 25). By 1935, another set of reforms gave the *sao hpa* greater representation in government, but with the advancement of Japanese imperialism in Asia, and clandestine operations commencing between the Japanese, Burmese nationalists, and Thai patriots, British Burma was not long for the world, nor were the Shan States as a Frontier Area.

Southeast Asian Nationalism and World War II

British colonialism's removal of the Konbaung monarchy and the rapid transformations of both the nature of the economy and social life itself did not come without increasing factionalism and dissent. Early Burmese nationalists—themselves relative elites within the Burmese economy—felt the rupture of the removal of their king and the subsequent British imposition of bureaucracy and secular education as further evidence of religious decline; for Burmese Buddhists, colonialism was not just a political and economic change but also a threat to their worldview (Turner 2014). Likely fueled by a tinge of jealousy that their own king had been violently taken away, in addition to growing modernist ideologies that saw hereditary monarchies as modes of the past, Burmese nationalists sometimes chided the Shan areas as feudal, backward, and ruled by helplessly old-fashioned oriental despots.[13] In one Burmese account, the Shan and Kachin leaders reigned supreme while the commoners were too busy with gambling and opium to develop any political consciousness. Burmese ire toward the leaders in the Frontier Areas was also stoked by the fact that the Shan *sao hpa* and Kachin *duwa* could rightly be seen as colonial collaborators.

Thus, in the early decades of the twentieth century, we can see an internationalizing economy in Burma and a peasantry increasingly dependent on the whims of the market. At the same time, there emerged a Burmese middle class embracing certain ideas about race, as well as international ideas about anti-colonial nationalism. Dobama Asiayone (We Burmese Organization) was comparable to other anti-colonial ethno-national movements. In French Indochina, the colonial encounter and European discourses about historical preservation incited Khmer nationalists to view their ethnic identity as a link to a common ancestral blood. By grabbing onto ideas about race, nationality, and historic rule—in addition to pointing to contemporary material inequities—Southeast Asian political movements garnered support by arguing that they were the historic rulers of the land, and their rightful authority was stolen by a foreign enemy. Their arguments that they were the rightful owners of the land did not, however, include a return to former dominions; they anticipated a modern, democratic society, but one in which Southeast Asians would be at the helm, both politically and economically.

The military upheavals of World War II ushered in massive political transformations throughout Southeast Asia. This chain of events was spurred not just by the war in Europe, which threatened the colonial Metropole, but also by the emergence of Japanese imperial power challenging European control over its colonies in Asia. After the Japanese invasion of Manchuria in 1931, followed by the annexation of parts of China in 1937, several Southeast Asian nationalist groups began to look eagerly to the Japanese "Greater East Asia Co-Prosperity Sphere" as a means by which they could wrest themselves from the yoke of European colonial domination. Burmese nationalists were no exception. The Japanese played on Burmese nationalists' aspirations, and they couched their ideologies in terms of "Asia for Asians" and suggested that the Burmese would be able to restore Buddhism through this new military movement.

A group of former Rangoon University student activists from the Dobama Asiayone founded the Communist Party of Burma (CPB) in Rangoon on 15 August 1939. The following year, the CPB sought to link up with the Communist movement in Shanghai (Lintner 1990, 5). In August 1940 they dispatched two of their key members, Aung San and Hla Myaing (Yan Aung), to sail to China. But, taking a Norwegian ship out of the Port of Rangoon, they ended up in Amoy, where they spent three unproductive months, until Major Kanda from the Kenpeitai (the secret police force

within the Japanese Imperial Army) found the young Burmese revolution-
aries (Yellen 2020, 129). Kanda invited them to Japan to receive military
training and to learn about the Japanese plans to extend their Greater East
Asia Co-Prosperity Sphere into Southeast Asia, and he later brought more
young Burmese activists to receive military training as part of the Minami
Kikan (Japanese Secret Service). This group of would later become known
as the "Thirty Comrades."

Meanwhile in Shan States, as part of their allegiance with the British as
rulers of the Frontier Areas, some Shan elite families actively served in the
British military. From 1940, a number of Shan princes served in the thirteenth Shan State battalion of the Burma Rifles (Simms 2017, 60). Kawn
Söng, the future leader of the Shan United Revolutionary Army, was a soldier in Detachment 101 of the United States Army.

The Thirty Comrades returned to Burma, where they subsequently were
able to amass an army of 3,500 Burmese sympathizers and called their organization the Burma Independence Army or BIA (Lintner 1990, 6). By February 1942 their numbers had grown to 4,860 men (Yellen 2020, 133). On
7 March 1942, the Japanese military and the BIA successfully took Rangoon. Two months later their ranks had swollen to 23,000 troops (Naw
2001, 88; Callahan 2003, 47). In the same year, the Burma Independence
Army was renamed the Burma Defense Army (BDA). The BDA got a boost
of popularity among Burmese youth when Burmese action movie stars
Kyaw Swe and Tin Pe joined the ranks of the BDA (Tetkatho Khin Maung
Zaw တက္ကသိုလ်ခင်မောင်ဇော် 2012, 62). However, the Japanese soldiers and the
Burmese of the BDA, which later transitioned to the Burma National
Army, were not well received by locals in the Shan States; in fact, many
Shan did not view them as a liberating force (after all, the Shan States were
Frontier Areas only partially under the thumb of the British Empire). For
the Shan peasantry, these groups were a foreign band of occupiers. Various
Shan history books record that the Burmese and Japanese armies treated
the Shan locals badly, raped women, abused children and burned entire vil-
lages (Sao Khwan Möng ᦷᦟᧂᦶᦉ 1986, 44; Khur Hsen ᦆᦴᦷᦉ 1996, 320).

Many of the *sao hpa* and their families, given their allegiance with the
British, fled the incoming Japanese and BDA/BNA troops. Some left the
country entirely, while others went into hiding. The Yawnghwe royalty,
for example, sought shelter in a village on Inle Lake (Simms 2017, 15, 60).
Groups of Chinese people who had long resided in Shan areas found it

suddenly necessary to assimilate as Shan. One of my fieldwork interlocutors—Aung Myo—detailed his family's experience during the Japanese occupation. At the time, they lived in a village a day's journey by oxcart from Panglong in Southern Shan State:

> My family told me that during the war, they once went for five days without eating a meal. They often didn't have rice to eat and so had to live on gruel made with bits of corn. The Japanese really hated the Chinese, too. They would often abuse or even kill Chinese families and children; it did not matter if they were just villagers. My family especially, they stopped speaking Chinese, they just used Shan and took down the Chinese altar in their house. They hid or got rid of anything that would make the Japanese think they were Chinese.

Aung Myo's family experience iterates that cultural groups will adjust their performances of ethnicity—their "situational ethnicity"—when it is advantageous to do so; in this case, merely to survive. However, in the Shan hills, as elsewhere, successfully changing one's social identity is not simply an act of the free will of the individuals; social gatekeepers will have their own sets of criteria for evaluation. Fortunately for Aung Myo's Yunnanese family, they were able to "pass" as Shan in the eyes of the Japanese. Some Yunnanese in Shan States went to the trouble of getting full sets of Shan tattoos to present themselves as Shan to the Japanese occupiers.

Although the Greater East Asia Co-Prosperity Sphere as marketed by the Japanese was initially attractive to some of the Burmese nationalists, the period of Japanese occupation, at the ground level, was hardly the Asian cultural and political renaissance they had been promised. Rampant warfare, hunger, and humiliation characterized the period.

Like the Burmese nationalists, the ruling military regime in Siam saw World War II as a timely opportunity to put into action some of its own political aspirations. The Thai prime minister and military general, Phibun Songkram, signed a non-aggression pact with the Japanese; he had an eye to "reclaiming" Tai territories that had been "lost" to colonial powers. This would have serious repercussions for some of the Shan States.

On 13 and 14 December 1941, Lt. Gen. Shojiro Iida of the Fifteenth Japanese Army in Thailand and Rear Admiral Naomasa Sakonju met with General Phibul Songkram to outline their military collaboration. They decided that Thai and Japanese joint forces would operate in Thailand, whereas the invasion of central and lower Burma would be the responsibility of the Japanese forces and their coalition with Burmese nationalists. The agreement stipulated that the Thai forces would operate along the northern region, up toward the Shan State of Kengtung, and west to Mandalay (Murashima 2006, 1061). In February 1942, the Siamese Air Force began operating sorties with the Japanese out of Northern Thailand. In one sortie, they attacked the Kengtung market. Siamese pilots escorted twelve KI 27 Otas and nine KI 30 Nagoyas in their bombing missions in the Shan States (Young 1995, 187).

In mid-1943, the Japanese presented two Shan principalities—Kengtung and Möng Pan—to the Thai government (Sao Khwan Möng ဝင်းခွာ၆မိုင်း 1986, 45).[14] The Japanese Imperial Army described these as "royal gifts for being a good friend and for giving passage to the Japanese in the invasion of Burma" (Sai Aung Tun 2009, 207). This action *infuriated* the *sao hpa* of Kengtung and Möng Pan, as they were not consulted prior to the execution of this decision. A group of *sao hpa* subsequently went to Rangoon to discuss the issue (U Ohn Pe ဦးအုန်းပေ 1984, 237).

Following the Japanese transfer of the Shan States to Thailand on paper, the Thai Army mobilized a garrison of soldiers, calling them Kongthap Phayap "Northern Army." They were dispatched to occupy Möng Pan and Kengtung, which the Thai government renamed the Saharat Tai Duem (Original United Tai States) and installed Thai rule of law (Thak Chaloemtiarana 2007, 26). This marks an important moment in regional ethnonationalist history, not only because discourse about ethnic closeness between the Thais and the Shan becomes part of the justification for Thai annexation of these two Shan States but also because military resources are mobilized to actualize that plan.

The Shan rulers—and the villagers in those so-called Original United Tai States—unsurprisingly, did not share this feeling of ethnic brotherhood. Both Shan elites as well as locals saw the Thai soldiers as an occupying force rather than long-lost kin. Though the Thai troops did not find much initial resistance in the acquisition of the territories, the soldiers tended to behave like settlers and were generally unpopular with the locals. They imposed new cultural norms on the locals, including forbidding the chewing of betel nut, prohibiting topknots for men, mandating new haircuts for women, and encouraging them to wear skirts instead of sarongs; in other words, the similar mandates of *siwilai* that the Siamese government imposed on its own subjects just a few decades ago (Thongchai Winichakul

2000). The experience gave Shans the feeling of being "second rate subjects" of the Kingdom of Thailand (Lintner 1994, 68), and for some, World
War II forced an awakening of the Shan nation (Yawnghwe 1987). As it
would end up, the only military operations that the Thai armies would see
outside Thailand during World War II would be these forays into the Shan
States of Kengtung and Möng Pan.

When the Burmese nationalists initially collaborated with the Japanese,
they had done so in the hope for independence, not to end up occupied by
another force. As Aung San had put it, "we invited the Japanese invasion of
Burma, not by any pro-Fascist leanings but by our own naïve blunders and
petty bourgeois timidity" (Naw 2001, 71). When tides started to turn, and
it was increasingly evident that they were on the losing side, leadership of
the Burma Independence Army sought to switch to the Allied forces; their
new group was known as the Anti-Fascist People's Freedom League (AFPFL).

As part of the Japanese unconditional surrender to the Allied forces in
August 1945, colonial territories were returned to Britain, including the
Shan States of Möng Pan and Kengtung.[15] Despite the return to colonial
status, Burmese and Shan politicians alike anticipated independence. Shan
politicians were well aware of international events such as the Atlantic Char-
ter of 1941 and the Tehran Agreement of 1943 (Department of Information
1986, 33). The British organized negotiations in London but only included
Burmese politicians.

In January 1947, Aung San and Clement Attlee signed the creatively
named Aung San–Attlee agreement, which would promise Burma independence within the period of a year (Naw 2001, xii). While Aung San was in
London, some Shan *sao hpa* sent a telegram to the British to iterate that
Aung San did not represent them (U Pe Kin 1994, 3). Although the Burmese patriots may have been thrilled to achieve their goal, the British
imposed a special clause: prior to granting the Burmese home rule, the
British demanded evidence of cooperation with the former Frontier Areas,
the very political leaders who had maintained their own relative autonomy
throughout the years of colonial rule. Would they be willing to throw in
their lot with a new Union of Burma? Under what conditions?

A New Title Deed for Shanland or a Nation-State on Layaway?

In the postwar period, political leaders in the Frontier Areas were concerned
about the future. In March 1946, Chin, Kachin, Karen, and Shan leaders

met in Panglong, near Loilem in Southern Shan States, to discuss their options. The war had left much of their infrastructure ravaged; they did not feel that the British supported full independence for these Frontier Areas, nor would the British admit them as dominions within the Commonwealth (US Congress 1975, 253).

The following February, on the heels of having signed his agreement with Clement Attlee in London, General Aung San and U Nu traveled to Panglong to meet with many of those same Frontier Area leaders. Aung San offered the leaders the possibility of a federal state and promised that they would have local autonomy, freedom, and equality within the Union of Burma. The phrase most associated with this sentiment is Aung San's declaration, "If Burma gets a *kyat*, Shan will get a *kyat*" (ဗမာတကျပ်ရှမ်းတကျပ်) (Hang Hseng Yawd ၅၁၆း၁၆ိင္ယ၀တ်း 1995, 1). The latter quotation is taken as evidence of the promise of equality in distribution of state resources. Another reading could reflect the fact that Aung San saw the Shan political leaders not only as the group best prepared for self-rule but also as the most capable of forestalling independence.

In the end, Aung San was successful in his trip to Shan States and returned with a document signed by himself and twenty-two Chin, Kachin, and Shan leaders agreeing to join the Union of Burma. The document, the Panglong Agreement, was signed on 12 February 1947 and offered the British sufficient evidence of cooperation from the Frontier Areas to grant independence to the AFPFL.

Aung San's legacy includes being the first Burmese politician to show concern for the ethnic minorities, and the Frontier Area leaders saw Aung San and U Nu as the only politicians who actively reached out to them in the difficult postwar time (Naw 2001, xii). Many Shan political leaders, to this day, insist that Aung San's intentions were genuine, and had he lived to see an independent Burma, he would have followed through on his promise to the Shan *sao hpa*. As one Shan author argues, "The Panglong Agreement and the formation of the Union of Burma was highly valued by all who participated in its signing, generating optimism for a prosperous, peaceful future" (Simms 2017, 78).

As with the characteristics of the region over the centuries, the idea of a united "minority" voice or sentiments was but an idea (or evidence of cooperation was merely a form to file for the colonial bureaucracy). One bold exception to the political movement to join a postcolonial union is that of the Wa people from the Northern Shan States. Their representative, according to records, abjectly refused to participate in any sort of nation-building. During the Pyin Oo Lwin hearings for the Frontier Areas of Enquiry, the three Wa representatives, Hkun Sai, Sao Naw Hseng, and Sao Maha, made it clear that they did not want to be part of any federation or modern political state.

Do you want any sort of association with other people?

Hkun Sai—We do not want to join anybody because in the past we have been very independent.

Sao Naw Hseng—Wa are Wa and Shans are Shans. We would not like to go into the Federated Shan States.

What do you want the future to be in the Wa states?

Sao Maha—We have not thought about that because we are very wild people. We never thought of the administrative future. We think only about ourselves.

Don't you want education, clothing, good food, good houses, hospitals?

Sao Maha—We are very wild people and don't appreciate all these things. (Qtd. in Lintner 2014)

For its legacy in Shan national sentiments, the Panglong Agreement also gave Shan elites further affirmation that the Shan constitute a legitimate nation (TRC 1990b, 2). More important than the Panglong Agreement, the Constitution, drafted in 1947, would extend specific secession rights for states:

Chapter X: Right of Secession:

201. Save as otherwise expressly provided in this Constitution or in any Act of Parliament made under section 199, every State shall have the right to secede from the Union in accordance with the conditions hereinafter prescribed.

202. The right of secession shall not be exercised within ten years from the date on which this Constitution comes into operation.

203. (1) Any State wishing to exercise the right of secession shall have a resolution to that effect passed by its State Council. No such resolution shall be deemed to have been passed unless not less than two-thirds of the total number of members of the State Council concerned have voted in its favour.

(2) The Head of the State concerned shall notify the President of any such resolution passed by the Council and shall send him a copy of such resolution certified by the Chairman of the Council by which it was passed.

204. The President shall thereupon order a plebiscite to be taken for the purpose of ascertaining the will of the people of the State concerned.

205. The President shall appoint a Plebiscite Commission consisting an equal number of members representing the Union and the State concerned in order to supervise the plebiscite.

206. Subject to the provisions of this Chapter, all matter relating to the exercise of the right of secession shall be regulated by law.

The constitution, with this chapter, was ratified in September 1947, the final year before independence. This right was specifically extended to the Shan and Kayah (Karenni) States, though the Chin, Kachin, and Arakan regions were given degrees of autonomy as well (Khur Hsen ခွန်ဟိန်း 1996, 374; Callahan 1996, 30).[16]

From the colonial period through World War II, the British recognition of Shan sovereignty in local rule gave additional reason for the Shan politicians to base their claim that they were the independent and rightful rulers of the Shan states. This even extended to their argument that the Shan were traditionally independent (M. Smith 1999, 64). This notion, however, fails to acknowledge the many instances in which Shan kingdoms were vassal states to various other empires, as well as the countless wars and skirmishes between various Shan principalities prior to British colonialism. But to the Shan politicians in 1947, the Panglong Agreement and Chapter X of the Union of Burma Constitution were documentary evidence that according to modern laws, they were the lawful leaders of Shanland, and in ten years, were it the will of their people, there would be a fully independent Shanland.

Conclusion: Passport to Shanland or the Dream of a Shan Nation-State Deferred?

Like the director of a film who assembles scenes into a story, it is inevitable that the nation will create a greater notion of continuity and community than actually existed or was even felt by the people referenced. Surely Mozart did not consider his music to be classical when he was composing it. The name "Shan" existed for hundreds of years before the British, but as a word used by the Burmese to designate other groups to the east, including the Lao and the Siamese; it was hardly an ideological and emotional adhesive that bound people together through a shared sense of race, ethnicity, or heritage.

Twentieth-century political leaders claim heritage with ancient kings and encourage others to bask in the former grandeur of their classical states. After basking, to throw in their lot with said politician. European colonialism with its attendant territorialization led to a shift in the grammar of sovereignty in the area. Historic glories became attached to contemporary power holders (or aspirants) through ideas about race and (re)conquered kingdoms and territorial (re)possessions. As such, the past serves as a repository for evidence of historic political power and thus legitimacy for some political leaders, and even more so for aspiring political leaders. The challenge for Shan politicians today is that "Shan" peoples are not united in their support (for said politicians). In the same way, they project onto the past a failure for Shan statelets to be united in their resistance to their neighboring "classical states" and, later, their new reincarnations.

Even within Shan historiography, one explanation for a lack of unity is particularly compelling:

> Unlike (Burmese King) Bagyidaw who ordered the chronicles to be re-examined and re-edited by scholars so as to make them more authentic, the Shan *sao hpa* failed to carry out a reassessment and re-editing of the old chronicles. The reason for the failure to bring forth an authentic chronicle was due to the fact that the Shan chiefs had never had the opportunity to unite among themselves. This explains the failure to re-examine and re-edit the chronicles. (Sai Aung Tun 2001, 3)

Read another way, historian Sai Aung Tun's observation suggests that there was not a politically powerful Shan figure to take over and subsume other Shan histories by writing one authoritative history of the Shan, hence the inconsistency regarding the years of the reign of Suerkhan Fa, or the number of theories regarding which statelets comprised the nine kingdoms of the Kao Hai Haw. One ruthless editor could consolidate the various chronicles and put their narratives together on the same page, thus overwriting the other purportedly "inconsistent" stories held by the weaker groups.

Whereas elite Burmese nationalism and cultural movements were initially predicated on the concern for a moral decline, or the loss of the patron of the religion at the hands of the British, elite Shan nationalism could not follow a similar arc. By maintaining the positions of the Shan *sao hpa* in the Frontier Areas, the British preserved the Shan leaders as the local patrons of the Buddhist *sangha*, though at a more cellular level. Shan *sao hpa* sponsored celebrations for auspicious events, founded temples, and supported monasteries in their Shan States. While the Thai king expanded his own authority by usurping that of the regional lords (and making everyone Thai), the Shan *sao hpa* had their fiefdoms effectively boxed in by British bureaucratic fiat and their history therefore similarly plural. It was later pointed out that Shan history, in particular, and more than for any other race, "has depended on the character and personal energy of the Sawbwa" (Tambiah 2002, 126). So, even if they wanted to, the Shan *sao hpa* lacked the institutional resources to make everyone in the Shan States "Shan" in the same way, though this may have become the aspiration of Shan politicians during World War II: they saw that they would be unlikely to be able to maintain their "congeries of statelets" in the Frontier Areas without the British in power.

The Panglong Agreement created a veritable title deed to Shanland. The agreement acknowledged that the historical right to a Shan homeland was in the hands of the Shan *sao hpa* and designated the *territory* upon which the future Shan nation would reference itself. The Shan national legitimacy project finds its part in Burmese history because the Myanmar government is its principal interlocutor and that which was supposed to allow it to separate from the Union of Burma. Shan ruling elites have had hundreds of years of political relationship with their Burmese counterparts. Their shared ritual language and understandings of political power allowed them to be peer polities in Southeast Asia.

It was during the colonial period that mapping and racial taxonomies created new kinds of boundaries; although many aspects of ritual languages of power were preserved, they began to flow through new pipes of ethnonationalism and territorial sovereignty. Some of the Shan *sao hpa* became united in ambition—and became "Shan," as it were—through the combined efforts of the British annexation and the imperial appetites of the Siamese/Thai. Shan elites anticipated a sovereign nation-state of their own because of empire-building, both European and Southeast Asian.

2

A Cold War Fusion of Elite Ideals with an Armed Insurgency

Especially since 1962, the Shans have been oppressed, humiliated, brutalized, violated, and domineered by an alien army. The army is alien in the sense that the Burman soldiers do not speak the Shan language. They neither understand nor respect the rights of the Shan people. They rape Shan women. Unfortunately, this has led the Shans to view the Burmans as an enemy or a hostile "race" and the Shans are not alone. Other non-Burmans share the same view.

—Chao Tzang Yanghwe, *The Shan of Burma: Memoirs of a Shan Exile*, 1987

So, if you're someone who is looking for somebody to blame for the revival of Shan nationalism, don't look far. The Burmese junta and Suerkhan Fa are each and both guilty, the former for their relentless and unceasing abuse of the Shan people, and the latter for remaining a symbol and inspiration for today's Shan youth, as he was for yesterday's.

—Khuensai Jaiyen

ON 21 MAY 1958, a motley group of thirty-two young men, calling themselves Num Hsük Han (ၶုမ်ႇသိုၵ်းႁၢၼ်) (Brave Young Warriors), drank holy water of allegiance and declared war against the Burmese central government. Their leader, Sao Yanta (also later known as Sao Noi), claimed royal Shan heritage as a brother of the *sao hpa* of Kengtung (Sao Khwan Möng ၸဝ်ႈၶႂၼ်မိူင်း 1986, 136).[1] He was famous among Shan patriots for his charismatic speeches and his ability to emote a romantic vision for an independent, prosperous Shanland. According to hearsay, a few Shan monks were so inspired by Sao Yanta's words that they added bandoliers to their prayer beads and fled to the jungles to join Num Hsük Han. Sao Yanta and Num Hsük Han represent the sparks that lit the latent embers to one of the longest-burning armed separatist movements in modern history. Shan patriots continue to celebrate 21 May as Shan Resistance Day. The moment represents a turning point in Shan politics: with the legal, constitutional method to repossess Shanland failing to deliver any tangible promise for independence, a few people started to take the process into their own hands. That armed movement would develop into a Buddhist nation-state-building project, expanding and flourishing in the interstices of other transnational territories in upland Southeast Asia.

At the brink of colonial independence, the Shan *sao hpa* were promised federal autonomy by the Panglong Agreement. Chapter X of the Union Constitution provided legal means for secession. But the military and political machinations of the 1950s would deny Shanland its entrance on the world stage via the legislated procedures as mapped out in the Constitution. Cold War geopolitics and the encroaching military nationalism of the Burmese central government altered the project for Shanland in two key ways: the government neutralized the hereditary power of the *sao hpa* and removed their influence from the licit political and economic sphere; and ongoing conflict and contestation prepared the soil for Shan armed resistance to sprout. Later, the transnational black market trade networks and migrant economies would prove essential fertilizer for the Shanland repossession project to blossom in the uplands.

Political scientist Mary Callahan has observed that for much of Burma's modern history, political power has been in the hands of those who are specialists in violence, be they the Tatmadaw, anti-government armed forces, criminal gangs, or paramilitary organizations (2007, 3). But the nation-states of Shanland were not built exclusively by brute force, nor did their purveyors survive through sheer might alone. Ideological alliances were also necessary between various groups in the Shan State for two principal reasons: the Cold War framing of these insurgencies created a nominal form and expectation of "surface compatibility" between armed groups and therefore justification of arms transfers and assistance; and for the groups that were engaged in an armed movement, the cultural and political ideals of the leadership do matter to those involved as ideological commitment does comprise an important motivating force. Although there was certainly forcible coercion and opportunities for profit within the operations of all these armed groups, aspirations for the movement's goals, cultural solidarity, and grassroots camaraderie all play crucial roles. Even though repossession is a violent act, it is motivated by a basic premise of rightful ownership.

Whether the party masquerading as the rightful owner is discovered to be a fraud is another story.

For the myriad armed groups in the past seven decades that have flown the Shan flag, advocated for Shan freedom, and included the term "united" as part of their name, the justification for mobilization of resources is two-fold: Shan armed movements are a response to contemporary strife and point to an enemy that has committed violence; and Shanland is presented as a bona fide sovereign nation-state that deserves a place in the international order. While contemporary war and violence are palpable, the ways in which the political movement articulates the origin of contemporary strife, as well as presenting itself as the vehicle toward a peaceful, prosperous future, are often more complex and subject to interpretation. In the 1950s and 1960s, incomplete nation-building projects and Cold War geopolitics turned the peripheries of Burma into ideological battlefields and logistical supply lines for numerous armed groups and (counter) insurgencies. As a result, the project for repossessing Shanland was both challenged and nurtured in dynamic new ways.

Following an overview of the political situation for the newly independent Union of Burma, this chapter examines how Cold War geopolitics came to bear on Burma in general and the ongoing project to repossess Shanland in particular. While colonialism preserved localized aspects of the political and cultural hegemony of the elite Shan *sao hpa*, these hereditary power holders (and the few members of their emerging middle classes) anticipated some of the transformations in the nature of sovereignty for Shanland. Some sold their political stake in Shanland, while others formed armed movements to establish embryo Shanlands amid a complex tapestry of dozens of armed groups with their intricate trade networks meandering the mountains of Shan State and its borderlands.

From the transitional context of independent Burma through the 1950s parliamentary democracy and the 1962 military coup by Ne Win, the second half of this chapter turns to a specific case study of Shan nation-state building: the formation of the Shan United Revolutionary Army (SURA) and the establishment of its borderlands base, Bang Mai Sung (Prosperity Town), by the charismatic one-armed General Kawn Söng. Key to this creation of a new Shanland is the way in which Kawn Söng not only crafted himself as a military hero and a Shan patriot but also positioned himself as both a Shan state-builder and Buddhist benefactor. To discuss this presentation of Kawn Söng and Shanland, this chapter draws on Shan-language publications printed by the letterpress and offset presses of the SURA, as well as recollections of former SURA soldiers. In order to enact a military and nation-state building project to repossess Shanland, the SURA made use of Shan historical narratives and discourses of Shan unity and legitimacy, as well as projections of new kinds of enemies in the context of Burmese military nationalism amid the Cold War. In sum, to be Shan is to be (an anti-communist) Buddhist.

A Newly Independent "Union" of Burma

Following the end of World War II, Burma was left with an infrastructure in shambles. But Burmese politicians had the promise of colonial independence: the very aspiration of Aung San and his comrades. Sadly, Aung San would never live to see this reality for which he fought so hard. At a meeting in July 1947—while the new constitution was being written—gunmen stormed the meeting room in the downtown Secretariat Building, bursting in with a spray of bullets, killing the young independence fighter and several other key politicians in one fell swoop. Nevertheless, the new constitution was ratified just two months later, and on 4 January 1948, Burma achieved its independence. The new Southeast Asian country joined the United Nations on 19 April 1948.

With independence, Burma entered its parliamentary democracy era and elected upper and lower houses of parliament as well as a president (Sao Shwe Thaike) and prime minister (U Nu). Because of the power and influence of the Communist Party of Burma (which was behind the political alliance that led to the current ruling party, the Anti-Fascist People's Freedom League [AFPFL]), Burma outwardly pursued a form of socialism; it distanced itself by rejecting Commonwealth status but still never actively affiliated with the Soviet Union.

Next door, the government of Thailand would become a stalwart friend to the United States and thus NATO countries, a stance that would crucially frame its relationship with Burma as well as the Shan separatist movements. This would also determine Thailand's future role as a key strategic ally for the United States and its military operations in Vietnam. The reasons for Thailand's stance are seen as pragmatic more than ideological: Thailand had United Nations membership; Thailand is largely agricultural; the sea transportation routes were mostly controlled by capitalist countries; and Thailand's economy was largely dependent on capitalist countries (Kasian 2001, 128).

Further, the postwar period would see an expansion of Thai ethno-nationalism. Especially with their alliance with the United States, the military nationalist regimes were resolutely anti-communist, equating party membership with being intrinsically un-Thai. Anti-communist rhetoric would be useful for the Thai state during the Cold War, not only to control internal rivalry but also to extend its domain outward (Bowie 1997, 72). Similar to Phibun's efforts to incorporate the Shan States into Thai hegemony as the "Original United Tai States," Thailand's military nationalism and anti-communism would invoke the Shan and their Tai-ness as inimical to communism.

While Thailand's notion of national citizenship conflated Thai ethnicity with Thai state subject-hood, the Union of Burma was founded with a plural vision for its multiethnic national population. The new national flag at independence featured a set of six stars in the upper left corner: one large star with five smaller stars surrounding it. The large star represents the Bamar ethnic group, and the five others the other most populous ethnic nationalities: Chin, Karen, Karenni, Kachin, and Shan. From the very start, the national image of the Union of Burma intrinsically depends on pluralism. As detailed in the previous chapter, the concept of *lumyo* as a moniker for race or ethnicity had been concretized through the census and colonial ethnological categorization, and now the various groups had representation in the Chamber of Nationalities. Anti-colonial nationalism and independence politics would further politicize these identities. The Constitution privileged members of these groups as indigenous races and therefore full citizens. But Burma still granted citizenship to other long-term settlers, and government policies were initially tolerant toward foreign business holders in the country.

Although the Panglong Agreement and Chapter X of the Constitution provided a legislated level of autonomy for the power holders in the former Frontier Areas, not all ethnic nationality leaders were on board the Panglong Unity Express at the time of signing. Some members of ethnic Karen leadership, for example, marginalized from the Panglong Agreement, were already organizing to separate from the union. They established the Karen National Defense Organization and were later joined by members of the Pa-O ethnic nationality in Shan State, which resented the power of the Shan *sao hpa*.

Further, there was another splinter group, the Shan People's Freedom League, which sought to remove what they saw as the quasi-feudal system in Shan State that had been preserved by colonialism. Some of the *sao hpa*, with support from Rangoon, dispatched their police to suppress these groups; this established additional precedence for the willingness of some Shan political leaders to work with the Burmese government.

However, the most powerful political organization in the 1940s was the Communist Party of Burma (CPB). Following the war, it still occupied swaths of lower and central Burma, and at the time of independence it had organized nearly all the trade unions in the country and commanded a peasant union of nearly a million members (Fink 2001, 46; Lintner 1990, 9). The organization spent three years as a legal party and, following that, forty-one years promoting armed insurrection in Burma (Man Poe Aye မန်းဖိုးအေး 2016, 22). The CPB would be a major player in framing the political and military battlefields for the Shan movements and the country's geopolitical situation for the ensuing decades.

Caught in the Crossfire; Stuck in the Middle

As the regime took office in newly independent Burma, internal conflict raged in its giant neighbor to the northeast. By 1949, Mao Tse-tung's Communist Party had emerged victorious in China, and Rangoon was the first non-communist country to recognize the new government. The Burmese government saw the need to tread carefully when it came to working with Beijing as there was concern that the Chinese Communist Party would support its counterpart in Burma (Lintner 1994, 98).

As a result of Mao's victory in China, troops of Chiang Kai-shek's defeated Chinese Nationalist Kuomintang (KMT) forces retreated, fleeing not just across the straits to Formosa/Taiwan but also over the southwest border of Yunnan Province and into Shan State. While fewer than two thousand KMT troops retreated to the Shan State in January 1950, they made alliances and received international assistance to build a counterinsurgency against Maoist China. They set up bases along the border with Yunnan and drafted soldiers from borderland groups, including Lahu, Wa, Ta-ang, Shan, and Sino-Shans (Lintner 1994, 99).

The Yunnan-Shan-Thai border Kuomintang forces, the majority of the foot soldiers of Yunnanese origin, received support from Taiwan and later the United States Central Intelligence Agency (CIA) as well as the Thai government. Starting with two thousand stragglers in 1950, by 1953 the Kuomintang presence in Shan State had swollen to twelve thousand troops. This systematic expansion was facilitated by air drops from the CIA, and the later extension of the Möng Hsat airstrip in Keng Tung Eastern Shan

State allowed for subsequent nonstop C-46 and C-47 cargo flights from Taiwan (Ministry of Information 1953, i, 11).

With thousands of troops in various armies along the Shan-Yunnan and Shan-Thai boundary, it was increasingly necessary that they find ways to support themselves. The outside logistical support and established trade networks across Mainland Southeast Asia created additional entrepreneurial opportunities. Opium had long been cultivated in the Shan uplands, and through the 1950s, its sale was legal in the Shan State; its taxation was a source of income for many *sao hpa* (Steinberg 2001, 215). With the KMT expansion in Shan State came ever-increasing poppy cultivation and opium trafficking. The opium itself was grown and harvested by uplands ethnic minorities, and the KMT would supervise and tax the mule caravans that carried the packages of opium gum from the hills to the border with Northern Thailand. From there, Yunnanese Chinese in Chiang Mai would organize the product's transfer and sale to powerful Teochew Chinese businessmen in Bangkok who were connected with the international crime syndicates to export the drugs to international markets (Lintner 2002, 243). The latter were entrenched, above the law, and able to carry out their illicit commerce because they would pay off government officials to ensure their businesses' smooth operations.

It was because of the Kuomintang's adversarial stance toward the Maoists (as well as the profit-making opportunities at every level) that the Thai government willfully ignored—at least in public—the drug trafficking, particularly since the KMT fought the Communist Party of Thailand on behalf of the Thai Army or, as the Thai government stated, contributed to the "maintenance of national stability." In the Thai government, the Kuomintang found an ally that would protect their trade routes and serve as an effective conduit for incoming supplies as well as a channel for the exportation of opium to lucrative markets further afield. There were particular Thai military and political strongmen who cultivated various alliances with the KMT: Pao Sriyanonda from 1953 to 1957; Sarit Thanarat from 1958 to 1963; and Kriangsak Chamanan from 1967 until the 1980s (Kanchana กาญจนะ 2004, vii, 261). As Bertil Lintner argues, "by 1955, the Thai police under Pao had become the largest opium trafficking syndicate in Thailand" (1994, 156). The coordinated transfer of that opium from the hills of the Golden Triangle was supervised by the Kuomintang.

However, these broader geopolitical concerns do little to explain what it might have felt like for the Shan local leaders, let alone the farmers, to have the iron curtain come crashing down on their rice fields, displacing entire villages, and rendering paddies into military grounds and swidden hills into poppy plantations. In some cases, the Kuomintang units respected local villagers, and regional traders made a handsome profit as a result of the KMT presence. Members of the Kuomintang sometimes justified their occupation of areas in the Shan States using the rationale that some of the Shan *sao hpa* historically had paid tribute to the Chinese emperor.[2] Furthermore, the *sao hpa* in the Kokang areas of the Northern Shan State were early to collaborate with the KMT (Chang 1999, 34).

Many villages in the Shan State, however, did not fare well at all. Stories circulated of KMT battalions that behaved like settlers, stealing and pillaging from the local people. The KMT justification that Shan *sao hpas* had formerly sent tribute to the Chinese emperor was a particularly bitter pill to swallow for the Shans who had looked forward to an independent, democratic future.

Nevertheless, while people in Shan State had a varied experience of the Kuomintang buildup, to the Rangoon government, the Kuomintang's presence signified but one thing: invasion, or as they called it, "The Kuomintang Incursion." In 1952 Burmese prime minister U Nu called upon the Shan *sao hpa* who still retained regional autonomy to come to a consensus and expel the KMT intruders. When Shan leaders failed to reach an agreement on the issue to the central government's satisfaction, the Tatmadaw (Burma Army) was dispatched to the Shan State to manage the situation. The Tatmadaw established martial law for many of the villages and engaged in armed combat with Kuomintang regiments (Callahan 1996, 30).

Some of the Shan leadership welcomed the deployment of the Burma Army. But for many others, especially local villagers, the underfunded, undisciplined soldiers of the Tatmadaw constituted yet another foreign occupying force in Shan State. Some platoons were particularly abusive in the rural areas, and civilians often found themselves caught in the crossfire between the Tatmadaw and the Kuomintang (Yawnghwe 1987, 112; Sai Aung Tun 2009, 207).

Although the Tatmadaw had been dispatched to take control of the Shan State for the central government, it lacked full capacity to do so. Their forces were simply inadequate for controlling the vast, complex mountainous region that is the Shan plateau. Sometimes they were simply expected to "live off the land." In some cases they would survive by selling military-issued equipment and rations to locals (in the event that they had supplies from Yangon), and in others they would just demand what they wanted from villagers.

As a result, the late 1950s saw increased militarization in the Shan State, with the various armies of the Kuomintang, Communist Party of Burma, and the Tatmadaw vying for control over territory and trade routes. The ongoing antagonism justified increased military spending, and the Burma Army was able to expand to become the most powerful political force in the country. In 1958 the Tatmadaw successfully orchestrated a "military caretaker" government in Rangoon and replaced U Nu's civilian regime for two years. Like many such strong-arm approaches, it came into power on the premise that it would cut out dead wood and efficiently clear the way for Burmese economic development. This would have direct and serious repercussions in Shan State.

With the continued ramping up of the military in Shan State, one can only imagine the effects that this ongoing war was having on the daily lives of locals, let alone any political aspirations for the future. Would they still have the chance to secede from the Union of Burma, as promised in the Constitution? What about the spirit of the Panglong Agreement?

Brave Young Shan Warriors Take Up Arms

For villagers in the Shan State, the tenth anniversary of national independence for the Union of Burma went by with little cause for celebration. The spirit of the Panglong Agreement promised Shan and Karenni politicians autonomy, and Chapter X of the Constitution gave ethnic nationalities the legislated right to secede from the Union of Burma following ten years' initial membership. But there was no concrete action in government to revisit the issue, let alone any call for a plebiscite. General Ne Win argued that some sections of the Constitution needed changing, as "age-old feudalism was directly connected to the spirit of the Constitution" (Sai Aung Tun 2009, 367).

With no vote taken and therefore no chance for a "Shexit" via legal means, a group of Shan patriots put together an armed movement to fight for independence from the Union of Burma. On 21 May 1958 they declared war on the Burmese government from Möng Pan, the famous Shan State at the Thai border that had once been a Japanese "gift" to Thailand. Num Hsük Han has gone down in history as the first armed Shan resistance to the postcolonial state. There is a distinct class character to it. It did not arise out of a specific economic grievance, nor was it broadly based in its composition. Early recruits to Num Hsük Han have been described as teens who left school for a national ideal (Cowell 2005, 9). Sao Yanta's (alleged) royal heritage added a powerful symbolic aura to the legitimacy of his claims. But it was a trader by the name of Baw Laeng Gung Na who would be the financial backbone for the early insurgency: he had made ties with the Thai police to facilitate the cross-border trade (Lintner 1994, 151, 152). In the earliest days of the movement, Num Hsük Han was rather ragtag: those given rifles carried only fifty bullets, while those with a carbine had only twenty bullets. When they went out on sorties, there were generally eight to ten soldiers to a line, one carrying the rice pot for the group and others with sacks of salt, fermented beans, and chili oil (Amporn อัมพร 2015a, 102, 103).

Num Hsük Han was joined by the son and nephew of Khun Kya Bu, one of the Shan signatories of the Panglong Agreement, adding to the idealist and elite aura of the movement (Simms 2017, 103). At this juncture, we can see notions of political idealism and choice—a positive idea of an independent Shan nation—fueling the fight against the Burmese central government. They still held onto certain aspects of Shan traditional symbolism and connections with royalty. However, the current *sao hpa* had gradually accepted a new reality: the colonial era of relative peace and autonomy was gone, and they would have to get with the changing times.

Trading the White Umbrella for a Golden Parachute

Seasoned Shan politicians and members of the Shan political establishment did not share the youthful exuberance of Num Hsük Han. Given that several *sao hpa* were in the upper house of parliament, they had to remain outwardly invested in parliamentary democracy of the Union of Burma for the time being, lest we forget that the Yanghwe *sao hpa* Sao Shwe Thaike was the president and speaker of the upper house. Years earlier, in 1952, there had already been a formal declaration of *sao hpa* that they were going to renounce their hereditary authority in favor of parliamentary democracy in the Shan State (Yawnghwe 2013, 197).

In 1959 the Rangoon government cut a deal with thirty-four Shan *sao hpa*. This political move partially stemmed from the machinations of Ne Win and his military caretaker government; Ne Win had stubbornly based his platform on "non-disintegration of the union." Although the Burmese military gave itself credit for orchestrating this transfer of power, in fact it had been on the table for years, and crucially, the Shan *sao hpa* themselves had not sought to separate from the Union (Yawnghwe 1987, 9; Simms 2017, 110).

The Shan political leaders were given cash bonuses and pensions in exchange for surrendering political autonomy to the Burmese authorities. This also included transferring their local police forces to the Burmese central government. From this point onward, Shan *sao hpa* would no longer have political or economic roles in the management of local affairs. These cash packages ranged from 50,000 to 5,000,000 kyat, a hefty sum in those days, and were calculated according to the maximum revenue that the individual state coffers would have been estimated to make for the following fifteen years (Khur Hsen ခိုးသိင်္ခ 1999, 132; Sai Aung Tun 2009, 374). This buyout was touted as a move to end "feudalism." Many Shan patriots, and particularly those exasperated by the Tatmadaw occupation, saw the move as yet another critical step toward military and cultural Burmanization of the area. In essence, the act was the equivalent of selling the title deed to Shanland at state auction.

As a direct result of patriotic indignation regarding the 1959 *sao hpa* power transfer, the ranks of Sao Yanta's Num Hsük Han soon swelled with former guardsmen and police of the Shan *sao hpa*. They did not appreciate being signed away to Rangoon. Numerous women also joined the ranks of the Shan insurgency. Several *sao hpa* who had taken Rangoon's retirement package demonstrated sympathy to Num Hsük Han; the 1959 surrender was not exactly voluntary, after all. Some of the funding for Num Hsük Han came from the prince of Kengtung (Sao Khwan Möng ဝင်းရွှေခမ်းမိုင်း 1986, 136; Cowell 2005, 4).

By the end of 1959, Num Hsük Han counted new recruits from various Shan towns as follows: Möng Yai (200), Kehsi Namsam (40), Möng Nawng (100), and Hsipaw (100) (Lintner 1994, 159). In November 1959, a combined force of Bo Mong, an ethnic Wa Union Military Police officer, a group of Wa soldiers, and the fledgling Num Hsük Han successfully took the town of Tangyan, only to retreat after several skirmishes with the Tatmadaw, who brought in aerial reinforcements (Yawnghwe 1987, 8; Lintner 2021, 42). But the initial symbolic victory at Tangyan inspired more Shan patriots to join Num Hsük Han. By 1960, their numbers are estimated to be 700 men.

One important point to note, however, about the history of Num Hsük Han and other armies that have been labeled "Shan" is that they were never strictly composed of ethnic Shan people in either their leadership or their rank and file. They would often represent the diverse ethnic tapestry that is Shanland; however, this is not to underestimate the resentment of the Shan groups that minority groups would have felt toward the Shan for their historic political power or acts of chauvinism. But the Shan did not reach the level of Tai cultural and ethnic hegemony that their neighbors, the Thais, were able to achieve in Thailand.

With continued fighting in Shan State, villagers were driven to the borderlands or sought protection from the growing number of insurgent militia. Local villagers were more and more likely to be affected by Tatmadaw, Kuomintang, CPB, and Shan separatist crossfire, recruitments, and requisitions of taxes, rice, supplies, and labor. Shan insurgent army ranks continued to swell not just from student idealists and civilians fleeing fighting but also from Shan defectors from the Burmese Tatmadaw. Militant nationalist groups continued to form: the Shan State Independence Army (SSIA) and the Tai National Army (TNA) both came onto the scene in 1960. Shan battalions collected taxes and contributions in kind and recruited soldiers. For the latter, their strategies differed from those of the Tatmadaw in the countryside. Because local Shan battalions knew the village headmen personally, they would know which families might have eligible soldiers. For the rural poor, joining one militia or another was hardly a voluntary act of patriotic will but increasingly became a requirement for household survival.

THE 1962 COUP AND MILITARY AUTHORITARIANISM IN BURMA

In 1960, following the military caretaker period of two years, Ne Win made good on his promise and returned political power to parliamentary democracy. Elections were held, and U Nu won again in a landslide victory. But this newly reelected regime did not last long. General Ne Win and his Tatmadaw, operationalizing the dictum of pushing for the "non-disintegration of the union," had neutralized the political clout of the former *sao hpas* though his payoff scheme and further consolidated his own rule in the process.

To give a measure of the strength of the Tatmadaw, whereas they counted just two thousand troops thirteen years earlier, by 1962 the Tatmadaw controlled fifty-seven infantry battalions, five regional commands, and more than a hundred thousand soldiers (Callahan 1996, 444). Government magazines and propaganda continued to present the Tatmadaw as the heroes of the people. Nationalist discourse emphasized that it was the army, as part of the Anti-Fascist People's Freedom League, that defeated the Japanese fascists during World War II. Tatmadaw military propaganda gave themselves the historical credit for leading the country to colonial independence.

Conversely, the Burmese government propaganda machine and some popular media presented the Shan *sao hpa* traditional leaders as evil dictators or the ethnic armies as rapists and murderers. Villains in Burmese popular motion pictures would be depicted wearing Shan-style pants, and paperback novels frequently presented Shan *sao hpa* as cruel and capricious despots. New war movies presented handsome leading men as Tatmadaw soldiers fighting the KMT (Ferguson 2012). When Ne Win's army staged a coup in March 1962, many people in central Burma (never having set foot in Shan State) supported the move. As with the promise of many strong military nationalist movements, there was a hope that a powerful army could bring peace to the country. The ongoing conflict and the Shan separatists were seen as "threats to unity," thus mobilizing the Tatmadaw for the actualization of a military coup (Steinberg 2001, 106).

The coup itself has been described as swift and well executed, though it was not bloodless.[3] On 2 March 1962, the Tatmadaw made a coordinated swoop and detained government ministers and prominent political leaders, including Shan *sao hpa* and their families. Troops surrounded government buildings, including Rangoon's Mingaladon Airport and the central railway station (Simms 2017, 110). Former president Sao Shwe Thaike was imprisoned and died there. The *sao hpa* of Hsipaw, Sao Kya Seng, was taken into military custody and never heard from again.

The coup itself was more than a military takeover of the government bureaucracy. Following the installation of the Revolutionary Council government, the new regime sought to lessen current foreign control of the Burmese economy and bring it into Burmese (military) hands; perhaps they had been taking lessons from the Thais next door. Although it was Burmese politicians who were given political control of the country at independence, the bulk of the country's economy was still largely controlled by Chinese, European, and Indian capitalists. The military coup was a method through which the army could not only take political control but also nationalize the economy. Ne Win's army took over ten private banks and twenty-four international banks (Silverstein 1977, 166).

Policy changes made it difficult for foreigners to get a tourist visa and all but impossible to get any sort of business or residence visa if one was not a full citizen of the country at that time. The 1960s saw a huge exodus of hundreds of thousands of foreign residents from the once-cosmopolitan city of Rangoon. Many formerly privately held enterprises were nationalized, and by 1964, major industries were consolidated into twenty-two official government-run trade corporations.

While Ne Win's military government nationalized the economy, making themselves the exclusive arbiter of commerce in the country, they reflexively created a black market. On the streets, the everyday supply of goods became known as "Trade Corporation Number 23." In the decades following the coup and the nationalization of the economy, anywhere from 40 to 80 percent of commerce in the country circulated on the black market (Chang 2004, 487). Therefore, those who could control the periphery, especially cross-border trade routes and access to manufactured goods from other countries, stood to benefit this expanding clandestine economy. Although the military coup justified itself with the claim that a strong army and central government would stamp out the civil war, the new government's economic policies gave the peripheral armed groups hitherto unseen power. Armies at the border started to tax increasing flows of illicit goods from neighboring countries to Burma, and these included everyday manufactured items from T-shirts to toothbrushes, men's briefs to monosodium glutamate.

While local militias benefited from the cross-border trade and the already robust supply lines of the Kuomintang becoming even more profitable, the Chinese Communist Party sought to keep these potential threats at bay and started to supply the Communist Party of Burma, a policy that would last until 1978 (Man Poe Aye မန်းပိုးအေး 2016, 67). With their new supplies of modern Chinese weaponry, the CPB successfully took over more territories in Northern Shan State, particularly ones formerly dominated by the Wa (Fiskesjö 2017, 340, 353). The Northeast Military Region for the CPB now consisted of five districts: Namkham, Kutkai, Kokang, Northern Wa, and Southern Wa (C. Smith 1984, 65). Further to this, as part of its People's Army, the CPB actively recruited Wa troops to its forces. By the late 1970s the CPB commanded an estimated fifteen thousand soldiers over a total territory of twenty thousand square kilometers (Lintner 2003, 184).

In 1963, already seeing the growing strength of these peripheral armies, the Rangoon government implemented a plan of control through military proxy: they established the Kakweye (KKY for short, meaning "defense") or home guard militia program. Through this program, local armed groups could sign up, as it were, and the government would promise them trade concessions, and sometimes weaponry, so long as they agreed to fight against the Kuomintang. KKY militia were given special "travel permits" to Thailand to fund themselves through the opium trade (Cowell 2005, 5). This system of military proxy, while from a Western political science perspective could be seen as the state surrendering its policing of an area to another group, for an underfunded army in a geographically and politically challenging geography, it would prove to be cost-effective. However, as seen in later years, it jump-started the career of more than one drug warlord in Shan State.

At the same time, the central government and the Tatmadaw did not surrender their entire sovereignty to the mercenary armies of the KKY. In the mid-1960s, the Tatmadaw instituted a new *hpyat lay hpyat* "Four Cuts" counterinsurgency campaign. The strategy behind the campaign borrows from the British practice in the Boer War and called for attacking the zones that were deemed to support insurgency; in other words, cut off the rebellion from its foundations. As the tactic was articulated in Burmese, "Cut food, cut communications, cut ties, and cut lives" (ရိက္ခာဖြတ်, ဆက်ကြေးဖြတ်, ဆက်သွယ်ရေးဖြတ် and သတ်ဖြတ်). In practice, civilian farms and villages were torched, and people were forcibly relocated. Through this brutal tactic, the Tatmadaw was able to push back the Communist Party of Burma in the north of the country as well as the Karen insurgents in the Irrawaddy Delta Area (South and Katsabanis 2007, 57).

By the mid-1960s, the Shan State still had thousands of troops of the Communist Party of Burma, various militia, and the Tatmadaw vying for power and control over increasingly lucrative trade routes; the KMT was moving toward the Thai border areas. Even if they were not supervising the heroin trade directly, they were all making profit off of it in one way or another. Kakweye (KKY) militias were also getting their hands in the gravy, profiting from their trade concessions. All the while, local people were left with less and less autonomy, and those displaced by the Four Cuts Campaign would often end up serving in yet another one of the dizzying number of militias. While the hopes to create an independent Shanland were still in the minds of some of the scholars and politicians, the changing circumstances made it hard to realize their peaceful independent ideal, though the enemies of the state were in greater abundance than ever.

In the 1960s and 1970s, in the Shan State alone, there were nearly forty independently operating militias, in various forms of alliance or competition with each other over territory and especially lucrative trade routes. To summarize, there were five major categories of militias or armed organizations operating in the Shan State:

1. The Burma Army, the Tatmadaw, ostensibly funded by the Burmese government but often inadequately supplied and forced to supply themselves by coercive "taxation" methods where they were locally stationed or by payoffs from traders.

2. The Kuomintang (KMT), or the soldiers of the insurrection against Mao's regime in China, supported by airlifted supplies from Taiwan, the CIA, the Thai government, and the profits from the opium trade.

3. The soldiers of the Communist Party of Burma, the largest political force following World War II and later armed by China, but also involved in opium trade networks.

4. State separatist or ethnic nationality militias seeking autonomy from the Burmese State. These include many of the Shan armies, as well as Pa-O, Wa, and Kokang, and were supported by sympathizers, taxing the black market, and the opium trade.

5. The Kakweye "home guard" militias, which were privately organized but sometimes given arms and trade concessions by the Burmese central government. These militias served as proxy forces for the Tatmadaw and often worked as counterinsurgents against other anti-state forces.

While this schema presents fives kinds of armed organization, this is an archetype if not a crass oversimplification of both the diversity of the composition of groups and their actual activities. On the ground, there are ample cases in which a Kakweye militia might merge and "rebrand" into an ethnic separatist organization or the Kuomintang forms an alliance with an ethnic separatist organization to extend its influence or protect its trade routes.

The Cold War geopolitics, the Tatmadaw's coup, and the nationalization of the economy created a key shift in conceptions of power. The *sao hpa* and the locally derived economies (or feudal modes) had started to become outdated through colonialism and the parliamentary democracy period, but the activities of the CPB, KMT, and numerous other armed groups and the ramped-up black market had further extended capitalist relations to the peripheries in new ways. Although various militia would still crucially depend on their local communities for rice and recruits, their increasingly powerful (and expensive) weaponry was sourced elsewhere, and their taxation of the black-market trade created the means toward modern state-building. However, how this drew upon nascent cultural foundations and Shan ritual languages of political power and prestige is best exemplified in the emergence of Sao Kawn Söng and the Shan United Revolutionary Army.

The One-Armed General and the Foundation of "Prosperity Town"

The Shan United Revolutionary Army is rooted in the cultural geopolitics of the Shan State in the 1950s and 1960s. It is from there that the SURA's charismatic and most-revered Shan freedom fighter comes into prominence. Like the most successful nationalists in the region, Kawn Söng gained military and political experience participating in an assortment of forces in the region, transgressing the divide of the Iron Curtain while he did so. Tracing his biography is helpful for situating the SURA in the political history of the Shan and its cultural ideals and for exploring the genealogy of the SURA as one of the various iterations of Shan nation-state building projects.

Kawn Söng was born on 20 June 1926 in Hta Naw Village, Lai Sak Village Tract, Hopong Township of Yawnghwe, Taunggyi District of Shan State. His parents, Lung Sang To and Ba Kyawng Chung, were peasants but were not poor. Kawn Söng was the third child out of twelve and spent two years as a novice monk at Mak Lang Temple. Through his religious education and polyglot exposure, he learned the Shan, Pa-O, and Burmese languages. Kawn Söng was a teenager when World War II erupted in Shan State. He joined Detachment 101 of the United States Army to fight the Japanese. According to his autobiography, it was this experience in the war that made him start to think seriously about international politics (TRC 1990b, 1).

In 1952 Kawn Söng joined the ranks of the Communist Party of Burma and fought as part of their rebellion in Shan State. As he reflected on this period, he would later claim that it was partly due to his devout Buddhism that he never fully adopted the ideology of the CPB. At the time, however, he was in agreement with the CPB's stance against the AFPFL and their push toward a modern political economy rather than one ruled by feudal lords. During his career with the CPB, Kawn Söng acquired the nom de guerre

Mo Heng, meaning "thunderclap" in Burmese. The name commemorated his fearless bravery on the battlefield and his charisma in public speaking and rallying the troops.

However, Kawn Söng's frustration with the CPB mounted. In 1956, with a group of Shan sympathizers, he established a splinter group called the Shan State Communist Party (Yawnghwe 1987, 209). However, Kawn Söng's SSCP was rejected by the Communist Party of China, and lacking the reinforcements that could have strengthened this army, the group surrendered to the government after two years. This series of events shattered Kawn Söng's aspirations for Shan independence through communist revolution (personal communication, Khuensai Jaiyen, 2020).

Kawn Söng was soon impressed by the idealism and cultural verve of Sao Yanta and Num Hsük Han. He joined this movement in its second year (1959), and his military and political experience was a big boost for Sao Yanta's ragtag group of students and dreamers. During a skirmish at a Burmese outpost at Huay Aw, Mong Ton, in September 1959, Kawn Söng suffered a severe injury to his left arm. Because of the remote location and mountainous geography, it took several days to get him to a hospital. The doctors deemed his wounds too severe to save the limb, and so they amputated it. Despite the loss of his arm, Kawn Söng would continue to fight on behalf of his ideal for Shanland and would become one of the most illustrious and beloved Shan patriots of the twentieth century.

With fighting in Shan State continuing through the 1960s, a faction of the student idealists, Kawn Söng included, was once again frustrated with what they perceived as a lack of distinct progress of Num Hsük Han in building a broad-based Shan political movement. Some students accused their leader, Sao Yanta, of being too authoritarian. Conversely, Sao Yanta saw the students as being strident and entitled: expecting too much too fast. The students' faction broke off and formed the Shan State Independence Army (SSIA). Ongoing battles in Shan State led to continued displacement and disorder. Thousands more locals in the state became involved in anti-state militias.

By April 1964, the three largest Shan rebel groups were the Shan State Independence Army, the Shan National United Front (SNUF), and the Kokang Resistance Force (TRC 1990a, 3). In a conference in Chiang Mai, Thailand, headed by Nang Hearn Kham, the Mahadevi, or Great Queen, of the Southern Shan principality of Yawnghwe, the three armies merged to found a united group, calling themselves the Shan State Army (SSA).

Kawn Söng was appointed chief of staff of this newly amalgamated army (Yawnghwe 1987, 209; Tao Pai Söng တၢ်ပၢ်းၸိင်း 2000, 1). A few other Shan leaders, most notably Saw Yanta, refused to join the SSA.

This merger signified a historic step toward a consolidation of Shan resistance movements, a coming together as Shan for a common goal of building a Shan nation-state. The fact that the meeting took place in Chiang Mai was prescient—not only was the city the important hub for Northern Thailand, but it also constituted a central node in the trafficking of goods on the black market from Burma through Thailand. But the symbolic alliance would not last.

Pushed by the ongoing conflict and displacement, and in particular the CPB conflict on the northern borders of the Shan State, Kawn Söng made a bold step to create a Shan movement separate from communism. Including a cadre of former Rangoon and Mandalay University students, in 1968 Kawn Söng founded yet another army: the Shan United Revolutionary Army (SURA). Furthermore, and importantly, the SURA was formed with the support of General Li Wen-Huan of the KMT, now based in Thailand. This comprised the first overt alliance between a Shan nationalist armed group and the Kuomintang. Some of the Yunnanese families in Shan State who had become "Shan" to avoid Japanese persecution in World War II were involved in the SURA at its founding and participated in building the alliance with the KMT.

This new group, like its key supporters and KMT allies, was staunchly anti-communist. But in drawing on Shan traditional notions of cultural prestige and political prowess, it was resolutely Buddhist and culturally literate in its assertions for a Shan nation. The new Shan United Revolutionary Army combined the reputation and leadership of Kawn Söng with the scholarly might and prestige of Shan intellectuals. Kawn Söng repeatedly emphasized the role of education in making for a modern army and modern nation (Witun วิทูร 2005, 32). Sao Naw Pha, the son of the Tawngpeng *sao hpa* and ethnic Ta-ang, joined the SURA, not only adding another layer of class to the multiethnic character of the SURA but also bringing with him political sophistication and his education from Germany (Simms 2017, 178).

Kawn Söng based the SURA on five principles: anti-communism, freedom and independence, democracy, unity, and peace (TRC 1990b). His reputation as a seasoned veteran of the Shan insurgency and a devout Buddhist continues to command considerable respect in Shan communities today.

On 25 January 1969, the SURA established its spiritual, logistical, and administrative capital right on the border between Chiang Mai Province, Thailand, and the Shan State (TRC 1990a, 4). It named the new capital Bang Mai Sung (Prosperity Town). Bang Mai Sung is adjacent to the town of Piang Luang, in Wiang Haeng District, Thailand. Its border gate would turn its headquarters into a black-market boomtown. Kawn Söng's SURA built its office buildings, schools, and a hospital in this border town. Like the traditional Theravadin political model, Bang Mai Sung contained both bureaucratic headquarters and a Buddhist temple complex, and similar to Shan villages in Shan State, the monastery is at the town's edge.

Within Buddhist cosmologies, one of the most important acts of merit a Buddhist can make is to establish a temple. Temples, replete with ordination halls, libraries, and pagodas, mark the physical landscape as Buddhist. The foundation of a temple could be considered a meritorious renunciation of the spoils of victory for a conquering king. For Bang Mai Sung, Kawn Söng founded Wat Faa Wieng Inn, a temple complex that straddles the geopolitical boundary between Burma and Thailand. Kawn Söng's vision was that Shan people on both sides of the border should unite in worship at the Buddhist temple. The abbot at Wat Faa Wieng Inn told me in 2005 that the temple was established because there is no horizon or boundary for the religion; anyone can come and worship there. Importantly as well, it sent a message to their neighbors, the Thais: the Shan are devout Buddhists.

As mentioned earlier, the Shan United Revolutionary Army was in an adversarial relationship with the Communist Party of Burma. One reason was that Beijing's support for the CPB would not recognize the ethnic divisions in Burma, so the Shan feared losing their autonomy in the process. Further, the leadership of the SURA had long been affiliated with the *sao hpa*, and therefore the rhetoric of privilege (let alone Buddhist religious hierarchies) was inconsistent with Marxist or Maoist ideology of a worker-based society or a peasant-based one. There was also the material reality that the SURA was in a strategic alliance with the KMT at Ban Mai Sung and was benefiting from the cross-border trade with Thailand. By maintaining an anti-communist front, emphasizing Shan ethnicity and Buddhism, the symbolic package of the SURA was attractive to Thai nationalist discourses.

Through Kawn Söng's speeches to the SURA troops, we can get a firmer idea of how the ideals of the nation-state building project were presented to its most important participants: the soldiers. As Kawn Söng argues,

> Our goals of patriotism and nationalism are not to cause oppression or suffer-
> ing to anyone. The Communist Party of Burma engages in class politics with
> the goal to defeat class difference within our Shan State. But, there is not a
> real working class in the Shan State. The Shan feudal kings are gone. . . .
> Against the Shan people's will, the Burmese have come to control our land
> completely. We are peasants together, us Shans, and we are united already, so
> the act of making a modern nation will not be difficult. (TRC 1990b, 17)

Kawn Söng's articulation of CPB rhetoric reflects his own years of experience within the organization. Furthermore, he runs up against the same
reality that prevented communist organizing in Burma in the 1930s: class
difference happened to coincide with national difference; many of those in
colonial Burma's working class were immigrants. Also, Kawn Söng may
well have harbored a tinge of resentment that Beijing had rejected his Shan
State Communist Party fifteen years earlier. Importantly as well, Kawn
Söng emphasizes the idea of historic unity of Shan, which is a relatively
recently created trope, and because of the Cold War has begun to make
inroads to local politics and broader awareness on the ground; these ideas
of ethnic affinity bear uncanny resemblance to the Thai government's
emphasis on *khwamphenthai* "Thai-ness" as an anti-communist discourse.

In another of his speeches to the troops, Kawn Söng asks rhetorically,
"Why do we Shan people need to be united?" And he lists the following
five reasons:

1. Because we are the same race. But, we can break up and fall to pieces and
   become ruined. We've turned our backs to each other for a long time
   already.
2. Because we are separated into many groups.
3. Because the Shan people and the Shan soldiers have already suffered
   greatly for our people.
4. Because many of us have died already and many more will die in the
   future.
5. Because we desire independence, that is our goal, and we want to build a
   peaceful and modern nation. (TRC 1990b, 8)

The sparks for the uprising were located in a combination of factors,
which included a lack of sovereignty for Shan political leadership and
ongoing military strife in the state. Kawn Söng's assertion here is relevant,

as it was in his speeches and political drive, which sought to connect Shan people to become a united force to liberate themselves from the oppression of the Burmese and ultimately to allow Bang Mai Sung (Prosperity Town) to flourish as a model for a Shanland to become.

Conclusion

Following the end of World War II, a number of Shan elites looked forward to peace and prosperity as part of their vision for an independent Shanland. The developments during the years surrounding the war motivated some to organize and prepare the infrastructure for a modern Shan nation-state. As part of this, some *sao hpa* envisioned themselves and their elite peers as being the stewards to Shan democracy. Joining the Union of Burma was not their ideal, nor was the prospect of putting their lot in with Thailand.

Aung San's charisma and directness were major contributing factors to Shan politicians' willingness to sign onto the Panglong Agreement. And rather than vilify Aung San after his death, there is a tendency among Shan political leaders to blame the subsequent Burmese military government for neglecting to follow through with what they have called the spirit of the Panglong Agreement. One Shan author argues that the Burmese had never been straight with the Shan about the issue of independence (Sao Khwan Möng ၸဝ်ႈၶႂၢၼ်မိူင်း 1986, 134).

Hanging on to the possibility of the Panglong Agreement seemed their most practical course of action. But it is almost inevitable that the Shan *sao hpa* would not have a unified response to the Kuomintang incursion, let alone a strategy that was in line with what the Rangoon government wanted. Nor might they have anticipated the ways in which the Shan plateau became a battleground for the Cold War. The ongoing war prevented their vision for Shanland being realized through political means.

As in previous centuries, the mountainous Shan State—with its steep slopes and deep gorges—continued to resist full, central sovereignty. Because of the advent of modern technologies of communications and transportation, various groups could maintain their fiefdoms through military strategy and black-market commerce. It was too lucrative as a crossroads. Through the complex coral reef, serpentine caravans of opium mules protected by various militia soldiers found their way to the Thai border.

In the context of the fight for Shanland, Kawn Söng was simultaneously stepping back from communist ideologies as he embraced aspects of Shan traditionalism and the Theravada Buddhist ritual language of political power. Furthermore, by emphasizing the Shan Buddhist worldview of the nation-state building project while acknowledging aspects of the Thai nationalist history of racial harmony and Buddhist devotion, Kawn Söng made the SURA ideologically compatible with the Thai government's anti-communist stance.

By the 1970s, the vision for Shanland comprised a powerful mix of Shan historic authenticity and spiritual sponsorship, amid a context of Cold War transnationalism, contested sovereignty, and cross-border logistical traffic. It was the incompleteness and fractious nature of sovereignty in the Shan State, together with the expansion of capitalist networks of the black market economy in the area, that served to transform modern Shanland from an elite golden city on the hill to an on-the-ground military and state-building project that would ultimately involve hundreds of thousands of people.

By establishing Wat Faa Wieng Inn on the geopolitical border of Thailand and the Shan State, Kawn Söng tacitly acknowledges that the Shan insurgency crucially depends on the economic and military conduit for access to Thailand. Making the border crossing a place of worship gives it an attractive symbolic package, iterating the notion that Shan and Thais are not only united in their "common" history and racial heritage but also in their contemporary lifetimes together as Buddhists. A popular Shan saying for lovers is that a happy couple is together today because of something they did in a previous lifetime: they made merit together at a Buddhist temple. Through the establishment of a Buddhist temple at the Thai-Shan State border, Kawn Söng draws people together in worship, thus creating the spiritual logistical apparatus for people to be soul mates in their future reincarnations.

3

Revolutionary Ink and the Shan Insurgent Culture Industries

Any race, wherever they might live, if they say they don't have their own written language, they will disappear for sure. Our race and our script, they go together naturally.

—Möng Kham Hkö Hsang (မိူင်းခမ်းꧡၵ်ꩬၢင် 2011, 95)

ၵွမ်းၵၢၼ်ၵိၼ်ꧡင်ꩶလၵ်,ဝၢꧡ် ၵွမ်းၵၢၼ်ꩬၵ်မ်လင်,မၵ် [Eating together makes the food delicious, working together makes the load light]

—Shan proverb

FOR THE ADVOCATES for Shan independence, the fight for Shanland is much more than a military battle to capture territory. It is a historical and intellectual struggle to preserve elements of traditional Shan language and lifeways, and to encourage people to respect and appreciate Shan culture. These are important building blocks to establish a distinct and modern nation-state poised for the future. While Shan historians and cultural enthusiasts readily point to the past glories of illustrious Buddhist kingdoms in upland Southeast Asia as the Shanland of years gone by, how these ideas are communicated and reinforced to a modern citizenry is a task for the mentors, parents and teachers, the educational system, and culture industries of the insurgent state today. In addition to everyday interactions, rousing speeches, and cultural festivals, it is through Shan print media, radio, music, and now digital video that the essence of Shanland is transmitted to the public, Shan soldiers, and potential sympathizers alike.

As the headquarters for the Shan United Revolutionary Army, Bang Mai Sung was a key strategic site, nourished by webs of trade stretching across the borderlands, further reinforced by the SURA's crucial alliance with the Kuomintang. But Bang Mai Sung was more than a military base. It was a center for Shan education, religious and secular, and a powerhouse of the Shan culture industries. In this sense, Bang Mai Sung was a cultural incubator for a national bureaucracy of the future.

As a black-market boomtown, well away from the scrutiny of the Burmese censor board, Bang Mai Sung enabled the SURA-sponsored culture industries to produce myriad publications in the Shan language, teach a Shan-language curriculum in schools, and distribute recordings of Shan music. Being far from the gaze of the soldiers of the Burmese state, members of the Bang Mai Sung public were openly able to learn to read and write in the Shan language and to buy and share popular Shan literature, including poems, novels, and comic books. They would also listen to Shan radio broadcasts, buy cassette tapes of Shan traditional and popular music, and, by the late 1990s, watch Shan videos and Karaoke sing-along videos on VCDs.

Shan language radio programs offered news and political discussions, public health advisories, and religious teachings. The radio also presented Shan rock songs, particularly recordings of Shan nationalist performers and especially the Shan songs that had been censored in Burma.

In addition to paper publications, another kind of inscription is significant to Shan identity: tattoos. Drawing upon centuries of traditional practices, Shan soldiers, women included, received sacred tattoos not only designating them as military personnel but also offering spiritual protection. People are not "inked" on industrial linotypes or offset machines but by Shan monks or ritual specialists. Within the insurgency the tattoos are an important medium for signaling eligibility and membership in the movement, while the tattoos themselves represent energies emplaced and encoded in their words and designs.

By focusing on Shan-language media production and Shan tattooing, this chapter considers aspects of the Shan insurgency often overlooked by political analyses of the ongoing conflict. Shan literary magazines, newsletters, and music recordings comprise media for learning about Shanland, its history, its geography, and its people. In this sense, they constitute artifacts of Benedict Anderson's notion of print capitalism: the platforms through which disparate groups can share a common idea of a nation or imagined community (1983). For the Shan United Revolutionary Army, their imagined community forged itself in the interstices of other dominant nation-states, and on top of that, the majority of Shan soldier-citizens acquired literacy in another language before learning to read and write Shan. Thus, the print capitalism of the Shan imagined community is already a joint venture, as it were, with other national media.

Following a summary of the history of the modern Shan written language, this chapter discusses the Shan United Revolutionary Army's use of this script as the basis for the bureaucratic written language of insurgent Shanland. In Bang Mai Sung, the SURA staff operated a linotype typesetting machine with Shan fonts and published the print materials for Shan bureaucracy, schools, and leisure reading. From publishing, attention turns to the Shan recording industry, which first emerged in Burma during the parliamentary democracy period. Following Ne Win's coup in 1962, as with much of Shan publishing, recording production shifted to the liberated areas of Shanland and to Thai studios for production and radio broadcast. Then, attention turns to a non-industrial, personal form of inscription: Shan tattooing. Tattoos are important Shan spiritual and cultural signifiers but took on additional meaning in the context of the SURA political movement.

To illustrate how insurgent literacy played out for people in the Shan United Revolutionary Army, the latter part of the chapter narrates the biography of Seng Kham, a Shan woman who left her Burmese government high school in 1978 to join the SURA in Bang Mai Sung. With special attention to her Burmese literacy and continued affection for Burmese music and films, Seng Kham's story highlights how some Shan patriots see their work as an inclusive project of political liberation, not one that aims to purge or suppress other cultural codes.

Scripting the Shan Future

Like the cellular congeries of squabbling states characterized in the first chapter, prior to the twentieth century there was never such a thing as a "Shan" language, nor a single Shan written script (there still isn't). Buddhist monastic education infused a relatively high level of literacy across the Shan plateau, but there was no mechanism to standardize the written language to make it mutually intelligible across the many polities that are today included under the umbrella term "Shan."

Among the myriad distinctions and local quirks, there are three main categories or families of scripts used to write Shan languages: Lik To Ngawk, or "bean sprout letters," created in Ahom, which were later principally used in the Northern and Western Shan States; Tai Khün, used in the Eastern Shan States, Kengtung especially, which bears considerable resemblance to

Lanna (Northern Thai) script; and Lik To Mun, or "round script," used in the Southern Shan States, including Taunggyi. To the untrained eye, Lik To Mun looks like the Burmese script, and the strong resemblance between the two comes from centuries of cultural contact as well as the use of the same writing tools and media.[1]

Shan scripts were imprecise and did not consistently represent the spoken languages (Renu เรณู 1998, 265). The inconsistency reflects linguistic diversity as well as the fact that written languages are intrinsically more conservative than spoken languages, which evolve more quickly. To be fair, we could ask why the written words *cough*, *dough*, *plough*, *rough*, and *through* do not represent spoken English consistently. For centuries, Shan elites and monastic communities had written on *parabaik*, fan-folded paper texts, and few older texts survive because the physical media deteriorates. In 1885 American Baptist missionaries had used the Southern Shan script, Lik To Mun, to construct the fonts for the first Shan linotype (Sai Kham Mong 2004, 141). During the colonial period, the British designated a modified version of that script as the official Shan script.

During the early decades of the twentieth century, as mentioned in the first chapter, students at the Shan Chiefs School in Taunggyi received a British bilingual education, but in the English and Burmese languages. Latching onto ideas of cultural romanticism—and having knowledge and appreciation of the lengthy literary history of their Shan polities—Shan scholars, poets, and cultural enthusiasts began to seek out modern ways to reinvigorate this aspect of their Shan cultural heritage. In the 1920s and 1930s, sometimes in conjunction with Buddhist temples, Shan cultural associations began to form.

In 1940, at the brink of World War II in Southeast Asia, a group of nine Shan literary scholars convened to standardize the Shan written language. They formed the Shan State Educational Committee (Pyanchayay Hnint Yinchehmu Tana ပြန်ကြားရေးနှင့်ယဉ်ကျေးမှုဌာန 1961, 157; Sai Htwe Maung 2007, 11). Their goal was to preserve the print language and make it more accessible to people throughout Shanland (Khur Hsen ၶိူဝ်းသိူၼ် 1996, 322). In so doing, the scholars modified the Southern Shan script (Lik To Mun), adding tone markers and some letters to make it more consistent with the spoken language. The result of their work was a new script called the Mai Sung Lik Tai "Prosperous Shan Script."

After standardizing the written script, those nine Shan scholars drafted school textbooks for years one to five. In the introduction to the textbooks, the committee spokesperson wrote that the purpose of the texts is "to enable the people of the Shan state, through education in the Shan language, to progress toward a modern political state" (Sao Hsai Möng ဝဵင်းသီႇႁၢင်ႈ 1962, iii). This idea is echoed by many advocates for Shan independence and cultural preservation. An officer from the Shan State Education Department took this a step further, saying that only through education could the Shan people survive as a race in the modern world (Sai Kham Mong 2004, 320). And for the Education Committee, creating a standardized, legible Shan script and teaching people to read and write using that script would establish that foundation for this modern form of Shan identity to survive in the twentieth century and beyond.

Although the Shan scholars who created the new written script could not have anticipated the various caveats of the Panglong Agreement nor those of the Constitution, they had established an important infrastructural element for an independent modern Shanland: a bureaucratic print language. Despite the Shan having their nation-state deferred, their script, the Mai Sung Lik Tai script, was adopted by Shan politicians, literati, and culture societies in Rangoon and Mandalay as well as in the various temple schools throughout the southern and middle regions of the Shan State.

Burma Print, Burmese Media

In the first decade of Burmese independence—also known as the parliamentary democracy era—the print media scene was considered to be one of the most lively in Southeast Asia. Popular presses whirred out over thirty daily newspapers, most in Burmese, but six in Chinese and three in English (Allot 1993, 4). In the 1950s, there were twenty Shan-language publishers throughout the country, which produced an estimated 250 different publications in the Shan language (Sai Kham Mong 2004, 340). Crucial to the success of these Shan media endeavors were the growing numbers of people in Shan cultural associations, especially those affiliated with Rangoon and Mandalay Universities. These cultural associations, as well as respected Shan literati and religious writers, later supplied some of the intellectual and creative labor that was integral to the Shan nation-building project under the Shan United Revolutionary Army.

During the 1950s, the Shan literary and cultural associations—though later deemed to be anti-Burmese subversives—could be considered more romantic traditionalists than producers of radical media per se. For example, President Sao Shwe Thaike had made it a project to transliterate the

Tipitaka into the Shan written script; previously, Shan monks had read Pali through printed versions in the Burmese script (Yawnghwe 1987, 7; Sai Kham Mong 2004, 262). Both Burmese and Shan alphabets are phonetic, and sacred texts are read in Pali—the point being, however, was that they were using these scripts to encode and therefore access the ancient language.

Although the Mai Sung Lik Tai script devised by the nine Shan scholars in 1940 had been well in use for nearly a decade, there were some modifications effected to incorporate more vowels and diphthongs. The new script was aptly called Lik Ho Hsö (Tiger Head Script), no doubt riding on the coattails of the great Shan empire builder Suerkhan Fa, who spent much of his youth as a surrogate tiger.

All this press freedom would gradually be curtailed by the Burmese government's clampdown on literacy and cultural expression. During the 1950s, the Shan language was made an optional language at schools in Shan-dominated areas, and therefore teachers would not receive pay for hours spent on Shan instruction. Concern about religion as practiced by Shan monks led to the 1957 formation of a Shan Buddhist Association. This group convened in Loilem, Southern Shan State, with 175 monks in attendance. However, after the formation of the Num Hsük Han armed resistance movement, any content in the Shan language could potentially be deemed even more politically suspect by the Burmese authorities.

With the gradual relinquishing of their political and economic role, many *sao hpa* found that they were no longer able to sponsor cultural events to the same extent as they had done during the colonial period. Ne Win's 1962 coup and subsequent nationalization of the economy would be the final death blow to the majority of Shan publishing in Burma. The high cost of paper made it all but impossible for the Shan cultural and religious associations to continue printing their materials. By 1969 the central government had ordered Shan civilian publishers to halt operations (Sai Kham Mong 2004, 340), the same year that the Shan United Revolutionary Army established Bang Mai Sung. Some of the literati whose works had formerly been sponsored by the *sao hpa* would later find employment with the Shan armed groups.

For a significant number of Shan educators, the increases in Burmese domination of the areas and suppression of the language made them redouble their efforts to educate future generations in the Shan language. Under Kawn Söng's leadership, the SURA was heavily involved in both

Buddhist practices and education for everyone in Bang Mai Sung; in an ongoing war, it was his prerogative to present the SURA as religious preservationists and himself as a Buddhist benefactor. In 1979 the SURA and the abbot at Wat Fa Wieng Inn sponsored a conference on the various versions of the Shan script (Sai Kham Mong 2004, 271).

By the 1970s, there were more than two hundred schools in Shan-liberated territories teaching the Shan curriculum.[2] Some of these schools would coincide with Shan temples, while others were separate buildings entirely. Many of the printed materials used in these schools were produced on the linotype and sometimes even sourced at commercial offset publishers in Thailand. The SURA publishers carried out supply projects for the local Shan villagers, which included the militia's invoice statements, and general bureaucratic paperwork, as well as wedding and funeral announcements.

The Shan United Revolutionary Army was hardly a ragtag rebel group but an army for a functioning state, with an ability to tax, issue receipts, and provide social services, including schooling and hospital care. The Shan paperwork and publishers were core to these processes. For a compelling example of the SURA's bureaucratic rationality, I obtained a February 1983 copy of the rates for the SURA's tax station in Bang Mai Sung, with fees assessed in Thai baht.

The duty chart offers a window into the kinds of items that the SURA would tax; items that were of basic necessity (cooking oil) and of daily use (tea leaves, coffee) and luxury items that would hold their value over a long distance (gemstones, ivory, and tiger skin). It reflects the nature of the transport (porter and mule) and suggests what kinds of high-value items would make their way from the Shan State to Chiang Mai Province via the SURA-controlled gate at Piang Luang. There is no explicit mention of opium; however, it was general practice that opium would be assessed at 10 percent of its value, though this could fluctuate.

A Case in Point: Operating a Shan Linotype Typesetting Machine

Operating a linotype typesetting machine was at the heart of the project to build Shanland as a nation-state. While Shan authors penned their poems, politicians their announcements and history articles, monks their *suttas* and Buddhist pamphlets, it was the everyday linotype operators who reproduced these messages. For most of the SURA typesetters and original authors, their first written language was Burmese. Those who had gone to convent schools

Rates, SURA tax station

1. High-grade goods, medicines, etc.	335 per mule
2. Low-grade goods	155 per mule
3. High-grade goods, backpacks	100 per porter
4. Middle-grade goods, backpacks	20 per porter
5. Low-grade goods, backpacks	10 per porter
6. Cows and buffaloes	210 per head
7. Coffee seeds	120 per mule
8. Tea leaves	30 per mule
9. One pair of elephant tusks	20 per viss (1 viss is about 1.6 kilograms)
10. Deer horn	20 per viss
11. Silver rupees, thin	30 per 100 pieces
12. Silver rupees, 100% pure	30 per 100 pieces
13. Silver rupees, double model	15 per 100 pieces
14. Silver rupees, low quality	15 per 100 pieces
15. Ivory, not in pairs	10 per viss
16. Gold	10% of value
17. Gemstones	10% of value
18. Small opium weights	5 per viss
19. Deer horn, low quality	4 per viss
20. Tiger skin	30 per piece
21. Tiger bones	5 per viss
22. Deer skin	4 per viss
23. Coffee seeds, porters	4 per backpack
24. Cooking oil	5 per tin
25. Kyats (currency notes)	2% of the value
26. Household goods for personal use	2% of the value

Source: SURA tax station, Bang Mai Sung, February 1983, Adrian Cowell Film and Research Collection, University of Washington Library.

or universities in Burma were literate in English. However, many only learned to read and write in Shan once they joined the SURA. One former SURA soldier, Seng Lao, had been a linotype operator at Bang Mai Sung in the early 1980s. As she explained: "You have to be able to do it, it's a skill. When I first saw people setting up the text, letter by letter, I could not make sense of it. . . . Many of the things that we would arrange would be based on handwritten articles, and we just went letter by letter. After practice,

I got it." As she detailed the process to me, she made a chopping gesture, as if she were mincing meat, but going right-to-left on the table in front of us. She was doing this to pantomime the act of typesetting: Shan is written left to right, but to typeset, one arranges the characters and slugs in reverse to contact the paper and print.

It was not entirely clear how the Shan United Revolutionary Army acquired a linotype and all the brass Shan fonts in the first place. One of the typesetters said that the SURA bought it from Lung Tang Kae, one of the Shan literary scholars from the Shan State Educational Committee. Lung Tang Kae continued to operate a Shan publishing house in Taunggyi, Southern Shan State, and today his daughter owns and runs a Shan clothing and memorabilia shop in the Taunggyi market. Another former linotype operator claimed that the brass characters of the linotype were actually modified Burmese fonts. The SURA had complete sets of Burmese fonts, since they produced many publications in that language as well.

The four informants I spoke with who used to work with the SURA linotype at the print shop at Wan Mai Sung all had at least a high school education (or part of a high school education) in the Burmese language, but their education in the Shan language was acquired via their affiliation with the insurgency.

Shan interlocutors estimated to me that only about 30 percent of Shan people can read and write in the Shan language. Therefore, the Shan insurgent publisher cannot only publish in Shan; it would not be able to recruit the many others who might have Shan sympathies but are illiterate in that language. The early editions of many of their publications were printed in both Shan and Burmese languages. Later Shan publications would include articles in Tai Khün (Eastern Shan script) as well as Thai and English.

The political leaders and bureaucrats of the insurgency held regular meetings to discuss their situation and plan for the future. Sometimes there would be official declarations and opening speeches in English, harking to the language of colonial bureaucracy and political speeches in Burma. Minutes of the meeting would be kept in Shan language. While the invoices, accounts records, and meeting minutes and agendas were important to the bureaucratic paper trail of the Shan United Revolutionary Army, the school books, other books, pamphlets, journals, and magazines provide an essential repository of historical ideas about Shanland. How do the media for a nation-state deferred create an imagined community among its people?

The elementary school curriculum is the logical place to start. Following the primers with the alphabet, by the second grade short readings include topic titles such as Our Shan Flag; School Opening Day; Grandfather Teaches His Grandchildren; Our Responsibility; Being Moral; What Will You Be When You Grow Up?; Ants Are United; Shan Basket Weaving; History of Taunggyi; The Hermit and the Rich Man; Good Student; and Electricity.

Each reading in the elementary school books is followed by comprehension questions. In terms of content, there is a balance between readings that emphasize Shan culture, history, and identity, such as those about the Shan flag, biographical readings about Shan heroes, including Suerkhan Fa, and other readings that deal with political ideals and citizenship but framed in general moral terms. These include readings about Buddhist precepts, the virtue of being a good student, and honoring and learning from one's elders. There are translations of Aesop's fables and articles about finding moral lessons in nature, such as ants working together because they love their species. For the illustrated stories, people are wearing Shan clothing, and traditional temples and architecture are also included. There are readings about science, such as electricity, gravity, and how a lever works. Finally, there are some aspirational readings about modern cities or modern classrooms, and the notion of *hküt kap* (ၶိုတ်းၵၢပ်ႈ) "with the times" is presented. In these readings, scientific knowledge and understanding of technology are put forward as important components of a sound education.

The elementary curriculum, as structured according to grade, brought Shan speakers to the written language through graduated lessons involving history, science, nature, morality, and aspirations. It is worth noting that all the lessons in the Shan curriculum tended to emphasize positive aspects of Shan culture; they did not deal with any bitter aspects of history, such as the Shan being denied a nation-state, nor did any of the readings present Burmese culture negatively.

Unlike the elementary school readings, the Shan United Revolutionary Army newsletters and journals were pointed with their critique of the status quo. In these articles, Shan authors discussed politics, social issues, and the role of the SURA. One of the journals is called *Söng Le'o* (ၸိူင်းလႅဝ်း), "Freedom's Way." It was started in 1984 and published annually until 2002. It is testament to the tenacity of the production team that the journal weathered a merger with Khun Sa's Shan United Army and later their surrender to the Burmese military. They stopped production in 2002 because the budget ran out. From local veterans, I was able to borrow and photo-copy nine of the nineteen issues, so my study of the content of the journal is based on those issues. My collection includes the first and last issue and is well distributed across the middle years of the journal's production.

The first issue, published in 1984, had a print run of a thousand copies, and was bound with a thin paper cover. Of the issue's sixty-eight pages, fifty-two are in the Shan language, while the remaining sixteen pages are in Burmese. The articles have features about the SURA itself as well as political position pieces about Shan unity and the ongoing struggle against the Burmese. Other articles include historical pieces and Shan poems. The issue includes drawings and comic illustrations.

One of the main articles in this first issue is a feature about the history of Shan warrior women. This correlates with the SURA recruiting women soldiers into its ranks. The text is adjacent to an illustration of a woman in a Shan skirt and headdress with giant swords in each hand, and on the opposite page is a poem about women soldiers, with a drawing of a woman in a SURA soldier uniform, her fist in the air. The article, titled "Sü Pün Ying Tai Hat Hān Hao Ta" (သိုပ်ႇပိူၼ်းယိင်းတႆးႇၵၢတ်ႇၷၢၼ်ႇၷၢဝ်းတႃႇ), "Connecting the History of Our Brave Shan Women," describes how Shan women have long held important roles, not just as fighters but also as intellectuals. Shan women have played a crucial role in resisting Burmese domination. The author mentions Nang Kham Lu, a Shan writer who contributed to the development and proliferation of the Shan written language and articulation of Shan culture. The conclusion of the piece instructs readers not just to respect and learn about the history of strong women but also to understand the current political situation in Shan State (Nang Lawn Tai ᢼᢠᢰ㠇ᨾᢰᢰ㠇ᨷ 1984, 27, 28).

Two years later, the print runs for *Söng Le'o* were three thousand issues, and production had moved to Chiang Mai, where they could make use of color separation for the cover, offset printing technologies, and gum bind-ing to produce a slick volume with sharper image quality in the photo-graphs (rather than the high contrast sketches they used previously). The 1986 issue contained 79 pages of articles in Shan and 16 pages in Burmese, and the 1988 issue had 77 pages of articles in Shan, 10 pages in Tai Khün (Eastern Shan language), and 67 pages in Burmese.

Numerous articles were dedicated to informing readers about what con-stituted the Shan Nation. For example: there is a 1986 article titled "Mana Sö Sat" (မုၼ်ႇᤅ㋞ႇ㠇㠇㠇), "National Pride." Of note, the author uses the term *sat* for nation (borrowing the Thai connotation of *chat*) rather than the Shan *hkö* for race or *möng* for kingdom/city. The author argues that the Shan people are indeed a true nation and should feel pride about this, as they have their race, civilization, language, religion, and great history of powerful kingdoms. But as the author Ta Mü Lek argues, at the present, national pride is weak among the Shan. The author attributes this situation to the fact that most Shan people are not literate in their own language. The Shan people feel that they are outsiders in someone else's home. In order to remedy this problem, the Shan people must rise up and create a strong and aggressive sense of national pride (Ta Mü Lek တၢမ္ၢိဝ်းလိၵ်ႈ 1986, 4).

An article published the following year, titled "National Symbols," argues that all countries, regardless of whether independent or subordinate to another country, will have their national symbols. Examples listed include the American eagle and the Russian white bear. The Shan have their albino tiger, and according to the article, it is the duty of Shan people to remind their fellow compatriots about their symbol and to have a deeper understanding of its origin and meaning (Hseng Küng Möng သႅင်ၵိုင်ႈ,မိူင်း 1987, 22).

In addition to providing a forum for Shan authors to reflect on their political project, the journal also presented reprints of international journalists' interviews with Khun Sa and commentaries about international events.[3] Through the SURA publications in the 1970s and 1980s, there begins to appear more widespread use of the term *sat* for nation, cognate with *jati* but taking on the semantic baggage of the Thai term *chat* for race or nation.[4] This semantic shift to adopting *sat* is a loaded one. While Shan people who are born in Thailand and are fluent in Thai incorporate many Thai neologisms into their everyday speech, members of the SURA are principally educated in Burma. This word choice by the Shan United Revolutionary Army writers is a method to tap into the additional power of race, sovereignty, and ownership that the term came to mean in Siam. As a resolutely Buddhist, staunchly anti-communist, pro-Shan movement, *sat* meaning rebirth, ethnic-nation, and homeland served as a more powerful affirmation of the Shan movement's authenticity of both their people and their territory. The notion also made their movement all the more legible to their neighbor, historical brethren, and Cold War ally, the Thai. Sharing common enemies (the Burmese and the communists) only reaffirmed this increasingly naturalized connection.

Shan Music of the Future

Although the importance of Shan literacy is frequently iterated throughout Shan books, pamphlets, and magazines, perhaps nowhere does modern Shan poetry connect with people at the emotional level more effectively than in the Shan-language songs sung in informal social guitar circles. This form of socializing (playing guitar, passing the instrument, chatting, and singing along) is immensely popular throughout Burma, including in Shan State. The informal circle requires neither attention nor participation; whereas in the West, often the pressure of "performance" on a guitarist and singer will tacitly require all the other people in the group to quietly listen and pay attention, in Southeast Asia, this is not always the case. Often people continue their conversations while one person plays and sings, or they might choose to sing along, or simply clap along with the rhythm.

In addition to providing a space where Shan insurgent print media production could flourish, the Shan Army–controlled territories encouraged youth to learn and sing Shan rock songs. For many of the soldiers in the Shan United Revolutionary Army, practicing guitar and singing with friends was an important leisure activity, and many of the best-known Shan language teachers and authors were also songwriters. Shan rock songs, along with popular music in Burmese, would be mainstays for the SURA; the former often were connected with political rallies, and the latter were played out of enjoyment and affection for various Burmese artists and songs.

In terms of discussion of modern Shan music, history essays on the subject place its origin at around the time of World War II. Some of the Shan literati who had standardized the script became key songwriters in the early days of modern Shan music, such as Lung Khun Ba Nyan of Hsipaw and Lung Kham Kong of Möng Nai. For some of the songs, they would adopt the melodies from popular Japanese, Chinese, and English songs and write new Shan lyrics to them (for the popular musical genre known as *copy thachin* in Burmese, see Ferguson 2013, 2016). Some of the songs would deal with themes of national pride, history, and language, while others would focus on romance and heartache. Following the war, Lung Khun Ba Nyan, along with a newly formed Shan Youth Organization, traveled to cities in the Shan State, taking a singing group with him. His most famous song from this period is "Hkö Tai Hkö Rasa" (ၵိူဝ်းတႆးၵိူဝ်းရၞႃ,လၺ), "The Shan Race Is a Royal Race" (Söng Kham Haw သႅင်းၶမ်းၸေႃ 2002, 9). Note, also, that this was penned in the early years after World War II, and that it uses the Shan term *hkö* for race rather than the later resignified term *sat*.

By the mid-1950s, Shan student associations at Rangoon and Mandalay Universities would be important sites for the promotion of Shan popular music. Shan groups were involved in student events, where they would listen to the latest records from the United States or England (Adams 2000, 140). While staying up-to-date with popular trends, Shan students in the 1950s made use of university recording equipment to record their own songs in the Shan language. The best-known band of this era was the group Sum Nam Hkong (ၸုမ်းၼမ့်ၶူင်း), or Salween Band. Khun Ung, a member of the band, also wrote the song "Kwa Le Nam Hkong" (ၵႂႃႇလႄႇၼမ့်ၶူင်း), "Visit the Salween River." Using Rangoon University's equipment, the Salween Band recorded numerous songs between 1956 and 1961. Their songs were even played on the Burmese radio airwaves, until Ne Win's coup put an end to that (Hsöng Kham Haw သိူင်းၶမ်းႁေႃ 2002, 11).

While groups such as the Salween Band or the songs penned by the Shan State Education Committee strove to instill in Shan listeners a sense of national pride, an affection for Shan culture and history, and a romantic appreciation of Shan nature, it was not until after the insurgency was in full swing that Shan songs became more militant in their content. With the likelihood of recording and broadcasting Shan songs in Burmese metropoles all but impossible, the Shan insurgencies offered a space, as well as funds for media production, through which Shan artists could propagate their art.

The two all-time best-known Shan popular singers are Sai Htee Saing and Sai Sai Mao.[5] They would each have illustrious careers in the mainstream Burmese popular music scene, as both men recorded numerous hits in both Shan and Burmese languages. The latter, Sai Sai Mao—Sai Mao for short— is the grandson of a Shan trader and spent the late 1960s traveling back and forth between Taunggyi in the Shan State and cities in Thailand. Through his travels in Thailand, Sai Mao got to know various Shan community leaders, many of whom had left the Shan State because of political problems.

Both Sai Htee Saing and Sai Sai Mao were involved in Shan radio in Chiang Rai, Northern Thailand, in the late 1960s (Hsöng Kham Haw သိူင်းၶမ်းႁေႃ 2002, 12). It was there that they came into contact with Sai Kham Lek, who is the most famous, most prolific Shan poet and songwriter in modern history. Sai Kham Lek was from a literary family, and two of his brothers and his sister are well-known authors in their own right. During the 1960s and early 1970s, the foundations for Shan political rock music were laid. One of these songs, "Kat Sai Hai Mai Sung" (Strive for

Progress), would end up being an anthem sung before New Year's events and every major Shan stage show in years to come (this song is discussed in chapter 8).

Political Rock 'n' Roll: Catharsis and Controversy

Shan political leadership recognized the value of converting revolutionary and cultural messages into modern tunes. One of these songs was "Lik Hom Mai Panglong" (The Panglong Agreement), which was written by Sai Kham Lek and sung by Sai Mao. They recorded the song at a studio in Bangkok in 1973, with the studio production and postproduction paid for by Ta Maha Hsang of the Wa National Organization (Hsöng Kham Haw သိူင်းၶမ်းႁေႃ 2002, 12; SHAN 2012).

In a 2012 interview, Sai Kham Lek offered some detail regarding his inspiration for the song. He saw a cartoon in the *Tai Youth Magazine* of the Rangoon University Shan Literary Society. In the cartoon, a young Shan man is climbing a statue of Aung San when the statue asks what the young man is looking for. He replies, "We'd just like to know if you had taken the Panglong Agreement away with you." Here are the lyrics of the song:

လိၵ်ႈႁူမ်ႈမၢႆပၢင်လူင် [The Panglong Agreement]

တႃႇတေႇတင်ႈမိူင်းၵွင်းၶေႃပုၼ်ႈတႆး
မၵ်းမၼ်ႈပၼ်ၵႂၢမ်းၵၼ်တီႈပၢင်လူင်
တေႃႇထိုင်မိူဝ်ႈလဵဝ်

When they established independence for the Shan people,
They made a promise at Panglong.
Until today . . .

ၽႂ်လႅၼ်ၽႂ် ၵမ်ႇလႃတ်ႈၵေႃႈတႆးႁူႉယူႇ
တႆးတေၵမ်ႇလႅၼ် မိူင်းတႆးၵေႃႈပႆႇလႆႈၶိုၼ်း
ပူၼ်ႉမႃးသိပ်းပီယဝ်ႉလူ မၢင်ၽဝ်ၵေႃႈပႃးလွမ်းၵႂႃင်ႇသၢၼ်ယဝ်ႉၵိုဝ်
ၵႂႃႇလႂ်ယဝ်ႉၵႃႉ လိၵ်ႈႁူမ်ႈမၢႆပၢင်လူင်

(Chorus) Who deceived whom? Without saying, the Shan already know.
The Shan don't deceive. Shanland has not yet been returned.
It has been ten years already. Has it been ruined? Gone with Aung San?
Where has it gone, the Panglong Agreement?

ခွတ်,တူင်,ရိုက်းလီက်း ဂိုုးတၢ,လွတ်းဆီ ယၢမ်းတိုက်းဧၢး
လဲးတိုက်းမျၢးဆၢင်ဂၶံယဝ်း ၸ်ၼ်ဝ်,ၸ်ၼ်ဝ်တေၢးလ်ဝိဝ်

To free ourselves from the iron chains, we had fought together.
They have fought each other already. So that today . . .
(Chorus)

လ်ိတ်,ၵၢမ်,ၵူင်း ၸ်းၵၢမ်,ဂၢၼ် ဝၶၼ်းၶိုင်းတေၢလဲးၸိၼ်ဆၼ်
တၢ,ေသၶီးၶၶၼ် ေတၢ,ထိုင်ၸ်ၼ်ဝ်းလ်ဝိဝ်

The sunshine won't fall. The Shan don't disappear. One day there will be a
    settling of this debt. Until today . . .
(Chorus)

The song skyrocketed to popularity among Shan networks, especially those along the borders, where insurgencies broadcast it over their radio channels. It is the most famous political song for the Shan, and its importance is emphasized with every generation—some have noted that there are young people who first learn about the Panglong Agreement because of the song (Hpu Twoi Hawk ၁ှုးတၢ်ၢ,ၵွၵ်း 2000, 10).

Sai Mao's recording of the Panglong Agreement song, in addition to his other recordings, which included Shan and Burmese renditions of Taiwanese star Deng Lichuen (aka Teresa Teng) songs, made him a rock star among Shan audiences (Ferguson 2015). Many of his Burmese songs would become hits in the mainstream scene in Burma. Sai Mao regularly performed in insurgent camps, and his songs were broadcast on Shan radio stations on the Thai side of the border or surreptitiously distributed in Shan State by sympathizers; he had gotten his start working in Shan radio in Chiang Rai.

A few years after the release of the Panglong Agreement song, at a performance in the Shan State, the Burmese military authorities seized Sai Mao. He was arrested and imprisoned for two years on the charge that he had dodged the Tatmadaw draft. More than one Shan informant told me that this was a ruse; the military had learned of his political content and wanted to censor him—not just to stop him but to make others cautious about making or distributing Shan revolutionary content. In 1976 he reached an agreement with the Burmese government: he would only perform songs that were approved by the Censor Board (Amporn Jirattikorn 2008, 47). In spite of his compromise with the Burmese authorities, Sai Mao continues to be tremendously popular among Shan people in Myanmar and exiles alike.

Today, the Panglong Agreement song is available for viewing on YouTube. In addition to the Shan version, there have been new recordings of the song in Thai.

Another musician who is beloved by Shan United Revolutionary Army affiliates is Sai Mu, from Möng Pan. For many, he is even more of a hero to the Shan than Sai Mao or Sai Htee Saing. Sai Mu was part of the SURA and an active teacher and writer. Many of his songs and their content were directly oriented to themes related to the Shan insurgency, culture, and nature. Though he did make some recordings in Burmese, he is much more of a star in the Shan music scene for his Shan songs. Even though many Shan people in Wan Kan Hai adored the other Shan popular musicians, for them Sai Mu was much more "one of us" than any of the others. Also, he was never considered a "sellout" the way some saw Sai Mao.

Sai Mu was born Sai Than Pe Le in Möng Pan, Shan State, in 1960. He attended middle school in the Sagaing Division in Burma, later moving to Bang Mai Sung in 1979 to join the Shan United Revolutionary Army. From 1984 until 1991, Sai Mu taught in the schools of the Shan resistance in the liberated areas of the Shan State east of the Salween River. In 1984 Sai Mu was also on the initial editorial committee that drafted the first issue of the journal *Söng Leʾo* (Freedom's Way). A year later, in Bang Mai Sung, he founded a rock band with the same name. It was during this time that he wrote and recorded songs with the Söng Leʾo band. Sadly, in 1995, Sai Mu passed away at the age of thirty-five in Wan Lak Taeng (Bün To Kep Sai Mu ပွိၼ်းတူၢ်ဝ်ပ်; ထၢ်းမူ 2005). His songs continue to be hits among Shan insurgents and exiles in Thailand. Even his former band, Freedom's Way, has carried on playing songs penned by him, and at one point had a small pub on the south side of Chiang Mai.

Despite his death at such a young age, Sai Mu's compendium of songs is vast and impressive. The songs range from the didactic (a song about the Shan alphabet) to the playful (a song about different kinds of poop), to the beautiful (ballads about nature and Shanland), to the revolutionary (songs about fighting for Shan independence). One Shan music enthusiast related, "Although Sai Mu the songwriter is no longer with us, we still use his song as our encouragement today." Multiple people in Wan Kan Hai talked about Sai Mu as a legendary musician "for the Tai." In this sense, the cultural intimacy and ownership is an important relationship; they don't just look at him as an artist who succeeded because he happened to be Shan, but rather they admire him because he worked for the Shan community. Although he recorded many songs in the Burmese language, he never achieved the mainstream success in Burma that Sai Htee Saing or Sai Mao did. He also never signed an agreement to perform only Burmese government–approved songs.

Sai Sai, a twenty-two-year-old Shan migrant in Chiang Mai, told me, "It's only Sai Mu's songs that really capture my heart. I'm sad that I wasn't born before he went to heaven. His music is beautiful and is always in my heart."

To give a brief sample of Sai Mu's repertoire, below are translations of three of his songs, which touch on themes of natural beauty, militant patriotism, and Buddhist philosophy.

သဝၢၼ်ဝပိင်းလူင် [Piang Luang's Nature]

ပိင်းလူင်ၵွၼ်းၶႆႇ. ၵွၼ်းယူႇ၀ီႇမီးလၢၵ်ဝၢၼ်ႈၼိုင်ႈ မီးၶဵ၊ တင်းတီး
သၢဝ်လီႈသေ၂၊တင်းမၢဝ်,ပရၢဝ်ႈ ၵွၼ်းယူႇ,ၶွမ်ႈၵၶႆ ၵၢမ်,မီးၼႄ့
ၶၢႆ..ၵွၼ်,မိူဝ်းၸ်တ်ႈ မီးၼႄ့ၼႃင်းထုင်းၼၵၡ မီးၼႄ့ၼႄၸ့တင်းဝတ်.ၡျင်းယူႇ,

Our Piang Luang has many different groups of people: There are Chinese as well as Shan, Lisu girls and Pa-O boys. We live together; nobody wants to go elsewhere. There are customs and traditions, culture and temples.

ပိၶၢႆတီႈၵွၼ်းသၢဝ်းမူၶၢႆ့သၢ၊လ့ ၵၢမ်,လၢင်ႈၶႃႇ.တီႈပၢႈၡ၊လ့
ၵိၶၢႆၶၵဝ်ႈတီးၼၵ၊ၵွၵႃ.လၢဝတ်ႈတီး ထုင်ဝ,ၶၵဝ်ႈတီးၼောႈတိုၵ်ႇ.ဝၢၶၢႆယူႇ,ၵ္ၢဝ်ႈ

It is a place of joy, we don't want to leave. We eat Shan foods and love the Shan nation. The Shan fermented bean is so delicious!

ပူၶၢႆ.သေၶႃၢဝ်းမ်ႈ ယိင်းၼၵၵ်ႈၵ၊ႈလၢႈၼႄႈၶၶၢႆ့ဝ်. ဝီးၼူၵၢႆ.ၼော
ထိုင်ၶိင်,လၢဝ်းၶၵ၊ႈၼၡူ၊လ့ယၵဝ်. ၵွၼ်းၵၶၢႆ,ၼောႈဝ်
ပၢၵ်ႈၵိီႇမၼၵ်းၶၵဝ်ႈၶၼ,လုင်းပၵ်ႈ

Following hot season the fields are plowed for the rain to come through so that Mr. Rice Farmer will be satisfied, and pay respect to the field and to the elders.

ယုၵ်.တၢင်,ထုင်းၼိူင်းၵၶၼ်လိ့မီးမၵ်ႈ လီမ်ဝၶၢႆးလင် ပိၶၢႆလွင်ဝ်ႈ;ထုင်းတီႈပိင်းလူင်ၵၵ်ႈ
ၵၢမ်,လိုမ်းလ၊ႈတွင်ဝ်ဝႃ.ၼောႈ,ၡဝဝ်ႈ သူၶလၵ၊ၵွၼ်းၼၵႃမ်.ၵၶၼ်ၡ်၊,ၶၵ၊
ယၢ၊ႈၼဝၢၼ်ၵဝၢင်းပိဝ်ႈၵၵၼ်ႈသူၡ်ၵဝ်ႈ

We hold our customs high for the future. It's done in regard to the customs and traditions of our Piang Luang. We won't forget; we remember them always. You and I are united together; don't part ways from me.

Piang Luang, as mentioned earlier, is the town adjacent to Bang Mai Sung, where Sai Mu lived and worked. Although the SURA (and the Kuomintang) made the place into a soldier town, Sai Mu has chosen to also describe its natural beauty and multiethnic character. The song neglects to mention any geopolitical problems or anything about the ongoing war. However, by extolling the idea of nature and interethnic harmony, the song keeps some of the goals and ideas behind the Shan insurgency as part of its theme, just not explicitly. As the lyrics of the song progress, we can see that the song communicates notions of peace, modernity, and Shan cultural values.

Moving away from natural beauty and peaceful coexistence, one of Sai Mu's songs more closely associated with militant Shan action is "Wan Tai Te Lawt Le'o" (The Day Shan Will Be Independent).

ဝၶႂႈတိုၼ်းတႄႇလွတ်ႈလႅဝ် [The Day Shan Will Be Independent]

တႃႇတေပီၶၼ်သေထေးလူင် ၵိုဝ်တေမၢင်းမွင်းမႃး
တႃႇတေဝၺၖတ်းမိုဝ်းမိုင်းၶီႇၵ်းပၶၼ်,ၵိုဝ်ပႃးယွၶၼ်းသူး
မၢင်းမွင်းပိုႇယူ,လွင်းတိုးၺႃ.ၶၼ်
လီႈယွၶၼ်းသူးယူ,ၵ်ႈတိုးၺၺမၽင်,ၶၼ်

To be a rich man, I have not hoped
To achieve Nirvana, I have not prayed for
What I have hoped for is for Tais to love each other
What I have prayed for is for Tais to be united

ယူ,ထင်လၺၵိုၶၼ်းလီဝၵိၶၼ်ၶဝ်ႈယေးလီဝ
ၶိင်,ၵၶၼ်ၼမႉတိုးတၵ်ႈၵိၶၼ်ယူ,ၶမ်ၶွၵ်ႈလီၵိၶၼၶ်.
ပီႈၶွင်ႈ.ၽိတိုးၽၵၼ်ပို့ၶၼ်းၵႃးလႃးႇယူ့ဝ်.
ပီႈၶွင်ႈ.လၢင်းၵၼ်ပို့ၶၼ်းၽိ့ၶၼ်းႏၢမ်ႈၶ်ႃႇ,ယူ့ဝ်.

We have had our place at the back of the house
For a long time, eating the rice from the granary of our Shan mother
Poor, desperate, stuck in an iron cage, brothers in argument with each other
Others perhaps take satisfaction in brothers hating each other
It's too much already

ဝၶၼ်းတိုးၵ့ဝ်းၽၺမ်.ၶၼ် ဝၶၼ်းတိုးၵ့ဝ်းၵ့ဝ်ၶၼ်းႅၶ့ဝ်
ဝၶၼ်းတိုးၵ့ဝ်းၵ့ၵ်.ၶၼ် ဝၶၼ်းတိုးၵ့ဝ်းတေလွတ်ႈလႅဝ်ႈ

On Shan day we will be united! On Shan day we will be independent!
On Shan day we will love one another! On Shan Day We Will Be Independent!

ၵၢဝ်ႇထိုင်ၶေမ်ႏၶွင်းသေ ၵွၼ်ၵၢၼ်တိတ်းမ်ႏပိုၼ်းၸလႇ
တꩡႇလၢတ်းလုၵ်ႇလၢင်းမꩡꩻဝꩻးလင် ꩡၼၼꩻပၢၼ်တၢင်းꩡလꩻ
ꩡမꩻမိုၵ်းတꩻꩡꩻꩻ၊တီꩻꩡ်ꩻꩡ်ꩻꩡ်ꩻသေႇ မုင်ꩻမွင်းပို၊ꩡꩻꩻꩡ်ꩻꩻတꩻꩻꩡ်ꩻꩻꩡ်ꩻ

Complain to the Salween River! Together write our new history!
Stake your claim for your children and grandchildren. Show the way!
Our Shan mother is in prison. Our objective is for Shan unity!

During my fieldwork in Wan Kan Hai, "The Day Shan Will Be Independent" was a mainstay for the evening rock band rehearsals, probably the most repeatedly played of any song. One of the other amateur musicians mentioned, in reference to Sai Mu's music, "When you listen to his songs, it doesn't make you hate the Burmese. But we still feel pain in our hearts because the Shan have suffered a lot." As an example of a song that reflects on the ongoing situation of Shan poverty, "The Song of a Worthless Poor Person" (ꩡꩻမꩻꩡ်ꩻꩡꩻꩡ်ꩻꩡ်ꩻꩡ်ꩻ), despite being a sober theme, is often played with an upbeat rhythm.

ꩡꩻမꩻꩡ်ꩻꩡꩻꩡ်ꩻꩡ်ꩻꩡ်ꩻ [The Song of a Worthless Poor Person]

ꩡိုတ်ꩻꩡ်ꩻꩡ်ꩻပီꩡ်ꩡꩻꩡꩻꩻမꩻꩻ ထုꩻꩡꩻꩻꩡꩻꩻꩡꩻꩡ်ꩡꩻꩡꩻꩡꩻ
ꩡꩻꩡ်ꩻပီꩡꩻꩡꩻꩡꩻꩻꩡ်မီꩻ ꩡ်ꩻꩡꩻꩻꩡꩻꩻꩡꩻꩡꩻꩡꩻꩡꩻꩡꩻꩡꩻꩡꩻꩡꩻ

I am born a human being, and I've seen a lot in this material world
But other things I haven't, such as having wealth such as others

ꩡိုတ်ꩻꩡ်ꩻꩡ်ꩻပီꩡ်ꩡꩻꩡꩻꩻမꩻꩻ ထုꩻꩡꩻꩻꩡꩻꩻꩡꩻꩡ်ꩡꩻꩡ်ꩻ ꩡ်ꩻꩡꩻꩻꩡꩻꩻꩡꩻꩡꩻꩡꩻꩡꩻꩡꩻ
ꩡꩻꩡ်ꩻပီꩡ်ꩻꩡꩻꩻꩡꩻꩻပိုꩻꩻမီꩻ ꩡ်ꩻꩡꩻꩻꩡꩻꩻꩡꩻꩡꩻꩡꩻꩡꩻꩡꩻ ꩡꩻꩡꩻꩻꩡꩻꩻꩡꩻꩡꩻꩡꩻꩡꩻ

I am born a human being, I've seen a lot already, but we poor people
We haven't had a lot thus far, we haven't seen wealth, not like them

ꩡꩻꩡ်ꩻꩡꩻꩡꩻꩡ်ꩡ်ꩻ ယꩻꩻမီꩻတꩻꩻꩡꩻꩻꩡꩻ ꩡꩻမꩻꩡꩻꩡꩻꩡꩻꩡꩻꩡꩻꩡꩻꩡꩻꩡꩻ
ꩡꩻꩻꩡ်ꩻꩡ်ꩻꩡꩻꩻꩡ်ꩻ ꩡꩻꩡꩻꩡꩻꩡ်ꩡꩻꩻꩡꩻꩻ ꩡꩻ၊ꩡꩻꩻꩡꩻꩡꩻꩡꩻꩡꩻꩡꩻꩻ
ꩡꩻꩡ်ꩻꩡ်ꩻꩡꩻꩻꩡꩻꩡꩻꩡꩻ မꩡꩻꩻꩡꩻꩡ်ꩻꩡꩻꩻꩡꩻꩻꩡ်ꩻꩡꩻꩡꩻ

Things I don't know yet, there are many, the song of a worthless poor person.
    Either proud or shy, they can get together and speak, because stones float
    when the bucket is not full of water, they do have a voice.

Although not directly advocating for a Shan political project, "The Song of a Worthless Poor Person" connects to Buddhist notions of birth, entering the world with nothing and leaving it with nothing. The tacit assumption is that many of the song's listeners will be economically disadvantaged, but the song gives them the hope that this will not always be the case, and allows them to reflect on their status of being born a human, which in the cycle of rebirth is considered high. Recalling the ongoing theme of cultural dissemination, what is compelling about this song in particular is that it acknowledges that the poor do matter. This statement is prescient, as it implies that the song itself is allowing this poor person to have a voice, to communicate his stories and aspirations to a larger community of Shan people. For amateur musicians in Wan Kan Hai, this was a frequent favorite in the jam sessions; people wouldn't request it by name but asked for it by singing the first phrase in the song.

Although this brief sample of songs hardly does justice to the vast compendium of songs and articles penned by this prolific artist, their themes are consistent with many of the values of the Shan insurgency: the natural beauty of Shanland, Shan peoples and customs, the ongoing state of oppression and injustice, and the need to organize and unite to correct the injustices.

While Shan modern music will often expound the virtues of the ancient Shan kingdoms and anticipate the wealth of an independent Shan nation, the differences between genres of the "modern" and the "traditional" merit further analysis. When Kyaw Myint, a guitar player and the former car driver for Sai Mao, explained about music in terms of genre, he talked about *ban kao* and *ban maü*, or "traditional" and "modern": "If you are playing the Shan long drum and the gong, that's traditional music. If you have a guitar, drums, bass and keyboard, that's modern music. Within those types of music, you can sing about anything you like, but usually songs about Shan politics or problems with the Burmese are sung with modern music. Besides, back when all we had was traditional music, we didn't have the same political problems."

The genres of modern Shan popular music came about in Burmese in the early years of colonial independence. But it was the insurgencies and the exiles in Thailand that made them boom. The key distinction made here is that modern music more effectively speaks to cosmopolitical notions of modernity and the nation. At the same time, modern music is able to incorporate nostalgia into a metanarrative about the Shan past and thus give direction to a future that includes a full-fledged Shan nation at the international order. One particularly representative example of the use of the

Shan long drum at a metonymic level is the popular song "So Tai So Taen, Laen Tai Laen Put" by the songwriter Sai Kham Hti, the younger brother of Sai Kham Lek. In the song, the lyrics detail the sacrifice of the Shan soldiers and claim that if the soldier dies, so will the sound of the Shan gong and the long drum (Sai Kham Hti ၵေႃႈၸ၀းၸၢ 1991, 111). The song itself, though, is played on guitar, bass, and drums. The point here is that the song refers to the sound of the gong and long drum as a metaphor for the hope of Shan independence.

One of the biggest Shan rock music recording studios is named SKT, short for Seng Kawng Tai, meaning the "sound of the Shan long drum." The icon of the studio, placed in the corner of its advertisements or on its CDs, is an image of a man in the Shan traditional costume beating on the long drum. While the music recordings produced by SKT tend to be rock music, featuring vocals, guitar, bass, keyboards, and drums, the content of the songs will occasionally invoke the long drum, even though they are not actual recordings of long drums, unless the sound is used as part of the background introduction to a rock song played on other instruments. Thus they use the modern music medium of rock to talk *about* the traditional long drum.

In these artifacts of popular culture, we can see the recurring thematic patterns of the projection of the Burmese enemy but also the romanticization of Shan nature and Shan foods. Repetition of Shan nationalist songs is an important way by which Shan people keep hope alive for a future Shan nation and something to strive for while they are pushed back from the core political and economic activities of two larger nations.

Revolutionary Ink: More than Skin Deep

In the twenty-first century, tattoos are thoroughly mainstream commodified decorations for many. They often include popular culture icons such as the Superman logo or Mickey Mouse, so their connection as a form of mass media is clear. For Shan soldiers in the 1970s and 1980s, this was not the case. However, it is useful to consider them as a form of media, even though they were neither produced nor distributed on an industrial scale as were magazines of music recordings.

Shan soldiers wore the Shan United Revolutionary Army soldier uniform, were taught to shoot guns, and learned to read and write the Shan script. All soldiers, including women soldiers, got traditional Shan tattoos, including those that designated them as warriors. Thus tattoos were an inscription

Illustration in *Söng Le'o* for Sai Kham Hti's song. Note that if a Shan soldier dies, the Shan gong and long drum collect spider webs. (Sai Kham Hti 1991, 111)

where the meaning was on the person, the individual, and, because of the modern insurgency, connected them to the modern nation-state building project while simultaneously connecting them to ideas of Shan cultural tradition and distinction.

Symbolic and mystical tattooing practices are common throughout Southeast Asia and date back centuries. For the Shan, tattoos are not decorations; they offer important protection against attacks and are considered a kind of vaccine against afflictions (Tannenbaum 1987, 695). Other tattoos, known as *sak yantra*, carry spiritual potency and meaning. In Mae Hong Son Province, Thailand, where there is a sizable Shan population that has been residing in Thailand for generations, not directly affiliated with the insurgencies, this type of tattooing has traditionally been common practice.

Tattoos carry gendered symbolic meaning for the Shan. For men especially, getting tattooed is often an important rite of passage. Tattoos serve multiple purposes: they protect their bearers, they ward off danger, and they cause others to have feelings of loving kindness toward them; further, some are used to prevent or cure illnesses. An elaborate set of tattoos is a marker of strength and virility. Traditionally, it was thought that a Shan man without tattoos would not be able to find a wife. There was a saying, "Yellow leg, get back away from our fields, otherwise our spirit of the field will flee" (Sai Htwe Maung 2007, 14). The "yellow leg" is the naked, untattooed leg.

The most striking Shan-style tattoos are known as "Shan trousers," which consist of a full set of tattoos covering the wearer's legs. The ink obliterates the natural flesh color entirely, thus the name "trousers." This particular custom seems to be dwindling, for when I was in Wan Kan Hai, the only men I saw with these Shan trousers looked at least sixty years old. However, many Shan comics and other illustrated stories include characters with these tattooed trousers on their legs.

For the more distinguishable patterns, other tattoos would be images of mythical animals, some with box grids featuring letters and numbers. Sometimes men would choose to have a certain animal tattooed on their skin in the belief that the animal would transmit particular characteristics to them via the inked images. A tiger would make one nimble; a Hanuman monkey would bring a long life, and a cat would make one stealthy (Conway 2006, 74). For warrior tattoos, the power of these tattoos also depends on the bearer maintaining Buddhist precepts; if the individual does not keep the precept, the tattoo would be rendered ineffective (Tannenbaum

1995, 94). But in Mae Hong Son, Thailand, Shan women would rarely have tattoos, except for preventing or curing illnesses (Tannenbaum 1987, 695). In some cases, it was said that Shan women only got tattoos if they were crossed in love (Sai Htwe Maung 2007, 15). Thus, the ongoing war was a game changer, at least for these women in the 1970s and 1980s.

The presence of a Shan military movement during the latter half of the twentieth century would change not only the ways in which the tattoos' significance would be deployed but also the gendered relationships of and for tattooing itself. The majority of the women who joined the SURA got tattoos. Both Seng Kham and Hseng Lün have elaborate tattoos up and down their arms, and Seng Kham once showed me the mythical animal tattooed on the small of her back. Although much of the mystic discussion of tattoos in Southeast Asia revolves around religious symbolism or allowing one to pertain to a spiritual or political community, Seng Kham's explanation about her tattoos was much more simple and straightforward: "I needed to show the other soldiers that I could withstand the pain." Furthermore, although it is sometimes custom that women would receive tattoos only in red ink, all former SURA women soldiers I met had black ink tattoos.

During the years of the SURA and up until the early twenty-first century, having Shan warrior tattoos was an important sign of membership in the military organization; they had spiritual applications and also were important status symbols for the Shan. As discussed in later chapters, these Shan tattoos became a liability for Shan migrants trying to assimilate in Thai society, or just to escape undue attention from soldiers of the state or judging Thais. Whereas the warrior tattoos set Shan soldiers apart from the general population and imbued them with special faculties, that "specialness" took on unanticipated, problematic new meaning in migration as power dynamics changed. In addition to the former soteriological meaning, in a hostile new climate the tattoos tagged the bearer as an ethnic outsider.

FROM SCHOOLGIRL TO REVOLUTIONARY SOLDIER

Möng Pan, in the Southern Shan State, is one of the scores of old chiefdoms once ruled by a *sao hpa*. In addition to the paddy rice production, Möng Pan's nearby caves had long been important sites for harvesting bat guano for making saltpeter (potassium nitrate), an essential ingredient in gunpowder. The town itself, located just to the west of the Salween River (though technically a small portion of Möng Pan lies east of the river), is only fifty-two miles north of the border with Thailand, but those fifty-two miles are as the crow flies over hills and mountains. Möng Pan is also significant in the history of World War II, as it was one of the two Shan States (the other being Kengtung) that the Japanese had transferred to Thailand as "Royal Gifts." During the latter half of the twentieth century, Möng Pan became an important connection with liberated Shanland, with its edges actively involved in supplying the Shan United Revolutionary Army. Lest we forget, Sao Yanta and the Num Serk Harn started the first Shan armed insurgency in Möng Pan.

In the 1970s, Möng Pan town was under the administrative thumb of the Burmese central government. It was another town paying Burmese taxes to Burmese tax collectors, obeying the orders of Burmese police, and, for the kids, attending Burmese government schools. Small shops sold (or rented) cheaply printed Burmese romance novels. Teens followed Burmese motion picture stars through the film magazines frequently rented from the various stalls at the Möng Pan market. Many of the Shan interlocutors who grew up in the area have fond memories of the major Burmese film stars, such as Win Oo, Wa Wa Win Shwe, Collegian Ne Win, or San San Aye.

Quite a number of the households in Möng Pan, however, quietly resented Burmese authority and had a son, cousin, or nephew who was armed and stationed in one of the hilltop camps of the SURA. In addition to the taxes paid to the Burmese government, local villagers would often be leaned on to support the SURA. For the insurgent camps to connect with the villages, they would send *kon pai möng* (ၵူၼ်းပႆမိူင်း) (literally "political person," but here more like a scout) to visit and seek assistance in the form of rice, money, or donations-in-kind such as volunteers (soldiers, cooks, or porters). These *kon pai möng* maintained the essential connection between the insurgency and the surrounding Shan communities upon which the ongoing war depended. They were able to slip into civilian communities undetected by the Burmese military and bring support for the SURA back to the mountaintop encampments.

Where the SURA took the personal approach and related directly to the village headmen or other families, the Burmese Tatmadaw was not so gracious. Aung Myo explained how the Burmese Tatmadaw would suddenly appear at an open-air film screening and round up able-bodied young men to be *luk hap* (လုၵ်ႈႁၢပ်ႇ) "porters" for their troops.

If someone at the film or big event with lots of people got word or saw the Burmese soldiers, it would be immediate pandemonium—people running away as quickly as they could. They knew how hard the Tatmadaw would work the porters. They needed porters for their gear and material, because over the mountains, they would go on routes where cars couldn't go, not even mules. The Shan wouldn't seize an event like that. At least not in the villages around Möng Pan or Pang Long. Instead, they would go and talk to the village headman, find out which families had young men that could do the job. Also, the Shan armies would not work the porters as hard as the Burmese. They would divide up the equipment and give the porter a more reasonable amount of stuff to carry. The Burmese would just work you until you were dead.

In 1979 Seng Kham and her best friend, Hseng Lün, were high school students at the Möng Pan government high school. Seng Kham was always a bit more aggressive and outspoken, although Hseng Lün had her moments as well. Seng Kham was the fourth child among ten and often took responsibility for looking after her younger siblings. Her father, a Yunnanese-Chinese man born in Mandalay before World War II, was the tax collector for the municipal government.

Seng Kham's father insisted that every one of his children, regardless of sex, complete school. He also saw the dominance of the Burmese state and believed it worthwhile that his children learn the ways of that nation. Seng Kham's mother, a Shan, once frowned on her daughter's time spent at school, saying, "What's the use of your reading and writing? You're just going to waste time writing love letters to boys!"[6] Perhaps her mother's words were just an attempt to admonish Seng Kham for not finishing her housework that day. But teenagers sometimes had plans entirely of their own. Seng Kham told me that she and her friends once skipped school because Sai Mao had just released a catchy new Burmese song, "I Can't Get Any Sleep These Nights" (အိပ်မရတဲ့ညပေါင်းတွေ). Rather than attend school that day, the teenagers bought the song's lyrics sheet and ran off to a hut to practice singing the song together until they had it "down."

As their high school was a Burmese government high school, staffed by Burmese teachers from elsewhere, sometimes the Shan students felt that they were treated poorly because they were Shan, or because they spoke Burmese with a Shan accent. For some Burmese teachers, being sent to teach in Möng Pan was the equivalent of being sent to the other side of the planet. Cultural differences, as well as the fact that many Shan resented the Burmese presence, would surely make it awkward to be a newly appointed high school teacher in such a context; some would overcompensate and rule over their classrooms with an iron fist.

Every morning, all the schoolchildren had to line up to salute the national flag. Although most children were not very politicized and went along with the ritual, those Shan children who knew of relatives and friends in the Shan United Revolutionary Army grudgingly submitted to this practice. One morning, Seng Kham got into a scuffle with a schoolmate, a Burmese boy who was the son of the local government official. According to Seng Kham, he had insulted her and called her a *Shan be-bok* (ရှမ်းပဲပုပ်) (Shan fermented bean, a staple ingredient in Shan curries), a pejorative to Shan people, and she was not going to simply take it without putting up a fight. Seng Kham and the boy got into a physical tussle, and she shoved the boy to the ground. Their teacher had to step in and break up the quarrel.

Rather than get to the bottom of things and hear both sides of the story, or punish both of the children, the teacher only punished Seng Kham. When she told me this story years later, she added that her problem at school coincided with an announcement posted by the Shan United Revolutionary Army: they were recruiting Nang Han "Brave Women Warriors." Seng Kham convinced Hseng Lün to leave Möng Pan and make the trek to Bang Mai Sung and join the SURA. They went together with another friend, Pö, who had a cousin already in the army. Even though Shan superstition considers three women together to be bad luck, the young women embarked on their journey anyway.

Although the political history behind the insurgency was something that was not clear to Seng Kham at the time, she was soon to get a truly experiential education through participation in the SURA. When the day came to leave, she packed very little. She had a long walk ahead of her. She had only heard hearsay about Bang Mai Sung. It was a Shan nation, where everyone spoke in Shan, and there were Shan schools, Shan factories, and a Shan publishing house. In some areas people even bought things with Shan currency.

The three teenagers set out early in the morning, just before they would have gone to school. They knew they had to head to the south, but they did not know the exact way. So, as many a trader had done before them, they asked villagers for directions as they passed through. Although it might have struck locals as odd that three young girls would be making such a journey on their own, they were determined, Seng Kham especially, to make it to this Shan capital in exile. They arrived at Wat Fa Wieng Inn Temple on the fourth day of their journey.

They could spot the pagoda from the opposite ravine and knew that the complex signified they had arrived in Bang Mai Sung. The spires of the Paya (pagoda) stand in a circle, and off to one side; on another hill is the temple school, and further up is the ordination hall that contains a large golden Buddha image along with several others placed near it. It was exciting to Seng Kham to realize that finally she was at the apex of the Shan separatist movement and standing on the crossroads of the Shan capital: the spiritual center of a movement that differentiated itself from two larger nation-states: the Burmese and the Thai. Shan flags were hoisted, and street signs were written in Shan script.

For Seng Kham and Hseng Lün, joining the SURA meant getting away from the stifling structure of a Burmese high school and looking beyond for a context where personal goals could be fulfilled. For them, joining the ethno-nationalist movement meant a solution to local frustrations; indeed they are relatively privileged in the scheme of things where surrounding areas are seriously impoverished. Seng Kham and Hseng Lün would meet many SURA soldiers who told horrific tales of younger sisters being gang-raped by Tatmadaw soldiers, entire villages burned to the ground, with all valuables, including livestock, taken or destroyed. It was their participation in the nationalist movement that connected the dots of the historical ideals to the problems of today, with the future Shan nation as the solution always further on the horizon. However, there was often a large gap in educational attainment between those who joined for cultural ideals or simply voluntarily versus those who joined because they fled other fighting or were fulfilling a recruitment quota. Further, many of the leadership had educational backgrounds in private schools, and some had university degrees from Mandalay or Rangoon Universities.

Latching on to a Shan future nation for many of the voluntary soldiers was a choice that involved a tinge of idealism along with a reality of frustration as a result of Burmese domination. The Shan liberated territories offered them a space where they could express themselves as they chose to in the Shan language, and also a place in which they were not compared with the same measuring stick as were the students in the Möng Pan government school. This is not to say life was easy or always fun. Twenty years

SURA soldiers in Bang Mai Sung, early 1980s. Hseng Lun is standing second from left, and Seng Kham is standing on the right. (Provided by Seng Kham)

later, Shan United Revolutionary Army veterans would look back on those earlier days with great fondness; but they also remembered what it was like being hungry during campaigns, struggling to survive on whatever game they could shoot, and seeing dear friends killed in battle.

CONCLUSION

Through participation in the insurgency, including learning the Shan written language in the schools in insurgent territories, Shan United Revolutionary Army soldiers grew to have a deeper understanding of what it would be like to live in a Shan nation-state. Because many of the SURA soldiers came to the Shan nation as teens or adults with roots in the incomplete cultural hegemony of the Burmese nation-state, their literacy and popular cultural appreciation reflects that background as well. After arriving in Bang Mai Sung, they learned the Shan script and read about Shan history in books written by its advocates instead of its detractors. For these SURA veterans, the late 1970s and early 1980s comprised the heyday of the Shan insurgency. Indeed, for the black-market economy at the bustling border towns, business boomed. Their economic and political movements were not under the thumb of the Thai state, so long as their monetary contributions sufficiently tickled the palms of the Thai police and army.

Modern nations, where most citizens will never meet each other, crucially depend on the dissemination of cultural ideas at the industrial scale. Printing and its distribution provide the logistical means, the platform, for the mass imagining of a national community. Although the development of scripts to write the Shan language took place in monasteries throughout the Shan plateau for hundreds of years prior to British colonialism, it was the introduction of the industrial printing industry—in connection with ideas about state-building and management—that took the process and its ideological implications to a new level. During the second half of the twentieth century, the conditions for the realization of that connection for the Shan nation gave them the gravitas for anticipating a Shan nation-state in the future.

It is the very printing of a language that enables it to have a kind of permanence that it did not have before, and, most importantly, that makes it "eternal" (Hobsbawm 1993, 61). The move to standardize the Shan print language was based on the present relationship with political power as well as the facility of adapting the current printing technologies in Burma to another script. That the *lik to mun* would be modified to become *the* Shan script is a perfect storm of political power and technical similarities. Further, the adaptation of Shan literacy within Burmese linguistic domination is not a massive leap for a Shan soldier who is already fluent in Shan and literate in Burmese.

With the anticipation that there would be an independent Shan nation, the Shan State Education Committee devised a standard written system for the schools and bureaucracies in advance of that; although political independence would be necessarily deferred for decades, the Shan separation movement allowed there to be a full dress rehearsal of that independent Shan nation-state: bureaucratic tasks were carried out entirely in Shan.

Shan publications, music recordings, and even tattoos could comprise what John Downing has called "radical media," in that they "express opposition vertically from subordinate quarters directly at the power structure and against its behaviour . . . [and] build support, solidarity, and networking laterally against policies or even against the very survival of the power structure" (2001, xi). However, because of the barriers to the Shan culture industries, an otherwise benign comic book or Shan translation of an Aesop's fable takes on radical characteristics since it might be published without a license and in a context in which even teaching the Shan language and script is suspect. In that sense, some of the Shan publications became radical not by their own volition but by the context in which they were distributed and read.

Burmese government policy indirectly thrust this print capitalist expansion on the Shan literati—the government diminished the role of the Shan *sao hpa* in its 1959 buyout and by relegating the role of the Shan movement to its narrow definition of "culture" ensured that this particular element of state-building could continue while others fell to the wayside. But the honorable and essential role of the Shan intellectuals has been repeatedly emphasized throughout the insurgency, in the Shan literacy project and the ongoing celebrations of Shan culture and history. Similarly, Shan authors are well connected with Shan musicians, and although Shan poetry has its own special place in Shan high culture, music bands are essential parts of every religious festival, and guitar culture has long been key to youth socializing in Southeast Asia in general.

The Shan warrior tattoos offer a corporeal affiliation with the insurgency, bounding the individual to the regiment but also, because of the experience of getting them (withstanding the pain) and what they represent, proving that the body has the necessary mettle to fight. In another vein, the tattoos serve as a symbolic reminder that fighting for a modern, independent nation-state is not an endeavor based on scientific, technical rationalism but draws upon aspects of cultural mysticism and traditional practices that are based on Shan spiritual ecumenism. The Buddhist *yantra* tattoos are not unique to the Shan, but in the context of the ongoing insurgency, where ethnic categories are increasingly politicized, the tattoos take on that additional cultural baggage.

Scripting the future Shan nation, it was the contradictory nature of nation-state building in mainland Southeast Asia, a quirk of indirect rule as well, that allowed the Shan elites to become empowered, but it was the cultural associations incubated by the Shan insurgencies that allowed those messages to be produced on a mass scale. Participating in that everyday reproduction, whether by teaching the Shan curriculum to kids or by practicing a Sai Mu song with other musicians, allowed people to learn—and indeed to reinforce—the idea that they were neither Burmese nor Thai but another nation that deserves respect.

4

Shanland during the
Reign of the Heroin King

Our Shanland is incredibly rich. Even though we eat and sleep every day
on this rich, golden land, our people are dreadfully poor.

—Khun Sa (TRC 1990a, 5)

DURING THE 1980S AND 1990S, the battle for Shanland made news-
paper headlines all over the world. This was not due to the Shan peoples'
unique cultural history or protracted struggle for autonomy but rather
because of the notoriety of one powerful, enigmatic leader: Khun Sa, the
so-called Opium King of the Golden Triangle.[1] In this period, Khun Sa
(known to his Chinese contacts as Zhang Qifu) amalgamated several
armies in Shan State—including Kawn Söng's Shan United Revolutionary
Army—to form the Möng Tai Army (MTA). At its apex, this force of more
than twenty thousand soldiers ostensibly posed the biggest challenge to Burmese sovereignty in Shan State. Its strength came from its numbers but also
from its massive supply of networks and firepower, largely funded by the
drug trade. At one time, the MTA supplied two-thirds of the heroin to the
global illicit narcotics market.

As the leader of the Möng Tai Army, Khun Sa presented himself as a Shan
nationalist, giving speeches about the Shan cause and sponsoring Shan
schools and religious events. Meanwhile, he made use of powerful criminal, business, and government connections to strengthen his empire and
amass tremendous personal wealth. In early 1996, much to Shan patriots'
dismay, Khun Sa surrendered the Möng Tai Army—its troops, weapons,
and territories—to the Myanmar military. This was done in exchange for
his own personal immunity and business concessions.[2]

Khun Sa's forfeit left a sudden vacuum of authority in Shanland. The
Myanmar Tatmadaw moved in and asserted its strength. An estimated three

hundred thousand villagers were displaced, many fleeing across the border and into Thailand. The Myanmar government moved ethnic Wa villagers down to the area from Northern Shan State and provided concessions for the government's ceasefire proxy, the United Wa State Army (UWSA), to establish additional bases along the Thai border.

From the time of their merger with Khun Sa's forces in 1985, the troops of the Shan United Revolutionary Army weathered these changes to their political and cultural project to repossess Shanland. The amalgamation and expansion of the Shan insurgency under Khun Sa were hardly minor tweaks to an existing bureaucratic structure. For SURA troops, this so-called merger was experienced more like a takeover: Khun Sa expelled—even executed— members of the former leadership and instituted major changes to the day-to-day running of the armies. This fostered discontent and drew cri-tique regarding the authenticity of their new leader's intentions. A number of former SURA elites and soldiers saw their cultural vision for an inde-pendent Shanland hijacked by a ruthless new authoritarian narco-army.

In this changing milieu, Cold War seismic shifts recalibrated the relation-ship between the economies of the uplands as well as the ostensible political goals of the various armed groups in the region. The Kuomintang was no longer the prominent player it had been in previous decades. The Commun-ist Party of Burma would later mutiny. New ethno-national forces would emerge, including the United Wa State Army, the most powerful army to enter into a ceasefire agreement with the Myanmar government. What does this all of this mean for the project to repossess Shanland?

To untangle how the movement for Shanland arrived at this surprising juncture, we need to consider how the SURA came to be part of Khun Sa's Möng Tai Army. To situate Khun Sa's enigmatic persona, this chapter starts with an overview of his biography, tracking his career and life trajec-tory through the changing fractals of Shan State politics during the Cold War. Then it discusses the merger between the Shan United Revolutionary Army and Khun Sa's Shan United Army. Attention focuses on the experi-ences of former SURA soldiers and their views (some with the benefit of hindsight) of how they experienced this massive political change. To gauge how the army and political project was presented to its participants, this chapter also explores the content of Khun Sa's speeches to the troops and how he and the MTA were presented and discussed in materials produced by the Shan-language publishers of the insurgency. Themes of authenticity and controversies over leadership come to the fore.

SHAN FREEDOM FIGHTER OR HEROIN KING?

Khun Sa looms larger than life. He is the most infamous figure in Shan history. A character of Hong Kong action films, he is also known to be vicious to any enemy. He built his reputation not only by commanding numerous armies but also by outsmarting local governments, foiling dozens of assassination attempts, and escaping punishment from the United States Drug Enforcement Administration. In sum, he is the notorious Opium King of the Golden Triangle. At the same time, he gave rousing speeches to his troops and presented himself as an adamant supporter of Shan freedom and independence. He could be charming and even jovial. All these personae attract questions regarding his true intentions. Many a news exposé starts with the puzzle, was Khun Sa a freedom fighter or an opium warlord? Somehow, he is expected to be one or the other. In the dynamic coral reef of Shanland, hardly anything is monolithic. If any lesson can be gleaned from the history of the region, it is that nothing is permanent.

On 17 February 1934, a baby boy named Sai Sa was born in the village of Bang Pa Pöng, Loi Maw District, Möng Yai, in Shan State. Sai Sa's father, Khun Ai, was the son of the chief of Loi Maw (Khun Yi Sai), who himself was a fifth-generation migrant from Talifu. The latter was once a Tai kingdom but presently is incorporated as part of Yunnan Province, China. Sai Sa's mother, Nang Seng Jum, was a Ta-ang Shan woman born in Loi Maw. Little Sai Sa lost his father when he was a toddler. Soon thereafter, his mother remarried. Her new husband was Khun Ki, the district chief or *myosa* of Möng Tawm District, not far from Loi Maw. Unfortunately, newly remarried Nang Seng Jum was not long for the world. She died when Sai Sa was only five years old. Sai Sa's stepfather initially took him in, but later the little boy was adopted by his paternal grandparents. His grandfather, Khun Yi Sai (chief of Loi Maw), took the little Sai Sa under his wing and taught him to read Chinese. He also gave his grandson practical skills in tea cultivation and horse and mule husbandry. Sai Sa started school, but the onset of World War II cut his formal education short (TRC 1990a, 1; Khun Sa 1992, 46, 47).

Loi Maw's location in the northeastern corner of Shan State put the small town in the path of the Kuomintang's retreat and along the supply lines for that army's efforts to gather reinforcements for its counterinsurgency. According to Khun Sa's biography, the KMT behaved like settlers in the area. In 1951 KMT soldiers showed up in Loi Maw to commandeer

Khun Yi Sai's pack of mules for their own use. As Khun Sa would later relate, his grandfather—with tears in his eyes—directed him to show the KMT which packsaddle would go on which animal. Khun Sa said that it was this experience in particular that made him resolve that the KMT were enemies that needed to be driven out of Shanland (Khun Sa 1992, 47).

Whether motivated by patriotism or by grudge, Sai Sa rounded up a group of his friends from Loi Maw and staged a raid on a KMT unit, allegedly taking thirty weapons. The KMT quickly retaliated and kidnapped his grandfather Khun Yi Sai so he would return the weapons. Sai Sa later fled to urban areas and began to resent Burmese domination of Shan State (Khun Sa 1992, 47). From his firsthand experience with long-distance traders coming through Loi Maw, his connections, and business savvy that he acquired from his grandfather's family, Sai Sa ventured out as a petty trader on his own, soon expanding to form his own militia. At one point, Kokang commander Olive Yang had taken Sai Sa in as a gopher for her militia, which was later in alliance with the KMT (Elliott 2006, 27–28).

During the 1950s, the Kuomintang ran the majority of the opium trade and had the most powerful armies in Shan State. Importantly, they did not engage in the opium cultivation themselves. They would compel villagers to do it; through quotas and violent enforcement, many villagers increasingly had to forgo rice cultivation in favor of the poppy. Most were already in debt bondage prior to planting. The KMT made their money protecting caravans of the opium product, taxing its transport and, later, getting it to refineries near the border so it could be processed into heroin. Sai Sa (or Zhang Qifu) found his way in these interstitial economies, making use of his Chinese-language skills to liaise with long-distance traders and to pay off the Kuomintang forces to protect his small but growing network (Ahram and King 2012, 179).

The Rangoon central government increasingly fought back. Throughout the decade, the Tatmadaw expanded its presence in Shan State and engaged in large-scale operations against the Kuomintang, starting with Operation Naganaing in February 1953. The Kuomintang defeated the Tatmadaw in a few weeks. In October of the same year, following another Tatmadaw attack, there was a KMT retreat into Chiang Dao District of Chiang Mai Province (Kanchana กาญจนะ 2004, 19). The following year the Tatmadaw launched Operation Bayinnaung (Callahan 2003, 159, 173). With the expansion of the Tatmadaw under the Military Caretaker period of 1958–60 came increased antagonism toward the KMT, and by 1958 there were more than three thousand KMT troops who had retreated to Chiang Mai Province (Gibson and Chen 2011, 235). Zhang Qifu and his Loi Maw militia were straddling each of these worlds.

On 16 January 1960, Colonel Maung Shwe, Tatmadaw commander of Eastern Strategic Command (Shan State), presented Zhang Qifu with an offer of special status as a chief of a volunteer militia: he would get trade privileges and assistance, but he would fight against the Kuomintang and the Communist Party of Burma. Interestingly, to the Burmese, he was Khun Sa, with "Khun" inherited from his grandfather's status as *myosa* of Loi Maw ("Khun" is a Shan title for royalty; "Sai" is a common term for young man). Zhang Qifu / Khun Sa saw terrific opportunity in this deal with the Burmese government and accepted it enthusiastically. By his own account, he was already supported by merchants who disagreed with socialism, and by 1963 Khun Sa's territories extended to Kengtung, which borders Laos (TRC 1990a, 2).

The Tatmadaw, with the assistance of their volunteer militias, expanded their control in Shan State. By 1961 the major groups of the Kuomintang were pushed out of Burma. They established bases just on the Thai side of the border in Chiang Rai and Chiang Mai Provinces, with the Fifth army of Tuan Hsi-wen in the former and the Third army of Li Wen-huan in the latter (Thaung We U သောင်းဝေဦး 2010, 165). With the shift in power, two of Tuan's officers, Zhang Suquan and Liang Zhung-ying, formerly of the Republic of China Special Forces and Battalion Special 111 (along with fifty other KMT soldiers), left the Fifth Army of the KMT and joined up with Khun Sa's Loi Maw militia. The two officers would go on to become key deputies for the growing army. The two were vital contacts for Khun Sa as they each had extensive strategic war experience in the region and were also members of the Intelligence Bureau, Mainland Operations Department (MOD) of the Ministry of National Defence, Taiwan (Gibson and Chen 2011, 243).

In the meantime, the Kuomintang presence in Thailand was tolerated, even encouraged, by the Thai government, as it served to collect intelligence for Taiwan, the United States, and Thailand (Lintner 1994, 194). The narcotics trade continued to grow. The KMT's supply networks for opium had long roots throughout the hills of the Shan plateau and depended on various militia to protect their caravans. Khun Sa's Loi Maw militia could be considered one of these protection armies for hire.

Following the March 1962 Revolutionary Council coup in Rangoon, the government instituted another new program to fight against its enemies: the Kakweye, or Home Guard militia (KKY), which had very much in common with the volunteer militia. In this program (as detailed in chapter 2), when a militia was willing to fight the Communist Party of Burma or the Kuomintang (or both), it would receive trade privileges, including the right to traffic opium, and sometimes even armaments. However, it would appear that many of these militia were perfectly content to carry on the opium trade rather than devote time and lose men to skirmishes with the Kuomintang or the communists. With the elaborate and reticulated trade routes of the uplands, there were pockets of opportunity for dozens of groups to profit.

Zhang Qifu operated the Loi Maw militia as a KKY force until 15 June 1964, when he rebranded the forces the Shan United Army (SUA) and established a base in Hin Taek, Northern Thailand, and up to Wieng Nguen in Wa territory in Northern Shan State. He would later return to collaborate with Rangoon in 1966. Zhang Qifu (Khun Sa) had remarkable skill at switching affiliations, hedging his bets to ensure he had powerful alliances to exploit when tides turned; as an investor, he maintained a diverse portfolio. This was not just due to his interpersonal skills, but also because of the wealth and power he was able to amass in the interstitial economies of the Shan hills. Khun Sa's rise to prominence in the region was attributed to the expansion of his trade networks and firepower that took place while operating as a militia for the Burmese government and the connections and profits made taking opium shipments to Thailand (Khun Loi Leng ၶုၼ်လွႆလႅင်း 1991, 166; McCoy 1991, 2; Renard 1996, 60). His powerful alliances extended beyond Mainland Southeast Asia: through his connections with the Taiwan Intelligence Bureau of the Ministry of National Defence, Khun Sa sent members of his Shan United Army to Taiwan for military and intelligence training (Gibson and Chen 2011, 254).

Zhang Qifu's (Khun Sa's) Loi Maw militia, the Shan United Army, was ostensibly established as a KKY outfit with sanction to fight the Communist Party of Burma and the Kuomintang at the behest of the Burmese government. However, there was a key resource issue: the groups with which they were supposed to be at war presented both a trade connection and competition over the opium business. While expanding your own business in the company of a powerful competitor, at what point do you fight back?

Later testimony suggests that Khun Sa felt particular resentment toward the Kuomintang, so in addition to military or business motives, there was an issue of personal grudge. He told the story of the KMT commandeering his grandfather's mules, and during his years commanding the Loi Maw militia, there was an incident in which the KMT raided his camp and put him in a pit for several weeks. The experience was humiliating and led to special resentment for the Kuomintang on his part (McCoy 1999b, 136). However, this resentment did not appear to extend to every part of the KMT; while he was in adversary relations with the Third Army, at the same time, he did work through his deputies with the Mainland Operations Department (MOD). The MOD has been responsible for controlling the guerrilla forces in China's south and southwestern border areas when serious activity began there in 1951 (Gibson and Chen 2011, 50). Importantly as well, Khun Sa had been working with the KMT in some capacity as their territories for the opium business did overlap.

In 1967 Khun Sa started to push back: in February he began to require that KMT caravans pay transit tax to his armies in Wa (Northern Shan) areas, and in June of the same year, he made an even bolder move that would erupt in all-out war (McCoy 1991, 356). Khun Sa had a mule caravan carrying approximately sixteen tons of opium en route to his buyer, Royal Lao Army general Ouane Rattikone, to whom he had sold opium the previous year. However, as was protocol, he would have to pay tax on the shipment to the Kuomintang. A shipment that big would attract a tax of 5 million baht, or the equivalent of US$240,000 (US$1.9 million in 2020). So the Loi Maw militia commander decided to take another route through Laos instead of going the more direct route that would pass through Kuomintang territory. The Kuomintang got wind of this tax-avoidance scheme and, in an impressive move, united the formerly bickering Third army in Chiang Mai Province and Fifth army in Chiang Rai Province and collectively dispatched their troops to surround Khun Sa's caravan of three hundred mules and its human complement of eight hundred soldiers or armed muleteers.

However, the Lao army got involved, sending reinforcements including helicopters that dropped five-hundred-pound bombs. Troops dug bunkers, and there was fierce fighting in the last week of July; Khun Sa's side lost eighty men. The Lao army allegedly took the entire opium shipment (worth 12 million baht, US$577,000 in 1967, or US$4.5 million today). The Kuomintang did not fare well either: it lost seventy soldiers and had to pay

187,500 baht to free the hostages the Lao army took from it (Kanchana กาญจนะ 2004, 152, 153). In spite of what seems like a massive defeat, Khun Sa became notorious. Meanwhile the Thai government became more sensitive about the drug-trafficking activities and started to require that local officials engage in more reporting to Bangkok.

At the same time, as detailed in the second and third chapters, the Shan insurgency movement, namely the Shan State Army, followed by the Shan United Revolutionary Army, had been gathering strength and expanding in the 1960s. While continuing to play the Burmese off the Kuomintang, in 1969 Khun Sa was approached to join forces with the Shan State Army and invited to a meeting to discuss this deal in Taunggyi, Southern Shan State. The Burmese government got wind of this and met Khun Sa upon arrival at the nearby Heho Airport on 20 October 1969; he was arrested and imprisoned in Mandalay on charges of treason (he had permission to traffic drugs, so that was off the table (Kanchana กาญจนะ 2004, 163). While in prison, he read Luo Guanzhong's *The Romance of the Three Kingdoms*, the fourteenth-century historical novel about ambition, empire, and breakdown.

In 1969–70, while Khun Sa was studying in his Mandalay cell, the Kuomintang (sponsored by the CIA) established a number of heroin refineries in the border areas (McCoy 1999b, 138). Although the first heroin refinery in the Golden Triangle was built in 1962, there was a growing market for the powerful drug, particularly among American GIs in the area: a captive audience, as it were, carrying the traumas of war on their minds and holding US dollars in their pockets. By the end of 1971, there were twenty-nine heroin refineries at work near the Thai border, the majority of which were protected by the KMT (Renard 1996, 58, 59). To ensure their raw materials made it safely through Shan State, the KMT established a network of eleven radio posts from its headquarters in Thailand on up to Lashio in Northern Shan State (McCoy 1991, 353). From the refineries to market, the Kuomintang, through its Thai government allies and overseas Chinese criminal networks, was distributing this highly addictive product to US troops in Vietnam and to international connections in China, Hong Kong, Macau, Malaysia, and Taiwan (Dupont 1999, 411).

However, the Shan United Army forces were not going to let their dear leader languish in prison any longer, especially with the heroin business in the region ramping up. One of Khun Sa's key deputies, Zhang Suquang (who was connected to the Intelligence Bureau of the Ministry of National Defence), coordinated the kidnapping of two Russian doctors in Taunggyi who were in Shan State to staff a Soviet goodwill hospital (Kanchana กาญจนะ 2004, 163; Kramer 2005, 42). To negotiate the hostage exchange with the Burmese government, Thai general Kriangsak Chamanan stepped in and was ultimately successful: Khun Sa was freed on 7 September 1974, though he had to remain under watch by the Burmese authorities. It may have been little coincidence that Kriangsak had been part of the Thai army that was dispatched to the Shan States during World War II. Kriangsak and Khun Sa would establish a profitable collaboration all the while presented as a Thai/Tai bromance.

A year and a half later, in February 1976, Khun Sa moved back to his base at Hin Taek and returned to the director's chair of the Shan United Army. The late 1970s marks a decisive shift toward the positive assertion of Tai identity—in concert with the Thai government—as part of his project; this is related to the army's powerful connection with General Kriangsak and others in the Thai military, as well as the changing machinations of the Cold War in Southeast Asia.

With the United States' withdrawal from Vietnam and thus Hanoi's victory, the Kingdom of Thailand read the writing on the regional wall and exchanged diplomatic recognition with the People's Republic of China on 1 July 1975 (Gibson and Chen 2011, 277). At the same time, however, the obvious presence of the Kuomintang on Thai soil was not just problematic because of the drugs issue but also because the Thai government would be seen as supporting a counterinsurgency against their powerful neighbor to the north. How to make the KMT appear benign? As the Thai government had done in previous decades with Chinese business elites, they would make them Thai.

Changing thousands of people's national and ethnic identity cannot be done with a snap of the fingers. However, granting bureaucratic privileges is an effective place to start. The Thai government offered special citizenship status to Kuomintang veterans. The policy was originally proposed in 1975, but it was not until 1978 that the Thai government would roll it out, with the criteria that those who had been good subjects of the kingdom would be qualified for Thai citizenship (Kanchana กาญจนะ 2004, 306). This order would ultimately affect fifteen thousand people in thirteen different villages throughout Northern Thailand (M. Smith 1999, 343). Partially owing to the fact that the majority of Bangkok's (and Chiang Mai's) business elites were of Chinese heritage but were culturally assimilated to Thai nationalism, members of the Kuomintang were gradually accepted within the Thai imaginary as Thai (Yos ยศ 2008, 66).

At the same time, while many members of the Kuomintang were formally accepting this Thai retirement package, those who remained active were expected to merge identity with the Shan insurgency. As part of his gesture to keep a good relationship with the local community, and to encourage long-term planning and state-building, the Shan United Army opened elementary schools for Shan children in the area and started teaching the Shan-language curriculum, the same one used in the SURA schools (TRC 1990a, 2).

With his SUA base in Hin Taek, Northern Thailand, and trade networks across Shan State, Khun Sa started to gain a larger proportion of the sauce. His profits were fueled by the black market in Burma and the ongoing money to be made through taxing and being involved in the trade of teak, gems, opium, and weapons, as well as everyday consumer items bound for Burma. In the Northern Thai city of Chiang Mai, going by the Thai name Chan Changtrakul, he established a jade trading company called Zhanghia. He made large contributions to the Thai state and toward General Kriangsak's political projects in particular.

The Cold War situation to battle communism presented another ideological opportunity for Tais to "band together," or rather for the ethnic ideology be presented as another form of strategic unity in the face of a nebulous enemy. The anti-communist rhetoric proved useful for Thailand both to extend its domain and to delimit internal rivals (Bowie 1997, 72). Government propaganda and popular media portrayed the figure of the communist as inherently un-Thai and diametrically opposed to the conceptual triad of Thai-ness: nation, religion, king (Thak 2007, 137).[3] By branding his militias as Shan, and therefore Tai, as Kawn Söng and the SURA had done before, Khun Sa rode this political wave, emphasizing to Thai authorities the supposed blood connection between Shan and Thai. Khun Sa even sought (but failed to obtain) royal patronage from the Thai king Bhumibol. His Shan military camps held parades in honor of King Bhumibol's birthday, and at one point, he even speculated that there should be one "official monarch" for all the Thai and Tai-lands.

However, the perception of racial brotherhood and cultural intimacy was not enough for a free pass to do business in Thailand. By the late 1970s, with the growth of the American War on Drugs, the business of the

Shan insurgencies (and the Kuomintang) on Thai soil was a continued embarrassment to the Thai government. Sensing this growing national discomfort about the drug trade, Khun Sa started to advertise that he would end the drug trade once and for all. In 1977 his officers drafted a bold proposal to Joseph Nellis, chief counsel of a US congressional committee on narcotics, to sell the year's opium harvest for destruction. This was refused, but later a letter of Khun Sa's was part of a report to the US Congress. In it, he offers to collaborate with the "International Drug Enforcement Organization . . . and on the 'humanity' stand, I have no other demand rather willing to fulfil my duty as a 'human being' should for his 'same species' aim at improving human welfare" (US House of Representatives 1978, 45).

Khun Sa's global recognition was increasingly problematic for the Thai government, particularly since he was overstepping the Thai government's authority in his bold plans to eradicate narcotics. In January 1982, the Thai government dispatched Border Patrol Police and paramilitary rangers to attack Khun Sa's base at Hin Taek. The Thais had more than a thousand troops as well as aerial reinforcements. After several days' engagement, Khun Sa's Shan United Army eventually retreated across the border into Shan State (Lintner 1994, 433; McCoy 1999b, 139). The SUA would establish a new capital in Shan State in the town of Homong.

During these attacks on Khun Sa's SUA, Kawn Söng's Shan United Revolutionary Army was still in its alliance with the gradually retiring Kuomintang; the SURA had been the KMT's "operative arm" within Shan State once the latter had settled in Thailand (Lintner 2021, 101). Although it might have looked on the surface like a peaceful retirement offer of citizenship privileges, the actual shutting down of heroin operations on Thai soil was much more violent, and various forces were in competition with each other. On 11 March 1984, Khun Sa sent a message to the KMT by dispatching a truck laden with explosives to destroy KMT general Li's compound in Chiang Mai (McCoy 1999a, 311).

In many cases (and this was true for the Shan United Army as well) the armies were not always running the heroin refineries themselves so much as making money off of protecting the opium supplies from the Shan hills. The heroin refineries were often controlled by Hong Kong or Macanese mafias. Although Khun Sa had become rich and powerful in the Golden Triangle, his income from opium was dwarfed by the profits made by the syndicates that shipped the heroin overseas (Renard 2001, 25). The push to retire all heroin manufacture within Thai borders did not end with the attack on Hin Taek. More than one informant was able to recall the violent destruction of Kuomintang and Chinese mafia operations in Piang Luang, Wieng Haeng District, Chiang Mai Province, in 1985. The Sua Pan Thai Rangers special forces were dispatched to kill dozens of people involved in drug production.

> They came at about three AM, all of them in black uniforms. The Shan soldiers had already got notice and so they were gone. The Thais had lists with the names and addresses of people that were involved in making drugs. They needed to have these big tanks of liquid, some chemical, to make "Number Four."[4] The Thai soldiers dug big pits and threw the dead bodies into them. Some of the pits had 13 or 14 corpses in them. . . . They were all killed by the Thai army, the Sua Pan.

In other cases, it was not clear whether the perpetrators of this swath of violence against the KMT or related drug production was related to the Thai Army. Another villager, Kyaw Myint, describes what he heard about the activities that frightful morning:

> Mae Tao Sao "Grandma Sao" was walking toward the intersection at the top of the hill, opposite the old SURA hospital early one morning. Two guys were sitting at the motorcycle taxi hut opposite the intersection. They shouted to the old lady, saying they were looking for Mae Tao Sao, and she replied back that it was her. They whipped out their guns, shot her and rode off on a motorbike. Mae Tao Sao was lucky though, or the gunmen were inexperienced, since they hit her in the abdomen and she was able to survive the assassination plot. Those guys who rode off, we never found out who they were, whether they were from the army, or were sent by a rival drug gang. Mae Tao Sao did oversee a shop that made drugs.

Kyaw Myint, who told me about "Grandma Sao," walked me to the edge of a shallow ravine, telling me that is where the bodies were buried. Some of the killings were attributed to the reckoning of mafia thugs, while others fingered the Thai Rangers. The experience of these extrajudicial killings traumatically punctuates the forced retirement of the KMT by the Thai government in this area, though those with stronger connections to the black-market trade networks and financial skills would end up working more closely with Khun Sa's networks. Although the Thai government attacks on Hin Taek and Piang Luang would destroy the heroin refineries there, the late 1980s and early 1990s would only see an expansion of the heroin outputs from the region. This spike in outputs would result from Khun Sa's monopoly over the Shan insurgency (by pushing back the KMT and amalgamating peer groups) and later the opium trade in all of Shan State. This would start with the merger of the Khun Sa's Shan United Army with Kawn Söng's Shan United Revolutionary Army in 1985.

FROM WOMAN WARRIOR TO CARPENTER'S APPRENTICE

As a result of this gradual retirement of the Kuomintang, the primary economic competitor to Khun Sa's trade from the Shan State through Thailand was fading in prominence. Conversely, Kawn Söng's Shan United Revolutionary Army lost its principal ally. On 3 March 1985, Kawn Söng and Khun Sa agreed to merge forces (M. Smith 1999, 343; TRC 1999a, 2). In retrospect, General Kawn Söng really did not have much choice; the SURA was surrounded by Khun Sa's SUA. This merger would signify a combination of the economic and military power of Khun Sa's armies with the cultural might of SURA's literati. In one characterization of the SURA before the merger, the "right-wing, staunchly anti-communist SURA concentrates its activities on Buddhist religion, construction of temples, and printing of Shan scripture" (Lintner 1984, 434).

After a brief period calling themselves the Shan State Army, the newly merged army was renamed the Möng Tai Army (MTA) in 1987. It would later become the most formidable nongovernment force in the region. In another analysis, the MTA represents an amalgamation of all the Shan groups that were not allied with the Communist Party of Burma (Rajah 1998, 140). The publishing arm of the MTA repeatedly emphasized the nationalist goals of the insurgency as being both anti-communist and pro-Shan.

For the former SURA soldiers, the merger brought many changes. Much of the autonomy that the SURA once enjoyed was quickly dissolved. One policy change that immediately affected Seng Kham and Hseng Lün—the teenage girls who left their high school in Möng Pan to join the SURA—was that the Möng Tai Army would not allow women to participate as soldiers. Women could serve the insurgency in other capacities, such as working as schoolteachers, in the print shops, or in the army hospital. But Khun Sa's executive fiat decided that women could not be soldiers.

Since being soldiers in SURA was all the work that Seng Kham and Hseng Lün had known for the past five years, and Seng Kham in particular was very proud of working hard and doing her job well, the sudden demotion left them angered and confused. They were disappointed by the new course that the Shan separatist movement was taking. They saw Khun Sa's military prowess and trade connections but were concerned about the genuineness of his dedication to the Shan cause and care for Shan villagers.

In a conversation, Hseng Lün told me that at this juncture, she worried that going back to Möng Pan would be risky, as the Burmese authorities likely knew of her affiliation with the insurgency. In addition to that, her husband, Aung Kyaw, was also a soldier, and they already had a toddler child. Since she had been shuffling her baby between friends and relatives, she decided that she could dedicate herself to childcare full-time. She also took in other children and started a kindergarten that would include basic instruction in the Shan language. This is an occupation that Hseng Lün has continued to this day, and she runs the largest Shan nursery school in town.

Seng Kham, on the other hand, was not as willing to put down her gun or to move to anything other than fighting for Shan independence. There was certainly much work to do in the army town, and one of the MTA leaders decided to hire a Thai carpenter to come to Bang Mai Sung to lead courses in furniture construction for some of the soldiers in their border encampment.

The classes were of interest to Seng Kham; she thought carpentry would be a useful skill to have, and she signed up for the Thai carpenter's classes. But an unexpected problem came up: one evening, the carpenter invited Seng Kham to come over to his room for some additional special lessons, or so he had told her.

When she arrived at his doorstep, he was masturbating and showed her his penis. He tauntingly dangled a red condom in front of her as part of his perverse joke. Seng Kham was not amused. She still carried her pistol with her, so she drew it and fired a shot over the Thai exhibitionist's head. As Seng Kham later told me proudly, "Oh, I wasn't going to hurt him. I just wanted to give the pervert a good scare."

When Seng Kham talked about the Thai carpenter, she laughed, still feeling that she did the right thing by firing her gun over his head. She explains

that the carpenter was a *pak kat long* or "cabbage," which is the Shan metaphor for dirty old man. As Seng Kham elaborates, "Look at the cabbage.
The leaves are ugly and old on the outside, but as you peel them away, they
get younger and fresher on the inside. He thinks he's like that."

For the other women in the furniture-building classes, especially the former SURA soldiers, Seng Kham was the hero for the day. The Thai carpenter had made inappropriate remarks to other women previously, but it was
Seng Kham who had the guts to confront him and his "cabbage" tenden-
cies. However, Seng Kham's actions would not go without punishment.
The carpenter reported Seng Kham for having shot her gun at him, and
the Möng Tai Army leadership took his side of the story. The MTA sen-
tenced Seng Kham to the brig for ten days. Seng Kham told me this story
when we were out for a walk together, and she showed me the valley where
this brig was located.

According to Seng Kham, the (male) superior officers thought that the
carpenter was more valuable to them, and Seng Kham as a (dismissed) soldier should simply stand punishment for her own actions so that the carpenter would continue to work for the MTA.

The End of the Cold War?
Ideology Turns Ethnic

The late 1980s ushered in massive changes to the political landscape of
Southeast Asia. A series of events in the late 1980s rocked the Union of
Burma to the core: a mass uprising, military coup, the Communist Party
of Burma mutiny, and a spate of ceasefire agreements with peripheral armed
groups. In 1988, spurred by a sudden government demonetization of the
Burmese currency, university students took to the streets in Rangoon, demanding political reforms. These students would become known as the 88
Generation, as they chose the auspicious day of 8 August 1988 for their
major protest. The demonstrations were met with violence on the part of
the military, and there was a massive bloodbath. Thousands of unarmed
protesters were gunned down by the army, many were imprisoned, and massive numbers of Burmese students fled to the jungles and sought refuge
with some of the insurgent armies in the borderlands. Chaos in the capital
led to the Tatmadaw staging a coup, ousting the Burmese Socialist Program
Party government, and installing a new military-led regime: the State Law
and Order Restoration Council, with the sonorous acronym of SLORC.

The new government adopted a new official name for the country: Myanmar. Although "Myanmar" was the country's name in the written language (Burma and Myanmar are cognates), this name change was disputed by some, including Aung San Suu Kyi, because of the undemocratic circumstances of the military government. Incidentally, Siam's name change to Thailand was done under no less authoritarian circumstances, to little international outrage over the name, surely iterating the importance of context.

In early 1989, the Communist Party of Burma effectively mutinied (M. Smith 1994, 60). With that, the newly named Myanmar central government initiated a number of cease-fire agreements with former insurgent militias. This strategy went in tandem with a plan to open the country up to outside investment and joint ventures, ending the nearly three decades of Ne Win's Burmese Way to Socialism inward-looking economic policy. In exchange for signing cease-fire agreements, former anti-state armed groups would be given special economic privileges. Between 1989 and 1996, military intelligence successfully negotiated a total of seventeen ceasefire agreements (Fink 2008, 448). Through these cease-fire negotiations, several groups were able to secure business concessions and became quite wealthy as a result.[5]

The largest of the Communist Party of Burma splinter groups was the United Wa State Army (UWSA); a group of Wa mutineers stormed CPB headquarters on 17 April 1989 (Lintner 2003, 185). Less than a month after their separation from the CPB, on 9 May 1989 the newly rebranded Wa group signed a ceasefire agreement with the Burmese government and was granted a special region in which to carry out its activities. The UWSA located its headquarters in Panghsan, the former base of the CPB in Eastern Shan State, bordering Yunnan Province. Although now ostensibly ethnic in its orientation, UWSA still carries with it structural survivals of the Chinese-sponsored CPB, namely a party-state structure, use of Chinese writing in its bureaucracy, Chinese trade connections and circulation of Chinese currency, and people—about ten thousand men from the CPB force became part of the UWSA (Lintner 2003, 185; Fiskesjö 2017, 353).

While other geographically peripheral players surrendered their status in favor of trade concessions during the early 1990s, Khun Sa's Möng Tai Army became the strongest stalwart anti-government army in Shan State. His army was the most powerful force in the Golden Triangle, an area that by 1989 produced 3,050 tons of raw opium, equivalent to 72 percent of the world's total illegal supply (McCoy 1991, 387). All the while, Khun Sa's speeches presented a fight for Shan liberation, seeking to give his troops the impression that he would fight for Shanland until the day he died. Behind the scenes, he maintained his contacts with the Myanmar government as well as the syndicates that took his products to international market.

THE SHAN INSURGENCY IN THE 1990S: PRESENTING POLITICS TO THE TROOPS

Although the ostensible merger between the Shan United Army and the Shan United Revolutionary Army to form the Möng Tai Army had taken place more than five years previously, tensions continued to grow between the former SURA factions and the new management. While the troop numbers expanded rapidly, few recruits were voluntary. Furthermore, the MTA officers were less likely to be the literary Shans or those connected with the hereditary *sao hpa* that had characterized earlier generations of Num Hsük Han or the SURA. However, the MTA continued to sponsor Shan schools, giving the soldiers an education in the Shan language, and they kept producing Shan journals and magazines as part of the newswriting and media outreach of the Shan cultural project.

The MTA publications provided an important forum to frame and address fundamental issues in Shan politics. In a 1991 issue of *Söng Le'o* (Freedom's Way), the author provides an overview of the history of Khun Sa's Loi Maw militia. Addressing the questions of many troops, particularly those of the SURA, the author iterates that the Möng Tai Army is not an army of Kawn Söng and Khun Sa but rather is an army for the Shan State and the Shan people (Khun Loi Leng ၶုၼ်လွႆလဵင်း 1991, 166). Another article in the same issue—as with many other political pieces published in the 1990s for Shan audiences—stresses the issue of unity among the Shan people. The author even suggests that should Kawn Söng and Khun Sa have a falling out, the Möng Tai Army would need to stick together (Sao Fa Lang သဝ်ႈၾႃႉ,လင် 1991, 53). Reading between the lines suggests such a fallout would mean Khun Sa's sole leadership of the Shan insurgency. Sadly, Kawn Söng passed away from cancer on 11 July 1991, so the situation played out the way that the author had suggested in that very same year.

The Möng Tai Army published a collection of Khun Sa's speeches. Like the other Shan-language publications, these transcripts offer a useful record to consider the ways in which Khun Sa communicated the ideological goals of the Shan project to his troops. In various examples of his speeches, Khun Sa would frequently remind his listeners of the goals for Shanland and Shan unity. Like the content of many books and articles released by the Shan publishers, the tropes of history and cultural authenticity form a crucial foundation to many of Khun Sa's speeches. Khun Sa iterates some of the key moments in Shan political history, particularly those that illustrate that the Shan are the rightful owners to Shanland, and that the Burmese government has suppressed the actualization of a Shan nation-state. In a specific reaction to one of the Myanmar government's plans for economic development of the border areas, Khun Sa interprets the measures for his audience of troops:

> Now the Burmese talk about developing the border areas. They won't be doing it for the Shan. They will make us Shan people lose even more, us impoverished people. They take us for poor stupid water buffalo. Some Shan haven't even realized this yet. Some have already become their slaves. Because we've been stupid, we've been their slaves for a long time. We don't understand that we have our land, our territory. We have our homes. We have our palaces. We have our lords. We don't need someone to come and lead us. Now is the era of democracy. Right now, I want us Shans to understand. Those who don't know will depend on the Burmese . . . others depend on the Chinese. But we don't need anyone's help, we can depend on ourselves. (Hang Hseng Yawd ႁၢင်ႈသိင်ႇယွတ်ႈ 1995, 4)

In addition to fostering pride and self-reliance among his Shan troops, Khun Sa summarizes some of the public works efforts and tangible accomplishments of the Möng Tai Army for the Shan people. Despite the fact that he himself was deprived of a formal education, he has the political savvy to recognize the importance of book learning. Back when he established his Shan United Army base at Ban Hin Taek, he invited Lung Khun Maha (Shan author and former president of Shan State Independence Army) to come work for him and even bought him a linotype machine to facilitate his publishing (Lintner 1994, 244).

At another level, the Möng Tai Army troops were increasingly composed of forced recruits from impoverished ethnic minority areas, thus the educational aspect of the insurgency sought to bring more of the troops closer to the ideological goals of Shanland. As Khun Sa says:

We have already opened schools for poor people. Some of our soldiers are peasants, those who don't have the skills to read. We need for them to have those skills. We have to teach them those skills, and give them knowledge. So we opened the schools. The Shan great masters have given us textbooks, and we need to make them relevant to our political work in the state, this state. . . . We know that if we get Shan independence, but if we don't have a teacher, we will just be exhausted and without a full nation. History has taught us that. Sao Möng Kawn has education, a great writer, and has written books that have educated generations of Shan people. We need to teach foreigners about our history and knowledge. Just like Saya Tun Oo (Burmese teacher), one of our great teachers is Sao Möng Kawn. If we are going to participate in politics, we have to study politics. If we study well, we will have good results. (Hang Hseng Yawd ဂၢင်းသိင်ယွတ်း 1995, 93, 94)

Through analysis of Khun Sa's speeches to his troops, we can see a repeated deployment of Shan cultural and historical ideas to foster pride in Shanland. The Spirit of the Panglong Agreement is also another important trope in Khun Sa's speeches (as with Shan National Day being celebrated annually to commemorate its signing). In one of his speeches to the troops, Khun Sa asks rhetorically: "Aung San came to the Shan State in 1947 and told us if Burma gets a *kyat*, Shan gets a *kyat*. What happened to that agreement? Has it been hidden away? Has it been torn up? Nobody knows. . . . We have been in a difficult situation, under the power of other nations for over 40 years" (Hang Hseng Yawd ဂၢင်းသိင်ယွတ်း 1995, 1). The extent to which these are Khun Sa's own ideas or those of his speechwriters is up for debate. However, one controversial topic consistently revisited is whether he was a true Shan, and whether the massive insurgent project was an endeavor that would bring benefit to the Shan people.

KHUN SA: AN AUTHENTIC SHAN FREEDOM FIGHTER?

Why should ethnic authenticity be an issue in Shanland? Within the Shan insurgency, many participants were fully aware of Khun Sa's chequered past, his work as part of the Loi Maw militia, business deals with and incorporation of Kuomintang personnel, and siding with the Tatmadaw, later the Thai government, then the Shan United Army. Former soldiers of the SURA told stories of how Khun Sa's tenuous loyalties were to those with powerful connections, and when those loyalties were threatened, they could be dropped viciously, even killed when it suited him.

It was no secret among the former SURA troops that Khun Sa maintained his business networks with Chinese traders and powerful international drug-trafficking syndicates; SURA had been funded through the narcotics industry as well. From the late 1970s onward, Khun Sa cultivated his image and presented his armies as Shan freedom fighters. However, among the Chinese businessmen and mafiosos with whom he plied his trade, he was not known as Khun Sa but instead was known as Zhang Qifu. Many of his Chinese partners in the jade trade considered him to be Yunnanese, not Shan (Chang 2004, 494).

This difference regarding Khun Sa's and Zhang Qifu's ethnic "presentation of self" raises an interesting dilemma: the extent to which his ethnic sympathies or affiliations mattered to those with whom he worked. Because of the diversity of cultures in the polyglot uplands of Southeast Asia, it is hardly surprising that Khun Sa would be fluent in multiple languages; for this, he was certainly not unique. If Zhang Qifu's Chinese business connections were eager to make a hefty profit through their deals with the man, they would be unlikely to reprimand him for not speaking the emperor's Mandarin. However, within the Shan nationalist project, there arose concerns that Khun Sa was not a true nationalist. But these critiques would question his "Shan-ness," asserting that he was not really Shan but instead Chinese. Class and power dynamics create the context for when ethnic authenticity matters.

Mawn Sai Hsük, in his article in the 1992 issue of the journal *Söng Le'o*, takes on the controversy of Khun Sa's ethnic authenticity in an interesting way. The article, titled "If You Don't Know How to Fix Things, Don't Place Blame" (ပေႃးၵၢမ်ႇမေႃမႄးယႃႇပႄၼ်း), points out that numerous Shan leaders have Chinese blood. As the author argues, "If they don't help the political situation of the Shan, whose situation are they going to help?" To add comparative weight to this argument, the author presents several other historical examples in which ethnic or national outsiders assisted in political movements. One such example is the revolutionary figure of Che Guevara, an Argentinian who helped the people of Cuba in their struggles. To iterate his argument, Mawn Sai Hsük points out that it was Khun Sa who built the Shan United Army, and that he continued to work for the Shan people at that time (Mawn Sai Hsük မွၼ်းလွႆသိုၵ်း 1992, 65). The upshot of Mawn Sai

Hsük's article is that people should not be concerned with the ethnic background of those who help the national cause but instead judge them for their work. This may have been a response to Karen politicians questioning the ethnic authenticity of MTA leadership.

Khun Sa, however, responded to these "Chinese accusations" in a different way. Instead of saying that his ethnic identity was not important, he insisted that he was a true person of Shanland, mentioning the names of his parents and encouraging any doubters to come and find out for themselves: "Some people have made the observation that I am Chinese—a foreigner—wondering about my race. But it is true, I am a person of the Shan land. My father was a leader in Loi Maw. His name was Khun Ai. My mother's name is Nang Hseng Jum and I was born in Wan Nong Jang in Loi Maw. Come close to me, stay near if you want to see me for real!" (Khun Sa တင်းခွန်သာ], 1989, 9–10).

Although Khun Sa was using evidence of his parents and birth village to argue that he was a child of Shanland, the suspicion among the other Shan nationalists of Khun Sa's Chineseness was not necessarily related to his ancestry. There was more concern as to whether he was playing a Shan nationalist for his own personal benefit, and if tides were to change, he might abandon the cause, just has he had done with various armed movements in the past. In terms of his ethnicity itself, another moot point is the fact that many soldiers in the MTA were of mixed heritage, though seldom was the ethnic composition of the foot soldiers, let alone the porters, scrutinized in the same way as that of the leadership.

Within military and political organizations, by installing their family members, friends, and affiliates to positions of political and economic gain, leaders not only protect their own positions by rewarding consent but also keep enemies at bay. This practice has been both criticized and criminalized in other public and professional bureaucratic structures as nepotism. Because of the nature of political relations and ethnic relations in the Shan plateau, and the fact that Khun Sa was ostensibly fighting for an independent Shanland, his nepotistic practices would lead to resentment on the part of his soldiers. However, sometimes those forms of resentment were channeled along ethnic lines as well—that somehow to be a true Shan freedom fighter, one would have to be a full-blooded Shan.

A veteran of the Möng Tai Army, Myint Aung, now living in a community of migrants near the border, explains his feeling toward Khun Sa: "Oh, Khun Sa is really Chinese. But in the beginning a lot of Shan genuinely loved him. He was talking big, but you could only move up in the ranks if you were Chinese. If you were Shan, you would only get so high. If you had one stripe on your shoulder [designation of the military] and you were Chinese, you would get a car to drive. But even a Shan with three stripes wouldn't even have a motorbike." Another SURA veteran, Sai Chuen, had a similar observation, corroborating the point that there was a glass ceiling for Shan officers in the Möng Tai Army: "It's a mistake to think that Khun Sa was in favor of a Shan nation and independence. Sure, he talked some great things about the future Shanland, but that was the front, the face. Behind, he was doing his drug business. Look at what happened, as he got more and more power. Fewer Shan people were able to have positions of power in his organization, and more and more of it was just Chinese people with big business connections."

Various articles in the MTA-sponsored news magazines and journals would seek to allay these concerns, but not about favoritism or nepotism on Khun Sa's part. The derision of Khun Sa in collusion with the Chinese or as Chinese himself emerged at crucial points: following the vast commerce networks established by the KMT in the Shan State, numerous Shan informants confided that they had initially supported Khun Sa because he represented a true Shan hero, and the idea of a Shan empire did appeal to them. However, other investigations suggest that Khun Sa may have been more interested in business and was instrumental as such in his deployment of Shan (or Chinese) ethnicity to advance his personal financial interests. Because he was seen to be manipulating his own identity for the purposes of personal gain, it was his identity that became scrutinized and blamed. It does raise the question, though, whether ethnic hypocrisy is a more terrible moral transgression than building a heroin empire, or whether it is simply an easier target to criticize.

Selling the Title Deed to Shanland; New Occupants' Violent Entry

Khun Sa's 1996 surrender to the Myanmar government was his ultimate betrayal to the vision for an independent Shanland. In the period leading up to this decision, the Möng Tai Army's networks were surrounded, other militias had signed ceasefires, and it appeared the MTA would not be able to realize its goal of national liberation any time soon. The Myanmar government had become much closer to China. In 1990, an arms deal for $1.4 billion worth of equipment soon established Myanmar's neighbor to the northeast as its biggest and most powerful ally (Mya Maung 1994, 449). In the years after, a series of regular arms shipments brought planes, amphibious tanks, rocket launchers, cruisers, and assorted equipment to Myanmar from China, and it became less feasible to remain a stalwart foe to the Yangon government. At the same time, both the heroin business and the newly booming methamphetamine manufacture and trade had begun to shift to the United Wa State Army, the strongest of the mutiny groups of the CPB and by then the Tatmadaw's most powerful ceasefire group (Ferguson 2010).

On 7 January 1996, Khun Sa presided over the Möng Tai Army surrender that was more like a media spectacle (Thaung We U သောင်းဝေဦး 2009, 204). Burmese helicopters delivered a few Tatmadaw generals and a dispatch of accompanying troops. The Mong Tai Army organized a Shan-style welcome for the Tatmadaw. This included a gong and long-drum ensemble, *kato* dancers, and children in Shan traditional costume to greet the generals and present them with flowers. General Tin Htut from the Burma Army was in attendance at this ceremony, which would be broadcast on Myanmar TV. On the dusty parade grounds were rows and rows of wooden racks, and upon those racks, soldier after soldier placed his rifle and then went in orderly fashion to sit behind the presentation of armaments. Also included in the presentation of arms were the Mong Tai Army's SAM-7 surface-to-air missile launchers.

As Khun Sa said to the troops: "We must join together in tears. You will have to suffer with patience during the next two years. After the mutiny, I wept until my tears dried up. I suffered as if my heart had been sliced out. It throbbed it hurt. Every time it ached, my tears flowed" (Cowell 1997).

As informants later learned, when Khun Sa was delivering his heartfelt speech, weeping for Shanland, his close contacts were in Yangon negotiating the terms of the ceasefire with the authorities. The Myanmar government would allow Khun Sa to retire in Yangon and continue his businesses, including in luxury hotels. The new businesses provided an effective front through which Khun Sa was able to launder his heroin fortunes and carry on as a legitimate businessman until his death in October 2007.

As one of the Tatmadaw generals had written about the surrender, once the drug war lord was gone, then the area would be able to develop and flourish (Thaung We U သောင်းဝေဦး 2009, 205). In January 1996, the Myanmar government issued an order: the inhabitants of 1,400 villages in eight townships in the Shan State were required to relocate in five days (Grundy-Warr and Wong 2002, 102). These approximately three hundred thousand people were deemed complicit with the Shan insurgency, although many of them who had contributed to the MTA empire in the form of sending taxes, rice, or soldiers did so not by their own volition.

The Tatmadaw itself took over some of the former Möng Tai Army bases, including the temple school at the former SURA capital at Bang Mai Sung. They made the school their base, started flying their Myanmar flag, erected spiked fencing, and even laid antipersonnel landmines in the ravine between the temple school and the other parts of the Shan temple complex. The former Shan spiritual center established by Kawn Söng was thus split in two by the Burmese military.

With their ceasefire agreement still in hand, the central government encouraged the United Wa State Army to come into the areas of the Shan State formerly held by the Möng Tai Army. These specific gains of territory, for the UWSA, were seen as the prize for having expedited the surrender of Khun Sa to the Yangon authorities (Callahan 2007, 29). Following the displacement, the Myanmar government repopulated former Shan insurgent areas with ethnic Wa peasants from the northern areas of Shan State.

Ravine between the borderland temple and the school taken over by the Tatmadaw. (Photo by the author)

Although the UWSA is in a ceasefire agreement with the Myanmar Tatmadaw, mainstream publications in Myanmar state that the Wa themselves "still maintain primitive culture" (Maung Pu Soe Chan မောင်ပုဆိုးကြမ်း
2014, 171.) Beginning in 1999 and continuing through to 2006, there were
massive waves of migration from the Wa region of the Northern Shan State
down to the South of the Shan State. There are a number of estimates as
to how many Wa people were moved, with one suggesting between 50,000
and 100,000 people (Fiskesjö 2017, 354) and another approximating that
126,000 people were moved from the Chinese border area of the Shan
State down to the Thai border (SHAN 2009).

WHAT WERE THEY FIGHTING FOR?

In hindsight, the machinations of ethno-nationalism that allowed Khun
Sa to accumulate massive material wealth are looked upon with great bit-
terness among former rank-and-file Shan soldiers. Many Shan veteran soldiers and affiliates iterated the point that Khun Sa used the Shan nation as
a facade to carry out his heroin-trafficking business behind the scenes. As
Kyaw Myint later noted:

> Khun Sa was the worst dictator imaginable. What he did was actually very
> clever. We Shan had been tired of watching them [the KMT] get rich while
> the Shan villagers had to sit paying taxes and suffering when the Burmese
> came to our village. Khun Sa and the MTA meant a Shan nation to us, but
> the more power he got, the worse he became. If he just didn't like your face,
> he could kill you. He became a worse dictator than the Burmans, and if
> anyone spoke up, he'd get cut, too. Of course we were disappointed that he
> surrendered to the generals, but he didn't really care about the Shan villagers
> like he used to say he did anyway.

Not "caring" about Shan villagers went so far as orchestrating massacres
in villages that had failed to meet the MTA's opium delivery quotas. Veteran soldiers, however, told stories of problems within the ranks. In a Thai-
language Shan issues magazine, the *Salween Post*, a former MTA soldier
corroborates Kyaw Myint's account: "After the surrender, everyone was tremendously disappointed. . . . The Shan people were just pawns in Khun Sa's
game, a bridge for him to walk across to do his drug business. Khun Sa
ruled the army like a dictator. You could rise in the ranks just on his whims.

He would kill ranking soldiers, the most capable people" (Witun วิฑูรย์ ลายอู๋ 2005, 33).

With the growing frustration and discontent with Khun Sa, his surrender of the Shan insurgency to the Burmese led to another group's decision to reinvent their vision for a future independent Shanland. This group, a former faction within the Shan United Revolutionary Army led by Colonel Yawd Serk, regrouped and vowed to continue the fight for Shan independence. This splinter force initially revitalized the SURA name but later adopted the name Shan State Army–South. They established their new base at Loi Taileng, a camp adjacent to the Thai border near Bang Ma Pha Village, Mae Hong Son Province. Since its formation, the numbers and resources of the SSA have been gradually growing; they now operate five base camps along the Thai-Myanmar border, and by 2018 they claimed an estimated ten thousand personnel (Thitiwut 2018, 88). However, many of their military engagements and skirmishes have been with the United Wa State Army, not the Myanmar Tatmadaw.

CONCLUSION

Today, former Shan United Revolutionary Army soldiers express frustration and dismay with the movement to repossess Shanland; they mention their former optimism, but they later experienced the massive disappointment of Khun Sa's surrender. Seng Kham's former husband was one of the SURA teachers who was murdered by higher-ups in Khun Sa's Möng Tai Army. Through interviews with veterans, as well as the study of controversies within the ranks as evidenced by contemporary articles in the Shan press, we can see, too, that the MTA soldiery was hardly monolithic, nor was everyone ideologically "on board" with the goals as articulated by Khun Sa or in agreement with Khun Sa's leadership. He increasingly ruled the Shan political project through fear.

Because ethnographic work on these periods involved interviewing people about how they remembered the insurgency, their commitment, and their hopes for the futures they once had, there should be a bit of caution taken. The former descriptions might give the impression that under the SURA and Kawn Söng, there was a true Shanland, and people enjoyed their time as soldiers there. Part of this impression is likely influenced by the tremendous disappointment of Khun Sa's surrender; he is seen as a sell-out, throwing Shanland under the bus in exchange for his own golden parachute (paid for with the massive profits from heroin). This is a major factor that would contribute to some former SURA soldiers looking on the early years as being closer to the ideas of a Shan nation. There is also the effect of distance: nostalgia for youthful idealism might create the idea that those times were veterans' salad days as young soldiers believing that an independent Shanland was just around the next corner. Seng Kham has kept a souvenir photo from her wedding at Bang Mai Sung. She and her groom, both SURA soldiers, are dressed in Shan traditional costume while they walk through a tunnel of their comrades' rifles. Her husband, Htee Leng, was one of the SURA officers murdered by Khun Sa's assassins.

The expansionist nature of the opium and heroin economies also brought Möng Tai Army accumulation to the hills of Shan State, incorporating more and more people into its leviathan. During a 2017 visit to a Ta-ang village in Chiang Dao District, Chiang Mai Province, I met a sixty-year-old man sitting on the bamboo veranda of one of the houses. He was practicing a traditional Ta-ang instrument, and I could not help but notice the prominent tattoos on his forearms, identical to those I had seen on many former Shan soldiers. As I soon learned, he spoke fluent Shan—as did nearly

Wedding photograph of Seng Kham and Htee Leng. Note the couple is in Shan traditional wedding attire, while they walk through a lineup of SURA soldiers creating a tunnel with their guns. (Provided by Seng Kham)

all the Ta-ang villagers older than forty years old—and he had been a soldier with the Shan insurgency. His reason for joining? "In our village, the Burmese Tatmadaw made raids from time to time. The Shan armies did as well. My parents thought that the only way I could survive would be to join one of the armies and get out of there. So, they signed me up for the Shan United Army when I was only thirteen or fourteen years old."

As Khun Sa's army acquired more and more soldiers in the late 1980s and early 1990s, an ever-smaller percentage of the troops were ethnic Shans, let alone ideologically committed to the vision for an independent Shanland. The Shan insurgency supported itself by taxing the black-market commerce that went through its territory, but it also would place demands on villagers. Where contributions-in-kind could not be acquired, families would send a son to join the army. If a soldier deserted, the army would return to the young man's family and demand that a sibling take the AWOL man's place as a soldier; even harsher cases included the soldiers coming to threaten or even kill the families of the AWOL soldier. These kinds of recruits were less likely than their high school– or university-educated Shan counterparts to rise in the ranks of the Shan military and, unlike the more idealist soldiers of the SURA, had few fond memories of their time fighting for Shanland, or for one militia or the other.

War creates extreme circumstances for people's struggle to survive, to be together with their kith and kin, and to have some living to look forward to. Where the gap between ideology and experience creates a kind of dissonance, people struggle to create a new vision for the future, but their vision is seldom given voice. As for the idea of cronyism, and Khun Sa populating the highest ranks of the MTA with his close business partners (who were Chinese), this is hardly unique, particularly within movements of and for ethno-national liberation in Burma. The Karen National Union (KNU) sought to present itself as a movement that was inclusive of peoples of all religious backgrounds, but their commander, Bo Mya, tended to fill his leadership positions with Christians like himself (Cline 2009, 597).

Scholars and journalists alike have repeatedly questioned whether militias in Shan State were fighting for a political cause or merely to maintain their narcotics trade networks (M. Steinberg 2000, 264). This suggests that the armies had either one goal or the other, as if political idealism can be separated from the corruptions of commerce. Returning to other popular binary questions, was Khun Sa a nationalist or a warlord? Was he Shan or was he Chinese? After reading many publications printed by the Shan presses during the Khun Sa years, including his speeches to the troops, as well as interviewing veteran soldiers of the Möng Tai Army, I conclude that the armies were fighting for both a political cause and to protect their trade networks. Khun Sa was a nationalist and a warlord, and he was Shan and Chinese. The Möng Tai Army was able to build and extend a nation-state predicated on an idea of historic presence in the region but fueled by the changing character of global geopolitics and illicit commodities. When considering whether ethnicity was a convenient ideological framework to present an economic relationship in a new way, I would respond, when is ethnicity *not* political or *not* economic?

The geographic and sovereign complexities of the Shan State abutting the growing capitalist economy of Thailand and the transnational illicit connections of the mafia networks for heroin came together to make a perfect storm for Khun Sa's army to effect a military coup of Shanland and later to hand over the keys to the kingdom in yet another business deal.

5

Little Brother Is Exploiting You

In June 2018, news from the Thai-Burma border captured the hearts of people around the world for eighteen suspenseful days. A boys' soccer team, the Wild Boars, consisting of twelve teenage boys and their twenty-five-year-old coach, was trapped deep in the complex labyrinth of Tham Luang Nang Non Cave in Chiang Rai Province, Northern Thailand. Authorities were alerted when the boys did not return home one evening. One of the boys had failed to show up to his own birthday party at his family's home. Locals soon discovered the boys' bikes and some of their gear at the cave entrance and surmised that the boys must be inside. Although they were on the cusp of rainy season, Tham Luang Nang Non Cave is prone to flash floods, so it was possible the boys might have ventured further inside the cave in order to escape rising waters. But were they alive? If so, how long could they survive?

The story of the trapped boys was soon breaking news on Thai television and quickly sparked international coverage as well. Within days, thousands of volunteers, including foreign spelunkers and geologists, came to assist at the site. Others provided time and resources to feed and accommodate the teams of newcomers. Water pumps operated round-the-clock to reduce the amount of water in the cave system. Pumped water flooded nearby fields, destroying local farmers' harvests. There was a real race against time to locate the boys. After several days' search, British divers discovered the group of boys on a shelf deep within the cave structure. The divers recorded their interaction on a smart phone, and later the video clip was broadcast on news segments worldwide. The boys and their coach were thin, but alive, all thirteen of them! One of the boys could speak some English and was able to interpret for the divers.

In the ensuing days, plans turned to nourishing the boys and figuring out how to extract them from the depths of the massive cave. In a glorious rescue, each of the boys—none of whom had any underwater diving experience—was given sedatives, connected to oxygen tanks, and attached to special stretchers. One by one, each was guided by a pair of divers through the crevices and complex tunnels of the cave. All the boys—and their coach—were rescued and taken to a nearby hospital to recover and build up their strength. The beautiful, happy ending was nothing short of miraculous.

During the captivating real-life drama, international news reports referred to the group as Thai boys, or the Thai football team, or even the Thai cave boys. Two books documenting the ordeal are titled *Boys in the Cave: Deep Inside the Impossible Rescue in Thailand* and *Great Cave Rescue: The Extraordinary Story of the Thai Boy Soccer Team Trapped in a Cave for 18 Days*.

The story of the boys' rescue was heartrending, suspenseful, and ultimately one of amazing heroism; it was ripe for Thai nationalist plucking. The event was described as "a chance for the nation to come together, regardless of social class or politics" (Massola 2018, 7). Hollywood filmmakers were soon scouting out the cave and its environs with their sights on turning the real-life adventure into a blockbuster movie. With so much media attention on the boys, it soon came to light that four of the boys were not Thai citizens. Now that the cave rescue had captured global media attention, the boys' individual stories of statelessness and quasi citizenship could expose the contradictions in Thailand's immigration and citizenship laws to the world.

The true adventure story books do briefly mention the situation of statelessness of the boys (Massola 2018, 11). The boy who was the interpreter for the British divers, fourteen-year-old Adul Sam-on, was born in the Wa area of Northern Shan State and speaks Wa, Thai, Burmese, Chinese, and English. He now lives in Mae Sai, Thailand. When he was only six years old, he had been entrusted by his parents to the pastor at the local Baptist church in Mae Sai. Adul's parents did this with the hope that the boy would get a better education than would have been possible in Northern Shan State. By dint of his academic prowess, Adul Sam-on received a scholarship to pay both his tuition and school lunches in Mae Sai. Two of the other Wild Boars were also from Shan State: Monkol Boonpiem and Pornchai Kamluang, both sixteen years old. Even their coach, Ekapol Chantawong, twenty-five, was stateless, despite having been born on Thai soil in Mae Sai Hospital. Though one of his parents was also born in Thailand, they did not have citizenship either. Ekapol's status "fell through the cracks" of Thailand's complex citizenship bureaucracy. For those whose bureaucratic status is not clear, the process of becoming a Thai citizen is expensive and laborious; for many more, it is simply impossible.

The boys' fame resulted in a number of high-profile international invitations: visit Manchester United Football Club in England and appear on the *Ellen Show* in Los Angeles. But without citizenship, the four boys would not be able to obtain passports, let alone apply for UK or US visas. Rather than reform their immigration laws, the Thai government made a hasty exception for the world-famous Wild Boars. The three boys were given Thai citizenship under Section 7, while their coach acquired citizenship under Section 23. All four received their Thai citizenship in a public ceremony on 8 August 2018, just in time for them to travel overseas with the team.

The boys' story keys into a dilemma for the Thai nation-state: their predicament and rescue are wonderfully enthralling for patriotic, emotional narratives, and they exemplify Thai-ness. The only hang-up is that they are not all "Thai" in the *bureaucratic* sense. Just scratching the surface, we expose some of the contradictions of Thailand's immigration laws. But what about those who never become famous? What about everyday Shan statelessness in Thailand?

Migrants and Refugees: A Recent Phenomenon?

With the nation-state and bureaucratic technologies for citizenship being relatively recent political inventions, its opposite condition, statelessness, is therefore a distinctly modern problem as well. For decades, Thailand has been a destination for economic migrants and refugees from Myanmar (as well as refugees from Vietnam, Laos, and Cambodia in previous decades), not to mention prior centuries or even millennia of human movement throughout the region. But the 1988 student-led uprisings in Yangon, the subsequent massacre of demonstrators, and uptick in political refugees from Myanmar, together with the end of the Cold War, precipitated new state approaches to migrants and people fleeing war. Thailand was not a signatory nation to the 1951 United Nations Convention on Refugees. Therefore it did not have a formal policy to assist and process people from Burma/Myanmar as refugees. In 1979 the Thai Immigration Act declared that anyone who "enters Thailand without authorization 'shall be punished by an imprisonment not exceeding two years and a fine not exceeding 20,000 Baht'" (Immigration Act B.E. 2522).

People fleeing war have been allowed temporary shelter on Thai soil and are classified as "persons displaced by fighting." Despite the hundreds of thousands of people in refugee camps along the Myanmar-Thai border, only at the end of the 1990s did the Thai government begin to allow the United Nations High Commission on Refugees (UNHCR) access to these people so they could receive outside assistance and potentially resettlement in third countries. There were 93,333 people living in the nine designated refugee camps across four provinces along the Thai-Myanmar border as of 31 December 2019 (UNHCR 2020). But there are an estimated two to four million migrant workers from Myanmar in Thailand, with varied forms of documentation, and estimates are difficult particularly regarding those who are stateless. The Thai government estimates that there are over 486,000 stateless people in Thailand, though nongovernment organizations (NGOs) argue this estimate is conservative (Paskorn Jumlongrach 2018). The Thai government has pledged that all stateless people will be registered by 2024.

Although Shan people have long been part of the cultural landscape of Northern Thailand, the first years of intense migration from the Shan State to Thailand coincided with Khun Sa's surrender, the massive displacement in Shan State in 1996–97, and the Asian financial crisis of 1997. In 1996–97, an estimated eighty thousand people migrated from Shan State to Thailand. The fact that a large percentage of these migrants were children and elderly people shows that it was not the usual labor migrant demographic but instead entire families fleeing war (Amporn อัมพร 2015b, 29).

Later migrants were affected by the expansion of attention from NGOs and international human rights organizations as well as the rise of Thaksin Shinawatra's Thai Rak Thai "Thai Loves Thai" political regime in Thailand. In July 2004, the Thai government issued a new policy by which all migrant workers, for a fee of 3,800 baht, would be able to register with the government and work legally in Thailand for one year. Many workers did so, and their numbers totaled 1,269,074 people; of those, 905,881 were Burmese (TBBC 2005, 6).[1]

However, the migration experience is much more complex than just having the right papers. Migration is juridical, but beyond that, it is cultural, it is value-laden, and it is frightening. In sum, being a Shan migrant in Thailand is expensive, both monetarily and emotionally, though dominant ideologies of Thai-ness suggest otherwise.

It is through the experiences of Shan migrants in navigating legal and ethnic categories that we learn how Shan people survive in an ethno-national political economy that categorically excludes them, and how their labor, both that which is remunerated and that which is not, is what bolsters both the contemporary Thai political economy and the cultural status quo. Therefore, this chapter also explores the symbolic and emotional work involved in surviving these economies. It is here that the challenge to remember— or the struggle to forget—Shanland is at its most poignant intersection. Ethnographic data demonstrate that Shan migrants in Thailand support the fight for Shanland materially: many current Shan State Army soldiers have past experience as labor migrants in Thailand; further, the SSA is partially funded by the remittance economy of Shan workers in Thailand. The migration experience of Shans in Thailand—the fact that they are refused citizenship and often treated poorly or even savagely by self-appointed purveyors of Thai ethnic chauvinism—creates animosity and reticence toward Thai assimilation. For some, this serves to reinvigorate Shan people's resolve to imagine as well as to fight for independent Shanland. It is these forms of emotional work, and intimate exploitation, that fuel the desire to keep alive the dream of Shanland.

Neither Refugee nor Citizen: Shan Migrants in Thailand

Unlike their Burman, Kayin, Kayah, or Mon counterparts, Shan people fleeing war in Myanmar and seeking refuge in Thailand are not classified by the Thai government as "people displaced from war." Although refugee camps do exist along the Thai-Myanmar border, the nine that receive UN humanitarian assistance—and for some refugees the possibility for resettling in third countries—are not designated for ethnic Shan people. Thailand's official refugee camps are organized according to the ethnic category of the people contained therein.

Why can't Shan people be refugees in Thailand? The reasons for this discrimination against Shan migrants are often nebulous. The following three explanations are the most common: the Shan have not faced persecution as an *entire* community (Ko Htwe 2009); to maintain amicable diplomatic relations with Myanmar, the Thai government has argued that the

Shan border crossers are not bona fide political refugees but economic migrants (Ko Htwe 2009; Pornpimon พรพิมล 2005); because of their linguistic and cultural proximity to the Thais, the Shan are perceived to be able to blend into Thai society easily and thus are not in need of outside assistance (Aphijanyathan Ropharat 2009, 13; Shukla 2004). These three reasons are deployed by the Thai authorities and popular media alike, some of which are more sympathetic to the plight of the Shan migrants than others. The fact remains, however, that the Thai economy benefits tremendously from the cheap labor of these migrants from Shan State.

Whereas official refugees are supplied and monitored through the UNHCR, the Shan people who cross the border must find their way on their own. The official refugees are required to remain in their refugee camps and are not allowed to work. They must wait for acceptance from a third country, such as Australia, Canada, France, the Netherlands, Norway, and the United States. In situations such as this, many refugees are left wondering whether it would be better to be a refugee trapped in a camp with food or a migrant seeking out undocumented (or semi-documented) employment, in constant fear of arrest or deportation. For Shan people crossing the border into Thailand, this is not a choice. Thus, Shan migrants have to confront the realities of trying to blend in as Thai and secure some form of employment in the country.

Increasing numbers of Shan migrants find themselves constrained and paying more into the Thai state in the form of fees and bribes in order to eke out an existence as alien workers. This form of money to the state is what I call "shadow taxation." The record of shadow taxation does not appear on any official government ledger, but it goes to agents of the state and depends on certain laws to exist. If there were no immigration laws, Shan migrants would not be illegal; thus there would be no necessary bribes to pay in order to travel to labor markets.

The migration and exile experience motivates Shan patriotism in new ways. Shan migrants experience condescension and cultural gatekeeping by Thais, and they are made aware that they are not welcome or accepted into Thai society. While their precarious status forces many to try to assimilate, and some do enjoy aspects of living in Thailand, daily discrimination and the emotional work of tolerating bigotry and condescension make some more steadfast in their hope for Shanland. The relatively free media within Thailand allows Shan people to watch Shan YouTube videos, and cities in Northern Thailand have Shan radio stations. Because of their tenuous situation, many Shan parents become more adamant in trying to ensure that their children retain symbolic aspects of Shan heritage, in the hope that if things do improve in Shan State, they might be able to return.

In a candid moment at a Wan Kan Hai temple festival kitchen cleanup, Hseng Lün turned and announced to the women across from her, "In my next life, I hope to be born a full citizen."

"That would save you so much time and paperwork from the district official!" responded Seng Kham.

Connecting Subjects to the State: The Thai ID Card

As a way of keeping track, the Thai government issues ID cards to people residing in the kingdom, both citizens and noncitizens. The Thai state has an elaborate taxonomy and classification system for noncitizen subjects. To be a full citizen is to be unproblematically "Thai," which is often seen as both a bureaucratic status and an ethno-racial identity. Nationalist ideology regarding the issue is so strong that Thai-ness, for many Thai citizens, is a taken-for-granted given rather than something that has been constructed or realized.

Groups of people are classified by location, place of entry, ethnicity, former political or military affiliation, as well as by time and type of migration into the Kingdom of Thailand. Aside from full Thai citizens, the Thai government has five official classification groups for non-Thai *chon klum noi* (minorities): Chinese, Hill Tribe, Vietnamese, Thai Muslims, and "others." This last category of "others" is further subdivided into three groups: *chin haw* Chinese, displaced people from Burma, and displaced people from Indochina (Pinkaew Luangaramsri 2003, 162).

In a conversation on the subject of non-Thai taxonomies, Sai Sai, a Shan cultural enthusiast from Kyauk Me, once commented to me, "Look at you with your passport all the way from the United States. Thai people call you a *khon tang chat* [คนต่างชาติ, person from another country]. Yet we Shan people are from right next door, they even say we are their brethren, but the Thai, they call us *khon tang dao* [คนต่างด้าว, person from another planet, or alien]. They should have better map-reading skills."

Because of the historic origin of these categories, the frequently shifting circumstances for migration in and to Thailand, and the changing regimes and bureaucratic apparatuses that process applications, there is often a great deal of overlap and inconsistency in the issuance of identity cards. The creation of categories was the result of bureaucratic fiat at the time, which had its own logic as much as seeking to "solve" a particular political issue (the special status given to former Kuomintang soldiers, as detailed in the last chapter, being an instructive case in point). Or finally, given the frequent regime changes in Thailand, a current regime will not touch the inconsistency of the citizenship laws, leaving it as an issue for the next government to deal with.

For migrants, this inconsistency affects them every day. In some cases, people will try to apply for one type of identity card even though their immediate peer groups and kinship networks might all possess another identity card. Older Shan migrants who are registered with the Thai government, such as Aung Myo and Seng Kham, carry a blue "highlander" identity card; more recent migrants have a green with red edges "public highlander" identity card. Other Shan migrants have applied for (and some successfully received) pink "Hill Tribe" identity cards as the application process for that particular card was more practical in that context.[2] It is not unusual for members of the same family, even children of the same parents born in the same hospital, just a few years apart, to have a different classification of noncitizen subject status in Thailand.

How people and their individual experiences as stateless measure up is very complex when one compares their everyday lives with the ways in which the bureaucratic law operates (Bohmer and Shuman 2007, 625). The plethora of ID cards and their categories confirms that ethnic categories in Thailand are not so much assertions of shared identity but rather constitute one of the state's powerful instruments of confinement and control (Pinkaew 2003, 157). Even so, the instruments of control are hardly complete; how the system restricts movement, controls access to labor markets, and allows one to obtain employment (or not) remains to be seen.

An important point about migration: the geopolitical borders at the edge of Thailand are not the only borders actively policed by the Thai state. A quirk of Thai immigration policy establishes many more borders between peripheral areas and urban labor markets. Migrants are expected to register themselves in the borderland districts in which they first entered Thailand. Once registered, they must apply for travel permission to leave "their" districts, thus creating another set of geographic zones of legality for migration within Thailand and, with that, another layer of bureaucratic burden and expense for participants. Furthermore, roadside checkpoints are set up to inspect these ID cards, registration papers, and travel permission papers of anyone entering or leaving a district. These are most intense along the channels of migrant labor. This is the equivalent of having your passport checked at the county line.

For Shan migrants in Thailand, these ID cards are essential to their daily survival. They are required to show the cards to soldiers of the Thai state at district border checkpoints, produce them for police officers upon demand, and present them before obtaining rental agreements. Currently they are required for buying a mobile phone SIM card at a convenience store. People are expected to have these cards on their person at all times and must pay stiff penalties if caught without them.

Aung Myo recalled a story where he was working with a team for a beekeeper near Chiang Mai in the early 1990s. The owner of the operation himself was a Thai citizen. The team of workers included migrants born in the Shan State as well as citizens. They moved the hives at night, and in one case the group was on its way to Chamtong District (fifty kilometers from Chiang Mai City) when they were stopped by police demanding to see their ID cards. None of the men had his card, and the policeman responded patronizingly, "It's not a *bat pracham ban* [บัตรประจำบ้าน, or "house" card] but a *bat pracham tua* [บัตรประจำตัว), or "person" card]. Adding injury to insult, the police took the whole group of men, including the Thai citizens, to the police station, where they spent two nights in lockup for the violation.

Because these government-issued ID cards are so crucial for Shan migrants, the common Shan slang term for them has become *hke'p to nao* (ခိပ်းတုၣ်ႀနဝ်း), or "fermented bean disk." A fermented bean disk is a brown, flat, dry disk consisting of pulverized fermented beans. It can be any size but is often the size of a CD.[3] It is a staple ingredient in many Shan curries, where it is ground and added to the sauce. When one is on the go, it can be added to rice for a bit of protein and salty flavor. Because of its popularity among Shans and ubiquity of it in Shan cuisine, the Burmese pejorative term for Shan people is *Shan pe pôk* (ရှမ်းပဲပုတ်), or Shan bean. For Shan people living in Thailand, the fermented bean disk, as metaphor, becomes the essential ingredient for interfacing with the Thai state. As discussed below, it is the "fermented bean disks" that are a source of great anxiety on the part of Shan migrants, and that are subjects of extreme scrutiny by agents of the Thai state.

GETTING TO THE LABOR MARKET: ON THE ROAD

Wan Kan Hai is on the Thai side of the border, a six-hour bus ride from Chiang Mai city. While there is an express van that takes about three and a half or four hours, the *rot pracham thang* (รถประจำทาง), or the "regular" bus, is significantly cheaper and makes as many stops as it is flagged to do so. The regular bus does not have assigned seating; it is a large vehicle, open in the back, and its long benches on either side can squeeze in upward of forty passengers. Once the bus is outside the city, if it is cramped, some passengers will climb up and ride on the roof. The regular bus in 2006 cost ninety baht or about three US dollars and generally would take about six hours on account of the many stops it makes along the way. In addition to stops where passengers board and alight, and the single stop for a toilet break and lunch at a noodle shop, the public bus also stops at all Thai government checkpoints. At these checkpoints, all passengers have ID cards (their fermented bean disks) and travel permission documents inspected by the Thai police or the Thai army, depending on the border being crossed. If there

A bus is stopped at a Thai government district checkpoint. Passengers must disembark and present their travel documents to the army. (Photo by the author)

are few passengers, the police or army will enter the vehicle and inspect the
ID cards and travel documents. If there are many, all are required to disembark, line up, and have their papers scrutinized one by one.

In a case I witnessed in 2006, a Shan man was traveling on the regular
public bus and presented his government ID card. When the army checked
his card and looked again at him, they still didn't believe that the man could
be a Thai citizen; he had an impressive set of Shan tattoos that peeked out
of his shirtsleeves when he extended his arm to hand his ID to the soldier.
I watched as they took him to the makeshift office to check his ID number
on the national system via their computer. When the soldier realized his
mistake (that the Shan man was actually a Thai citizen), he handed back
the ID card and apologized by putting his hands together in a *wai* gesture
of respect. So, even when one does have complete documentation, there is
no assurance that the bearer will be free from harassment; there is an ongoing micropolitics of how people are seen and scrutinized according to
prevalent stereotypes. More than one (male) Shan informant commented
to me that the Thai police would readily turn a blind eye and not check the
migration documents when the border crosser was a beautiful young woman.
If she would smile and flirt with the police, that was her *hke'p to nao*, or
"ID card."[4]

The road is mountainous, and when this journey became a trope of in-
quiry for my research, I often rode in the regular bus. On days when the bus
was filled to the brim, with other passengers on top, there was little room to
sit, let alone move. The passenger compartment was structured such that
when all the benches were occupied, others could stand in the aisles, holding on to the rails bolted to the ceiling. Traversing the winding roads in the
mountainous areas, passengers become nauseous, children especially so.

Given the constant motion, the physical discomfort, and the emotional
distress of potentially interacting with not only the Thai Army at the district
checkpoint but also the Thai police at their own checkpoints, the journey
into urban Thai labor markets provides for crucial and fecund migration
humor on the part of the Shan. Similar to the pantheon of jokes about
Shan porters for the Tatmadaw, these anonymous tales offer a way to talk
about stress and all-too-common trauma. So people told jokes about other
Shans traveling on the bus to Chiang Mai.

In one example of this brand of gallows humor, a couple of Shan villagers are caught at the district border checkpoint and are told that they must
get down off of the bus to go to the *rong phak* (โรงพัก), or "police station."

These perhaps fictitious Shan people are excited and say, "Well, if we are going to the *hung hpak* [ၛင်းဟၵ်း), or "food hall"], we should buy sticky rice first!"

The joke refers to a common but anxiety-ridden moment, where the policeman can wield the authority of the Thai State over the helpless Shan migrants. The comic relief comes from the linguistic understanding: *phak* in Thai means "rest"; thus "police station" is literally "police rest hall"; but for the Shan *hpak* would mean "food," usually an already-prepared curry dish, thus the meaning "police food hall." The simple twist enabled by the misunderstanding takes the situation from frightening to benign, hence the displacement effect is successful and allows Shan to laugh at the presumed misfortune, because they "get" the joke, even if its subject is suffering because of it.

Although this joke is based on a linguistic misunderstanding, there are other jokes that have to do with the ways in which Thais notice and identify Shan people as outsiders. The journey is not merely legal or logistical: it is symbolic. While everybody knows that the bus connects the border area to Chiang Mai City, the pressures to comply with certain expectations become greater as one nears the urban core. Also present are potential culture clashes. Seng Kham related one such experience to me.

The bus was jam-packed, and it was only getting worse. This six-hour ride would likely turn into an eight-hour one, and several people had already got out their plastic bags in anticipation of motion sickness. There were people squeezed in the front cab, packed in the cavernous two-rowed back, and also about two dozen people sitting on top of the vehicle. Seng Kham was on her way to work as a vendor at the Night Bazaar in Chiang Mai; a connection of Mattana's (a close neighbor back in Wan Kan Hai) owns a stall on the popular tourist thoroughfare.

Near Chiang Dao District, a few Thai university students got on board. They struggled to find a place to sit, so Seng Kham took charge; she made space next to herself and the Lahu woman on her right.

The two young women said thanks briefly and, with their stylish name-brand adventure wear and backpacks, sat down. They started to talk with each other about their visit to the cave and gossip about their current university course, complaining about the amount of homework expected from them.

Seng Kham started to feel annoyed that the young women did not seem a bit sensitive to the fact that they were in the company of others who had a much harder lot in life than they do. Seng Kham always wished that she could have gone further in her studies. Her street smarts far surpassed those of her former husband, Htee Leng; he was just from a well-to-do family that was able to send him to Mandalay University. These women had an even bigger, more modern university than the one back in Mandalay, and they griped about having to do too many readings for a class.

Seng Kham stretched her arm, which she had pinned uncomfortably to her right side as she sat squeezed in next to the students on the bench. As she stretched, she inadvertently pulled back her shirtsleeve, and her Shan tattoos drew the attention of the young Thai women. While the tattoos are invaluable within the Shan social milieu, once Shan become migrants and travel to urban Thailand, the cosmological significance of the markings is lost on some Thais. Even though they have their own spiritual tattoos, these tattoos rarely are seen on women. Some Thais are likely to ask ignorant questions (at best) or will discriminate, badger, and persecute (at worst) Shan people whom they see in Thailand.

"Ohh!! Why do you have tattoos on your arms?" asked one of the young women in all earnestness.

"I got them in prison," Seng Kham replied as she showed her forearms to the girls in sardonic pride.

"What were you in prison for?" asked the woman, in logical follow-up.

"Killing someone!" Both of the Thai women's jaws dropped, and a number of Seng Kham's fellow villagers giggled quietly.

The women were awkwardly silent for the rest of the ride, to Seng Kham's unusual delight. In another iteration of naive Thais asking her about her tattoos, Seng Kham told one Thai that she wanted to catch AIDS. This odd joke played on the Thai stereotype that the spread of HIV in Thailand was the result of migrant sex workers or people with unhygienic drug and tattoo practices. All the more frightening is that Seng Kham is a female migrant. This incident, as Seng Kham told me, took place in the mid-1990s, right when Thailand was scrambling to get a grip on the AIDS scare, and the Shan, as migrants from "Burma," were demonized for spreading the virus. Migrant workers who engaged in sex work (even those forced to work in brothels) were scapegoated for spreading the virus within Thailand. But Seng Kham has steered control of this condescension back in her own favor by exacting a kind of comic revenge on her interlocutors.

Although few Shan migrants would have the savage wit and quick response that Seng Kham has, other interlocutors often vented about their experiences with common questions they experienced in Thailand. They sometimes called the stereotypical assumptions or odd questions *ngö ngö nga nga* (ငိူဝ်ႈငိူဝ်ႈငႃးငႃး), which is Shan for "naive" or "dumb"; in social psychology, these would later become known as "micro-aggressions." But the stereotypes, assumptions, and awkward questions only scratch the surface of the difficulties that Shan migrants experience in Thailand. Frustration and annoyance are compounded when accompanied by real legal and material marginalization, especially when class and power differentials silence the rebuttal from the abused.

A Stateless and Undocumented Travel Guide

In April and May of 2006, the official of the district that includes Wan Kan Hai decided to stop issuing any travel permission for holders of the "green with red edges" or "public highlander" identity card. Other migrants could still obtain travel permission. Many of these card holders were Shans who were registered in Wan Kan Hai and surrounding areas but had jobs or engaged in daily work in Chiang Mai. According to the district official, there had been a number of problems with document forgery. Thus, they decided to stop issuing travel permission altogether. Some speculate that the government official knew that the police and the army made more profit when migrants were not allowed to travel at all: bribes can be a great deal more lucrative than legal travel permission fees.

While travel permission was suspended, Seng Kham's twenty-two-year-old nephew, a short but athletic man named Sai Pit, paid her a home visit in Wan Kan Hai. Wearing some well-fit jeans and a dark-green army jacket, he cautiously entered the house and sat on the bamboo matted floor near the sofa, facing his aunt. He had recently traveled from Möng Pan, Shan State, and crossed the border into Thailand. Now he sought his aunt's advice.

"I would just like to find some kind of work in Chiang Mai. Any kind of work will do. I have a 'green with red edges' card, but I don't have travel permission. The government district official is not issuing the permission. . . . How long will this last? Should I try to go anyhow?" Sai Pit had borrowed money from his family back in Shan State in the hope that he would be able to repay them in kind and also earn additional profit while working in Chiang Mai.

Seng Kham heaved a belabored sigh and told her young nephew that he was better off waiting to travel than undertaking the journey without the proper permission paperwork from the district official. She told him that it was the government's job to issue these permits. It was a source of legitimate income for the district, and the hiatus would not go on forever.

Sai Pit thanked his aunt for her suggestions and joined the family for an evening meal. He knew other Shan youth in Wan Kan Hai, and following the meal, he thanked his aunt once again and went out to join his friends. "He's not going to wait, he's itching to go," commented Seng Kham. "I bet he will get opinions from a bunch of different people, then choose the point of view that most suits what he wants to do right now, which is go to Chiang Mai as soon as he can."

For the migrant lacking travel permission papers like Sai Pit, the best-case scenario is that the official would not notice him, and he would pass through. He might just be stopped and not be allowed to continue his journey. At worst, he might be taken to prison, fined, and deported. Most cases of incompletely documented migrants fall somewhere along this spectrum of possibilities, with negotiation for a shadow taxation payment greasing the wheels of the journey.

Because of these risks, most inadequately documented migrants avoid taking the *rot pracham tang*, or "regular bus," altogether. They know that the commercial vehicle will stop at every checkpoint, and one cannot avoid state surveillance. Shan migrants know how to get in touch with a van driver whose specialty is to take undocumented people to Chiang Mai (or further afield). For the same trip, one that costs 90 baht on the standard bus, it costs 4,500 baht on these "special" vans. Like the "coyotes" at the Mexico-US border, these van drivers help migrants evade the normal expected surveillance and border enforcement of agents of the Thai state. Because of the illegal nature of the service, as well as the vulnerability of the people paying for it, the cost is high.

In some cases, such van drivers pay a flat bribe of 1,000 baht per migrant to the Thai officials at each checkpoint. In euphemism, Shan people call these payoffs "giving pictures of the king." This moniker is quite literal in the sense that every Thai currency note has a picture of the Thai king on it, but it also suggests the sacred representation would have a unique aura that would affect its recipient and allow lenience to its giver. In other cases, the vans drop passengers prior to arriving at the checkpoint, where the migrants have to take a side path on foot through the forest and later reunite with the van further down the road. These are part of the expected scenarios, as the end result is that the migrants eventually and successfully arrive in Chiang Mai, where they find their way to construction sites, domestic work, brothels, or other places where they might engage in paid work.

Just a few days after Sai Pit's visit, Seng Kham received a phone call from her young nephew: he was calling from Chiang Mai prison. He was captured by the Thai police and, lacking proper travel documentation, was taken to lockup. Even though he paid 4,500 baht for passage to Chiang Mai, rather than bribe the officials or evade their surveillance, the driver simply pulled up to the checkpoint and presented the Thai police with a vanload of undocumented migrants. As Seng Kham explained to me, that van driver probably received a payoff from the police, or if not, he had already pocketed the 4,500 baht fee from each passenger, and police bribery would cut into his profits. Clearly, this driver had no intention of continuing to work among this particular Shan community. As Seng Kham learned from Sai Pit, not only was her nephew arrested for not having travel documentation, but the police also relieved him of all his cash. More likely than not, the police operated with the assumption that Sai Pit would have contacts in the area to bail him out. And that burden then fell on Seng Kham.

Seng Kham received Sai Pit's call for help with a mixture of frustration, anger, and sympathy. While she wished that her nephew had followed her initial advice and waited to get travel permission, she knew that his opportunities still would have been limited. And because she was his aunt, she was obliged to retrieve him from the Chiang Mai prison (and pay his fine to get him out). Having navigated the bureaucracies of Thailand many times herself, she knew the difficult and arbitrary nature of some of the checkpoint laws and enforcement officials. Although Sai Pit's case is extreme in that he lost all of his money without entering a labor market, for Shan people in the borderlands, it is all too common. Most every Shan migrant in Thailand has experienced a similar misfortune at some point.

Sai Pit's story is illustrative of the fact that most individual migrants depend on a larger social network for advice and help. The bureaucratic obstacles and sudden and costly problems create strain on those networks. Seng Kham and her husband made their plans to go to Chiang Mai right away to post bail for Sai Pit. They visited the district official to acquire travel permission. They were able to do so because they both have "blue" ID cards, not the "green with red edges" cards that were on the "no go" list (the card held by Sai Pit).

Seng Kham and Aung Myo borrowed Aung Myo's younger brother's truck for the trip to Chiang Mai. The brother, Myint Aye, earned his living as a driver, and most of his jobs were for the Shan State Army. Thus, the truck saw heavy use, as he would take rice sacks up to the nearby mountaintop camp to feed the soldiers there. For the journey to Chiang Mai, they decided to take with them their two children: Intalaeng, the eight-year-old; and Sai Mong, the eight-month-old. After borrowing the pickup truck, Aung Myo parked it in the driveway as Seng Kham played a Sai Mao tape while the family got ready for their journey.

On another occasion, when I was traveling to Chiang Mai with a group of migrants in the same old Toyota pickup, loaded with people and objects (both in the cab and in back), we listened to a tape of Sai Mao songs during the journey. My contacts were relieved when I volunteered to do the driving. For Shan migrants, even their driver's license is only valid within the district. Getting caught without a valid driver's license could require giving the Thai police more "pictures of the king." From Wan Kan Hai to Chiang Mai, there were no fewer than three army and police checkpoints along the road. As we approached the first district checkpoint, the bright-orange traffic cones and a red-and-white wooden barricade guided our lane over to the left, where a Thai soldier in a dark green beret and full fatigues held one arm out, gesturing me to pull over.

At the checkpoint, one of the men in uniform started to walk up to my window on the right side of the truck. As he did this, I fished in my bag for my passport. Seng Kham, however, quickly grabbed the volume knob on the cassette deck and turned down the music so it was completely inaudible. "I don't want the Thai soldiers to think we're Burmese!" she told me in haste. When I made eye contact with Seng Kham for a moment, she herself laughed at what she had just said. "OK maybe they won't think you're Burmese" she conceded, and we shared a laugh, partially at the soldier's expense, who was already perplexed by the fact that a foreign woman was driving an old Toyota pickup truck, loaded with Shan villagers, through the northwest mountains of Thailand.

At the checkpoint, it was Seng Kham, a person intimately familiar with both Burmese and Thai contexts, who turned down the volume of the Burmese music so that the Thai soldier wouldn't hear it. Although the soldier might not even have recognized the lyrics of the songs as being in Burmese, Seng Kham certainly knew that they were in Burmese and, crucially as well, knew the ways in which the Burmese are considered the "evil enemy" in the Thai popular imagination. In the often harrowing situation of the Thai army checkpoint, it was necessary for the Shan migrant to be as benign, compliant, and "Thai" as possible. Purging the pickup truck of Burmese elements for the sake of the Thai soldier meant that the Shan can be Tai or Thai, but certainly not Burmese.

To return to the story of Seng Kham's nephew, Sai Pit, later that day Seng Kham and Aung Myo showed up at the Chiang Mai prison and posted bail for Sai Pit, who was given a temporary pass to return to the border areas. Humiliated and completely out of money, he offered a huge, grateful *wai* to his aunt (also implicitly knowing the whole time that he should have followed her initial suggestion to wait before going to the city). Legal boundaries partially create the geographies, but it is personnel of the state who enforce, and therefore earn their living from, their policing. The zones are bureaucratic, legal as well as cultural. But within these areas are a number of self-appointed cultural gatekeepers whose sense of cultural belonging and gender can depend on how they police others.

If You Want Food, Just Order Food!

Nang Lao, Hseng Lün's twenty-year-old niece, has been living in the Northern Thai city of Chiang Mai for two years. She moved from Möng Pan to Wan Kan Hai with her parents four or five years earlier but now has been working in the city and pursuing an urban lifestyle. Nang Lao has taken to many aspects of Thai consumerism, popular music, and fashion. Like Sai Pit, she has a "green with red edges" identity card that registers her in the borderland district that includes Wan Kan Hai. And, like Sai Pit, she must apply for travel permission every time she leaves the district. But unlike Sai Pit, she was already in Chiang Mai when the district official issued the travel permission hiatus. As a result, she simply stayed put.

Nang Lao, the fashionable young woman that she is, recently leased a silver Honda motorbike. She was able to obtain the leasing contract from the dealer using the citizenship documentation of a Thai friend of hers but with the agreement that the bike was Nang Lao's responsibility to look after, and most crucially, to make the continued payments to the dealer. After spending a year or two doing sundry jobs, Nang Lao got word from another friend that one of the restaurants in the Chiang Mai airport was taking on more wait staff. The restaurant was an American-style sandwich shop and sports bar called Champion One. Eager at the prospect of working in the cosmopolitan setting, and already fantasizing about cashing in on hefty tips from wealthy foreigners, Nang Lao readily accepted.

A few weeks after Nang Lao started working at Champion One, I was in Chiang Mai. So on her day off, we met for lunch at a local noodle shop. I asked her how the new job was going. She replied that it was generally OK, not too difficult, though some customers were better than others. When she took the job, she worried that she would have difficulty communicating with foreign customers, as her English skills were rather rudimentary. But the restaurant's menus were in Thai, English, and Chinese, and if that didn't make things clear enough, each food item had a corresponding full-color picture, so customers could order food without speaking a word of *any* language; they could just point to the photo.

Because Nang Lao had spent some of her teenage years, as well as all of her young adulthood, in Chiang Mai, her Thai was completely fluent, and she had full comprehension of both Central and Northern Thai languages. But she had a very subtle Shan accent when speaking Central Thai, as her Shan tones would occasionally infiltrate her pronunciation of Thai long vowels. In any case, her Thai was excellent, so it surprised me a bit to hear her tell me that she had more problems with Thai customers than people of other nationalities.

Nang Lao never mentioned having a language misunderstanding with the Thai customers, but she told me that every once in a while, a Thai customer would remark that she "didn't speak Thai clearly." In Thai linguistic hierarchy, at least according to the Bangkok-centric bureaucracy, as well as government elementary schoolteachers throughout the country, only the privileged Central Thai accent is considered to be "clear" speech. This is a commentary applied to people from the provinces as well. Whether the comment is intended (or received) as pejorative depends on the situation. For Nang Lao, this comment would frequently include thorny follow-up questions, such as "Are you Thai?" or "Where are you from?" Particularly inconsiderate customers even asked about her immigration status or type of documentation.

If Nang Lao told customers where she was born, the Shan State, sometimes Thais would comment, "Oh, so you are Burmese?" or "You don't look Burmese." Nang Lao hailed from a family that supported the Shan insurgency, and whenever Thai customers were insensitive to the differences between Shan and Burmese, it annoyed her. Often, as well, Thai customers didn't consider the Shan people as part of the pan-Thai/Tai ethno-national rhetoric that made them *phinongkan*, or "ethnic brethren," evidence that not every morsel of nationalist history taught in Thai schools was avidly remembered by all citizens and self-appointed patriotic gatekeepers throughout the land. Occasionally, some Thais even talked about the Shan as a "hill tribe." In anticipation of these kinds of derision, Nang Lao experimented with new ways to respond to these uncomfortable intrusions.

One afternoon a middle-aged couple walked into the restaurant while Nang Lao was working. The man wore designer sunglasses and a light-blue polo shirt with the collar turned up. The woman donned fashionable beige slacks with a starched linen shirt and a designer silk scarf around her neck and shoulders. She was also carrying a Louis Vuitton handbag. She had been talking on her mobile phone from down the corridor and carried on the conversation as she walked beside the man in the polo shirt. Nang Lao welcomed them to the restaurant and walked them to a free table near the window, placing two laminated plastic menus on the table for them. The couple sat down, all the while the woman continuing her phone conversation. The man picked up one of the menus and scanned the food items pictured on the single card.

"Oh, so this is just *farang* [Western] food that you have here," said the man, glancing down the list of sandwiches and hamburgers.

"If you would prefer to eat rice instead of bread, the other restaurant down the corridor has Thai food. But these are delicious sandwiches," Nang Lao replied with a smile. "Would you like to order something?"

"Ehhh . . . I'll have a Heineken," said the man. Nang Lao looked to the woman, but she carried on with her phone conversation. The man looked back at Nang Lao. Almost on cue, he asked, "Where are you from? You don't speak Thai clearly."

Nang Lao bit the inside of her bottom lip to stifle her annoyance and replied, "I'm from Chiang Dao. You know, we speak Northern Thai."

Rather than end it at that, the man decided to push the issue a bit further. "Ok, if you are from Chiang Dao, you should know the name of the *nai amphoe* [district government official]. What's his name?"

Flustered, and in fact quite embarrassed by this form of interrogation, Nang Lao hastily replied, "He he he he. Oh, I don't know, I've been in Chiang Mai for a long time now."

The woman had decided to pause her phone conversation and told Nang Lao, "I'll have a lemon juice and the tuna sandwich; here, this one" as she pointed with her carefully manicured fingernail to the photo on the laminated menu. Relieved because the topic had been changed, Nang Lao turned her attention back to the man again and asked him if he would like a sandwich, too, or just the Heineken.

It was but a day or two after the incident, and Nang Lao told me the story in acute, vivid detail. "I bet he doesn't know the name of his district official but thinks it's OK to interrogate me about that. If he wants to order food, well, then just order food!" As she retold the story, her frustration was palpable; she clenched her fists in exasperation, thumping the top of the table for emphasis. I'd known Nang Lao for several months and knew she was close friends with people affiliated with the Shan State Army and was proud of her Shan heritage. Two of her cousins were SSA soldiers, and her aunt and uncle both fought with the SURA. Nang Lao readily joined Shan temple festivals and events in Chiang Mai and tuned in to Shan radio as one of the broadcasters was another old friend. But none of this was relevant to her while waiting tables at Champion One at the Chiang Mai airport; she would rather not discuss her Shan history and identity and continued to explain why not.

"The people from Bangkok are the worst. They act like they're so smart, but don't know the difference between Shan and Burmese and just assume we are all the same. What's even more *hsuk hsak* [ဟြက်.ဟြက်., Shan for annoying, or a hassle] is knowing that the guy in the polo shirt thought that he was being clever and flirtatious by asking me about Chiang Dao, even though he was doing that right in front of his wife!"

"How do you know she was his wife?" I asked.

"Because they weren't talking with each other!" she replied, almost triumphantly, and for the first time in several minutes, she smiled.

Given Nang Lao's interest in the latest fashions, and her occupation, it was her imperative to try to minimize the perceived difference between Shan and (Northern) Thai. At home, Nang Lao proudly identified as Shan, but she saw no contradiction in "acting" Thai on the job to avoid awkward or difficult conversations. Her frustration with the customer, however, seemed solely to revolve around the man's interrogation of her accent and to find out if she was "really" from Chiang Dao.

I was particularly impressed with Nang Lao's detailed description of the fashions of the Bangkok couple, down to the polo shirt and the designer handbag, and mention of the manicured nails. Once I had bought a pair of Levi's jeans from the open-air market and had them in a plastic bag at one of our lunchtime meetings. Nang Lao immediately wanted to have a look at my recent purchase. Pulling the blue jeans out of the plastic, she said within five seconds, "These are fake. Look at the rivets." I had only spent the equivalent of US$15 on the jeans, so perhaps I should not have been calling them Levi's. It had not occurred to me to inspect the rivets to authenticate the jeans prior to purchase, because, frankly, I didn't really care about the brand.

Even though the cost of the items owned by the Thai couple in the restaurant, such as the designer handbag, polo shirt, or genuine Levi's, was astronomically beyond what Nang Lao could afford on her waitress salary, her detailed knowledge of the objects implied a subtle aspiration for this kind of symbolic capital. Perhaps she saw fashion knowledge as a way to leapfrog the perception that she was from "the hills" or was somehow less modern than her elite Bangkokian interlocutor. By dressing the part, Nang Lao could avoid provoking the kind of condescension that a "hill tribesperson" inspires in the imagination of many Thais. A middle-aged Thai woman made the observation that she thought many young migrant men from Myanmar were *lo fiao* (หล่อเฟี้ยว), or "stylishly handsome." Itinerant labor makes their bodies fit and trim, but wearing fashionable clothing and having a great haircut signifies urban modernity, something that relatively privileged Thai citizens would take for granted but that is scrutinized for the migrant.

But for migrants, fashion knowledge and stylish clothing is insufficient for acceptance as Thai, though it might help one blend in superficially. Other pieces of symbolic baggage might be harder to transform. The man's phrase for accusing Nang Lao of not speaking Thai clearly is a direct translation of *phut phasa Thai mai chat* (พูดภาษาไทยไม่ชัด), whereby the notion of "clear" speech actually means speaking the language with the privileged Central Thai accent. It was that very accent that has been established as a privileged core component of Thai national identity (Mukhom Wongthes 2003, 30). Even though people in the provinces, with their respective varying accents and speech patterns, are very likely to communicate with each other with greater ease in their local languages, the nation's ideological linguistic hierarchy places such importance on speaking with the Central Thai accent that any variation from that specific privileged accent is regarded as "unclear."

One lecturer in the Faculty of the Humanities at a Northern Thai University discusses the issue: "Some Northern Thai parents want their children to speak Central Thai only. Instead of speaking their native language with their kids, they speak Central Thai with them. But what good does it do if they are speaking unclear Thai with their children?" In this example, the Northern Thai parents believe that speaking Central Thai with their children will give the kids a future advantage in a society that privileges the Central Thai dialect and its attendant pronunciations. But according to this teacher, the children's speech will still be stigmatized as they will be speaking the Central Thai dialect but with a Northern Thai accent.

At the home of a friend in Bangkok, I became acquainted with her maids: two sisters native to Thailand's northeast region, Isaan. The two women spoke their local language with each other but used Central Thai with their Bangkok employer (herself from Trang in Southern Thailand) and her family and with me when I visited. One of the maids, Kai, told me a story about another houseguest whose language skills flipped her expectations upside down. Takako, a Japanese researcher who had done fieldwork in Laos, came to visit. Takako is fluent in Japanese, English, and Lao. Kai speaks Central Thai and Isaan. With Lao and Isaan being mutually intelligible, Takako and Kai, one might expect, would communicate in those languages.

To her delight, Kai told me the story, giggling often: "When Takako came, I spoke Thai with her because, you know, speaking Thai is more polite. But then, I was amazed, she only speaks Lao. She's from Japan, but she really could speak Lao, she knew all the Lao words for different kinds of fish! It felt strange to me to speak Lao with a foreign guest." Kai had internalized the linguistic hierarchy that Central Thai is the proper, polite, and public language. Instead of using what is considered the "proper" speech, she was speaking with Takako in what might be considered some rural hillbilly dialect instead of "standard" language.

Language and accent in particular are often used at the micro-level to assess one's "authentic" Thai-ness, as demonstrated by the incident between the man in the polo shirt and Nang Lao in the airport restaurant. It is not an ethnic barrier just for Shan migrants but is also experienced by Thai citizens from other regions. Nang Lao's transactions took place in a context where she would constantly have to interact with people from different backgrounds. Furthermore, we could imagine that the Thai customer who picked on Nang Lao would have been more likely to remember his manners if she were a wealthy entrepreneur or a business client. Would our Thai man in the polo shirt jeopardize a million-dollar jade deal with Khun Sa by criticizing his accent or challenging him with a Thai bureaucracy trivia quiz?

The Most Intimate Interlocutors:
Shan Cinderella and Thai Prince Uncharming

In addition to working at construction sites, farms, restaurants, and brothels, Shan women and girls are overrepresented as domestic workers in Chiang Mai. For a migrant from Shan State, working as a maid is seen as a desirable way to send money home: one often receives both room and board and a monthly wage. But as is expected for someone who would be marginally documented, the wages are often low, and in some cases, conditions are terrible. Maids seldom have any recourse if their salaries are docked or if they are abused, especially if they are not fully legal workers in Thailand to begin with. As a form of cultural contact, live-in maids offer a unique ethnographic perspective on politics of class, ethnicity, and gender at their most intimate levels. Where maids are ethnic Others, their domestic labor frequently includes aspects of ethnic assimilation.

The story of a young Shan woman, May, presents a number of challenges to ideas about ethnic intimacy and what Shan identity represents in the Northern Thai context. May and her parents migrated to Mae Hong Son Province following the massive displacements after Khun Sa's 1996 surrender. In 2012 she took a job as a maid in a Northern Thai middle-class home in a housing development in Saraphi, just south of Chiang Mai. The household consisted of Arpa, seventy-three; her husband, Chatchai, seventy-six; and their forty-five-year-old son, Somchai. Arpa and Chatchai's daughter had married a man in the Thai police, had moved to Bangkok several years previously, and was raising a son.

Decades ago, Chatchai had invested in real estate in central Thailand, and this paid off handsomely. By Thai standards, the family was quite well off. Arpa had achieved a master's degree and spent part of her career as a government employee. Arpa's extended family owned homes in the same housing development, so she and her two sisters, brother, and neighbors socialized often, eating meals at one another's houses, watching TV, or sometimes taking trips to the temple or the market. There was an informal group of neighborhood women in their seventies and eighties, and cooking meals and eating together was one of the main foci of their lives, as was catching up on the neighborhood gossip; their social network was reminiscent of a rural village, where many of them used to live.

Unlike his parents, Somchai was neither ambitious nor enterprising. Typical of Southeast Asian stereotypes, as the youngest son, Somchai had been frequently indulged and doted upon. In unfair contrast, it is often the daughter who does all the housework while sons like Somchai just hang around, only opening their mouths when they want food (as the stereotype is characterized in Thai). Somchai never displayed much ambition and perpetually dropped out of any university or degree program he started. At the age of forty-five, he only had a high school certificate. He was still living at home, which was certainly not unusual in Southeast Asia by any means, but by his fifth decade he had no established career of his own, despite his parents clearly having the means to pay whatever tuition fees his program might require. He did have an impressive collection of vintage Doraemon toys, so he was not completely without interests.

Within several months of having taken the job as a maid in the household, May became romantically involved with Somchai. One of Somchai's aunts related, "After lunch, he would ask May for a massage, and the two of them would stay in his room for a long time." As the "massages" continued, the extended family and the neighborhood got wind of the gossip. It was eventually made clear to the family that the relationship was more than just a tryst: Somchai was serious about May and wanted to get married. His mother, Arpa, however, would have nothing of it. His father was irate. Their initial ire was out of middle-class expectations for their son. They viewed a maid as someone who cleaned the house; perhaps a nonserious fling would be fine, but a maid was not someone you marry. Ethnicity did not seem to play a defining role in Arpa's rejection of her son's relationship, or at least that was how the discontentment was originally articulated.

As Mu, Arpa's fifty-year-old niece (and Somchai's cousin), explained the situation to me:

> Look at Somchai. An educated Thai woman would not be interested in getting together with him. He's so spoiled and lazy. Just talk with him, he lacks *sanae* [เสน่ห์, or charm]. But for an impoverished Tai-yai girl, marrying him is marrying up. And May would be prepared and more willing to take care of him; she has to deal with it. An educated Thai woman, she would prefer to live on her own and be independent rather than be with a guy like Somchai, even though his family has money.

In this case, Mu articulated the complicated ways in which class, status, and ethnicity can intersect in intimate expectations in Northern Thailand. Arpa's rejection of May as a prospective daughter-in-law could derive from the fact that May entered the relationship as a maid (but class identity cannot be completely disentangled from ethnic identity). Arpa had certain ambitions for an appropriate pair for her only son.

As an economically independent middle-class woman who has known her cousin Somchai for all his life, Mu saw May's decision to get involved with the guy as a rational decision based on her insecure status in Thailand. By marrying (and later having a child with) Somchai, May was sacrificing her own enjoyment and personal freedom in favor of long-term financial and legal security for herself and her family in Thailand—a feminine virtue of patience and sacrifice for the greater good and future merit within a Buddhist cosmology as well.

A middle-class Thai woman with her own economic security would have the relative privilege to pursue relationships that she enjoyed. As evidence of Mu's assertion, middle-class women in Thailand are increasingly choosing not to marry and have children. These women can preserve their autonomy by staying single, a status that has less stigma these days than it did in prior decades.

Finding the situation with his parents untenable, Somchai surprised the entire extended family and their friends by taking a stand against his mother: he and May moved out of the family home and got their own place together. They lived on their own for two years, until Arpa relented and decided to allow the marriage, ultimately accepting May as a daughter-in-law. The family threw a large festive wedding and invited their extended family and friends in the Saraphi neighborhood, and May's extended family attended the event as well—the latter all wearing pink as a form of sartorial solidarity. Members of May's family spoke Shan when they were together at the reception tables, though they greeted Arpa and others on the groom's side in Central Thai.

Although one might interpret this as a successful resolution to an ill-fated romance of a Northern Thai Montague and a Shan Capulet, one aspect of the relationship still remained taboo for Somchai: May's status as Shan. On numerous occasions, Somchai would go out of his way to insist, "May is *THAI*!"

As I got to know this extended family, who themselves interacted with each other in Northern Thai and Central Thai fluidly and interchangeably, I saw that Somchai and May spoke only Central Thai together. Somchai's extended family knew of my research work and experience speaking in the

Shan language, but they actively discouraged me from approaching May and speaking in Shan with her.

At a social meal attended by two of Somchai's aunts and his uncle, I pressed the issue: "But I've spent a lot of time learning Shan and appreciate the language and culture. Wouldn't May be happy to chat with me in Shan?"

"Somchai doesn't see it that way," his aunt retorted quickly.

The visible presence of May's relatives all in pink at their wedding and also speaking Shan together, unsurprisingly, gave plenty more juicy details for Arpa's neighbors and extended family to talk about; the love of May and Somchai (and the parents' initial rejection of the relationship) was a real-life soap opera. Arpa's elder sister, Ampika, in particular, was eager to chat with the neighbors. She freely told her peers about the Shan family, describing their clothing and their attendance at the wedding. Later Somchai came by his aunt Ampika's home to reprimand her: "May is *not* Tai-yai. She is Thai! Stop gossiping to everyone that she is Tai-yai!!"

Although the neighbors well knew the circumstances of Somchai's relationship with May, he was uniquely focused on trying to control the discourse about her ethnicity. His anger at Aunt Ampika and policing any suggestion or interest in Shan-ness suggest that his masculinity was threatened by the public knowledge that his wife was ethnic Shan. While Aunt Ampika was discussing May as Shan as a matter of fact, not intentionally passing judgment, Somchai's anxiety was hinging on the notion that he might not be perceived as "man enough" to attract a Thai woman.

Conversely, Somchai did not try to police the neighborhood discourse about May's class background. He never reprimanded Aunt Ampika for telling the neighbors that he married their maid, though this action—for many middle-class Thais—could be considered taboo. Then again, Aunt Ampika had met May when she started working at the house, and there were multiple eyewitnesses that she was the maid. For Somchai to try to deny that fact would have been even more preposterous.

Even though ethno-national discourse creates a romantic notion of Thai-Tai intimacy, there are aspects of that intimacy that are not always comfortable. Ethnic difference is fine and presentable when it is manifest at a temple festival, or as an exotic new delicacy on a plate in a restaurant, or on display as tourist art, but it becomes uncomfortable and even inappropriate within the betrothals of respectable middle-class families.

CONCLUSION

Although Thai patriotic history embraces the Shan as ancient blood relatives, the current bureaucracy and the experiences of Shan people migrating to and working in Chiang Mai tell a very different story. Everyday encounters reveal other forms of legal and economic privilege, which also demand the symbolic and emotional labor of ethnic assimilation. While the state sets up its legal mechanisms for conferring and policing citizenship and access to labor markets, ethno-national ideologies and homegrown chauvinism and bigotry have created and empowered cultural gatekeepers at the local level.

It is the very incompleteness and sudden changes in policy regarding migration and its legal status that serve to vary the income for state officials in their shadow taxation of Shan migrants. When travel permission is granted, the local authorities collect application fees; when travel permission is not granted, the police and army collect bribes along the way. In both cases, employers remunerate stateless workers with substandard wages and conditions. Whereas a political or bureaucratic analysis might focus on bureaucracy, economy, and labor, at these checkpoints the nature of their very operation is highly personal. For many Shan, it is a symbolic minefield, and the anticipation of those mines' location has everything to do with one's own knowledge and fear, often based on experience.

It was nationalist discourse and administrative fiat on the part of the Thai government that decided that all those speaking Tai languages shared a common language, regardless of the degree of mutual intelligibility of those languages (Keyes 2002, 1179). While Shan, Thai, and Northern Thai are in the same language family, the languages are only mutually intelligible at a very basic level. In any case, and this has everything to do with value-laden aspects of Thai chauvinism, Shan people are much more sensitive to the differences between their language and that of Bangkok Thais than are the Thais (Eberhardt 1988, 9).

But one of the justifications for *not* conferring refugee status on Shans fleeing war is that Thais consider the Shans linguistically and culturally similar and therefore not in need of outside assistance. Although it might be true that it is easier for a Shan migrant to learn Thai than a Karen- or Burman-speaking counterpart, the reality of migration is much more complex. It is reductionist to look at language ability alone as a sole deciding factor in the experience of migration (Amporn Jirattikorn 2007, 16).

Many Shan migrants living and working in Chiang Mai, such as Nang Lao, are able to blend in; she dresses well and is up on the latest trends in Thai pop culture. Her Shan identity is something that she prefers to reveal only in certain contexts and, logically, in places where she would not be judged negatively. All these aspects are not likely understood or appreciated by the Thai guy in the polo shirt who felt empowered to quiz Nang Lao because of his superior status as an older, richer Thai man—he was a customer. To him, Nang Lao was "just" a cute young waitress.

Where the emotional labor of ethnic assimilation is often shouldered by the minority, there can be work for one who is a member of the majority but in an intimate relationship with the minority. There is an important role to be played by the cultural ally, a person who is a member of the majority but advocates for a minority group and criticizes acts of bigotry among the majority. Allies can be powerful agents of change. Many Thais fit this description of an ally and actively work to make Thai society more accepting of Shan people and Shan culture. But Somchai was not one of them. He would prefer that nobody talk about his wife's Shan-ness.

With all the legal, economic, and cultural barriers to survival in Thailand, what of the struggle to repossess Shanland? While there is undoubtedly a tremendous diversity of experiences among the hundreds of thousands of Shan migrants working in Thailand, there are ways in which many of these experiences feed into the Shan insurgency, both economically and culturally.

First, numerous Shan State Army soldiers had themselves formerly been migrant workers in Thailand. The grinding reality of being second-class Thai subjects, both bureaucratically and culturally, drives young Shans back to the borderlands to join the SSA.

One young soldier I interviewed at Loi Tailaeng on Shan National Day celebrations, Sai Chuen, spoke fluent Thai and told me why he had moved back to join the SSA: "I was always afraid to go out. I never knew when the Thai police would stop me and try to take a bribe. Or, if I paid for the work permit, then I would have to work for weeks just to pay back that debt. I wanted to send money to my family back home, but often it was too hard to save any money, or get enough to send home. Also in the SSA camp, I'm welcome as Shan."

Shan migrant workers support Shanland through their remittances, both directly and indirectly. Some send donations of money directly to the insurgency, while others make Buddhist merit by presenting donations at Shan temples that are affiliated with the Shan State Army. Shan migrants indirectly support the insurgency by sending remittances to their families in the border areas (who themselves support the SSA) or when they send money to families whose homes are in the taxation territories of the Restoration Council of Shan State (RCSS), the bureaucratic arm of the SSA.

Recalling Hseng Lün's comment that she would like to be a full citizen in her next lifetime, we can see how her struggles with Thai bureaucracy have framed how she envisions a higher rebirth. She will continue to make merit at her local Shan temple at Wan Kan Hai. She does not describe her future incarnation as a citizen of Thailand but instead as a full citizen, a crucial difference.

6

We Are Siamese
(If You Please)

How many times have you seen the Thai people come visit us here and smiiiiilleee and tell us we're *phinongkan* [siblings], only to treat us worse than dirt when we look for jobs in the city, or even just speak their language with a bit of an accent?

—Seng Kham

RECENT DECADES HAVE SEEN continued expansion of Thailand's domestic tourism industry, a development that has not only transformed regional economies but also has changed the ways in which Thais think about other places and peoples in the country. Four decades ago, it would have been all but unthinkable for urban middle-class Thais to choose to visit their country's uplands or border areas. The Communist Party of Thailand controlled significant swaths of territory, and the mountainous borderlands of the country were seen as wild and dangerous. For wealthy Thais in the 1960s and 1970s, leisure travel—the idea of *pai tiao*—generally meant one of three things: to go stay at the homes of relatives in another province, to make merit at famous temples or religious sites, or to visit places that were perceived as developed and therefore prestigious, with Europe or the United States topping the list for those with the means. Rural places with peasant economies or ethnic minorities did not carry much cachet for Thai leisure tourists. For example, the northwestern province of Mae Hong Son, which borders the Shan and Kayah States, was once characterized as the Siberia of Thailand (Tannenbaum 2002, 141). Better roads and infrastructure and increased middle-class spending power, together with shifts toward consumerism of different forms of "Thai-ness" and positive orientation to "exotic" cultural experiences, mean that more Thais are actively seeking difference in their own country. These encounters are spurred by leisure travelers, journalists, and businesspeople alike.

The majority of the Shan adults in Wan Kan Hai were born in Shan State, and the political history of the town is prominent, particularly as the current village leadership and the most established households of the community were involved with the Shan United Revolutionary Army. That aspect of the town is a draw for a few Thai visitors; an occasional researcher or journalist will come to interview the locals about the political history or the contemporary struggles.[1] However, the more mainstream expectation for Wan Kan Hai, as an ethnic minority village in the uplands (in addition to the allure of the geography, the mountains, and the climate), is to see displays of cultural difference, "ethnic" attire, and pleasing performances of music and dance, or to try on locally made clothing and to sample Shan foods. Reciprocally, locals get to know what visitors might like to see or buy, so there is a push to create performances, present difference, and offer consumer opportunities for foods and curios. But how these items represent "Shan-ness" can be different, depending on the visitor, and there can be disagreement within the local community as well.

One key aspect about Thais who visit Wan Kan Hai: they are a self-selecting group. Unlike Nang Lao's customers at the airport, or the mainstream Chiang Mai public who Shan migrants encounter on a daily basis, Thai tourists in Wan Kan Hai will have an awareness of Tai-yai as a distinct group, and others may have some knowledge about the history of the insurgency. Nonetheless, the Thai tourists do have their own cultural expectations of Shan-ness that they project on villagers in Wan Kan Hai. Class difference and experience play an important role in framing these interactions. How the Shan people perform that Shan-ness, and what that performance means to them, are yet to be seen.

Therefore, this chapter explores how Shan people anticipate and mediate these visits by Thais. With guests in town, Shan seek to present their history, their identity, and themselves in ways that communicate an important message to the Other (and to each other). It is in the context of economic and social tension that we see how identity—and perceptions about identity—are interstitial, unstable, and socially contingent (Willford 2006, 120). We can further consider what it means for Thais to visit a Shan village that is in the national periphery, has its own history of political insurgency, but is now seen as subject to the Thai nation-state. Although the ideology of cultural similarity and *phinongkan* Thai/Tai siblinghood is repeatedly invoked, it is in the asymmetry of these cultural interactions that

Shan people disproportionally experience the contradictions of this ideology and sometimes suffer as a result.

THAI CULTURAL TOURISTS IN THAILAND

In a style characterized by former Thai prime minister Chatchai Choonhavan in 1988, the Cold War stomping grounds of Southeast Asia have been subjected to a concerted attempt to "turn battlefields into marketplaces." The growing market for cultural tourism in these former battlefields is part of this trend. Whereas temples and monuments—such as the historical parks of Sukhothai or Ayutthaya—comprise major sites for projecting the historical legitimacy of Thainess, through commodification via the construction of tourist attractions, other aspects of cultural pluralism come into focus.

During the 1990s, partially under the aegis of promoting regional tourism, the Thai state began to sponsor "festivalized" displays of ethnic diversity in various regions throughout the country. In her detailed ethnography of Khmer localism in Surin, Thailand, anthropologist Alexandra Denes explains how the Thai state's relatively recent acknowledgment of Khmer history and ethnicity within the borders of Thailand has facilitated these performances of Khmer ethnicity, including music, dance, and elaborate costuming. However, the Khmer-ness presented is based on a Thai hegemonic vision of a past in which Khmer people are loyal subjects to a Thai court (Denes 2006).

Thai tourism discourses have also profitably exploited internal Others through hill tribe tourism. Advertising brochures promote such places as "remote and unspoiled." Tourists are encouraged to "see the tribesmen in their own surroundings and study their actual way of life" (Cohen 1996, 68). Often in the form of village visits, treks, or homestays, hill tribe tourism was initially only advertised to international tourists and emerged as a major market in the 1970s and 1980s. But today one can find increasing numbers of Thai urbanites visiting Hmong, Lisu, Akha, and Lahu villages and going on treks to other non-Thai villages in the northern mountains. According to guesthouse data collected by the government Ministry of Tourism and Sports, in 2016 the number of Thai tourists visiting Mae Hong Son Province was over triple that of all foreigners combined: Thai tourists totaled 607,113, and all foreigners totaled 193,549 (Ministry of Tourism and Sports 2016). Thailand's Siberia has become much more crowded than it used to be.

Although the statistics demonstrate the increased popularity of domestic tourism in Thailand's periphery, the raw data do not describe the ideological and cultural processes that are at work when urban Thais interact with these so-called internal Others. In addition, Thai citizens' understanding of their supposed connected history with the Shan, as siblings by origin myth, will sometimes frame their expectations of the people of Wan Kan Hai, not just in terms of performative culture but also as an expectation for political alliance and cooperation. While the Akha and Hmong "hill tribe" people might be seen by Thais as a distant cultural and civilizational Other, the Shan, as Tai-yai, are sometimes expected to be a kind of Other in time or a vestige of Tai culture before modernity. For example, a Thai tourist, an office clerk named Nok, described her visit to Kengtung, in Shan State as *"just like* Chiang Mai 100 years ago!" For someone to be able to relate her eyewitness comparison of Chiang Mai in 1915 to Kengtung in 2015, Nok certainly wears her years well.

For many Thai people with specific interest in Shan culture, and who would make a trip to Wan Kan Hai as tourists, a common motivation involved a feeling of ethnic empathy, and especially the notion that Thai and Shan are *phinongkan*, or "brethren." This inclusion has also been thought of as part of the "transnational Tai community—even family" that is projected onto people based on linguistic similarity, purported historical connection, and aspects of shared culture (Walker 2009, 21).

This romantic notion has also been critiqued in a broader shift in cultural values toward Thai internal Others. As detailed in the first chapter, twentieth-century nationalism in Thailand sanctioned Bangkokian urban modernity and Central Thai speech as privileged cultural forms to the detriment if not attempted erasure of regional languages and expressions. This also extends to clothing and comportment that were encoded as *siwilai* (Thongchai Winichakul 2000). But not everyone in the Thai capital stayed on that political and cultural bandwagon: the upheavals spearheaded by the student revolutions of the 1970s, as well as touristic economies and neoliberal cultural configurations, have altered this dynamic, and for many have upended ideas about prestige. Whereas the student activists had focused their political attention and mobilization on the injustices and inequities in the country due to the successive military regimes, they also demonstrated their aversion to mainstream aesthetic manifestations of status and hierarchy. Partially in distain for established aesthetics of urban elitism, as well to embrace the styles popularized by American folk music singers such as

Bob Dylan and Joan Baez, middle-class Thais started to take on new kinds of fashion. For example, groups of Thai student activists since the 1970s (as well as plenty of Thais today, some more politically involved than others) chose to wear indigo-dyed farmer's shirts, jeans, and flip flops instead of starched and pressed university student uniforms (Haberkorn 2011, 82). This move was not only a symbolic rejection of the student—or middle-class—status but also an act of solidarity with the peasants.

This positive sentiment toward the down-trodden and reversal of the "prestige ladder" resonate with the nationalist ideology that started to view the countryside as a "reservoir of an idyllic Thai past" (Tannenbaum 2002, 143). Although participants might think of this symbolic stance as a gesture of empathy with or solidarity for their rural or ethnic counterpart, it can also be interpreted by those peasants or ethnic others positively, but this is not always the case. The symbolic bridge is fraught, especially in situations where legal, economic, and cultural differences are considerable.

Post-1970s Thai interest in—and affection for—both rural people and Tais in other countries are less characterized by military prowess but rather are of scholarly and cultural interest (Reynolds 2003, 24). Thai academic work in ethnic studies has been characterized by three waves: studies that were influenced by older "race and tribe" studies, suggesting that cultures are fixed and timeless; studies of cultures as superstructure to political economies; and studies of cultures that place importance on the diversity of identities facilitated by late capitalism, cultures of consumerism, and migration (Yos ยศ 2008, 15). Thai academic and popular books about the Shan often reflect this contour.

Tai groups outside Thailand are of interest to ethnic studies for the way they fit into the migration myth and for cultural and linguistic similarities across Thai/Tai groups. Tai cultural resilience and preservation are main tropes in this research. As one Thai historian of the Shan writes, in nations in which ethnic Tais are a minority, such as Burma, China, Vietnam, and Malaysia, the modern state uses technological and mass communication means to swallow Tai minorities (Sompong สมพงศ์ 1998, 232). One Thai scholar writes that Burmese culture, or Burmanization, has penetrated every area of the Shan State, and Shan kids with Burmese friends are ashamed of their status as Shan. Therefore, the Shan language is eroding and is being replaced by Burmese (Renu เรณู 1998, 265). Another summarizes that Shan migration to Thailand is a result of the Burmese government's treatment of ethnic minority groups (Siraporn 2012, 148).

When Thai studies scholars shift their focus to Tai groups in Thailand, the prognosis for Tai identity changes. Based on fieldwork in Piang Luang village in Chiang Mai Province, near the border with Shan State, one Thai master's thesis making use of Barth's theory of boundary making argues that the Shan use markers of Shan identity such as language, culture, and dress in an effort to delineate an ethnic boundary between themselves and other groups, particularly the Burmese (Wandi วันดี 2002, 78). Another scholar argues that the Thai "festivalization" of ethnicity gives Shan migrants in Northern Thailand a context where they can affirm their cultural identity by wearing their traditional clothing, speaking their language, and practicing their performing arts. In addition to this, they assert their feelings of ethnic closeness with Thais, as being on Thai soil enables them to enjoy an openness of cultural expression (Pannida พรรณิดา 2011, 114).

Thai popular writing about the Shan also emphasizes Thai-Tai historical closeness. In one Thai-language book about the Shan insurgency, the author argues that the late sixteenth-century Siamese King Naresuan is still highly revered by Shan soldiers as he is written about in Thai history as having united the Siamese and Shan kingdoms (Nipatporn นิพัทธ์พร 2006, 72). Thai news segments have noted that the Shan State Army reveres the Thai king, thus uniting Shans and Thais in both respect for the monarchy and Buddhism (Spring News 2016).

Whereas the last chapter focused on Shan legal, economic, and cultural experiences of entering Thai labor markets and Thai families in urban Chiang Mai, this chapter considers examples of Thai engagements with Shanness in Wan Kan Hai, on the periphery of Thailand, but in a town where Shan people comprise the majority. Thai ethno-nationalist rhetoric is predicated on this idea of *phinongkan* "brethren," or connection with other Tai groups. Thai academic and popular interest in Shan culture has also been coupled with the kinds of nostalgic empathy mentioned above. However, this pan-Tai connection or kinship is not necessarily felt or reciprocated in the same way by the other various Tai groups. It is in the complex dynamics of touristic meeting grounds that these ideologies play out. Analysis of these interactions offers loaded evidence of how some narratives and experiences might be silenced in favor of the more powerful.

Ethnic Performance and Cultural Brokering

While war and poverty forced most Shan migrants to become acquainted with Thai culture in the past several decades, Thai touristic interest in the

Shan is more recent. With the movement for "festivalization" of Shan culture, there have emerged certain culture brokers: individuals who are adept at presenting cultural events and displays to outsiders. One of the earliest—and most consistent—Shan culture brokers whom I got to know in Northern Thailand is a Shan ambassador of sorts. Everyone in Chiang Mai who is involved in Shan literary production, whether connected to the major Shan temples in Northern Thailand or to academic study of the Shan, knows this forty-five-year-old Shan man whom I'll call Sai Sai. He has considerable expertise in Shan performing arts and is an articulate teacher. He speaks fluent Shan, Burmese, and Thai and is also proficient in English. Sai Sai is akin to the "go-to person" when Thai scholars want to attend a Shan event or find out about Shan rituals.

Born in Kyauk Me, Northern Shan State, Sai Sai has been living in Thailand for the past two decades. He is small in stature and quite nimble; thus he is able to dance the *kinnaya* with grace. The *kinnaya* (in brief) is a mythological half-human, half-bird creature, and the human dance performance is a mimicry of the courtship between the male *kinnaya* and the female *kinnayi*. When one performs such a dance, the costuming includes elaborate fan-folding tail-feathers. The figure and the costuming are prevalent throughout cultural events in Burma, too. But for people in Northern Thailand, the *kinnaya* is often seen as an expression of Shan cultural identity (Siraporn 2012, 154).

Sai Sai's enthusiasm and passion for the Shan performing arts is infectious, so it is no wonder that scholars and patrons of the arts enjoy consulting with him about these subjects. He is wonderfully charming and loves a good story. He is skilled at explaining Shan cultural differences for people of varied backgrounds to understand. Sai Sai pays regular visits to the various towns and villages with large Shan populations in Thailand, meeting with elders of the community and also teaching traditional Shan dance and music to local youth. As he says, he loves to teach Shan kids to appreciate their own culture, but he welcomes any student eager to learn about various Shan performing arts.

When he was staying in Wan Kan Hai for a few weeks, I had the privilege of studying the Shan written language with Sai Sai and also tagging along on the back of his motorbike to attend one day of a funeral ceremony and cremation of an important Shan monk in an adjacent town. In addition to learning more about Shan history and arts, I was delighted by some of the quirks of his sense of humor. For example, he had a song (in

English) that went, "We are the Buddha club. . . . We are the Buddha club," which he would sing in a comic falsetto, while squinting one eye to hold an imaginary magnifying monocle and with his other hand a small object (a pretend Buddhist amulet) up to his invisible monocle. It was Sai Sai's way of making fun of Thai amulet collectors. Although amulets are big business in Thailand (not just in terms of revenue but also for the spiritual protection that some are believed to provide their bearers) Sai Sai seemed to revel in irony of the seriousness of amulet micro-inspection. His gestures to animate the song reminded me of some performances that I had seen at a Mandalay *anyeint* comedic variety show performance. Nevertheless, when at the temple, Sai Sai is a devout (and serious) Buddhist.

During one of his visits to Wan Kan Hai, a Chiang Mai–based scholar put some cultural tourists—a group of middle-class Northern Thais—in touch with Sai Sai. He told them that he had been teaching Shan traditional dance at the local high school and invited the group to come visit and see his students perform. The Chiang Mai–based group set the date and hired a van for the dozen people to make the three-and-a-half-hour trek along the mountainous roads to Wan Kan Hai to see the kids' performance.

Sai Sai held his dance classes in a small, free-standing recreation classroom located opposite the school sports field on the high school grounds. The rec classroom was far enough from the main school building that the loud percussion music would not be too distracting to the regular classes. Inside, student desks were pushed to the side, so Sai Sai and his teenage students had space to practice their dances on the concrete floor. The school owned a set of Shan long drums (*kawng*) and gongs (*mawng*) to provide the background rhythm for the dances that would follow. The guests from Chiang Mai were warmly welcomed by Sai Sai, and they found seats in the rather haphazard pile of desks. The guests were mostly in their twenties and thirties, and a few were middle-aged. They were kind and engaging and were not expecting any sort of "red carpet" treatment; from the interactions they seemed glad to be there and genuinely interested in seeing Shan high school kids performing traditional Shan dances.

For the Shan students' performances, one of the boys squatted beside the *mawng*, a set of a dozen gongs mounted on a rectangular wooden frame.[2] The frame has a striking device similar to that of a bass drum pedal on a rock band drum kit. But this *mawng* has a lever hitched to a pedal drive that connects with multiple beater mallets. With one push of the lever, multiple gongs are struck. The boy formed a straightforward, fast-paced downbeat, operating the lever that struck the *mawng* with repetitive pushing motions.

With the regular *mawng* strikes forming the basic structure, another teenage boy stood with a five-foot-long drum slung over his shoulder. With his palms he struck the drum face, offering patters of offbeats and paradiddles to give complexity to the mechanical downbeat of the *mawng*. While the teenagers created the base rhythm, Sai Sai joined with a pair of cymbals to punctuate the offbeats and added additional syncopation to the small percussion ensemble. These small ensembles have become the signifier for Shan events and dances as well as a way to welcome VIPs to a Shan village. Some luxury resorts in Shan State have these ensembles to welcome arriving guests.[3]

A series of short dance performances ensued, with girls dressed in the *kinnayi* costume and boys in Shan-style jackets, baggy trousers, and turbans dancing a long-sword dance. The visitors from Chiang Mai were fully attentive to each performance, offering polite applause when each teen bowed in a respectful *wai* at the end of her or his number. The performances lasted about forty-five minutes in total, and at the conclusion, the guests went around the room, each sharing his or her impressions of the performance. A few of the comments are as follows:

> The dance is beautiful and very special. It's lovely that you have the opportunity to take care of your traditional culture.
>
> It was a special chance to come to your village and see your show. Please keep practicing these cultural performances and teach them to your children. Seeing the different kinds of culture helps us to remember that we are *phinongkan* (siblings).
>
> The Shan character is lovely.[4]

Each of the twelve guests had a turn, and all the opinions were much like those above, some verbatim repetitions of what the previous person said; everybody was positive and supportive of the performance, lavishing praise for the dance's beauty. More than one guest used the term *phinongkan* (siblings) as a way to express empathy and connection with the Shan. After all the guests had spoken, Sai Sai shared his opinion about keeping up Shan performing arts: "Especially when we have to fight the Burmese to have autonomy, keeping our Shan identity is a challenge. When kids and teenagers come to Thailand, often they want to grow up and be just like the Thais, dressing like the Thais, and speaking only the Thai language. But I want them to learn to love their own culture. It's like we're different leaves on different trees. The greater the diversity of leaves, the more beautiful the forest." The guests smiled and nodded in agreement with Sai Sai's comment. Before the group departed the school grounds to go back to Chiang Mai, they thanked Sai Sai profusely, encouraged him to keep up the work, and presented the school with an envelope containing a monetary donation. After the session, Sai Sai and I went to Seng Kham's house to chat with her and Aung Myo about the event. They noticed that the visitors did not give the high school students the chance to share their opinions about the dance. It was as if their performance was their sole contribution, and the "opinion sharing" on the part of the guests was the reciprocal gift for the students. I saw Sai Sai also mutter under his breath that next time he would make sure that the students were encouraged to actively talk about their feelings about the performances to their guests; he realized it would be valuable for the kids to explain to the guests how they themselves felt about their own performance and what learning these Shan traditional dances meant to them.

In many regards, the group of Chiang Mai cultural enthusiasts was earnest in its appreciation of the Shan dances. Not many middle-class urbanites would go to the trouble to hire a van for a day's excursion to visit a border town like Wan Kan Hai. Although within Western cultural studies discourses, there is a great deal of sensitivity—with ample reason—for issues of cultural appropriation, the cultural enthusiasts from Chiang Mai who visited the Shan teenager's dance performances were lovely and kind in their support, and Sai Sai (as well as the high school student performers) were thrilled that the group took a serious interest and traveled to see them. In this case, I am reticent to offer a critique that would be cynical about the event, as not all such events involving performances of culture difference are bitter or exploitative, even though the participants may be very well aware of their sociological differences outside the context of the performance or any discourse of "Thai privilege." During the visit, there was no discussion of the poverty in Wan Kan Hai, the struggles of Shan migrants in Thailand, or any other social or political problems; the visitors' experience was bracketed to include just the lovely show.

Let's Work Together in
Your Sufficient Economy

While the Chiang Mai cultural tourists' objectives were fulfilled by their one-day trip, other urbanites' forays into the borderlands have longer-term goals. Several months later, another group, consisting of businesspeople from Bangkok, made plans to visit Wan Kan Hai. They claimed to represent an environmental NGO concerned with sustainable, organic agriculture. I call the NGO Planet Preservation. The director of Planet Preservation, whom I call Khun Maew, is a well-connected member of an elite Thai family that owns a department store chain. She is in successful liaison with scholars at a local university as well as some officials in the Ministry of Agriculture.

When Khun Maew's team contacted the village headman and told him about their plans to go to Wan Kan Hai for a preliminary visit, they indicated their intention to establish a long-term agricultural project for the village. The villagers would grow vegetables using certified organic methods, and Planet Preservation would be concerned with getting the products to market. Although Khun Maew told villagers that she was visiting Wan Kan Hai in the capacity of the director of Planet Preservation, she later insinuated that she might be able to sell the produce in the supermarkets at her family's retail chain.

The evening before the Planet Preservation visit to Wan Kan Hai, Sai Möng Mao, the village headman, announced on the village loudspeaker that there would be a town hall meeting. Four men convened the meeting, and one took the minutes in Shan script. There were about forty people in attendance, approximately evenly divided by gender.

Mattana quickly took command when the topic of a welcoming reception came up. They were to prepare various foods for the guests, and she started to delegate responsibility. There was a sense of eager anticipation that a group of Thai VIPs would be coming to their village soon. But the enthusiasm wasn't universally shared. One of the co-convenors of the town meeting, Yee Thip, was much more doubtful about the intentions of Khun Maew and her Planet Preservation group, and he was the first to air a bit of skepticism:

Ok, so we have these important people from Bangkok coming here tomorrow, and then they have their experts. They are going to tell us, "You need

to do it like this. You need to do it like that.⁵" What are we going to do? Are
we going to say something? Are we going to talk about the many problems
that we have here? What about the undocumented migrants? The refugees?
The people with AIDS? What about the poverty? Are we going to tell them
about all of it, or are we just going to smile and give them the impression we
all love one another, and then they'll go back to the city thinking we are so
happy? What about the problems?

At this point, there were some murmurs in the group, and Seng Kham
interjected, "Right, and for these products, who is going to pay the licensing
rights? Who is going to inspect the produce to see that it's really pesticide-
free?" Nobody responded directly to the questions of either Yee Thip or
Seng Kham. While Mattana and her gang were avidly discussing the next
day's menu and entertainment lineup, Yee Thip and Seng Kham's concerns
hovered in the room, like a fog that everyone knew was there but was trying to ignore.

It was exciting to have such rich and powerful guests coming to town.
But would they actually help the community, or would they exploit it once
again? Even if their plans might have been self-serving, there may have
been some opportunity to benefit by collaborating and welcoming this
private-sector assistance. In any case, Yee Thip and Seng Kham's inter-
ventions demonstrated genuine concern that the Shan people might have
been out of their depth regarding the technicalities of the NGO's plan and,
once again, might be potentially vulnerable to future exploitation as the
result of a bad deal.

THE BIG DAY

The planned arrival time of Khun Maew's big entourage was not clear to
many of the people involved in preparing their reception. Some of the
Wan Kan Hai villagers said that the visitors would arrive at the gathering
hall at ten o'clock that Saturday morning. Early that morning, a group of
villagers consisting of nine women and two men were milling around, all
wearing *hko Tai* traditional costumes, usually reserved for weddings and
temple events. Women wore fancy multicolored, layered, wrapped turbans
on their heads, and fitted long-sleeve shirts with matching skirts with em-
broidered stripes. Horizontal stripes are characteristic of Southern Shan
while vertical patterning of the embroidery represents Tai Mao style. I was
even wearing my own colorful Shan outfit to be in sartorial uniform with

the other women. The two men were dressed in their baggy Shan trousers, but complemented by T-shirts rather than their finest Shan jackets.

At the northern side of the hall, the women brought out folding tables and started to arrange displays of local products, including hand-woven skirts similar to the ones that they were wearing. Hseng Lün set up a little pyramid of plastic jars of her homemade roast chili with dried shrimp, tamarind, and garlic. She even had labels printed in Shan and Thai on the face of each jar.

Several young girls, all around ten years old, were each in colorful *hko Tai* costumes too. Nang Mya told the girls' mothers, who were standing on the other side of the table, "Wash that *thanakha* off the girls' cheeks! We don't want them to think we're Burmese!"

Thanakha is a species of tree bark that, when ground and mixed with water, makes a yellowish-beige paste that is a useful skin cream. It is popular in Burma and can be seen on the faces of people throughout the country, especially women and children, though anyone working outdoors uses it. It is practically ubiquitous, being a natural, effective, and inexpensive sunscreen and skin toner. *Thanakha* is sold at markets in the Shan State and can be bought in Wan Kan Hai, as well as other towns in Northern Thailand, Chiang Mai included; it is sold either as a branch or as a ready-made paste in jars. But because of its omnipresence in Burma, Nang Mya is concerned the Thai guests might see the Shan kids as suddenly less Shan and more Burmese.

Seng Kham expressed disdain at Nang Mya's insistence that *thanakha* be removed from the children. I saw her frown in annoyance at the comment, and with her characteristic knowing tilt of her head, she made a side comment to Hseng Lün, "So what!? Shan people wear *thanakha* all the time! It doesn't make them Burmese."

Despite the border spaces comprising a special zone where Burmese symbolic elements are able to circulate as part of Shan daily social life, the impending visit of Thai VIPs created a desire by some to present themselves as "pure" Shan, somehow completely uncontaminated by Burmese elements. Where to draw the boundaries? Many forms of ritual performance as well as sartorial styles are related to those in Burma as well as China. The Poi Hsang Lawng ritual (detailed in chapter 8) is Brahmanic but incorporates a great deal of styles that are also common to the ritual in Burma. But in Thailand, these same performances and aesthetics are presented as distinctly Shan cultural practices.

As lunchtime approached, the Shan people at the reception hall were told that Khun Maew's group was not supposed to arrive until one. Then three. Then it turned out that they were being shown around by members of the Chinese community on the other side of town. It was not until dusk that the group's parade of SUVs finally pulled up to the event hall. The villagers had set up a Shan *gawng* and *mawng* ensemble to greet the arriving party. Stepping into the event hall, Khun Maew and her group walked over to the reception tables, each lavishly decorated with displays of various Shan handicrafts, traditional clothing, and agricultural products.

The guests, fawning over the cloth and the various items placed on the tables, bought a large number of the wares, dropping money quickly. It was remarkable to witness this flurry: they would grab the textiles with one hand and then toss some banknotes on the table with the other hand. Their motive, it seemed, was to show such appreciation for the goods that they would delightedly pay any price for them.

Hseng Lün, who was staffing the table, however, stood in awkward silence. She did not initially reach for the 1,000 baht bank note Khun Maew dropped on the table without acknowledging her. Hseng Lün was more accustomed to careful discussions with customers to haggle the price of every transaction. But now, this woman just tossed what would be a week's income for many Shan people like it was an empty peanut husk.

The wealthy visitors were ebullient in their appreciation of the environs, the Shan clothing, and the cool mountain climate. With their effusive praise also came effusive suggestions. They encouraged locals to build up their tourism infrastructure and to always wear Shan traditional clothing.[6] In her talk to the community, Khun Maew told the people at Wan Kan Hai that they did not need to migrate to the city. In fact, if they collaborated and sold their organic produce through her new scheme, they would have enough income. She iterated Thai king Bhumibol's plan for *sethakit pho piang*, or "sufficiency economy."

In her speech to the villagers, Khun Maew explained the goals of Planet Preservation. She told them that the NGO was a foundation with combined sponsorship from both state and private interests and was concerned with agricultural development, ecology, and looking after the planet. The group had projects in a number of politically sensitive areas, including border areas and the deep south. Planet Preservation did demonstrate commitment to Wan Kan Hai by constructing a new water reservoir tank for villagers' use. Nearly all of the visitors in the Planet Preservation team were from Bangkok, with the exception of a few from Chiang Mai. Their group had a videographer recording the visit, especially focusing on Khun Maew and her speech.

Later, Yee Thip, who was the most vocal member of the Wan Kan Hai community to express skepticism about Khun Maew and her entourage, offered further comment when I asked him what he thought following the visit: "Here they are, coming to our village in *paen khon ruay*, 'rich people's plan' [*he interjects in Thai*] just looking around, and telling us to cooperate with their expert plan like it will be so good for us. Yeah, they mention the king's *sethakit pho piang*, 'sufficiency economy.' We need enough to survive, but Khun Maew, isn't she from one of the richest families in Thailand? Is that her 'sufficiency economy?'" Despite this skepticism, as well as that which he voiced at the town hall meeting, Yee Thip still collaborated and talked with the people from Planet Preservation. He had a degree from the University of Mandalay, worked in the SURA bureaucracy for years, and was fluent in Thai. His literacy, experience in political organizing, and language skills made him a useful contact for Khun Maew and her elite group, none of whom was conversant in the Shan language. In this sense, more than a culture broker, Yee Thip might have been positioning himself as a local "fixer" for Khun Maew and Planet Preservation. He was not just explaining the Shan context for the visitors but was also helping them implement their plans. Yee Thip's involvement stemmed from a desire to ensure that Wan Kan Hai would be treated fairly. But to what extent would Khun Maew's team trust the opinions and suggestions of Yee Thip or defer to their own experts?

AN ORGANIC HARVEST

Just a few weeks after the first visit of Khun Maew and her entourage, after supper Ko Siew paid Aung Myo a visit at his home. Ko Siew was a short, pock-marked, rough-looking, chain-smoking man (who smelled like it) in his early fifties and a member of the Chinese community on the other side of Wan Kan Hai. Aung Myo brought out the kettle and gave his guest hot tea as they sat in red plastic armchairs and talked together on the veranda. Ko Siew knew of Aung Myo's modest lychee fruit orchard and brought up the subject. He told Aung Myo that the fruit would fetch a handsome price if he were to sell it as certified organic produce in Bangkok. Ko Siew iterated that selling it locally, or even in Chiang Mai, would not be nearly as lucrative. Ko Siew also said that he had a connection who could help

Aung Myo get his produce to a dealer in Bangkok. He said he would arrange everything, including the transportation of the crates of harvested lychees to Bangkok. All Aung Myo needed to do was harvest the fruit and load it onto the truck.

A few days later, Aung Myo recruited Hang Mit and Nang Oo, the young couple who lived around the back of their home, to help with the harvest. They needed to complete the picking work in one day and then load it all in a truck to send to Bangkok. Nang Oo was not accustomed to this kind of labor but happily agreed to join, not just to do a favor for a friend but also to earn a bit of cash. So Aung Myo and his two young helpers set out to pluck all the ripe fruit from the trees, pulling bunches of lychees from the tree branches.

Not long after their work was complete and a few dozen plastic stackable crates were filled with the fruit, Ko Siew and a truck driver came along to pick up the wares. He also had several reels of yellow plastic tape with a Thai symbol and a "certified organic" icon printed all along the length of it. Ko Siew handed Aung Myo a reel and told him to wrap the boxes with the tape. Then, they finished loading the truck. Aung Myo had never met the driver before; Ko Siew and the driver spoke in Chinese.

That evening, exhausted from the long day's work, Aung Myo chuckled and commented that Nang Oo's fingers must be sore from all this work. As promised, Aung Myo paid his young helpers 200 baht each for their day's work.

Two days later, Ko Siew paid Aung Myo a visit at his house. They sat drinking tea, and Aung Myo waited to find out how much they were able to sell the lychee harvest for in Bangkok. During their conversation, Ko Siew received a call on his mobile phone. It was the driver, who said that the market in Bangkok would not buy Aung Myo's lychee harvest because it was *suk guen pai*, or "overripe." According to Ko Siew, Aung Myo would need to pay for return transport to get the lychee harvest back to Wan Kan Hai. Ko Siew passed his phone over to Aung Myo so he could talk with the driver directly. They spoke Thai together. Aung Myo was exasperated, asking, "How can the lychees be overripe? We just harvested them!" There was a long pause while the driver was speaking back from the other side. Then Aung Myo responded, "If you want money to transport the lychees all the way back here, we'll have loss on both sides. Instead, help us out and just dump them somewhere."

As far as we knew, the driver agreed to dump the produce, and Aung Myo ended up losing money on the cost of the driver (via Ko Siew) as well as the wages he paid to Nang Oo and her husband for their harvesting work, not to mention the lost income from the entire lychee crop. There was no evidence that the lychees were overripe, and in this case, Aung Myo didn't have a leg to stand on, since everything was organized by Ko Siew.

A few days later, Aung Myo was chatting with the guys at the motorbike taxi stand about the predicament. Sai Lek almost guffawed, "*Oh lo lo lo lo*, you did business with Ko Siew? Nobody over on the Chinese side of town works with him. He's no good."

"I don't understand how it could happen! We're from the same village!" retorted Aung Myo the following week during the morning meal. (Aung Myo's frustration also stemmed from his own foolishness: not to get the lowdown on Ko Siew from the usual town gossip machine before agreeing to sell his lychee harvest through him.) This deal gone bad may have been the first shipment of "certified organic" produce to leave Wan Kan Hai.

Planet Preservation's Persistence

Khun Maew and her entourage of experts from Bangkok continued to visit Wan Kan Hai on and off for the next few years. With each visit, though, the plans were met with decreasing enthusiasm on the part of the locals in Wan Kan Hai. As before, some of the villagers were more willing than others to cooperate with Planet Preservation. But others who had participated before simply did not show up, and fewer and fewer dressed up in their *hko Tai* Shan finery to meet the entourage of SUVs. Nang Mya explained this decreased interest: "OK, so they want us to plant leafy vegetables for their organization. But last year, they said that if we all plant it, it would flood the market. But then, if we don't do it at all, they'll think we aren't cooperating. What are we supposed to do, then?"

Another one of Planet Preservation's projects was to rent a rice paddy for collective agriculture, and according to Wan Kan Hai villagers, part of the crop would be remitted to Planet Preservation. Some of the Wan Kan Hai villagers did not see how this project would differ from capitalist share-cropping and were not enthusiastic about participating.

In another visit, Khun Maew and her entourage brought a video crew, and she gave a speech about encouraging organic food production in the area. As part of the project, Shan villagers from Wan Kan Hai lined up, and she presented each of them with small sacks of a certain species of seed. A few paces in front of Khun Maew was a man shooting video of this seed presentation. After Khun Maew and her entourage had left, more villagers were expressing skepticism about the NGO and its grand plans. Some cynically commented that the seeds were a meager gift for such a rich entourage to give to poor villagers. Sai Lek at the motorbike taxi stand commented about her rhetoric for poverty alleviation. The environmental aspects sounded great, he said, but the most desperately poor would not want to work with Khun Maew and her project because they are living hand to mouth, or as the Shan say, "search in the morning, eat in the evening" (ႁႃလဝ်ႈၵိၼ်ၶမ်ႈ). If they stopped doing what they were doing to try a new plan, what would they eat that night? What if her marketing plan didn't work? Khun Maew could afford *to choose* to take risks. The impoverished Shans would not voluntarily take such risks, though gambling is another story, ironically. For the other villagers who were more optimistic about the project at first, their interest tapered off over the subsequent two years, as did Preservation Planet's visits to the area.

A couple of weeks after one of the subsequent Planet Preservation visits, some of the guys at the motorcycle taxi stand were chatting about Khun Maew and her entourage. One of them brought up the Burmese expression *ba-ze hma hpaya hpaya, lek hma kaya kaya* (ပါးစပ်မှာဘုရာဘုရာ။ လက်မှာကရာကရာ။, the mouth talks holy, the hands dance around), a sonorous and graphic way to describe someone who is two-faced. Sai Lek interjected, reminding the group (and perhaps for my benefit as well) that the Shan equivalent of this expression is *hsop sem kon hsom* (သူပ်းဢိမ်းၵွၼ်းသူမ်း, sweet mouth, sour ass). Then the conversation shifted to various instances when people had been swindled or when they suffered after hearing about a deal that was too good to be true, like that of Ko Siew and his plan to "help" Aung Myo sell his lychee crop in Bangkok. Although Ko Siew was Chinese and Aung Myo was Shan, there was very little mention of an ethnic network, other than Ko Siew talking about his business contacts in Bangkok who could sell the lychees as certified organic. There was certainly a symbolic cachet of organic food being sold in a supermarket, instead of the usual "fresh market" in Southeast Asia where produce is often sold by its farmers or close family members.

Moving from disappointment with Khun Maew's group, conversation returned to a familiar trope: Shan people who were struggling but were themselves to blame. Drinkers and gamblers were frequently chided for keeping the Shan down; these difficulties were articulated in Buddhist terms, as these constitute transgressions of the five *sila* (precepts) to which every

Theravada Buddhist is bound. Seng Kham's frequent source of frustration was her younger sister, who lived with her husband and kids in a cheaply built bamboo house twenty-five meters from Seng Kham. They technically did not have their own address and house registry. For electricity, they ran an extension cable from Seng Kham's household electricity. The husband, despite having the relative advantage of Thai citizenship, instead was the source of strife, because of his proclivity for drinking and gambling. From Seng Kham's house, one could hear the couple's frequent squabbles; Seng Kham was often frustrated, feeling obliged to help her sister but unable to intervene or discipline the drunk, gambling husband.

Another major trope was the perceived lack of unity and common direction among Shan people; people do not help each other the way they used to, some would say. Kyaw Myint once contrasted Shan unity (or the lack thereof) with that of the Chinese. As he said, "Look at the difference between ants and bees when they are in trouble. The bees are the Shan. If you set a fire under a beehive, the bees all rush around buzzing and flying in all directions, *zuh zuh zuh zuh zuh* [*he waved his arms about as he onomatopoetically imitated the sound of bees flying all about*]. The ants, if their nest is in trouble, they get organized in a line and get all the eggs out."[7]

Arguably, the stereotype of the Chinese with their reputation of being organized and shrewd businesspeople (among the Shan, anyway) could have had a role in Aung Myo's decision to work with Ko Siew; Aung Myo himself was from a Chinese family near Panglong and could speak the language fairly well, though his primary language was Shan, followed by Thai. It was illuminating to learn later that Ko Siew had cheated people in the Chinese community, not just Shan people.

The last visit of the Planet Preservation caravan took place in 2011. Khun Maew and her entourage pulled up to the village and met a group of Shan villagers in the gathering hall. Part of the plan this time was to give the village headman a seed grant of 100,000 baht (at the time about US$3,300). After a welcoming ceremony, Khun Maew's entourage stood in a U-shape when she presented a white envelope to Sai Möng Mao, the village headman of Wan Kan Hai. They both looked to the camera while each held a side of the envelope.

After the photo-op was complete, Sai Möng Mao started to put the envelope into his sack for safe keeping. Khun Maew interjected, "Oh, the money's not in the envelope. We just needed that to take the picture. We will do an electronic bank transfer to deposit the money in your account later. It's safer that way."

Years later, the villagers had yet to receive either a bank transfer or a return visit from the entourage of Planet Preservation.

CONCLUSION

For the Thai nation, the hills of the North represent a zone where Thais can go to experience cultural difference without crossing an international boundary. If they consider themselves cosmopolitans, these tourists may see their position as one that embraces cultural diversity and as adoptive of a stance that is reflexive and metacultural in response to divergent cultural experiences (Featherstone 1990, 9). There is an aspect of prestige to the stance, and cultural tourists (and anthropologists alike) may flaunt their cosmopolitanism on their sleeve or as a scarf, much like a designer brand. But being cosmopolitan is not the exclusive preserve of the urban, rich, or educated. The highlands of Myanmar have also been characterized as cosmopolitan spaces for the kinds of social interaction, diversity and, indeed, cultural crossroads that they present (Robinne 2020, 291).

However, whether one has an articulate stance as reflexive and metacultural, or is an "everyday" cosmopolitan such as a local trader or barber who is comfortable working with people from varied cultural backgrounds, there is still an important difference in relative privilege and agency in one's "cosmopolitan-ness." It matters whether one's cultural flexibility is through privilege or through necessity for survival. Refugees, diasporic peoples, migrants, and exiles "represent the spirit of the cosmopolitical community" (Breckenridge et al. 2002, 6). Thus the penalties are greater for the vulnerable Shan if they offend the Thais (particularly the rich and powerful) than the other way around. But as a zone that can incubate a diasporic sense of "Shan-ness," Thailand is not a neutral territory, some sort of blank slate and welcoming place for Shan people to manifest whatever forms of cultural identity that they had suppressed when under the authority of the Myanmar military government.

There is an ongoing trope among Shan that iterates the fear that they will disappear and be forgotten. Their decades-long and never-ending war in Myanmar and the difficulties they face as migrant nonrefugees trying to survive in Thailand offer ample evidence to support the fear. When they do have others taking an interest in them as Shan—such as the tourists interested in the high school kids' dance—there often is genuine gratitude; it is nice, after all, to have others recognize and even enjoy some things that are your cultural pride.

However, the cultural performances and ethnic intimacy create more of a Thai fantasy of *phinongkan* siblinghood than a lived reality for Shan people in Thailand. Recall Seng Kham's comment from the beginning of this chapter: "How many times have you seen the Thai people come visit us here and smiiiiilleee and tell us we're *phinongkan* [siblings], only to treat us worse than dirt when we look for jobs, or even just speak their language with a bit of an accent?"

When there is little at stake, or there is a social or political advantage to presenting a happy image of ethnic unity, then that picture will be deployed. It is not always done with devious intent; in some cases, it could be genuine and earnest. The Thais can further iterate their privilege with the Shan through expecting performances of Shan-ness, with part of the display being the underlying ethos of presenting themselves as grateful subjects of the Thai state.

An illusion of ethnic closeness can sometimes be used to create an artificial rapport for business to take place, one on which Khun Sa sought to capitalize decades earlier. But again, as we see when comparing the experiences of Shan migrant workers in Chiang Mai with the experiences of Shan villagers discussing their interactions with Thais, this is situational as well. Where and when politically and economically powerful Thais want to emphasize difference (or similarity) depends not only on the context of the interaction but also on the perceived class and social difference at the personal level.

Like Phibun Songkram's use of pan-Tai racial ideology to try to incorporate Tai peoples residing in European colonial territories in Southeast Asia, Khun Maew's entourage was seeking to bring new forms of neoliberal capitalism to the periphery and to sugarcoat it with a rhetoric of *phinongkan* sibling-hood. For many Shan, this talk is not so sweet to their ears and is only made increasingly sour by their enduring poverty in the face of Khun Maew's wealthy entourage. The frequent presence of videographers and promotional brochures for Planet Preservation indicated a potential public relations angle to these activities, perhaps having value as a demonstration of corporate social responsibility for the powerful Thai conglomerate.

However, the notion of *phinongkan* Thai/Tai siblinghood is still meaningful for Shans themselves. As Aung Myo once explained, "*Phinongkan* 'brethren' is what the Thais say is the relationship between themselves and the Shan. We're brothers because we're both Buddhist, our languages are similar, and we originally migrated from the same place in China. But we went our separate ways later."

"But in Thai, we Shan are the Tai-yai great Thai, and they are the Thai-noi the lesser Thai, so who's the older brother and who's the younger brother then?[8] Isn't it obvious we're greater?" responded Seng Kham.

Even though some Shan people understood the notion of Tai-yai as being the greater, or the older sibling, they would not necessarily remind powerful Sino-Thai Bangkokians such as Khun Maew of that angle on the issue. The Tai/Thai migration narrative almost willfully ignores exogamy along the way, or that non-Tai speaking groups would become part of multilingual Tai towns. Pointing out that Seng Kham's Chinese father only started learning the Shan language in his teens, or that Khun Maew is third-generation Chinese, shows the irony of iterating an ancient migration story in which none of their actual ancestors would have participated (even if it were true).

Nevertheless, the territorialized nation-state of Thailand is an everyday reality, and despite their struggles to get by, or to adjust their comportment to certain Thai expectations of Thai-ness (or Shan-ness), occasionally Shan will take the stance that they are guests in "their" house, meaning the Thais' house. Opinion is not universal regarding the relationship between Shan and Thais, and in reference to the more than a hundred thousand refugees from Myanmar in various camps in Thailand, Nang Mya described the Thai government as generous in allowing all the people to stay. Her opinion about Thailand's refugee policy (or lack thereof) was likely tempered by her memory of various clearance operations in Myanmar, particularly the mass displacement of more than three hundred thousand people in Shan State in the late 1990s. In this sense, even when they are guests in their siblings' land, Shan people intuitively know that it is not the same as being in their homeland.

7

Rockin' in the Shan World

As NIGHT FALLS on the mountainous borderland town of Wan Kan
Hai, in Mattana's family compound just up the road from the motorbike
taxi stand and the former Shan United Revolutionary Army hospital, the
flicker of florescent lights pulses through the cracks of a cinderblock room.
This structure is ostensibly a study, but the desk and bookshelves have been
moved to one side. On the opposite wall, two sets of amplifiers and a drum
kit face each other, and a few young men sit together on a bench. Mike and
music stands are in the center of the concrete floor. On the inside of the
metal sliding door are chalk-written the five Buddhist precepts, scrawled in
the Shan script.

This room serves as the practice space for a neighborhood pickup band,
and a dozen villagers are crowded inside. Mattana, now in her fifties, and
Nang Oo, in her midtwenties, chat as they flip through the worn pages of
a songbook. In a red sling on Nang Oo's back sleeps a toddler boy, oblivi-
ous to what is going on around him. Even when his mother is singing a
rock song on the mike, he sleeps.

The teenager on drums not so subtly demonstrates his eagerness to get
started by tapping his drumsticks on the rim of the snare drum. After listen-
ing to a bit too much unsolicited advice about the correct rhythm of a song,
another young man divests himself of a guitar, handing the instrument to
his older advice-giver, taking care not to entangle its cable in the top of the
music stand. This casual band's repertoire intermingles Shan, Thai, and
Burmese language rock songs with only minutes in between as they switch

instruments and regroup. When the songs boom, they spill their reverbera-
tions down the mountainside, penetrating the walls of the teak, bamboo,
and concrete homes throughout the area.

Here in Wan Kan Hai, playing in or simply attending the practice sessions of the pickup band is a regular activity, often a nightly one for a core
group of rock music aficionados. The band is entirely informal, seldom
playing with the objective to perform, even though some of its participants
have played and sung at local events and fairs. Mattana is the homeowner,
letting friends and neighbors use the space to play music together. Former
and current Shan insurgents, their friends, and their families come to socialize, sing songs, and have fun. Some don't play instruments or even sing.
But for the music fans, there is something sublimely exciting about "plug-
ging in" to an electric amplification system and broadcasting sounds out
into the night; the music itself travels as far as its sound waves will take it
across the mountain ridge. Anticipating this reverb effect seems intrinsic to
the rock musician.

Although the repertoire of the band shifts according to the preferences,
language skills, and caprice of those players who happen to join the band
on a particular evening, one specific pantheon is always played: the songs
of the legendary Shan resistance songwriter Sai Mu, whose biography was
discussed in chapter 3. A perpetual favorite is Sai Mu's catchy hit song "Wan
Tai Te Lawt Le'o" (ဝၣ်းတႆးတေလွတ်ႈလိဝ်ႇ, "The Day Shan Will Be Independent").[1] There is often so much enthusiasm for playing the song that after
the band has completed the verses and chorus, they will repeat the chorus
ad infinitum, thus rattling the contents of immediate neighbors' refrigera-
tors and competing with the sounds of household television sets within a
half kilometer of the little room:

> The day Shan are united!!! . . . The day Shan will be independent!!! . . . The
> day Shan love one another!!! . . . The day Shan will be free!!! . . . The day
> Shan are united!!! . . . The day Shan will be independent!!! . . . The day Shan
> love one another!!! . . . The day Shan will be free!!! . . . The day Shan are
> united!!! . . . The day Shan will be independent!!! . . . The day Shan love one
> another!!! . . . The day Shan will be free!!!

"The Day Shan Will Be Independent" is an easy song to play. It has a
straightforward rock beat, and the guitar part only requires three chords
(A-D-E). Undoubtedly the ease of learning to play and the catchy chorus

add to the appeal and accessibility of the song for the amateur musician. On one evening, when I am at Seng Kham and Aung Myo's house, a few houses down from Mattana's, we chat, but the music echoes in the background. With further repetition of the chorus to "The Day Shan Will Be Independent," Aung Myo chuckles while repeating the line, and asks rhetorically, "They're never going to get that day, are they? Will it ever come?"

Aung Myo does not see Shan liberation on the immediate horizon, but the continued popularity of the song hints at the idea that the Shan nation might not be so far away, and singing the song serves to keep the desire for an independent Shanland alive among Shan migrants. It also presents a positive, even jovial image of the deferred nation-state. The fact that the group of amateur musicians works together to produce the song could also be seen as a microcosm of greater Shan unity, or a collective vision for the future Shan nation. A tacitly understood political point, however, is the fact that they are playing these songs on the Thai side of the border. When they lived in the Shan State in Myanmar, they might very well have faced arrest for playing such a politically charged song.[2]

When I first became interested in this practice band, Seng Kham took me to meet Mattana. It was only my second or third day in Wan Kan Hai, and I had heard the echoes of the music the night before. Mattana was friendly and encouraging, and she perked up when I told her I liked to play popular music, too, and had played bass in bands off and on since high school. Mattana's response was simple: "When you hear the sound, come on over!"

It was through two years of intermittent band practice that I came to know various people in the community and their relationships with music. Discovering the variety of musical genres that these Shan migrants to Thailand enjoyed, Burmese popular music in particular, allowed me to use music—talking about it with interlocutors, seeing how people made music, and playing in the band with them—as a method to learn about other aspects of peoples' lives and personal histories. Playing music can elicit qualitative aspects of Shan pasts in Shanland, and in Myanmar, and can demonstrate mastery of—and affection for—another cultural code: Burmese rock music and the Burmese language.

Unlike the cultural performances detailed in the previous chapter, the sessions at Mattana's shed were not played to the expectation of others or strangers; they were not specifically performances of Shan-ness per se, although Shan songs were certainly a key part of the music jam sessions. The variety of music played tapped into broader interests and histories and comprised a form of socializing that is multilingual, even cosmopolitan. Therefore, the first section of this chapter explores the musical practices and preferences of Shan people in Wan Kan Hai, situating it in their everyday lives, getting to know people and their music. Attention is paid to the ways people approach music, whether as a hobby to cultivate or as a pleasant and nostalgic way to connect to happier times. From experiences in the jam sessions at Mattana's shed, I also look at the sociality of the rock band and consider how Shan migrants use their musical knowledge as a way to express cosmopolitan connections. Here I consider my own embeddedness and how my presence and participation could evoke different forms of musical performance and cultures.

Finally, public performances of Shan music, in the form of social visits between villages and festival-style concerts, offer evidence of how Shan-language music has found itself a key niche for expressive culture among Shan people in the borderlands. Although it is fleeting, amplified music presents the band with the chance to assert a kind of sovereignty, connecting their sounds and their message to all within earshot. Practicing and jamming popular songs offers a way for Shan people to unite in a form of sound production, and one that expresses a kind of social self that borrows from but also appropriates ideas beyond nations and national cultures as well.

LOCAL REPAIRMAN BY DAY, SHAN ROCKER BY NIGHT

Hang Mit, age thirty-three in 2005, was born in Taunggyi, Shan State, but has spent nearly all his adult life in Thailand, engaging in construction work, itinerant farm work, and electronics repair. He is completely fluent and literate in both Shan and Thai languages as well as Burmese. He only speaks Burmese reluctantly, perhaps because he is less confident in that language. In Wan Kan Hai, he is the local electronics repairman, fixing everything from VCD players to televisions, to household circuit breakers, to video game controllers.

Hang Mit lives with his wife, Nang Oo, and their toddler son in a humble home. It is a single cinderblock room underneath a bigger corrugated metal roof. The structure is atop a rough concrete floor. Inside their one-room home, there is plastic matting and one bed. There is a behemoth tube television, replete with a receiver, VCD player, VCR, and massive speaker system, all engineered and assembled by Hang Mit. The entertainment system is the largest object in the room, second only to the bed.

The small family uses the outhouse of the adjacent home for their toilet, and there is a bathroom with a reservoir tank for taking splash baths as well. They were able to build this cinderblock room on land owned by relatives who were already well established in Wan Kan Hai. This kind of living arrangement is typical among Shan communities, where relatives from the Shan State migrate to Thailand and build these types of residences adjacent to contacts who have been in the country longer. It is common to see makeshift electric powerlines strung from one house across to a nearby shack, like that of Seng Kham's sister. Many other extended families share close living quarters, and typical as well, some may not seem related but are living in the same household or connected by a shared electric bill.

At Hang Mit and Nang Oo's home, on the veranda area, there is evidence of at least a dozen electronic and mechanical repair projects in progress and various other parts and pieces that I could not identify. It was a veritable appliance hospital of sorts, with a stack of television chassis in one corner, a gutted motorbike in the other, and whatever project du jour in the center of the work area. When I visited, it was a disemboweled VCD player on the metal folding table in the middle of the veranda, with a soldering iron on a stand to its right and an open Burmese-language electronics repair book behind.

Visiting various homes in Wan Kan Hai, I sometimes saw Hang Mit engaged in a repair project, such as running a lead to extend an electric power outlet, taking apart a circuit breaker, or performing various other electronic wiring projects that needed tending to. I wondered how he gained all this technical knowledge about home electronics and mechanics, especially since electric utility service is so spotty in Shan State. Far fewer people had electricity in their homes, let alone elaborate entertainment systems. When I asked him about this, he quickly corrected me: "What? Burma is the best place for learning about wiring! The government service is so inconsistent that you learn to light a home on a truck battery, or to have a step-down transformer to adjust the current. When government electricity works, you have to be more careful about surges, too. That teaches you more than here, where things are just replaced, and people don't know how to make do." And making do was clearly something Hang Mit thrived at. He had a stack of Burmese-language electronics repair textbooks in the corner of their cinderblock home. He had no formal training in electrical engineering or electronics repair, but everyone I talked to praised his skills. In addition, and through spending time with Hang Mit and being there when he installed an extension for a new clothes washer at Seng Kham's house, I observed that he had a careful, calm knack for explaining to other villagers what repairs they needed or why he could not fix something to do what they wanted. I'm not sure what the electrician's equivalent to a doctor's good "bedside manner" would be, but this was undoubtedly part of the reason that Hang Mit was Wan Kan Hai's "Mr. Fix-It."

When he talked about electronics or technical concepts with others, Hang Mit rarely used technical language (though he would have certainly learned plenty from the repair books). Instead, he often employed accessible metaphors. For example, in 2005 I was curious why he was still doing VCR repairs. By that year, it seemed that the VCD disk had all but completely replaced the videotape as the platform of choice for home video consumption. New (and rental) VHS tapes were gone from the shelves of the shops, making way for the much cheaper and more sophisticated VCDs and DVDs.

Hang Mit told me that it was important to keep the VCRs working for two main reasons: it's not possible to buy new ones anymore, and a lot of people still have tapes that they want to watch. (An additional tacit reason, too, was that Hang Mit still had his knowledge of VCR repair.) And, he added, there are certain advantages to the older magnetic format: "When you put in a disk, and the VCD has a flaw, or a problem somewhere on the disk, the whole thing stops, you don't get to watch anything. But the videotape, there might be a part that you won't see, you'll miss a bit, but the tape continues to walk." Perhaps there is a verb in Shan to describe the reeling of magnetic VHS tape from one spool to the other, but Hang Mit's use of the term "walk" described it quite well. How he was paid for his repair work was often up to negotiation, and the remuneration process for Hang Mit's work often carried social meaning beyond direct pay for services rendered.

One afternoon, when Hang Mit and I were talking over a cold glass of Coke at the table in front of his home, a pair of young boys—probably ten and eleven years old—from up the road stopped by, asking for their video game controller. They had brought it to Hang Mit a few days earlier for repair. From the conversation between Hang Mit and the boys, I learned that one of the boys had thrown the controller on the floor, thus damaging the circuitry for some of the buttons. We can presume he did this out of frustration from having lost at one of the games. Hang Mit told the boys that he had repaired the controller, and it worked fine, but he would not give it back unless they asked their mother for his repair fee. The two boys looked down at the ground, avoiding eye contact for a heavy pause, and kicked the dirt around to dally. But one eventually said "OK," and they left Hang Mit's work area.

"If I repair it for them, and just give it back, they will keep breaking it. I'll be stuck doing this work for free," explained Hang Mit, with an authority no doubt from repeated experience with these boys. The boys' mother was a family friend of Hang Mit's; he could very well have done the fix for free as a favor. I noticed that for many of his friends, he did minor repairs for free. "Now they have to face their mother's reprimands in order to get the money to pay me for the repair. I charge half of what the electronics repair shop in town charges, but these kids, of course, don't think about that. They should take better care of their things."

The nominal fee to repair the video game controller was more didactic than essential. If Hang Mit returned the fixed controller before collecting the fee, the boys wouldn't tell their mother that the controller had been broken. Thus, demanding payment took the social moment farther from the relationship between Hang Mit and the neighborhood boys, but to the relationship between the boys and their mother. While Hang Mit might be able to scold the boys for not looking after their things, it would not have the same force or authority as a mother reluctant to pay for repairs because of the boys' carelessness.

In addition to home electronics and machinery, there were also three gutted guitars in Hang Mit's work area. He built his own acoustic guitar and fitted it with a pickup for an electric amplification system. Hang Mit had an extensive cassette tape and VCD collection of Sai Mu's songs and recorded performances. He loved to describe the thematic content of the song lyrics as well.

When I stopped by for a social visit, I would sometimes find Hang Mit sitting at the table on the veranda, with a guitar in his lap and a small cassette player in front of him on the table. This was his way of practicing Sai Mu guitar solos. He would fast-forward the tape to the beginning of a guitar solo portion of a song, listen to it, try playing it back himself, then rewind the tape and listen again. He would repeat the process until he had got the solo "down." On several occasions at the evening jam sessions at Mattana's place, Hang Mit would get the band to play the same song he had been practicing earlier in the day, so that he could try out the solo with a live backup rather than just the cassette player.

Hang Mit was quite skilled at the guitar, though he never joined a formal band or performed at any festival. He saw the skill as a hobby and as something to do with friends. Many evenings he would turn up at Mattana's house and simply socialize with other people in attendance, not stepping up to play or sing any song. His wife, Nang Oo, as I would learn, was much more enthusiastic about singing at these informal jam sessions.

When I first met Hang Mit and Nang Oo in 2004, they had been married for about four years, and their son was two years old at the time. Nang Oo was twenty-six and had grown up in Panglong, Shan State, the town made famous by the Panglong Agreement. She moved to Wan Kan Hai because of her marriage to Hang Mit. Nang Oo recalled that her mother was reluctant to let her go to Thailand; her mother feared her daughter would be forced into prostitution. She would never do such work, she assured her mother. When I met her, her time was largely devoted to looking after their son, tending to two hogs in a pen behind the cinderblock home, and teaching children at a local orphanage run by a Catholic nun, Maesha "Teacher" Mary.

Nang Oo was never a Shan militant herself but supported the idea of Shan independence. As she later told me, it was only after she moved to Wan Kan Hai that she learned to read the Shan script and started to sing various songs in the Shan language. She did not really care for Sai Mu's songs until she got together with Hang Mit. Nang Oo has a bachelor's degree in zoology from Taunggyi University, Southern Shan State. On one occasion, when I asked Nang Oo about her interest in zoology, Hang Mit interjected and explained, "Oh, Nang Oo doesn't like to study very hard, and zoology was appropriate for her because all she had to do was look at pictures of animals." In the public university system in Myanmar, like that of Thailand, one's major sometimes is not related to one's interests or career ambition. Entrance exam scores determine the range of options available to a student, and once the student starts school, even after a successful year, changing majors is not possible.

In spite of her husband's teasing, Nang Oo lit up with enthusiasm when she told me about her years at Taunggyi University. She started to talk about the wonderful friendship she had with five women in her class. "Five best friends?" I asked. She smiled and laughed in response and explained a bit more.

Every day, or so it seemed, this group of six students would go out together, visit each other's houses, snack together, sing songs, or go to tea shops. They might also go on an afternoon excursion to Inle Lake or the temples surrounding Taunggyi, just to spent time together. They were in the same major, though Nang Oo neglected to mention them studying together. As Nang Oo told me, "Every single day, the six of us, we would go here, six people, we'd go there, it was always us six people."

In contrast to her present life, it made sense that Nang Oo would be nostalgic for her university days. She jokingly referred to her daily chore of chopping up banana trunk to feed the pigs as "zoology." She and Hang Mit also raised several chickens for eggs and meat. Lacking the travel documentation to work in Chiang Mai, her sources of income were the cash she received teaching as well as her earnings from the occasional child-minding that she did for neighbors. She later did sewing piece work. Hang Mit had his income, too, but neither could truly depend on a regular salary, so some periods were leaner than others. When the pigs Nang Oo fed daily were fat enough to go to market, later that day Aung Myo broke the news of the sale to me, saying that "Hang Mit and Nang Oo are rich today!" They sold the pigs for 3,000 baht each. So having the cash equivalent of US$200 drew the moniker of "rich" in this village. Then again, this was the equivalent of a month's pay for a Shan construction worker in Chiang Mai.

As I got to know Nang Oo, and became better acquainted with her musical tastes, the various artists and genres that she liked, I realized that her most intense interest in music lay in Burmese popular songs. At her home one day, she handed me a notebook; it was her personal book of favorite songs. As I scanned through the pages of carefully handwritten Burmese song lyrics, she commented rhetorically, "The Burmese songs are pretty, aren't they [kwam Man hang li na]?"

Impressed by her meticulously kept songbook, but seeing only words on the page and not knowing their tunes, I handed the book back to Nang Oo and asked her to sing one of her favorites. Responding with a smile, she thumbed through the book, found her choice, and sat up in her chair to project her voice as she started the first verse of the song. The tune was oddly familiar, but I couldn't quite put my finger on it until she got to the chorus, when I was suddenly flooded with more than the elation of the winning contestant in the bonus round of *Name That Tune*. The chorus is none other than the melody of the one-hit wonder "I've Never Been to Me" by Charlene, which was originally released in 1977, but a 1982 rerelease of the song went all the way to number three in the United States and number one in Britain, and then it went on to become a camp anthem in Britain and Australia. It was later released as a Japanese popular song, "Love Is All" by Megumi Shiina, in 1993.

But Nang Oo was not singing "I've Never Been to Me," even though the melody was the same as the Charlene hit. Instead, she was singing "Ma Ne Maung" (မနဲမောင်, "Elder Sister and Younger Brother"), a hit by the Burmese popular singer Nwe Yin Win. This song is an example of the pervasive Burmese popular music genre *copy thachin*, or "copy song." *Copy thachin* comprises renditions of international popular songs that have been refitted with Burmese lyrics penned by Burmese poets and recorded by Burmese popular recording artists. It emerged as a major part of the popular music industry as a result of the Ne Win government's ban on imports. Through these Burmese-made renditions, musicians (and fans) could keep up with international trends. *Copy thachin* was institutionalized in Burma and has taken on a cultural life of its own, with popular singers and bands followed by their adoring fans. The genre, however, is not without its controversy in contemporary Myanmar, but it has been a mainstay for musicians and fans for decades (Ferguson 2013, 2016).

After Nang Oo finished singing "Ma Ne Maung," I applauded and thanked her. Then I asked more about the song, what it meant, and why she liked it. She explained it was true to the meaning of the Burmese lyrics: it is a song sung from the perspective of an older woman, singing to a younger man (Maung, "little brother" or younger guy), telling him a bit about her history, and encouraging him to find his own way and to discover love on his own. I was curious if Nang Oo identified with the song in any way, wondering if there was a meaningful connection she made with the lyrics. She said, "Sure! I have a younger brother!"

But her story about her younger brother had nothing to do with themes of nostalgia or affection as depicted in the Burmese song. Nang Oo was the middle child in a family of three back in Panglong, and as she told me more about her younger brother, I could sense her feeling of frustration with the guy. Nang Oo's parents had bought three plots of land back in the Shan State as an investment for each of their three children, but the brother had failed to become financially independent and continued to sponge off their parents. This was out of the young man's own laziness, insisted Nang Oo. His life was very comfortable back in Panglong, she indicated, because their parents indulged his every whim. Nang Oo explained that the song's feelings had nothing to do with her family, but that she liked the song because the melody was pretty, and she had long been a fan of its singer, Nwe Yin Win.

Although the song "Ma Ne Maung" was a *copy thachin* rendition of "I've Never Been to Me," it was clear that the new Burmese thematic content had very little in common with the English-language original, and Nang Oo had her own reasons for liking the song. Even though Nang Oo knew that the song was a *copy thachin* cover of a Western popular song, her appreciation of the song didn't hinge on the international translation but rather had to do with her own affection for Burmese popular singers. This does not mean, however, that Shan people only had an accepting and appreciative stance toward *copy thachin*. Explorations, out of both appreciation and ambivalence toward *copy thachin* as well as other Burmese, Shan, and Thai genres of popular music, were carried out through their reworkings on the concrete floors of the rock jam space in Mattana's compound.

Another serious enthusiast of Shan and Burmese rock music in Wan Kan Hai is Sai Lek. He is a thin man of forty-five years, with dark features and wide, alert eyes. He is a veteran soldier of the Shan United Revolutionary Army and later the Möng Tai Army. Before joining the SURA, Sai Lek was a student at Mandalay University and now is the leader of the local disabled people's association. In the early 1990s, while on a campaign with the MTA, he stepped on an antipersonnel landmine and was nearly killed. His right foot and ankle were blown off entirely, and later the rest of his leg below the knee needed amputation. Now he works in a small workshop making prosthetic limbs for others in need. Although Sai Lek makes full molded limbs, he often chose to wear just a wooden peg leg; perhaps it was lighter and more comfortable than the full prosthetic. I frequently saw him on his motorbike, riding across town, or hanging around the motorbike taxi stand, chatting with the guys there.

In addition to being close friends with the other SURA veterans, Sai Lek was a steadfast participant in village events and present at every Town Hall meeting. He is respected among the community of Shan scholars and independence sympathizers for his articulate understanding of Shan politics and history. Early in my fieldwork at Wan Kan Hai, more than one villager had told me that if I wanted to learn more about Shan political history, I should go talk with Sai Lek. This detailed knowledge could be chalked up to his level of education and extensive experience in the Shan insurgency but also to his curiosity and ability to seek out information. He is a bookworm, with an extensive collection of books, including many

Burmese books about history and political science. Sai Lek's interest in learning and passion for history clearly applied to popular music.

As a student at Mandalay University, Sai Lek was both an avid guitar player and a fan of 1970s Burmese rock music, called "Stereo" songs. He said that after joining the Shan United Revolutionary Army, during the long stints at camps, playing and singing songs with the other soldiers was the main form of nightly entertainment, especially once it was too dark to read; often the trade through the border checkpoint from Shan State would contain cassette tapes and song books, precious items for Sai Lek, as joining the Shan political movement had partially cut him off from the latest releases of his favorite musicians or stage shows in Mandalay.

Sai Lek was a veritable jukebox of Burmese rock songs from the 1970s and 1980s, and it seemed that he could play song after song for hours without repeating a single tune. He was a regular participant at the jam sessions at Mattana's house but would only play a few songs after others played. He respected the casual nature of the pickup band and let others have their chance on the guitar and at the mike. He also liked the chance to chat with his friends.

Sai Lek, with his encyclopedic knowledge of Burmese popular songs, would play guitar and sing songs that were his old favorites. He frequently asked me to accompany him on bass, and for those songs, I would follow his cues. He would play, and I would keep in step with his barre chords, playing the bass part in line with what he was playing, or watching his left wrist start to curl upward so I could anticipate that he would play C, or the back of the hand up and the ring finger out in a way that suggested the next chord would be a D, and so on. The more songs we played together, the easier it was to play bass to his guitar, not just from recognizing tunes, but also knowing some of his personal quirks to playing. Different people will have different "go-to" positions for the same chords. Rock-and-roll standards follow a familiar progression, so that made accompaniment easier for me. With practice, and as my familiarity with his styles improved, we would play other songs.

In the rock jam situation, the bass must sync with the drummer to create the foundation rhythm while staying in tune with the chord progression of the guitar. Playing a new song is an act of anticipation to keep in step: you have to know what chord is coming next to play the right note on time. If you're late, the rhythm is off, and if you're wrong, the band is out of tune. There is also a skill to getting back into the groove after you've made a mistake.

Sai Lek, having played in numerous bands over the years, was sensitive to these issues, too, and I began to notice that he would often choose Burmese *copy thachin* songs to play when I was on bass. When I knew the international song, playing the bass part was much easier, as I would not need to focus on what Sai Lek was doing to know what notes to play next. He also would encourage me to sing along with his Burmese songs. It was during fieldwork in this Shan village at the Burma–Thai border that I got back into playing John Denver, the Beatles, Creedence Clearwater Revival, Albert Hammond, Carpenters, Elton John, Everly Brothers, and Paul Anka songs, to name a few, because these were artists for which Sai Lek knew the Burmese *copy thachin* renditions of their tunes.

Our musical fusion, however, was not always successful. Sometimes Sai Lek would play a song, and I would be following him along on the bass, but still trying hard to stay focused on his left hand so I could anticipate the chord that was coming next. Whenever I recognized a *copy thachin* song as a familiar tune, I could just settle into a more comfortable rhythm of playing; I think it is safe to say that the music is better when it just "flows." Anxiety and excessive focus sure can kill a nice groove. When I failed to recognize Sai Lek's cues for a *copy thachin* song, it was both awkward and a bit frustrating. I would still try to follow what he was playing and singing, but I felt a tinge of disappointment on his part, as if this was a body of knowledge that I was supposed to have, but I was failing to meet expectations.

Because the jam sessions in Wan Kan Hai were so fluid, and people would take turns on guitar (and bass, and drums, and at the mike), villagers encouraged me to play different songs, so I played some of the various popular songs that I knew, mostly Top 40s and classic rock songs that are well known on the US pop charts. Frequently, Sai Lek and Nang Oo would be quick to let me know if there was a Burmese *copy thachin* version of the song I was singing. They would always tell me with a sense of triumph, too, as a way of saying, "Oh, that's not new to us."

Needless to say, learning about Hang Mit, Sai Lek, and Nang Oo's tastes in music, and seeing how they actualized them through collecting tapes, songbooks, and practice at Mattana's house, were tremendously enjoyable. At a village meal the day after one of the many band jams, I sat next to Sai

Lek at a bench as we ate noodle soup together. Probably for the umpteenth time, I told him I enjoyed the songs and told him that it was terrific that he had such an extensive musical repertoire and memory of various songs; I basically said again that I had fun. He responded: "Playing music together for us Shan people, sure we do it because it is fun, and we love to play songs. But it's more than that. You come from America, I come from the Shan State, but we can play the same songs, even if they are in different languages. When we know the same songs, we can *pen saü kan* [share hearts]." I do not want to overestimate this statement as some sort of achievement of ethnographic intimacy on my part; it does not imply acceptance as "one of them," but rather it suggests what it might mean for people from very different backgrounds to play music together and to already know the same melodies. Sai Lek, a Shan former insurgent soldier who has lost his leg fighting the Burmese, can spend his leisure time playing Burmese songs and sing songs with a woman from Chicago. For Sai Lek, along with much of the elite membership of the Shan United Revolutionary Army, being educated meant being fluent in Burmese. Many of the history and political theory books that people in the SURA studied were written by Burmese authors or were Burmese translations of international authors, including those of the Naga Ni, or "Red Dragon," anti-colonial book club of 1930s Rangoon.

And here, in Wan Kan Hai, Burmese symbolic capital still carried cachet, especially to older generations or to people like Nang Oo, who has her Taunggyi University degree, loves Burmese popular music, speaks Shan fluently, but only speaks halting Thai. While the concrete floor of the band practice room at Mattana's house offered an important social space for various kinds of popular music jam and resignification, various forms of public performance were deeply meaningful in Wan Kan Hai. Rock music was also used to create and accentuate relationships between Shan villages, creating a special relationship for Shan communities in the Thai periphery.

ROCK MUSIC AND
CROSS-VILLAGE COMMUNITAS

On holy days, members of the community unite in worship at the local Buddhist temple. On one particular day in September, many of the residents of Kong Long, the next town over, came to Wan Kan Hai to make merit at the monastery. Later that evening, groups of Wan Kan Hai residents piled into the back of pickup trucks to pay a return visit to their neighbors in Kong Long. The latter town was a four-kilometer journey across the mountain ravine from Wan Kan Hai, and there were many mutual friends and family relationships between the two towns already. Whereas for the religious event at the temple earlier that day, the majority of visitors were older women, for this truck ride, the participants were mostly men ranging in age from about twenty to fifty. Their spirits were high, and there were bits of gossip and laughs (and small flasks of whisky) shared by those standing or squatting in the backs of the pickup trucks during the short ride.

In one of the trucks was a Shan gong and long drum ensemble, and their syncopated rhythm emanated as the noisy and jovial caravan wound its way down the mountain from Wan Kan Hai toward Kong Long. Once the first truck arrived near the edge of Kong Long village, its passengers disembarked, jumping out of the back of the pickups and onto the tarmacadam. Straight from a long day working in the rice paddy and still donning his T-shirt, sweatpants, and shin-high plastic work boots, Sai Chuen walked first, carrying two straw effigies of horses. The straw ponies are small, probably about 50 percent larger than a domestic cat.

Sai Chuen placed the little straw ponies in the middle of the road and then took a couple of steps backward. He was presenting the two critters as a ceremonial offering to the people of Kong Long. Just then, the gong and long drum players and instruments had found a place on the road, and

Shan percussion ensemble at a merit-making event. (Photo by Sai Leng Learn Kham)

begin to play, *gonggg gonggg gonggg thud-th-thud thud gonggg thud gonggg gonggg thud th-th-thud thud . . .* , the traditional Shan-style welcome accompaniment. Sai Kham, a resident of Kong Long and the lead singer of the Kong Long Shan rock band Wan Maü (literally "New Age" or "Modern" in Shan), grinned and walked to the straw ponies. He picked them both up and waved to the gathering of Wan Kan Hai folk, shouting, "Come!! Eat!!"

Sai Kham led his guests, most of whom he has known for decades, over to the side of the road closer to the village, where party preparations awaited the neighbors. A picnic awning was set up. Under the awning were four picnic tables, with plastic chairs beckoning occupants. On the table were teapots and trays of porcelain teacups. As people moved in to sit down, out came three women carrying trays with plastic bowls of steaming *kao sen Tai makua hsom*, or "Shan noodle soup," known in Burmese as *Shan kao swe*. Behind the tent where the picnic tables were set up was the backdrop poster advertising Sai Kham's band, Wan Maü. The Shan gong and long drum ensemble continued their percussive activity for some time, but gradually Sai Kham and his band members picked up their instruments and started to hammer out a few Shan rock tunes. While everyone ate, the amplified sounds of the rock band quickly drowned out those of the Shan gong and long drum but intermittently created a cacophony of overlapping sounds. At one point, Mattana fronted on vocals for the band. Later on, Sai Lek stepped up to play guitar and started to sing a Sai Mao song known by Nang Oo and Mattana, who sang along, while others clapped to the rhythm.

At one point in the evening, Hseng Lün's husband, Aung Kyaw from Wan Kan Hai, stepped up to the microphone. Seemingly without needing a cue, Sai Kham and the other members of his band put down their instruments and walked away from the makeshift stage. Aung Kyaw asked the audience if they were tired of the *dung dung dang dang* music, implying the sounds of the Shan rock. Following this comment, he started to sing Sat Tai, or a form of Shan performances in Shan language related to court music, the term *Sat Tai* being shorthand for retelling of the Jatakas, or stories of the Buddha.

Following Aung Kyaw's performance of Sat Tai, the rock band returned, and a pair of men who had been working in the fields got up to dance. The two men were still wearing their shin-height rubber boots, mud-caked trousers, and grubby T-shirts. The two guys danced comically, almost like a free-style "worm" or "noodle" of sorts; it reminded me of hippies dancing at a psychedelic concert. It must have been intentionally ridiculous, and the guys seemed to be reveling in their silly performance. I heard Aung Myo, in all seriousness, comment to his neighbor, "They must have learned to dance like that in the city. People in Shan villages never dance like that."

The evening's activities embraced a number of key aspects of the contemporary Shan social self: merit-making, traveling in groups, gestures of sociality, and, of course, making music and having fun. When Sai Chuen presented the straw horse effigies to the people of Kong Long, he was doing so on behalf of everyone from Wan Kan Hai. By accepting the straw horses and inviting the people of Wan Kan Hai over for food and music, Sai Kham extended reciprocity to the people of Kong Long. The rock music has entered the scene of such village interactions in the past few decades. Although music is not the showcase, it offers the backdrop to neighborly camaraderie, and that backdrop blends modern Shan rock with Burmese songs as well as the more traditional Shan song styles.

Throughout my stay in Wan Kan Hai, nearly every significant ritual or event, with the exception of funerals, would have a requisite Shan rock band performance with music in the Shan language. Shan rock music provides an invaluable backdrop (and sometimes foreground) to major events in Wan Kan Hai. The importance of Shan rock music is intimately tied to the history of the Shan insurgency, the development and proliferation of Shan print media, and, more recently, the economies of digital media reproduction. The Shan rock music also works together with what are considered more traditional rituals of social solidarity. How it is tagged depends on the performers and the audience. Especially in the context of the temple festival, Shan rock music becomes the major social draw for the night's entertainment.

At these larger events, Burmese music is absent. For example, on New Year's Eve in 2005, 2015, and 2019, Piang Luang village—adjacent to the former headquarters of the Shan United Revolutionary Army and Bang Mai Sung—sponsored a commemorative concert for Sai Mu. More than a dozen well-known Shan rock musicians from both the Shan State and Thailand came to the border town to perform in this stage show. In addition to the show itself, there was also a museum-style picture display booth, which showed Sai Mu's intimate connection with the insurgency. On the stage bills, posters, and advertising flyers, he is billed as Khu Sai Mu, or "Teacher Sai Mu."

This kind of festival or event specifically to honor special teachers dates back to the 1970s in the Shan State. The Shan cultural associations would host these Poi Khu Mo Tai, or "Shan Teacher Festivals." The practice is common for great Burmese literary figures as well, but the fact that Sai Mu was also a popular rock musician means that the rock concert component is particularly apt for this occasion. For the New Year, bands and singers perform Sai Mu hits. There is one main backup band, and Shan female singers take turns at the mike. Fans can purchase synthetic garlands to present to the singers as gestures of appreciation. Adjacent to the stage show are carnival-like games of skill, such as darts, ring toss, or throwing a ball to knock down a triangular stack of empty beer cans. But the modern rock band takes center stage, and attention focuses on the lead singers and guitar players.

This Shan-tagged modernity is both distinctively Shan through its use of certain tropes and signifiers, such as the direct mention of Shan past prosperity, and the Shan long drum, but it also is in tandem with global modernity, in that it harks to the idea of a nation through the medium of rock music. Although the guitar got its sixth string in Spain, there is not a single country on the planet that does not have local musicians who know how to play it. Therefore, in advocating for the Shan nation through the medium of rock music, Shan musicians, songwriters, and music aficionados not only look forward to a future where a Shan nation exists but also anticipate a Shanland that is *recognized* by others. With music, being Shan is neither forgotten nor perceived as esoteric, and an upbeat rhythm and catchy tune make that vision desirable.

CONCLUSION

The repossession of Shanland is not just a military project; it is an intellectual and cultural assertion of Shan-ness, with enemies much more nebulous than just Tatmadaw soldiers with guns drawn. When Shan migrants struggle to survive in Thailand, they are burdened with the emotional work of trying to act Thai. For many, they are forced to purge their public social selves of any elements that would attract undue attention or suspicion. Although Shan people themselves see nothing odd or contradictory about enjoying Burmese popular culture, many have come to realize that this can create dissonance if they are trying either to assimilate to Thai society or to present themselves as Shan to Thais.

A case in point: When I met with some Thai students at Chiang Mai University and told them about my research experience playing music with Shan villagers, I named some of the songs we played, including Thai, Shan, and Burmese songs. A few of the students were taken aback. One said, "Burmese songs? Why aren't they proud of their Shan-ness?" The Thai student was surprised to hear that Shan people might like Burmese songs; her tone gave me the impression that she didn't believe me.

Later that same afternoon, I mentioned this interaction to Sai Naw, himself a former Shan State Army soldier now living in Chiang Mai. "Many Thais don't know how to differentiate," he said succinctly. Sai Naw, twenty-two, is quite fashion-conscious. He was wearing a rugged silver chain necklace; fitted black T-shirt that showed off his trim, muscular body; and ripped blue jeans with a leather belt. On the internet, he went by a chat handle, "M16" and included a photo of himself as a Shan State Army soldier holding a rifle, with the distinctive rectangular SSA soldier's cap on his head. Now he uses gel to create a spiked look for his hair, a style like that of a Japanese anime character. I often found him watching VCDs of Japanese cartoons with Burmese subtitles.

But what are the Thais not able to differentiate? I ask Sai Naw to elaborate a bit further. He explains, "Sometimes the Thais think that everyone from Burma is all the same, like Shan and Karen and Burman, they call us all 'Burmese' [คนพม่า], and then, there are other Thais that know we are Shan and there are different groups in Burma. But they think that because we are Shans and Shans are Tais then we hate *everything* Burmese."

What Sai Naw has put his finger on is that Thai ethno-nationalist ideology about Tais in other countries leaves little room for multiple cultural relationships and codes. Sai Naw knows that for many Shan people (himself included), a political stance is not an indicator of pop culture taste, nor does a decades-long war intrinsically make all Shan people purge their social selves of all Burmese elements. It was Thai nationalist history that cultivated the figure of the evil Burmese enemy, but most Shan adults in Wan Kan Hai have a much more nuanced relationship with Burmese people and Burmese culture. And why shouldn't Nang Oo be allowed to cherish the memories of her Taunggyi University student life, going to Burmese teashops, watching Burmese movies, and singing Burmese pop songs with her five best friends? What makes this border zone important for popular culture practices is that Shan people constitute the majority, and while Shan symbolic elements flourish, people still enjoy practicing Burmese rock songs or, indeed, flaunting their Burmese cultural capital even if it was au courant in their previous lives in the Shan State, Mandalay, or Yangon.

Conversely, I later carried out some field research about Burmese popular music in Myanmar. In a discussion of the topic of 1970s music with a fifty-year-old Burmese man in Yangon, Maung Soe, he asked how I came to know about these various songs. I told him that I first learned about Burmese music from Shan United Revolutionary Army veterans, as some of them were fans of many Burmese rock musicians (Sai Lek probably gave me the best hands-on "crash course" in Burmese rock music I could ever wish for). My Burmese interlocutor "corrected" me, letting me know that since Shan soldiers are fighting against Burmanization, they want to preserve Shan culture, so they do not want to practice Burmese songs. I realized that the second part of Sai Naw's assessment about "not being able to differentiate" clearly applied to Maung Soe too: he was fully convinced that ethnic minorities hated *everything* Burmese.

One evening in Wan Kan Hai, Seng Kham, a neighbor, and I watched a VCD of a Burmese movie, in this case, a *thone pwint saing*, or "love triangle," romantic drama. Hoping to elicit some feedback about her interpretation of the plot, the characters, or the meaning of the movie itself, I asked Seng Kham what she thought of it. "Oh, we're not against them," she said as she gestured toward the cellophane envelope of the Burmese VCD sitting on the table in front of us. "We are against the government only. Besides, if we don't know their language, how are we going to defeat them?"

Through playing music with Shan people in Wan Kan Hai, I was able to tap into pleasurable memories of people's lives in Shan State and Burma, giving a more complete picture of their cultural practices. When I interviewed Sai Lek about politics, he provided a very thorough historical analysis of the SURA and the MTA. But by playing music together, I learned that his memory of playing Burmese popular music and his skill in recalling these numerous songs is an important part of who he is. Hang Mit, on the other hand, is not such a fan of Burmese music—he prefers Shan singers, especially Sai Mu—but he does not see anything wrong or contradictory with Shan people who do like Burmese music, as he knows it does not reflect a political stance.

While many Shan have found a relatively safe harbor in Thailand, they often face acute forms of discrimination by the Thais, and their tenuous legal status often forces them to take the worst jobs under the worst conditions, facing police harassment or imprisonment if they are caught outside their registered district without the correct travel documents. The Burmese regime, for Shan nationalists at the border, is their ideological enemy from which they want to separate, but Thailand is now their host, albeit a fierce, condescending, and exploitative host for many. Music offers a chance to be together and imagine a different world, and to rehearse a vision of a future as well. Indeed, the jam space at Mattana's house offers a place to assert a cosmopolitan Shan social self despite the ongoing fight for political and cultural survival in hostile environments elsewhere.

8

Future Shan Kings or Ethnic Poster Children

ရှမ်းရှင်ပြုအလွယ်လေး [The Shan Poi Hsang Lawng is simple] တမူးရလို့တပဲလျှူ
တို့ရှမ်းတောင်သူတ္တနိုင်ရိုးလား [If they get two annas (¹⁄₁₆ of a rupee), they use one anna to make religious merit (donate at a temple); can anyone match those Shan hill people?]

—Burmese idioms

"BECAUSE YOUR SON has ordained, after you die, you will hang onto his robe and be pulled up to the next station for your future rebirth," Phü explains to a group of friends gathered at Seng Kham's house. They sit on the bamboo-matted floor, encircling a low round table that has a light-blue plastic basket of boiled peanuts in the center. The women take turns reaching for peanuts, husking them, eating the nut, and depositing the husks into a growing pile on the table. As Phü explains her point to the group of women, she raises both fists together and mimes the gesture of clenching onto an imaginary robe. "As his mother, you get the first place. But, if your son ordains after he has already married, then you lose first place on the robe to his wife."

Seng Kham retorts, "What are you worried about? Somchai is only eight years old!" The others laugh at Seng Kham's quick wit.

"Poi Hsang Lawng [ပွဲးသၢင်,လွင်း] is going to be huge this year, maybe a hundred Hsang Lawngs!" says Phü as she reaches for a peanut out of the basket. She removes the husk while looking at Seng Kham. "Did you hear? This year, Nang Nge's son will be a Hsang Lawng too."

The group of women falls silent (but only briefly). Poi Hsang Lawng is arguably the "most Shan" of Shan Buddhist rituals; it is definitely the most lavish of events. It is a mass ordination of young boys into novice monkhood at the beginning of rainy season. As part of the ritual, there are several days of ceremonies, feasts, and entertainment; it's ritual by day, carnival by night. The ornamentation and decorations of the boys are so elaborate and fabulous that numerous books and magazine features about the Shan include photos of the event so readers can get an idea of what "Shan-ness" looks like. Images of Hsang Lawngs—meaning "novice-monk-in-becoming" and used as a name for the boys themselves during the ritual—grace the covers of academic books about the Shan. The Hsang Lawng, as the focus of the religious ritual, has become an icon for Shan-ness and a poster child for national ethnic diversity.

Back to the topic at hand for our table of chatting women, Nang Nge' is well known in Wan Kan Hai, but mostly for her sad situation. Nang Nge' is thirty-two years old and was born in rural Shan State. She is one of the most impoverished people in Wan Kan Hai and has five children, each from a different father. As if being poor, stateless, and a single mother of five were not enough of a struggle for this young woman to face, Nang Nge' is HIV positive, as are her two youngest children.

Back in Möng Pan, Nang Nge' grew up as an orphan, and at fifteen, she had been the clandestine girlfriend of a Möng Tai Army officer. Nang Nge' got pregnant at fifteen or sixteen and had to live off the meager amount of money her boyfriend (inconsistently) gave her. She left him for another

Entourages carrying their Hsang Lawng. (Photo by Sai Leng Learn Kham)

boyfriend, who in turn left her. Her second pregnancy coincided with Khun Sa's surrender and later the mass displacements in the Shan State. Nang Nge' moved with other MTA refugees across the border to Thailand but could not support herself, let alone her small family of three. Being uneducated, speaking only Shan, and with few other options, she sold sex. On some occasions was able to become the girlfriend or "minor wife" to a married man, a desperate way to try to have a more stable income. For some women, getting pregnant and having a man's child is a calculated strategy to acquire stability, to solidify a precarious relationship. Nang Nge' and her children live in a tiny bamboo house, across a ravine and rice paddy from Wan Kan Hai. The house lacks electricity, and she gets around town on foot. But Nang Nge' stays in Wan Kan Hai only part of the year; other months she works in a brothel in the coastal town of Rayong. The brothel owner has connections with a van driver who would organize transport for Nang Nge' but with payment terms that required Nang Nge' to work for "the house" for a certain number of clients before she could start to keep even part of the money she earned. While Nang Nge' works in Rayong, her eldest daughter looks after the younger children.

Having faced desperate times, and knowing how others have it worse than themselves, most villagers sympathize. Dang, who operates a modest hair dressing salon across the road from the village meeting hall, had once been a sex worker in Chiang Mai, but she was able to save some money, move back to Wan Kan Hai, and start the small business. Neighbors in Wan Kan Hai do help Nang Nge' survive, especially by giving her children food to eat or contributing so that her school-age kids can attend the migrant school. When she joined a local support group and started getting health checkups and anti-retroviral drugs from a local NGO, Nang Nge's status as HIV positive was "outed" to the small community. The guys at the motorbike taxi stand have their masculine banter about her, noting that Shan State Army soldiers seem quick to find out when she's back in town, or discussing the water buffalo herder's rainy-day tryst with her. They discuss her not by name but as "the AIDS person." But when asked, they claim not to discriminate.

Back at the gathering at Seng Kham's house, Aunty Bu interjects with another anecdote. A few months ago, she was at the sundry goods shop up the road and saw Nang Nge' there. Nang Nge' had bought a few things and was lingering at the shop. Meanwhile, the shop owner and her friend had their attention focused on the TV on the cabinet behind the counter. While they watched, they animatedly discussed the program. Nang Nge', with her purchases in a plastic bag in one hand and her toddler child in a sling across her back, stood adjacent to the counter. She was watching the TV to find out what the others were talking about.

A few minutes went by, and the shopkeeper noticed Nang Nge' still standing in her shop. She cast a disapproving look and eventually said, "You've got what you came for, so why don't you just go on your way? I'm not prejudiced toward you, but other customers will be reluctant to enter my shop because you're hanging around."

The women at Seng Kham's house share their opinions about Nang Nge' being ejected from the shop as related by Aunty Bu. Seng Kham frequently worked with an NGO dealing with AIDS education and outreach, the very support group that Nang Nge' joined, and has extensive experience working with HIV-positive people.[1] "Maybe I should talk with the shopkeeper. She was perfectly happy to take Nang Nge's money but won't let her watch TV? HUMPH!"

Despite the "topic not yet being finished," as they say in Shan, Phü steers the discussion back to the upcoming Poi Hsang Lawng, asking, "How many envelopes have you received thus far this year?"

Seng Kham isn't sure. "More than fifty," she replies. The envelopes are sent out in advance by the Hsang Lawng–sponsoring families to solicit donations from various people in their social network. The monetary donation—a meritorious act—helps pay for the meals, preparations, and the lavish outfits donned by the young boy during the days of the ritual. One group of families pooled their resources to sponsor four boys' ordinations. For each day of the ritual, they planned to slaughter an entire pig and for friends and family to feast on the finest cuts of pork each day.

This year Wan Kan Hai's Poi Hsang Lawng festival will feature the ordination of eighty-six little boys. Shan migrant workers from Chiang Mai and Bangkok will return to their relatives in the borderland village for the event. Even relatives from Shan State and as far away as Mandalay and Yangon will travel to Wan Kan Hai to partake in the ritual and its many festive celebrations. While Seng Kham's group of friends sits eating peanuts and exchanging village news, Nang Nge' is on her way back from the brothel in Rayong to attend her son's ordination. She, out of all people in Wan Kan Hai, is most desperate for the merit boost that a son's ordination will bring. This is her hope for the future.

Whereas the central goal of the Poi Hsang Lawng ritual is the ordination of young boys into the novice monkhood, in the Shan community at

Wan Kan Hai, the massive series of events takes on multiple powerful meanings beyond its orthodox intent. Its many messages are complex, intertwined, and highly subjective; the days of ritual, blessing, and carnival include various activities that connect to the Shan political project, the Thai nation-state, and the Burmese Army. Like the Shan communities themselves, Poi Hsang Lawng transgresses multiple frontiers of meaning.

Therefore, this chapter first provides a brief overview of the Poi Hsang Lawng and its orthodox meaning and structure as a Brahmanic ritual event that also reenacts part of the biography of the Lord Buddha. Then it considers how the economies of sponsorship operate in the context of a Shan village, a node on a broader web of networks of precarious Shan subjects across upland Southeast Asia. As an important, embedded part of Shan Theravada Buddhist practice, the Poi Hsang Lawng has long been part of the ritual language of Shan statecraft and aspects of its economies of sponsorship and includes symbolic nods to political power. But with newer ideas involving race, ethnicity, and political power come new stops on the itinerary: monuments of the nation-state, representing the contemporary zeitgeist of racialized territory. Finally, the precarity (and resilience) of the Shan community also hijack some of the religious infrastructure to create a cathartic political message for Shan people themselves, creating novel platforms upon which to imagine their own cosmopolitical futures.

The Festival for the Novice in Becoming

The Poi Hsang Lawng (ပွဲသၢင်္လွင်း) is rooted in Theravadin Buddhist and Brahmanic ritual symbolism. The etymology of the Shan term hints at its plural genealogy: *Poi* is a Shan pronunciation of the Burmese word *pwe*, meaning "festival" or "event." *Hsang* is the Shan word for novice monk (derived from *sāmaṇera*, Pali for "novice monk"), often referred to with a term of respect: *Sao Hsang*. *Lawng* is from Burmese, *laung*, meaning "in the process of becoming." In Burma, the event is called a *Shin Pyu Pwe*; the Thai term used for the event is *Buat Luk Kaew*, or "Jeweled Prince Ordination."

The overarching structure of the Poi Hsang Lawng is that of a coming-of-age ritual for a young boy: his first ordination as a novice monk. The story and the costuming animate a portion of the biography of Lord Buddha: his transition from being a prince to becoming a *bikkhu*, or "learned mendicant." In brief, when Prince Siddhartha was born, his father (the king) was told by a fortune teller that the boy would grow up to become either a great king or a possessor of resplendent knowledge. His father, hoping the boy would become a great king, sheltered little Siddhartha from the suffering of the world, giving him a lavishly rich childhood and hoping the pleasures of wealth and indulgence would win the child's heart over to the lush life. One night, the prince stole away from the palace, discarded his princely attire, cut his hair, and became an ascetic. It was during this time that he first saw an old person, a sick person, and a dead person; he had been sheltered from life's eventualities. Then, after meeting an ascetic, Prince Siddhartha decided that the way out of the inevitability of age, suffering, and death is to escape the cycle of rebirth, the *samsara*, through deep insight, eventual enlightenment, and getting to nothingness, or *neikban* (nirvana). The fortune-teller was right: Prince Siddhartha would become a possessor of resplendent knowledge, and he became the revered Lord Buddha. The days of the Poi Hsang Lawng present a festivalized version of this story.

In the first days of Shan Poi Hsang Lawng, the boys embody Prince Siddhartha during the palace phase: they wear elaborate, colorful outfits, replete with laboriously applied makeup and ornate headdresses. The more lavish, extravagant, and ornamental the festival is in the here and now, the better and more beautiful is the future that awaits in the next lifetime; it's a way to sample future riches. Because Prince Siddhartha left the palace on a horse, the Shan boys' feet are not to touch the ground. For all the days of the ritual, they are carried on the shoulders of men, or sometimes on horses (or nowadays on the beds of pickup trucks, but not during ritual processions).

Despite the event's variety of practices over hundreds of years, today's Poi Hsang Lawng, when it is practiced by Shan people, is considered within the dominant national gaze (for both Thailand and Myanmar) as presentation of Shan Buddhism, synonymous with the idea of festivalized culture discussed in chapter 6. For Shan communities in Thailand, its flair, beautiful ornamentation, and ceremonial aspects make it a popular tourist attraction, to Thais and others. Shan people in Mae Hong Son, many of whom are long-term residents or citizens of the Thai state, have grown used to these performative aspects of ethnicity; thus they see their representations of Shan-ness as facing outward to the Thai Nation (Tannenbaum 2009, 177, 182). It has also been observed that the Poi Hsang Lawng in Mae Hong Son represent a tenuous power balance between the centripetal force that attempts to absorb Shan Buddhism into the structure of the nation-state and the counter-force that is trying to reduce differentiation within Shan society (Murakami 1998, cited in Yasuda 2008, 37).

In Chiang Mai, where Thai and Northern Thai are culturally dominant, the Poi Hsang Lawng takes on characteristics of an ethnic festival as much as a Buddhist ritual. The spatial geographies of the procession are organized to include key city landmarks, including Thapae Gate and the Three Kings Monument commemorating the founding of Chiang Mai (Eberhardt 2008, 58, 59).

A similar dynamic can be observed in Myanmar, where Shan are presented as another *taingyintha*, or "indigenous group," within the national pantheon. Similarly, the Myanmar government exploits the Kachin Manau festival, with Myanmar Airways increasing its flights to the area to bring in more tourists (Sadan 2013, 422). In this sense, the Poi Hsang Lawng, as it is seen from majority perspectives in Myanmar and Thailand, has expectation heaped onto it as a "Shan" cultural event par excellence. Because the Shan Poi Hsang Lawng is also a Buddhist ritual, the attractive variant on the dominant religion also presents the Shan as lovely, docile, and loyal subjects to their sovereigns.

There is a set itinerary for the days of the Poi Hsang Lawng; various villages and towns with large Shan populations are careful to schedule their events so as not to clash with the others. The boys and their entourages tour around the area, visiting temples, shrines, and monuments, and in the evening attend a carnival that also includes Shan rock music. For this year's group of eighty-six boys and their entourages to complete the schedule of events, the logistical arrangements are massive. The days of the event close with the boys' ordination as novice monks, and they usually remain as novice monks for the following week and sometimes longer.

Making Merit and Facilitating Its Transmission

Although the boys are the center of attention throughout the days of the ritual, the event is more of a rite of passage for the sponsoring adult than it is for the boy (Eberhardt 2006, 90). Part of the meaning was aptly described by Phü—the mother is able to move to a higher rebirth by holding onto her son's robes. As Phü described her location as "first place" because her son had not yet married, there is another argument that posits that children are more apt to transmit merit than adults (Thirapap ธีรภาพ 1995, 112). When I spoke to the boys themselves, in addition to the most common reason for participating, "I want to do it," many said, "I am doing it for my mom." The boys do have a tangible idea of the amount of resources, time, effort, and money that goes into sponsoring their merit; as vehicles for merit, they are anything but automatic transmission. For the days leading up to and including the Poi Hsang Lawng, we can look at the boys as the symbolic hubs, and the spokes that radiate outward connect each boy to their immediate families but also to greater social networks, including those who help in the preparations and logistics of the event as well as to those who make modest donations and place them in the envelope boxes at their respective stalls.

But for the various sponsors, being a spoke on many networks of expectation is a lot of work. Presenting monetary donations to fifty or more families can stretch one's household budget. Seng Kham, being a prominent, established member of the community in Wan Kan Hai, has a large social network. I recall the stack of envelopes on her living room desk as well as her response when two teenagers pulled up to her house on a motorbike with (yet another) envelope: "Sigh, put it on the pile over there."

For a devout Buddhist, the Hsang Lawng donation envelope is a gift solicitation that one cannot refuse; to do so would shun the merit-making of your friends and neighbors, an act far more offensive than showing up to a party empty-handed. While the stack of white paper envelopes continues to pile up on Seng Kham's desk, she also thinks about the relative means of the various families sponsoring a Hsang Lawng ordination.

Although Seng Kham's Buddhist principles are strong, and she will hold up her end of the bargain, her own life struggles give her some trepidation regarding the massive expense of the event for many others. She enjoys the big celebration, but she does not like to see so many of her neighbors spending beyond their means, only to suffer for their lack of economic prudence later on. It must be difficult to watch them spend all their money, going into debt bondage, not just for the merit-making but also because the event produces a spirit of competitive one-upmanship among the participants; everyone wants to be richer and more lavish than their neighbors. Few are immune to the bug of conspicuous holy consumption.

Sometimes the profligate spending for the festival gives unsympathetic Thais the impression that Shan migrants are actually rich, or that their situation is not as desperate as various NGOs and migrant advocacy groups would otherwise lead them to believe. However disdainfully some may view the religious spending of the impoverished Shan, there is a religious logic that makes such excessive spending a good investment for the future.

In his study of Buddhist festivals and religious spending in Burma, anthropologist Melford Spiro argues that big spending is a rational decision and a sound investment for two reasons: meager income and general economic instability in the Burmese context have made economic savings highly unlikely to bear any long-term gains (we can say the same for Shan migrants in Thailand); and religious spending confers merit, which potentially results in a higher rebirth in the future. Furthermore, lavish festivals with delicious foods, resplendent jewels and silks, and professional entertainment are much more pleasurable than staying home and saving every penny and give a "taste" of what a rich future might be like (Spiro 1966, 1163–68). In sum: spending money on religion is the soundest investment one can make, as it means prestige in the present and a more prosperous future life (Spiro 1992, 97).

This Buddhist logic certainly is manifest in many of the Hsang Lawng sponsors and in what I observed attending the festivities in Wan Kan Hai. But others will disagree with Spiro's conclusion that religious spending is always a sound investment for impoverished Buddhists. In 2007 the management committee of one of the Shan internally displaced camps made the unilateral decision that their Poi Hsang Lawng was *not* to be a lavish event. They would still have the ritual, but spending was capped, and the boys would be in plain clothes rather than the ornate costumes. The Hsang Lawng still completed the religious ritual of ordaining as novices following the days of parading and blessings of the festival.[2] We'll have to wait for the next rebirth to test their hypothesis that the frugal festival can still confer merit.

RITUAL DAYBREAK IN WAN KAN HAI

Early in the morning of the first day of Poi Hsang Lawng, the ritual procession starts: the boys, carried on the shoulders of their human horses and shaded by their umbrella bearers, perambulate the Wan Kan Hai temple three times before going inside. Two men carrying a *kyisi* (brass gong) on a bamboo pole lead the slow parade, striking it intermittently so that everyone within earshot will know that meritorious activities are taking place. The previous day, the boys' hair was cut and their heads were shaved by their sponsors, with the initial strokes of the safety razor made by the monastery abbot. While the shaving took place, the boys held a giant lotus leaf in the palms of their hands, receiving the shorn locks. Once the haircut was complete, the leaf was rolled up and presented as a souvenir spring roll of human hair for the boy's mother to keep.

In today's parade, the first boy prince is atop a pony, while the rest are carried on the shoulders of men. The boys' attire is nothing short of opulent. They don colorful silk costumes and elaborate headdresses. They are also fully made-up, replete with foundation, lipstick, costume jewelry, and bangles. Yellow Thanakha has been applied to the boys' faces, some with ornate dotted patterns on their foreheads and cheeks.

Then, the eighty-six little Hsang Lawngs and their families are crowded into the main temple in Wan Kan Hai, a teak structure with a broad main floor and the Buddha altar featured in the center. The boys and their families are seated around small tables, each replete with various foods. The ritual dictates they are to eat twelve kinds of food. Mothers hand-feed their little princes, placing the food directly into their mouths. During the lavish feeding of the boys, it becomes clear that ritual excess has already begun to take place, at least for one little boy. A Hsang Lawng in a bright-blue costume and white headpiece stands up from the breakfast table and quickly makes his way to the corner of the main temple room. His belly heavy with all the food, he needs to vomit, and his family follows him quickly with a plastic bag, comforting the boy as he squats to retch. As part of their orthodox ceremony, the boys recite the Pali suttas that they have been practicing for the last several weeks.

Following the morning ritual at the temple, the boys and their entourages head over to their temporary "home base" for the days of festivities: the high school soccer field. Temporary bamboo platforms containing partitioned booths have been set up to accommodate the boys and their families. Families who have pooled their resources to jointly sponsor more than one boy have their princes together in a booth. It is like a theater green room of sorts: the family stows multiple sets of attire for the boys and keeps their own supplies for the events that follow. Different from Poi Hsang Lawng traditions in villages in Shan State, where entourages go house to house to pay visits to individual merit-makers, the "home base" of the bamboo booths on the soccer field serves to centralize this process.

Each Hsang Lawng has a number, and at the front of each booth is a wooden mailbox with a slot on top and the corresponding number of the Hsang Lawng pasted on it. While at the booth, the Hsang Lawng is on display, seated in full regalia in a chair next to the mailbox. It is there that he personally receives individual merit-makers, frequently relatives, neighbors, or friends of the family (with their envelopes). When someone shows up with an envelope containing a donation, they place the envelope in the mailbox and then receive the Pali blessing from the Hsang Lawng. It is at this phase that Seng Kham takes her accumulated envelopes—appropriately stuffed with cash—to visit the various Hsang Lawng booths; close inspection of the different boys' costuming and chatting with the sponsoring families are part of the fun of the event.

The system of the centralized booths set up on the soccer field means that individual household visits are no longer part of the Poi Hsang Lawng. But there is still ample and abundant parading through town. Everyone wears their finest *hko Tai* Shan clothing and participates by carrying ornamental objects, ceremonial silver bowls, and ornate *ton paday*, or "money trees," made of plastic ribbon straws and formed in the shape of bushes. Bearers carry framed pictures of the Thai king, and others carry Buddhist flags, Thai flags, and Shan flags. There is a cacophony of sounds throughout the parade. A Ta-ang music and dance ensemble joins the parade. Groups with their percussion instruments are often not in synch with the next part of the parade. Hsang Lawng bearers and umbrella bearers bounce to the rhythm, others dance to the music, while some carry silver bowls of puffed rice and toss the rice at the Hsang Lawngs to celebrate the occasion.

Although people have been taking photos of the event throughout the day, at the soccer field comes the first grand group portrait of the eighty-six little princes. This photo-op features the boys together with the Thai government officials. These same officials, from the police, army, and government district bureaucracy, are the ones responsible for monitoring the movement of Shans into labor markets. They derive their income from Shan applications for travel permission, registry documents, and drivers' license paperwork; these are the agents of the state that constrain Shan peoples' lives in Thailand.

Taking souvenir photos with the government officials is a significant reversal from Shan migrants' day-to-day interactions with the Thai state during the rest of the year. Other Shan Poi Hsang Lawng events in urban Chiang Mai include visits to prominent Northern Thai temples in order to receive blessings from those abbots, a practice that has been described as a strategy for Shan migrants to publicly display their willingness to respect the local authorities (Eberhardt 2007, 8). This is also the case in Wan Kan Hai, as the Hsang Lawng bearers line up with the Thai officials; they are presenting themselves in full Shan-style regalia, and the Buddhist ritual gives it an attractive symbolic package, as it were, for the Thai officials to attend the Shan event.

DAYTIME MERIT-MAKING
TURNS TO NIGHT-TIME PARTY

At dusk, the soccer field starts to transition from a site of merit-making to one of carnival and revelry. Vendors operate booths selling snacks and refreshments (including beer and whisky), as well as children's rides and assorted "games of skill" with prizes. Even the otherwise serious and practical Seng Kham gives in to the spirit of the festivities: she walks up to a booth with a ring-toss game. She puts some cash on the counter to receive three plastic rings, which are about the size of the circumference of a drink can. A meter and a half from the counter is a table with an arrangement of nine Chang Beer bottles, the large 620-milliliter size. The objective is simple: toss one of the rings so that it lands on and encircles the bottle neck, and you win the bottle of beer. Of course, the game looks easy; that's the point. After three sets of unsuccessful attempts, Seng Kham moves on. She has already spent more than enough to buy a bottle of beer and refuses to give into the temptation to chase her loss.

At one of the other carnival booths, about a twenty-meter walk from the ring-toss booth, is a dart game. One young Hsang Lawng, in full regalia, is standing on the table with three darts in his left hand as he winds up to throw another dart with his right. He is aiming for a wall on which a few dozen pear-sized balloons of various colors are taped. Each color balloon corresponds to a different prize, and the Hsang Lawng has his sights set on the yellow balloon that represents a plastic AK-47 toy gun. In the economies of these "games of skill," not every dart launch can equal a prize, and unfortunately for our Hsang Lawng at the table, he has been utterly unsuccessful for some time. After running out of darts, the eminent prince tugs at the sleeve of his uncle, while making a whining sound. Almost on cue, the uncle hands over another twenty baht to the booth attendant, who gives three more darts to the little boy so he can continue playing. Not long thereafter, "Pop!" He successfully bursts a yellow balloon, and the carnival attendant hands the little boy his much-sought-after prize: a plastic AK-47.

For the Hsang Lawngs this year, plastic guns are "the" toys to have. Atop their bearers at the carnival, the boys play "cowboy" and pretend to take aim at each other. It seems anathema to the spirit of Buddhism and making merit that the Hsang Lawngs would be carrying plastic guns—such symbols of violence—as they ride on the shoulders of their bearers. But for the community, they are still little boys after all, and in their roles as lavish princes, indulging them means catering to their every whim. They animate luxury in order to actualize a stark contrast to the austerity they take on as novices once the festivities are over.

As night falls at the soccer field–cum–carnival, on the main stage we can see the beginnings of a rock concert. A young man wearing jeans, a black T-shirt, and shiny dangling chain connecting his belt loop to his wallet saunters over to the stool behind the drum set. Pulling a pair of drumsticks out of his side pocket with his right hand, he riffles through his spiked hair with his left hand as he sits down. Grabbing one stick in each hand, he gives each cymbal and drum a ritualistic tappety-tap-tap, and the bass drum a thud-thud-thud before looking to the other guys in the band. The four players—on drums, keyboard, bass, and guitar—are all men in their twenties. They wear jeans, T-shirts, army jackets, and, in general, attire that speaks "rock" in any international context. The lead guitar player has gelled his hair into a spike and is wearing a mechanic's work shirt and jeans. The keyboard player is wearing a bomber jacket, jeans, and a chain wallet. As the guitar player warms up with the band, he tests out some solos, using fuzz distortion. As he hits the high notes, he gyrates his head in a punkish gesture to show how he is "in" with the rock music. For a minute or two, each of the other band members adjust their instruments and get them set up to play.

All the while, the announcer is testing out the mike and welcoming people to the Poi Hsang Lawng. A few people are standing around the stage, but there is not yet a full audience of onlookers. More people are coming, including Hsang Lawng bearers with the little boys riding atop their shoulders. Several minutes later, a column of young men and women files onto the stage. They are all in traditional Shan clothing: the men in baggy Shan trousers and jackets, while the women in hand-woven skirts and with carefully wrapped headdresses. They walk onto the stage and form a *U* to face the audience. Prior to starting their song, the *U*-shaped group of young men and women bow and pay respect in unison, giving the audience a respectful *wai* before they start their performance.

The drummer taps out the one-two-three-four intro, and the band launches into an upbeat rhythm. From their *U* formation, the performers clap to the downbeats. The audience, particularly the Hsang Lawng bearers, starts to bounce to the rock music. The Hsang Lawng boys flail about on the shoulders of their bearers. Many of the boys have their plastic guns, and so they play with these, brandishing them from their positions of privilege above the crowd.

For the first number, as is de rigueur for all Shan rock concerts on the Thai side of the border, the group sings "Kat Sai Hai Mai Sung" (Strive for Progress) written by Sai Kham Lek. The song is not a national anthem so much as it is a Shan nationalist song that is used to open all stage shows.

To the upbeat rhythm, the singers pipe in with the lyrics:

The sound of the Shan gong and the Shan drum
Resonates everywhere, When Shan people meet
They have joy in their hearts and happiness
For they share a heart, and whatever they do it gives them strength
Our Shan brethren will be united until the end of history!

Prosperity! Prosperity one day! Our Shan kin will be great!
The Shan race, don't let it die, the Shan land, don't let it disappear.
Strive . . . for the future generations, make the Shan people with the times.

Great hearts beat in the Shan people
Our ideas are far-sighted
Don't let our ancient history become impoverished
Bear the weight, when we see we can strike back
We are able to build a great nation!

With the band playing music and people dancing, the excitement is infectious. As the rock concert continues, the increasingly drunken celebrating continues into the night. While the backup band remains the same, the featured singers rotate, with various Shan rock singers and male and female crooners all making their appearances and singing various Shan hit songs. As a gesture of appreciation, fans can buy a woven plastic garland to be placed on the singer. Particularly well-known (and attractive) female singers are sometimes rewarded with so many garlands during their performance that they look like haphazard stacks of multicolored inductor coils, their heads poking out the top to sing into the mike.

Aung Myo told me that the revelry sometimes includes "stealing" Hsang Lawngs away from their entourages. During all the wild dancing and celebrating, the boys are typically passed from bearer to bearer as a matter of course to share the responsibility of carrying the boys. Some of the boys, especially the twelve- and thirteen-year-olds, are surely a burden to carry, let alone bounce while dancing at a concert. Thus one with intent to trick might take the boy away as a good-natured joke to play on the boy's extended family. The revelry continues late into the night, and either by devotion or by adrenaline, the entourages and the boys are able to arise the following morning to continue the ritual.

Morning Monument Worship

The religious dimension of the Poi Hsang Lawng ritual follows its orthodox intent: the boys learn the *suttas*, while their parents seek sponsorship, merit, and blessing at various sites. They maintain the basic arc of the story of Prince Siddhartha becoming a *bhikku*. The geographic adaptation of creating the bamboo booths as a "home base" for the days of festivities is new; for eighty-six Hsang Lawngs (plus entourage), it makes better logistical sense to centralize the collection of donation envelopes than to have the entire group go to each and every house in town.

Today, the boys forgo their human horses in favor of pickup trucks. This morning the eighty-six boys and their bearers, umbrella bearers, and greater entourages travel eighteen kilometers to a hilltop monument: the statue and shrine of the sixteenth-century Siamese king Naresuan. This next stop on the Poi Hsang Lawng schedule of activities is an acknowledgment of Thai-centric ethno-national history.

On the way there, in the back of one of the pickup trucks, I chat with Yee Thip, asking about his memories of Poi Hsang Lawng when he was a teenager in Shan State. He tells me that when he participated in Poi Hsang Lawng events in Möng Nai, the entourages didn't go to national monuments. I ask him the natural follow-up question: so why are we doing this now? Yee Thip gives his characteristic cynical grimace (the little twitch of his nostrils and a forced tiny frown of sorts—a sign to others that some tart words are coming soon) and says, "Why not . . . it's an excuse to add something to the plan. . . . But I think this 'Thai thing' makes it [Poi Hsang Lawng] look good. Maybe the Thai will sponsor more ordinations. But they'll never be so generous to give us Shans any citizenship rights."

On the road to becoming a monument, King Naresuan has gained mythical status within Thai nationalist discourse. He is commemorated for having united Thai and Tai kingdoms to fight back against Burmese armies. Naresuan was born in 1555 to Maha Thammaracha, was taken as a hostage to Bago (Hanthawaddy), and was raised in the Burmese king Bayinnaung's court, only to move back to Siam after his sister was presented to the Burmese king as an exchange. Naresuan is famous for his victory in a 1593 elephant duel against the Burmese crown prince (Wyatt 1984, 102). In addition to indexing a Burmese enemy, the figure of Naresuan also represents historical "unification." He did not allow princes to rule over provinces, a move that consolidated his own power, and his strategies also inspired administrative centralization in Burma (Wyatt 1984, 105; Seksan Prasertkul 1989, 34; Reid 1993, 261).

Thus, in the midst of the Cold War buildup of Thai patriotism—predicated on nation-religion-monarchy, the historic "evil enemy" being Burmese or the intrinsically un-Thai communist—King Naresuan was a useful symbol of a glorious king who defeated the Burmese armies more than once and invaded the Burmese heartland twice (also incorporating areas of the Shan States). He was the perfect Thai hero king (Sunait Chutintaranond 1992, 92). The Thai-Tai unification idea is also projected onto Shan history. In one popular Thai-language book about the Shan, the author argues that Shan people have close feelings for Thais partly because King Naresuan came up from Ayutthaya to help the Shan fight the Burmese (Nipatporn นิพัทธ์พร 2006, 10). A more critical analysis of Thai-Tai "brotherhood" ideology posits that Thais have mesmerized the Shan through their folklore stories of common ancestry (Niti Pawakapan 2006, 44). People such as Yee Thip (if I could describe anyone as "unmesmerizable," it would be him) will be suspicious of any romantic view of history coming from Thai patriotic discourse.

Yee Thip's assertion that national monument worship is a new addition to Poi Hsang Lawng peregrinations is easy to verify: the statues themselves are twentieth-century creations. The statues of Thai kings started with King Chulalongkorn (Rama V) commissioning Georges Ernest Saulo to make an equestrian statue of His (own) Majesty, which was unveiled in 1908 (Niti นิธิ 2004, 81). Not long after, in 1914, King Vajiravudh (Rama VI) went to the site of a purported victory of Naresuan's in Suphanburi Province and commemorated it, saying that Naresuan had "secured our national freedom and made our nation respected by the Burmese and the Mons" (Peleggi 2007, 195).

Four decades later, on that same site in Suphanburi, Thais built a bronze statue of King Naresuan. The unveiling ceremony in 1959 included speeches by Thai military top brass, including Sarit Thanarat and Thanom Kittikajorn. Sarit said, "The armies of the king do not know the words fear or loss.

The blood in the Thai soldiers in this era was full of the spirit of sacrifice for the nation" (Anusorn Don Chedi อนุสรณ์ดอนเจดีย์ 1959, 13).

Today there are dozens of statues of King Naresuan throughout Thailand, and their numbers continue to increase. These monuments of kings are effective as symbols in that they are worshipped for their spiritual capacities but also represent the essence of Thai society (Wong 2000, 70). In this sense, the worship of the statues of great Buddhist conqueror kings—as exemplars of their races and national heroes—has become part of the ritual language of modern Southeast Asian nation-building. The late 1980s saw the beginning of a special prosperity cult of King Chulalongkorn statues: people worshipped the statues and asked the king for money or success. The cult is not about the king as a historical figure but rather what he represents in the social imaginary of Thais (Stengs 2012, 55).

To return to the Poi Hsang Lawng parade, the pickup trucks head along the main road to the entrance to the King Naresuan monument. At the entrance are two giant concrete roosters, one on each side of the driveway up to the shrine.[3] Through the gate and up the hill, the pickup trucks stop and allow the Hsang Lawngs and their entourages to alight in front of the steps to the monument. The building that houses the Naresuan shrine also has concrete rooster figures in front of it, as well as inside at the altar itself.

As part of the procession, the boys and their bearers line up once more to pose for photographs in front of the shrine, with the bronze statue of King Naresuan looking out over the tops of the lines of Shan migrants. Following the group photo shoot, each individual Hsang Lawng entourage enters the shrine building to take photographs with the bronze effigy of the sixteenth-century king. The religious ritual further sacralizes this Thai patriotic interpretation of regional history. Although Yee Thip is doubtful, his perspective has become the minority opinion among many younger Shan who have not grown up with cynical distance from Thai patriotic history; within Shan-language history books, Naresuan is mentioned, though his virtues pale in comparison to those of Suerkhan Fa. The former is presented as a Thai king, whereas Suerkhan Fa is the Shan king who united the Tai.

REVELRY BORDERING ON AGGRESSION: FACING THE ENEMY

From figures of Thai-sanctioned history, the next destination on the itinerary moves to a contested space: Wat Fa Wieng Inn, the borderland temple founded by Shan United Revolutionary Army leader Kawn Söng in 1969. This is the temple complex Kawn Söng established with the explicit purpose to straddle the Thai–Burma border. He wanted Tai people from both Thailand and Shan State to unite in worship; the current abbot explained, too, that Buddhism has no boundaries. It was also a not-so-subtle reminder to the sovereign states of Myanmar and Thailand that *this* area is Shanland.

After the massive displacements from Khun Sa's surrender in 1996, the Burmese Tatmadaw took over the temple school and used it as their outpost. They erected fences and laid antipersonnel landmines in the ravine between the temple school and the rest of the temple complex. It is here that the geopolitical boundary between the Thai side and the Myanmar side is most apparent—it is not a wall per se but a small ravine cut between the buildings of the temple complex.

The nickname local Shans have given to this Burmese army outpost is *sun hsat*, or "zoo." The Burmese soldiers are isolated, and themselves become a spectacle. At one point, not long after they established the temple school as an outpost, the Burmese army had a message relayed to the Thai Army that they did not want people taking their pictures. The annual festivities and the catharsis of Poi Hsang Lawng revelry make this request utterly impossible to fulfill, even if the Thai Army wanted to do so.

Today, after making the trek up the steep hill to the temple complex, the various pickup trucks find places to park, and the revelers disembark. According to the printed schedule, they are expected inside the temple to receive the abbot's blessings. But an eminent digression is afoot: everyone walks to the edge of the ravine to look at the Tatmadaw base "zoo" on the other side. From the side, we can all see a few Burmese soldiers casually sitting on a bench, one in a uniform with an AK-47 held to his left hip. Another Burmese soldier is sitting beside him, wearing nothing but a Burmese *loungyi*, smoking a cheroot cigarette, all but ignoring the revelry and pandemonium on the other side of the ravine.

As more and more revelers in the Poi Hsang Lawng arrive at the top of the hill, the number of Shan people staring at the Burmese soldiers swells. While some people are off at the sides, talking to each other quietly, more and more bearers take their Hsang Lawngs to gaze at the Burmese soldiers. One of the Hsang Lawng umbrella-bearers lifts his retracted umbrella and holds it on his shoulder for a moment, cocking it as if it were a rifle, and then fires a pretend shot, even pantomiming a rifle recoil to the amusement of the others around him.

The people gathered facing the crevasse are soon joined by some percussion ensembles. A group of men, casually smoking cigarettes and cheroots as they play the drums, sets up their ensemble opposite the Burmese soldiers on the hill. They start to play an upbeat rhythm, all the while staring at the Burmese soldiers as they hit the long drum, strike the gongs, and crash the cymbals together in overlapping unison. It is clear that they are providing an unsolicited performance for the Burmese soldiers.

A few men start to dance in front of the ensemble again, intentionally in the view of the Burmese soldiers. The dancing is styled after the Shan sword dance, with their shoulders bent in a crouching, attack position, and their arms sweeping in martial arts stylized arcs.[4] One of the dancers pulses forward and shouts "HA!" in the direction of the Burmese soldiers. He continues his dance, with a grimace on his face. He concentrates on his dancing, but the amusement of shouting, almost growling, at the Burmese soldiers in front of all his friends has overtaken his emotions. His wide grin is one that he cannot retract for several minutes.

Once everyone has calmed down just a bit, the abbot of the temple calls the group in to receive his blessings and recite *suttas*. While many of the group have come inside the ordination hall to sit behind the Hsang Lawng as they pray, others stay outside and continue to gaze at the Burmese soldiers.

In the previous year, yet another Naresuan statue was built, just behind the chedi at the Wat Fa Wieng Inn temple complex. Sitting on his throne, regal bronze Naresuan gazes across the temple grounds. Taking King Naresuan's orientation as the starting point, at his immediate one o'clock is the *chedi*, and at twelve o'clock, further across the land mine–laden ravine separating the two halves of the temple, is the temple school that the Myanmar Tatmadaw currently occupies. It is not a coincidence that Naresuan is facing the Burmese military.

In 1996, at the Shan State–Thai border town of Tachileik, the Myanmar government unveiled a new statue of Bayinnaung, the sixteenth-century Burmese king who led armies to defeat the Siamese capital of Ayutthaya in 1569. The town (and this Bayinnaung) is located opposite the Thai town of Mae Sai, at the northern edge of Chiang Rai Province. The giant King Bayinnaung, the heroic leader of Toungoo Dynasty and symbolic of Burmese prowess, stands in battle regalia, sword on hip, arms folded, and stares southward at Thailand. A few years later, following a skirmish at the border in 2001, Thai Lt. Gen. Wattanachai Chaimuenwong set plans to erect another Naresuan statue in Mae Sai. As he said, "We want to pay gratitude to King Naresuan who brought us victory in the fight against the Burmese troops. Without King Naresuan the Great, Thais would have no land in which to live" (Rungwaree Chalermsripinyorat 2004). The two nations erected a bronze warrior king staring contest across the geopolitical border between Myanmar and Thailand.

The new Naresuan statue at Wat Fa Wieng Inn was also built following a border skirmish between the Thai Army and the Tatmadaw. As the Hsang Lawng procession circumnavigates the *chedi*, they are literally positioning themselves between the gaze of the Burmese soldiers and the Naresuan statue. During this ritual, both figures are silent. It is the Shan percussion ensembles that are heard for miles beyond the mountaintop temple grounds where they are gathered. The state's gaze is silent, but the sounds of the stateless boom, if only for a brief period of revelry.

THE CARNIVAL ENDS AND AUSTERITY RETURNS

The last morning of the Poi Hsang Lawng has the boys taking on the golden robes and performing their first ritual as *sao hsang*, or novice monks. No longer on the shoulders of the bearers, the boys now walk on the ground, but barefoot, as Lord Buddha did as a mendicant. The morning procession is an act of walking and receiving alms from devotees and, in turn, reciting reciprocal blessings.

The *sao hsang* carry black lacquer alms bowls with metal lids, and villagers—many dressed in some of their finest *hko Tai* outfits—hold stacks of green twenty-baht cash notes to place in the boys' bowls. Before each placement, the women hold the note up and, with a quick flick of the wrist, make small honorary *wai* of sorts, to indicate they are not presenting the money to an average human but to a novice monk. The boys serpentine around the temple, and following the line of villagers lined up, monks also present the individual *sao hsang* with twenty-baht notes as part of their first round. Unlike the others, the monks just place the notes directly in the boys' bowls; they do not carry out the honorific flick of the wrist as do their commoner counterparts.

Following another session of *sutta* recitation and prayer in the temple, the boys are to stay on and live in the temple as novice monks. The majority will occupy this new role for only a week, while some of the more devout will stay on for years. During the last days of the revelry, the boys are visibly exhausted. During the morning prayers, many of the boys are yawning and struggling to stay awake. I notice a few of them actually stooped over and nodding off during the ceremony.

While the novice monks stay on in the temple, all the people who came in from elsewhere return to their workplaces: the orange orchards, construction sites, or, for Nang Nge', the Rayong brothel where her everyday secular work will resume.

CONCLUSION

People often turn to religion when they have very little power themselves to change their present situation (Keyes 1983, 3). Difficult political and economic circumstances are indeed a sad reality for many Shan people today. Participation in Poi Hsang Lawng is more complex than a cry for help, although desperate circumstances in this lifetime comprise an important motivation for making merit. Poi Hsang Lawng is a cathartic and spiritually enriching festival, though Shan participants do finish the event much poorer financially than they started. While the Poi Hsang Lawng is often viewed as a religious reckoning of Shan-ness in a contested border zone, there is the question of whether it represents bona fide political militancy or instead an ephemeral subordination of the Shan nation-building project to the Thai gaze. Does the event ultimately reinforce the grip of the Thai state and neoliberal capitalism over the Shan migrants? Was the Poi Hsang Lawng just bread and circuses with some local fermented bean flavors and Shan music and dance?

The ongoing war in Myanmar has indirectly fueled Thailand's economy for decades by supplying it with desperate and cheap labor. Sectors of business and the government have reaped tremendous profit from the transnational illicit narcotics business. Shan people returning to their normal jobs in the lowest echelons in the Thai economy ultimately benefit Thai capitalists, the mafia, and the state. Therefore, from a material point of view, the Poi Hsang Lawng ritual is quite conservative. The war has also brought capitalism to the countryside through its commodity networks and the purchase of armaments and supplies, plus the sale of narcotics and the taxation of the black-market trade. Likewise, war sponsors Shan merit-making events, temples, and Poi Hsang Lawng. It returns capital to the borderlands in the form of a remittance for the future. In this sense, the insurgent states still carry with them aspects of the ritual language of Theravadin states of prior centuries, just adapting to black-market capitalism and hindered by the further constraints of citizenship laws. These, in turn, create new shadow economies for accumulation through dispossession.

Where the ritual language has taken on new roles is in the commodification of its packaging, as it were. With the festivalization of regional ethnicity in Thailand, the Poi Hsang Lawng is presented as a happy, colorful, benign celebration of Shan culture and Shan variation on the dominant religion: Buddhism. Touristic features in airline magazines, TV programs, and local businesses readily exploit the advertising potential of the seasonal event.

Because of this attractive packaging, Poi Hsang Lawng offers a special moment for Shan people to be hypervisible in contexts where they are otherwise an invisible minority. Thus government officials posing for photographs with Shan Poi Hsang Lawng participants in full regalia presents an image of ethnic harmony within the purview of a benevolent, welcoming state. As noted in ethnographies of Poi Hsang Lawng events in Chiang Mai and Mae Hong Son, an important theme in the processions is this stance toward the Thai state: the Poi Hsang Lawng in essence helps present the Shan as good T(h)ai subjects (Eberhardt 2008).

The Poi Hsang Lawng events in border areas offer important differences, in that the political geography is not the same, and the majority population is recent migrants from the Shan State, many of whom have close affiliations to Shan political separatist movements. Aspects of the festivalized culture and presentation toward the Thai state do exist, and the inclusion of the Naresuan monument on the festival's itinerary can be taken as a meaningful nod to Thai ethno-national history. Like the Shan United Revolutionary Army leadership's appeal to ethno-racial politics in the 1960s and 1970s to differentiate it from communism, today's Shan appeals to Thai-sanctioned history emphasize the ethnic closeness, the same narrative espoused by Thai patriotic discourse. Whereas the Poi Hsang Lawng in Chiang Mai is clearly oriented to face the Thai state, the location of Wat Fa Wieng Inn on the geopolitical border—with Burmese troops in a small border base—allows the event to face the Burmese too. Ironically, however, their work is trapped between the Thai nationalist history and the projection of the Burmese enemy.

The movement of people from urban Thailand back to the border areas stimulates the local economy through the massive ritual spending. On the other hand, many of the booth operators are from elsewhere and take their profits away with them. The monastery economy, however, is an important consideration: through supporting important Shan temples and circulating

Shan monks from Shan State to Thailand, they solidify and reinforce the networks of Shan state-building through their connections with the religious institution. The same monks who carry out services for Poi Hsang Lawng in Chiang Mai or Mae Hong Son will also work with those at Shan State Army bases, contributing to the monastic education and Shan language education of novices as well as the broader Shan community of each. They keep the Shan cultural economy circulating.

Finally, and perhaps most importantly for the cultural spirit of the event, in the nightly carnival and rock concerts, the future Shanland is now! It is brought to the present through the amplified sounds of the bands and the euphoric dancing of the Hsang Lawng bearers and the wild revelry in front of the stage. It is the format of the Buddhist festival that "tells [them] that it is possible, in future existences, to experience the pleasures of the human realm of which [they are] presently deprived, or the even greater pleasures of the heavenly realms" (Spiro 1966, 1170).

For Nang Nge', watching her son Pok become a novice monk not only fills her with pride but also gives her a shred of hope to hang onto, that she might be pulled along by his robes and taken to a higher status in her future rebirth. Just as the opening song at every night's rock concert encourages Shan people to "Strive for Progress," the entire week's events give people the symbolic basis to strive to envision a future Shanland, a Shanland that understands and acknowledges the present condition of Shan people and iterates their current subservience to other nation-states but puts the karmic wheels in motion to repossesses Shanland for the future.

CONCLUSION

Finding the Shan Nation, Building a Shan State

Soldiers are exhausted, working hard for the nation, working for our land, the land of our mothers and fathers. Some soldiers from Möng Yang haven't seen their families for eleven years. Some from Möng Hsau haven't seen their families for seven or eight years. Although Tai groups might live in distant locations, we are kin, we are close, so we should be together. The Shan army is the army of our land; we who are of the Shan race, we need to understand that.

—Khun Sa, 29 January 1994 (Hang Hseng Yawd ဟၢင်းသိင်ယွတ်; 1995, 17)

The Thai government is clever compared to the Burmese one. We Shan have been at war with the Burmese for so many years, but the more they beat us down, the more we keep fighting. The Thai also oppress the Shan people, treating us like animals, but they somehow figured out how to make our children want to be Thai.

—Sai Sai

IN 2015, WAN KAN HAI started to experience acute water shortages. Toward the end of the dry season, before Poi Hsang Lawng, local homes did not have tap water for daily use. Several villagers equipped themselves with additional reservoir tanks as a short-term solution. After two years of this seasonal drought, Sai Möng Mao called a town hall meeting to discuss the issue and announce a plan to resolve the problem.

While Wan Kan Hai is technically on the Thai side of the border, the nearby forested mountains on the Shan State side comprise a watershed containing valuable springs. The temple at the border makes use of water from the Shan State side; there is a small turbine in a local stream to generate power for the temple as well as the temple school, which is now the Tat-madaw base. Sai Möng Mao and his consultants proposed a new project that would involve the Shan community and the soldiers of the Shan State Army: tap one of the springs in the adjacent mountains and pipe water to supplement Wan Kan Hai's dwindling supplies.

This is hardly the first time in recent history that Wan Kan Hai has taken resources from the Shan State side of the geopolitical border; actually, it happens all the time, even with the ostensible shutting of the official border gate. People forage and hunt game, and with the border being relatively porous, there is a great deal of undocumented crossing. But this particular pipeline was the largest effort in the area in the past few decades. When village leaders proposed the water pipeline plan at the town hall meeting, Aunty Bu raised the concern, "What if the Burmese take the opportunity to poison our water?" In spite of their own history with the Tatmadaw and its abuses, the others at the meeting shrugged off Aunty Bu's hypothetical sinister scenario as far-fetched.

To organize the funds to build the new pipeline, the village council cal-culated that each household on the eastern, predominantly Shan side of the village would contribute 1,500 baht, while those on the western, predomi-nately Chinese side would contribute 3,000 baht each.[1] The location of the two sides of the village on opposite hilltops would mean a split of the pipe-line, diverting the water to each side. After emptying their village reserve fund and seeking household contributions, they had acquired approximately 900,000 baht for the project. The village headman coordinated with the Thai district-level government organization องค์การบริหารส่วนตำบล, referred to by the Thai acronym Aw Baw Taw, to send an engineer to survey the area, create a drawing, and plan the installation.

With the plans from the Thai engineer and supplies trucked in from Chiang Mai, soldiers of the Shan State Army carried out the heavy labor, hauling the pipe and supplies up to the mountain and installing the pipe to feed the village. As Kyaw Myint explained, "The Thai government proba-bly would not have been able to carry out this work. It's not in their territory. And besides, the Thais don't know where the land mines are, so the SSA would be better to do this work anyway. The soldiers are strong, because they are doing military exercises every morning. They can do the job."

During the project's implementation, Seng Kham took lunch to the soldiers, out of care and camaraderie. The completed pipeline starts as an eight-inch diameter pipe from the catchment at the source, narrows down to five inches, and is three inches in diameter at the point at which it splits at the T-junction to send water to the Chinese side of town and the Shan side in smaller household pipes. On the way to a tract of homes, bright blue sets of PVC pipes are still visible.

Why was Wan Kan Hai running out of water in the second decade of the twenty-first century? Villagers' consensus was that the water shortage came as a result of rampant deforestation in the area. Along the roads to the village, I noticed more fruit orchards as well as some commercial fish ponds. Some Shan pointed to the increased use of irrigation-intensive agriculture. One Shan interlocutor went so far as to suggest climate change was to blame. "It's big business that cuts down the forest," commented Sai Leng. "The Shan migrants have neither the equipment nor the resources to get the bigger trees. We only harvest bamboo or banana trees for our daily use."

Even so, the provision of water for the local villagers in Wan Kan Hai reinforced the role of the Shan State Army as a group committed to the local community. Although they took the job as mercenary hydrologists, they had both detailed knowledge of the territory and the trust of the community; they were able to follow through and complete this important work. In addition, many had worked on construction projects in Chiang Mai, thus plumbing and septic tank installation was a skill some possessed. The Shan village is on the periphery of the Thai state, but villagers' ability to organize and their connection with the Shan State Army allowed them to make the project happen. They can bring water to Shanland.

While the Shan State Army bases maintain their relationship with the surrounding community, the question remains: what allowed Myanmar and Thailand to emerge on the world stage as full-fledged internationally recognized nation-states, but not Shanland? We might look at it as a perfect storm of history. Tai-speaking statelets, variously vassal to other empires, predated European colonialism by hundreds of years, but it was the British who mapped the Shan States as Frontier Areas, creating a bureaucratic distinction that effected tangible differences in territory and political authority. Ontological changes in categories of community and race further reinforced this divide. While Burma's ethno-nationalism was forged as an anti-colonial struggle, the incorporation of the Frontier Areas as part of the Union might very well have been an afterthought, an appendix, or, more precisely, Chapter X to the Constitution.

Meanwhile, Siamese/Thai adoption of European discourses of race and nation crucially affected the future of Shanland in two ways: by connecting

The PVC water pipes installed by the Shan State Army. (Photo by the author)

Shan people to the Thais by ideas of blood, the Thais put forward a political model whereby Shans and Thais are inextricably and naturally bound to each other historically and therefore should—according to the Thais—be united in a future empire; and by making use of the idea of ethnic kin, Thai Cold War policy would later frame Shan insurgencies as ideologically acceptable (though it would later deny Shans fleeing war the ability to acquire refugee status). Thai national discourse would appropriate Shan-ness in one more way: Thai patriotism sees the Shan in Myanmar as politically dominated by the historic colonial enemy of the Thai nation, the Burmese, and therefore a Tai group in need of "rescue."

The Shan elites during British colonialism, though they may have been the object of T(h)ai nationalist discourse at the time, had little interest in the political ambitions of their neighbors to the southeast. They had their own interpretations of race and heritage, though from their boxed-in cellular Shan States they had not developed imperial ambitions in recent centuries, though some had absorbed their neighbors. For the Shan chiefs of the early twentieth century, the center for modern prestige was a continent away and was one where people wore suits, played tennis, and had afternoon tea in English gardens. On the other hand, Shan and Thai elites were still sponsors of Buddhist religion and ruled over domestic rice paddy economies. However, it was the Siamese who built a territorial nation-state that violently absorbed many former vassal states and made them Thai, though only within its geo-body (Thongchai Winichakul 1994). An attempt was made to absorb two Shan States into Thailand during World War II, though these were reverted back to British Burma's Frontier Areas at the close of the war.

In sum, anti-colonial struggle forged Burma's ethno-nationalism, while elites integrated the Thai race and nation from above. The Shan elites were in collaboration with the British, but prepared for self-determination, only to have a protracted internal conflict stoke the symbolic powers of ethnic identity.

Was Shanland somehow late to the party compared to its neighbors? In a way, it was. At the close of World War II, Shan politicians were not interested in joining their Thai counterparts, as they feared becoming completely absorbed and ruled as part of Thailand. Joining with the Union of Burma included a legislated caveat that they would be allowed to vote for independence following ten years' initial membership. In hindsight, going with Thailand might have brought greater material stability (though at the end of World War II, Burma's economy was more advanced than Thailand's), but at the expense of local autonomy.

That meeting in 1947 in which Shan *sao hpa* agreed to put in their lot with Aung San and join the Union of Burma represents a critical juncture. Shan politicians and intellectuals still hold a tenacious grip on what they call the "Spirit of the Panglong Agreement." I had a long conversation on the subject with Sai Leng, one of the key organizers of SURA, who has a medical degree from the University of Mandalay. We discuss whether it was Aung San's true intention to grant the Shan State full independence. With Sai Leng, I speculate about what Aung San *really* wanted to do. I suggest that perhaps he only got the agreement as a bureaucratic exercise, that he just wanted independence for Burma and did not plan to extend rights to Shan States until the British made him do so. Since Aung San was killed prior to independence, we have no evidence as to whether or how he would have followed through with the plan or dealt with the changing circumstances. Sai Leng responds with interest and states:

> You can say that as a free thinker. But how could I suggest something like that? Aung San is their national hero, and Shans rally about the Spirit of the Panglong Agreement. So, when they ask whether I think Aung San was genuine, I have to say, of course he laid out the plans for Shan independence in the Spirit of the Panglong Agreement. If he had not been killed, he would have fulfilled the promise and given the ethnic nationalities the chance for independence.

Sai Leng has a nuanced understanding of history but also the political savvy to recognize the ways in which the political movement of which he is part depends on a certain interpretation of that historical event. For the Shan political movement, a nation that seeks to repossess its state, the Panglong Agreement represents the title deed, and Aung San's intension is that the Shan are the rightful owners of Shanland. The ten-year agreement was a temporary lease of Shanland to Burma, as it were.

Putting together a timeline to demonstrate the paths in history that deferred Shanland's entrance to the world stage is instructive but inadequate for the goals of Shan nation-builders today. Such a timeline narrates a story of Shanland's past, and its injustices, but does not present the Shan people with historic agency. If the mistakes of the past are highlighted, then people today can be taught not to repeat them. In this case, the recurring trope of the congenital lack of political unity on the part of Shan has such a political purpose.

In a Shan-language history book, the author argues, "We Shan have been slaves to others for a long time. We have also been lords, but as lords we have not been united" (Möng Kham Hkö Hsang မိူင်းခမ်းၶိုဝ်းသၢင် 2011, 55). Specific events and processes are pointed to as evidence of this disunity; for example, from the third Anglo-Burmese war, "the great potential for resistance in the Shan hills was never fully realized because there was a fatal lack of unity among the Shan chiefs at the crucial moment of British invasion" (Ni Ni Myint 1983, 105). Another interpretation of the colonial imposition in Shan States points out that among Shan *sao hpa*, an outside arbitrator was necessary as the Shan princes "would perish rather than submit to their own kind, even for the sake of unity" (Saimong 1965, 147).

From another angle, this situation or the evidence of cellular political histories in the region provide ample evidence that linguistic similarity (and among the elites at that) is not sufficient basis for political alliance. Blaming long-dead Shans for their historic disunity is a nudge to Shans to unite in the present. The figure of the Shan warrior king Suerkhan Fa is presented as great *because he united Shan kingdoms.*

With ethno-national discourse, then, groups with the same language, heritage, and even "blood" are to be together in the same nation-state. One Thai scholar of the Shan makes the observation that Shan-ness "doesn't manifest itself in the same way, not the same sense of unity as with the Thai. The lack of unity has allowed Burma to exercise influence" (Shalardchai Ramitanondh ฉลาดชาย 1998, 23).

The Shan have not actualized the kind of ethno-nationalist ideology promulgated by the Thai. Their political power has historically been cellular, plus they don't have the infrastructure or power to make everyone in the Shan State fully Shan, let alone Shan in the same way, even though they have sufficient historical evidence to point to. In a conversation with a former Möng Tai Army teacher, Kyaw Myint, he explained to me, "Each of the *sao hpa* would have just one area of Shanland separate from the other." As he is talking, with his index finger he traces a line on the bench where we are both sitting, drawing an imaginary boundary between himself and me, "but the Thai king has all of the Thai people respecting him alone. That's how the Thai and the Shans were different."

Another woman, Thuzar, from Wan Kan Hai elaborated further: "When some Shan move back to Shan State after living in Thailand for a long time, they take pictures of the Thai royal family with them. They put the photos up in their homes there. The Myanmar government does not like it; they don't have a king anymore. But as you see in Thailand, every home has pictures of the king. It's just something everyone does."

The Siamese elites were able to succeed at this project because of a subordination process that happened decades ago, so there is the tacit racialized notion that the Shan lords should have done this. When discussing Thai cultural unity in the present, many conversations willfully ignore the various principalities that were hostile to Siamese subordination, or even the fact that this idea of "unity" is predicated on violence. The increased use of monuments to warrior kings, namely Naresuan, Suerkhan Fa, and Bayinnaung for the Thai, Shan, and Burmese, respectively, offers bronze evidence of this shift in ethno-national statecraft. They come to represent the national and racial unity of "their peoples" in history as a strategy to mobilize them in the present. Again, the racialized nation is projected onto history.

The awakening of the Shan nation can be charted from a colonial beginning and the classes of the Shan Chiefs' School through to a Cold War kaleidoscope of black-market economies and shifting allegiances. With the formation of the cultural associations in the first half of the twentieth century, the Shan nation was an elite project. The Kuomintang incursion, followed by the Burma Army occupation and continued decades of war, pushed the peasantry in the Shan State in various directions and forced many of them to join one armed group or another. Groups such as the Shan United Revolutionary Army offered a cultural and patriotic alternative to the chaos and oppression of the foreign occupiers. The Buddhist, patriotic vision of Kawn Söng made the Shan movement attractive to the Thai government as well. Khun Sa's Möng Tai Army offered a similar vision, although its size and international connections brought it more power and firepower. Nevertheless, Khun Sa's armies were able to maintain Shan liberated territory and kept media production and education in the Shan language going.

I was once at a Shan literary event at Chiang Mai University in 2007, and a monk giving a presentation asked the audience rhetorically, "Lanna (Northern Thai) language has its own script, but how many Northern Thai people can read and write it?" Although approximately six million people speak Northern Thai, their literacy is only in the Central Thai script; only a handful of monks and scholars are fully literate in Northern Thai. Spinning this another way, we could argue that it was due to Thai unity that Northern Thais are not able to read and write their own language.

Today temples, landmarks, and tourist attractions around Northern Thailand have signage in Northern Thai script for aesthetic effect (though always in tandem with Central Thai and often romanized for foreigners). Northern Thai restaurants have menus printed in Central Thai using Lanna-esque fonts. However, these are only superficial uses of the written script; there was never a modern movement with the force to make Northern Thai the primary language taught in schools or the bureaucratic print language of Northern Thailand, as was the case with Shan.

For the Shan people now living in Thailand, the fight to maintain a sense of Shan community is not waged with guns as it is in Myanmar. There is not a Shan State in Thailand; in fact, the Shan people who have been in Thailand for generations have largely submitted to being Thai, even if Thai is not their first language. The settled Shan in Mae Hong Son often have the privilege of Thai citizenship; especially those Shan who move to Chiang Mai or Bangkok are fully assimilated as Thai and often eschew mention of their Shan heritage when in the company of Thais. Recall Nang Lao, the Shan waitress at the Chiang Mai Airport. For her, acting Thai is necessary for her survival just to do her job and receive her wage. When the Shan do present themselves as Shan, it may be when they return to Mae Hong Son for Poi Hsang Lawng—this and other cultural events or touristic ethnic displays fit the country's idea of festivalized culture.

But cultural appreciation and embracing the ideology that Shan and Thai are racial siblings can be a double-edged sword: Shan might be considered ethnically closer to the Thais, but in this way, they have been forced to surrender their political and cultural autonomy to Thai-ness. Many Shan people have the unfortunate and frustrating experience of being lumped in with the Burmese in the eyes of Thais, a status they go to great lengths to avoid. For those Thais who do acknowledge the difference of Shan people, and respect it, there is sometimes the accompanying attitude that the Shan are deeply authentic and that modern urban life is not appropriate for them. This perspective comes from an acknowledgment that Shan peoples' lives as semi-documented poorly waged laborers in the Thai economy is a form of terrible exploitation. But Khun Maew and her rich entourage announcing to a group of impoverished Shan people, "You don't have to migrate to the cities," comes off as patronizing to many. There are class dif-ferences that undergird perceptions about ethnic difference. The fact that a "development" NGO would promise great prosperity and then gradually lose interest, in addition to their repeated ostentatious displays of wealth and privilege, again reminds the Shan that while some Thais might enjoy the romantic image that they and the Shan are historic brethren, the image is fine and comfortable to the better-off Thai so long as it does not challenge their place of privilege.

Many Shan people are neither willing nor able to become Thai, and some resent the behavior of other Shans who seem to be forgetting their Shan heritage. It is no coincidence that migrants from Shan State now working in Thailand constitute a major source of funding for the Shan State Army, or that many soldiers themselves have been migrant workers in Thailand. When Shan workers in Thailand send remittances to their families in the Shan State who reside in the taxation areas of the Restoration Council of the Shan State, they are indirectly supporting the Shan State Army. Some Shan migrants choose to contribute directly via their networks of contacts in Thailand.

For many, the dreams for an independent Shanland are predicated on contemporary misery. But imagining a Shan nation does not mean purging oneself of dynamic social history or social capital, even if it held greater currency in another place and time. As shown by analysis of Shan appreciation of Burmese popular culture, people in Wan Kan Hai, in spite of being politically opposed to the Myanmar government, still love Burmese rock songs and have affection for Burmese film stars. Exploring Shan migrants' relationship with personal histories through popular culture practices demonstrates that their social lives are more complex than some hackish ethnonational analyses might suggest.

For some patriots, an independent Shanland still lies on the horizon. The characteristics of that country have changed according to the times, as have the tactics for its repossession. Shanland is already complete with the necessary prerequisites of a modern nation-state: a history, a print language, a government, a monetary system, and schools teaching a complete curriculum in the national language; it can even deliver plumbing to its residents.

One of my trips to the Shan State Army base of Loi Taileng was organized by a Shan monk who goes by the name Philip. We rode up the mountain together: he in the front passenger seat of the four-seater pickup truck while I was seated in the back. After general chit chat and talking about Shan politics, Philip told me, "Jane, when we get Shan independence, we will issue you a Shan passport." Reflecting on the motives behind his gesture, I knew Philip's offer did not come from a desire to compare the potential bargaining strength of Shanland with that of my other citizenships (being a dual national and carrying Irish and United States passports, I already have access to numerous labor markets and tourist visas-on-arrival). Instead, Philip wanted to remind me that he anticipated that Shanland would have the full accoutrements of a modern nation-state, and the infrastructure to connect its citizens to the world; his gesture was to tell me that I would be welcomed to that community. I must say, I do love the idea of being a citizen of Shanland, and if Shanland does achieve independence in my lifetime, I plan to use this publication as evidence to hold Philip to his word (assuming he has a modicum of political power by then).

While optimism for a fully independent Shanland is far from universal among Shan people—including those who committed decades to that project—the possibility of realizing that vibrant future is periodically stoked by booming rock concerts and carnivalesque revelry at Buddhist festival events. Such cathartic events punctuate a mundane reality that is dominated by harrowing struggles just to get by, from the millions of Shan peasants in the Shan State to the hundreds of thousands of migrant workers trying to eke out a living on the fringes of the Thai economy. While the fun of revelry offers a sample of the delights of a higher rebirth in the Buddhist cosmology, the cachet of modern music along with other components of Shan cultural visibility gives them a platform for the anticipation of a Shan nation that is recognizable to others in an international community. In that sense, repossession is complete, and Shanland has been returned to its rightful owners.

NOTES

Prologue

1. This discrepancy in years is noted across various sources, including sources by Shan authors. David Wyatt, who relied on Burmese records, puts Suerkhan Fa's reign at 1152 to 1205; Yos notes that Chea Yanchong claims it was from 1336 to 1364 (Yos Santasombat 2001, 5). Khur Hsen's Shan-language history book agrees with Chea Yanchong's dates: 1336 to 1364 (Khur Hsen ၶိူဝ်းသႅၼ်1999, 149), while Sai Aung Tun writes that it was from 1220 to 1250 (Sai Aung Tun 2009, 16). Another Shan historian, Sao Yanfa, has put the reign at 1311–64 (Khuensai Jaiyen, personal communication, July 2020).

2. The latter Burmese name is also permanently associated with a Shan *nat* spirit of the same name (Ko Myo Shin).

Introduction

1. According to Myanmar's census scheme, Shan State contains thirty-three ethnic nationality groups.

2. The most recent nationwide census in Myanmar was in 2014, and as of today, the data regarding ethnicity have not yet been released. The construction of the categories and their implementation have been controversial (Ferguson 2015).

3. For Shan languages and their distribution, Murakami defines them as follows: (1) Tai Long, in central and southern Shan State; (2) Tai Nü, the northern Shan State / Yunnan border area; (3) Tai Khün, eastern Shan State; (4) Tai Khamti, northern Kachin State; (5) Tai Lue, the Sipsongpanna area of Yunnan Province, China; and (6) Tai Yuan and Khun Mueang, the Lanna areas of northern Thailand (2009, 82–83).

4. Also romanized Möng Maw (in Shan: မိူင်းမၢဝ်း).

5. I use the most typical romanization of the Shan king Suerkhan Fa, which would be romanized from the Shan as Hsö Hkan Fa (in Shan: သိူဝ်ခၢၼ်ႇၾႃႉ).

6. I make use of the older Wade-Giles romanization for Kuomintang (instead of Guomindang) as Shan interlocutors and texts use the abbreviation KMT frequently; the choice is to reduce confusion across acronyms.

7. "Shan" in Burmese is သျှမ်း or more commonly ရှမ်း. This may also reflect the British using Portuguese maps, so the term's romanization may well have been by the Portuguese, only to be copied by the British.

8. In Thai: ไทใหญ่ "great Tai." Another theory posits that the lowland Thais called upland groups *Tai yai* because they perceived them as savage (Niti นิติ 2004, 7).

9. Further studies of different groups "becoming" Tai include those of Izikowitz (1951) and Condominas (1990).

10. There is an important caution to be taken in contemporary anthropological work on race, to be wary of a tendency to step back from racial arguments in "glib deconstructionism" while at the same time failing to engage with histories (and presents!) of racism within the practice of the discipline and its analytical procedures (Allen and Jobson 2016, 129).

CHAPTER 1. PASSPORT TO ANCIENT SHANLAND

1. The dates of Suerkhan Fa's legend do not consistently line up here.

2. Southeast Asia by 1600 had one-seventh the population density of China, and, by contrast, in China land was used as a means to exercise control over people (Scott 2009, 65).

3. Nicholas Tapp (2000) uses the metaphor of the honeycomb to describe the various Tai states. While I like the image, it implies a certain regularity to it and relatively discrete boundaries between states.

4. From an evidentiary perspective, it would seem logical that the powerful centers would be the parties sponsoring the authorship regarding their polities. Importantly, this paradigm of the Mandala, the Galactic Polities, has offered a legitimating historical narrative to creating an image of a happy, just kingdom, where even slavery was not as oppressive as one might think. Katherine Bowie's (2018) use of oral history offers an important counternarrative to this idea that the ancient kingdoms were so prosperous and kind to their subjects.

5. Like the Shan, the Kachin are considered the majority ethnic group in one of Myanmar's fourteen administrative regions and, as such, have a named state: Kachin State. While part of the area had formerly been controlled by Shan *sao hpa*, a group of Kachin chiefs had usurped their power, and by the nineteenth century, the area was largely controlled by Kachin chiefs (Lintner 2003, 177; Sadan 2013, 51).

6. In the Thai context today, various cultural demonstrations are understood by Thais as iconic of Shan ethnic identity, a prime example being the Poi Sang Lawng ritual ordination festival (which is derived from Brahmanic rituals). However, for

Shans, sometimes it is referred to as a *khöng Man* ခုံင်းမာခင်း "Burmese thing" as it became incorporated into Shan cultural practices by cis-Salween Shan polities with extensive cultural contact with the Burmese.

7. A point of interest: eleventh-century Mon and Khmer kingdoms looked at Tais as the barbarians for their lack of cultural sophistication (Keyes 1977, 4).

8. In cases where individuals did not know the discrete term for their language, the enumerator filled in the blank on their behalf, as happens today. The exercise codifies the enumerators' perceptions, too, offering yet another subjective aspect of the process that should be taken into account.

9. A recent mass-produced popular history book, *Paen Din Thi Sia Pai* (Lost territories), exemplifies this stance. It contains fourteen chapters, each describing the way in which that respective territory became part of a state other than Siam (Wipan วิพันธุ์ 2008).

10. The irony of Siamese royalty placing themselves at the top of a racial order of a *chat* Thai is that one does not have to go far back on the Chakri family tree to find Chinese branches. This is not unlike Benedict Anderson's observation that the late British Empire had not been ruled by an "English" dynasty since the eleventh century; its dynasties were Normans, Welsh, Scots, Dutch, and Germans (Anderson 1991, 83n). As usual, the rules for the commoners do not apply to the royalty.

11. During the 1880s, it was noted as well that *sgaw* Karen language coined a new term, *dawkawlu*, which is a conjunction of "the whole of a kind," but started to take the meaning of "nation" (Fujimura 2020).

12. "We Sawbwas" uses the Burmese pronunciation of the Shan term *sao hpa*. The Tawngpeng prince might have had to eat these words: in 1946 he would become president of the Shan Chiefs Council, the group that signed the Panglong Agreement in 1947 (Khuensai Jaiyen, personal communication, July 2020).

13. Next door in Siam, the 1930s saw the end of its absolute monarchy at the behest of local bureaucrats; Burmese nationalists similarly looked to new political models rather than a return to the monarchy of old.

14. They did not transfer the entirety of Möng Pan State to Siam, only the trans-Salween part, which is Mong Ton Township today (Khuensai Jaiyen, personal communication, July 2020).

15. Thailand had acquired other colonial territories from Indochina and Malaya, and these were also returned to the French and British colonial authorities, respectively, with the close of the war (Haseman 1999, 158).

16. It was written elsewhere in the constitution that the provisions of Chapter X did not apply to Kachin State.

Chapter 2. A Cold War Fusion of Elite Ideals with an Armed Insurgency

1. This name is related to his monk (Pali) name, Sonanta. Some later referred to him as Saw Yanta (the "Saw" derived from the Burmese pronunciation of "Sao") or even "Sawn Ta" (Khuensai Jaiyen, personal communication, July 2020).

2. But historically Shan rulers would often pay tribute to other more powerful kingdoms as well; historical tributary relations, as we have seen across Southeast Asia, become compelling fodder for contemporary imperial ambitions.

3. According to one of Khun Sa's speeches in 1993, more than eight thousand people, including Shan intellectuals, were imprisoned during the period of Ne Win's coup (Hang Seng Yawd ႁၢင်ႈသႅင်ယွတ်ႈ 1995, 3).

Chapter 3. Revolutionary Ink and the Shan Insurgent Culture Industries

1. Many argue that the similarity of appearance is because this Southern Shan script is derived from the Burmese script, including ethnologue (Eberhard, Simons, and Fennig 2021). A historian of the Shan scripts, Sai Kham Mong, instead argues that the similarity in appearance is not because the Shan script is derived from the Burmese script but rather because they are both derived from Brahmi Nagari script (Sai Kham Mong 2004, 80). I cannot argue one way or another, but it does illustrate, yet again, that the written language is an important signifier of heritage and authenticity for these nations. I put the Shan version in the main text to provoke.

2. This figure was according to SURA informants; also, what comprises a "school" is subject to interpretation, as detailed above.

3. The next chapter contains portions of Khun Sa's speeches, translated from some of these books.

4. Khuensai Jaiyen has pointed out that there is a song by Kengtung Shans written in the late 1950s titled ဝၼ်းၼႆႉပဵၼ်ယိင်ႈယႂ်ႇ, ပီႈၼွင်ႉႁဝ်းလၢတ်ႈတီႈလဵၵ်ႈမျႃးႁူပ်ႉထူပ်း ၵၼ် that uses the term *sat*, but it was later with the SURA that the term gained widespread currency as an idea of ethnic race or nation (Khuensai Jaiyen, personal communication, July 2020).

5. What was interesting in talking about the two most famous Shan recording artists in Burma, Sai Htee Saing and Sai Sai Mao, was that many Shan people felt they had to proclaim which of the two was their favorite. One SURA woman even told me that while she was a Htee Saing fan, her former husband liked Sai Mao. They are no longer married, but for unrelated reasons.

6. This comment is not without precedent in Shan tradition. The art of the Shan love letter *lik hkew* (လိၵ်ႈၶဵဝ်) or "green letter" was a poetic form used by a boy to woo a girl. This was of such importance that sometimes there were village "green letter" writers that could be hired freelance, as it were (Sai Htwe Maung 2007, 24).

Chapter 4. Shanland during the Reign of the Heroin King

1. The Golden Triangle is the moniker given to the borderlands where Burma, Laos, and Thailand meet. The United States Drug Enforcement Administration (DEA) named it as such because the high-value transactions of the black-market economy in the area used gold bars as the medium of exchange.

2. The Burmese government refused to extradite Khun Sa to the United States, despite the DEA putting a $2 million price tag on his head.

3. The historical precedent for this is located in the 1952 Anti-Communist Act in Thailand, which, in turn, is based on un-American activities legislation, which argues that communism is simply un-Thai in its ideology and as a way of life (Thongchai Winichakul 1994, 6; Peleggi 2007, 17). The fact that Chinese and Vietnamese constituted the majority of communists in the country, especially in the early days, meant that the communist menace could readily be portrayed as foreign, and therefore un-Thai (Kasian 2001, 18).

4. This is the shorthand for Heroin Number Four, or the most pure and expensive form of the drug.

5. For example, the National Democratic Alliance Army–Eastern Shan State (NDAA–ESS) was given autonomy by the Burmese government to operate Special Region 4, or what is known as Mongla. This autonomous region, from the 1990s onward, was home to casinos at which wealthy Chinese and other international tourists would cross over to engage in high-stakes gambling. Since its heyday, Mongla as a location for high rollers has been eclipsed by the Laotian border town of Boten, in Luang Nam Tha Province.

CHAPTER 5. LITTLE BROTHER IS EXPLOITING YOU

1. This was not broken down according to ethnicity; Shan people are included in this total.

2. I learned of some Shan migrants who had successfully acquired "pink" or "Hill Tribe" identity cards by claiming to be Lahu, as they perceived that they would have better prospects for acquiring Thai citizenship than if they had kept the "displaced Burmese national" ID cards.

3. The fermented bean disks are sometimes jokingly referred to as *CD tuen*, or "pirated CD."

4. Incidentally, in the approximately thirty times that I made this trip between Chiang Mai to Wan Kan Hai over my two and a half years of fieldwork, I never saw the Thai police or army neglect to check a woman's card. It very well could be that this perception that pretty women "have it easier" with the police has been amplified by folklore. But there is also the possibility that the Thai police would be more thorough and consistent in doing their job when a foreigner is watching.

CHAPTER 6. WE ARE SIAMESE (IF YOU PLEASE)

1. Other sites in Thailand have used the political history as a key "selling point" for tourism. For example, Doi Mae Salong in Chiang Rai Province has a Kuomintang museum, and Ban Hin Taek, also in Chiang Rai, has a Khun Sa museum.

2. I realize this is a bit confusing in translation, what with the *mawng* being a gong set and a *kawng* being a drum.

3. As describe in chapter 1, one of these percussion ensembles accompanied the first hoisting of the Union Jack on the flagpole at Möng Nai; in chapter 4, I describe how it played to welcome the Tatmadaw helicopter of Burmese generals to accept Khun Sa's surrender.

4. This speaker used the Thai term *nisai* นิสัย, which could also be translated as "one's nature."

5. Yee Thip switches from speaking in Shan to Thai just for this sentence to emphasize this point. He took on a very nasal tone of voice, almost whining, as he mocked a Thai accent, saying, "You need to do it like this, you need to do it like that," or in Thai ต้องทำอย่างนี้ต้องทำอย่างนั้น. The switch of language and tone, even the grimace that he made while he said the sentence, accentuated Yee Thip's sentiments of frustration as a result of bad experiences working with Thais.

6. Khun Maew did not acknowledge that the beautiful Shan clothing that everybody was wearing was the type reserved for special occasions; Shan villagers wouldn't ever wear wedding finery or temple festival attire to hang around town, let alone work in the fields.

7. I later realized that he may have appropriated this metaphor from one of the stories in the Shan elementary school reader for grade 2, which offers the unity of ants as a moral lesson from nature. The reader, however, does not ascribe any human ethnic nation to the ants (and there is no mention of bees).

8. It has also been argued that the appellation Tai-yai comes from a perception of the upland groups as being savage in comparison with the lowland Siamese. Also of note is that the Tai have never called themselves Tai-yai (Niti นิติ 2004, 7).

Chapter 7. Rockin' in the Shan World

1. The full translation of the song is in chapter 3.

2. In 2007 a young man in Taunggyi, Shan State, was arrested by the Myanmar police for singing this very song.

Chapter 8. Future Shan Kings or Ethnic Poster Children

1. The Shan Women's Action Network (SWAN) provided modest resources and education for reproductive health in Shan migrant communities, and Seng Kham was one of the founding members.

2. The Shan refugee and internally displaced people (IDP) camps are, to a significant extent, dependent on income from international donor organizations. The decision to hold modest Poi Hsang Lawng may have come from the desire to maintain their assistance.

3. This harks back to a legendary cockfight in which Naresuan's cock is alleged to have defeated that of Maha Uparaj, the son of Burmese Toungoo king Bayinnaung.

4. Shan-style martial arts *lai hke'n* လၢႆးၶေႃႈ are considered part of Shan traditional cultural practices, with young men learning their skills from an established master. They were expected to learn as a form of practical knowledge and

self-defense, but during the BSPP/SPDC years, the Burmese government prohibited it (Sai Htwe Maung 2007, 18).

CONCLUSION

1. The differing taxation rate not only reflects the coincidence between relative wealth and ethnicity but is also directly reminiscent of the Thathameda tax paid in Lashio, Northern Shan State, during British colonialism: Europeans, Indians, and Chinese all paid ten rupees, while Shan and Burmese paid six; Taunggyi, in the Southern Shan State, however, had no such tax distinction (*Shan States Manual* 1932, 91, 98).

REFERENCES

Adams, Nel. 2000. *My Vanished World: The True Story of a Shan Princess.* Cheshire: Horseshoe.

Ahram, Ariel I., and Charles King. 2012. "The Warlord as Arbitrageur." *Theory and Society* 41:169–86.

Allen, Jafari Sinclaire, and Ryan Cecil Jobson. 2016. "The Decolonizing Generation: (Race and) Theory in Anthropology since the Eighties." *Current Anthropology* 57 (2): 129–48.

Allott, Anna J. 1993. *Inked Over, Ripped Out: Burmese Storytellers and the Censors.* New York: PEN American Center.

Amporn Jirattikorn. 2007. *Living on Both Sides of the Border: Transnational Migrants, Pop Music and Nation of the Shan in Thailand.* Chiang Mai: Regional Center for Social Science and Sustainable Development.

———. 2008. "Migration, Media Flows and the Shan Nation in Thailand." PhD diss., University of Texas at Austin.

Amporn อัมพร จิรัฐติกร. 2015a (2558). ประวัติศาสตร์นอกกรอบรัฐชาติ 55 ปีขบวนการกู้ชาติ ไทใหญ่. Chiang Mai: Center for Social Science and Sustainable Development.

———. 2015b (2558). พื้นที่สาธารณะข้ามชาติ การเมืองเรื่องพื้นที่ของแรงงานอพยพไทใหญ่ ในจังหวัดเชียงใหม่ เชียงใหม่ มหาวิทยาลัยเชียงใหม่.

Anderson, Benedict. 1978. "Studies of the Thai State: The State of Thai Studies." In *The Study of Thailand: Analysis of Knowledges, Approaches, and Prospects in Anthropology, Art, History, Economics, and Political Science*, edited by Eliezer B. Ayal, 193–247. Athens: Ohio State University Center for International Studies.

———. (1983) 1991. *Imagined Communities: Reflections on the Origin and Spread of Nationalism.* 2nd ed. London: Verso.

Anusorn Don Chedi อนุสรณ์ดอนเจดีย์. 1959. อนุสรณ์ดอนเจดีย์ สุพรรณบุรี คณะกรรมการ อนุสรณ์ดอนเจดีย์.

Aphijanyatham Ropharat. 2009. "The Human (In)Security of Shan Migrant Workers in Thailand." Bangkok: Research Institute of Contemporary Southeast Asia.

Appadurai, Arjun. 2019. "Traumatic Exit, Identity Narratives, and the Ethics of Hospitality." *Television and New Media* 20 (6): 558–65.

Asa Kumpha อาสา คำภา. 2006. รัฐฉานและคนไทใหญ่ในช่วงสมัยอาณานิคม ไทยคดีศึกษา 3 (2): 82–130 กรุงเทพ.

Ashin Thukameinda အရှင်သုခမိန္တ. 2008. ရှမ်းတိုင်းရင်းသားတို့၏ယုံကြည်ကိုးကွယ်မှုနှင့်ဓလေ့ ထုံးစံများ ရန်ကုန် သာသနာရေးဝန်ကြီးဌာန.

Aung-Thwin, Michael Arthur. 2011. "A New/Old Look at 'Classical' and 'Post-Classical' Southeast Asia/Burma." In *New Perspectives on the History and Historiography of Southeast Asia*, edited by Michael Arthur Aung-Thwin and Kenneth R. Hall, 25–55. London: Routledge.

Banerjee-Dube, Ishita, ed. 2008. *Caste in History*. Delhi: Oxford University Press.

Barth, Fredrik. 1969. Introduction to *Ethnic Groups and Boundaries: The Social Organization of Culture Difference*, edited by Fredrik Barth, 9–38. Boston: Little, Brown.

Bohmer, Carol, and Amy Shuman. 2007. "Producing Epistemologies of Ignorance in the Political Asylum Application Process." *Identities* 14 (5): 603–29.

Bowie, Katherine A. 1997. *Rituals of National Loyalty: An Anthropology of the State and the Village Scout Movement in Thailand*. New York: Columbia University Press.

———. 2018. "Palimpsests of the Past: Oral History and the Art of Pointillism." *Journal of Asian Studies* 77 (4): 1–23.

Breckenridge, Carol A., Sheldon Pollock, Homi K. Bhabha, and Dipesh Chakrabarty, eds. 2002. *Cosmopolitanism*. Durham, NC: Duke University Press.

Brubaker, Rogers. 2004. *Ethnicity without Groups*. Cambridge, MA: Harvard University Press.

Bün To Kaep Sai Mu ပွိုန်းတူစ့်က်ပ်; ၐၢးမူး. 2005. Pamphlet handed out as part of the New Year's celebration.

Byrne, Jennifer. 2016. "Contextual Identity among Liberian Refugees in Ghana: Identity Salience in a Protracted Refugee Situation." *Politics & Policy* 44 (4): 751–82.

Callahan, Mary. 1996. "The Origins of Military Rule in Burma." PhD diss., Cornell University.

———. 2003. *Making Enemies: War and State Building in Burma*. Ithaca, NY: Cornell University Press.

———. 2007. *Political Authority in Burma's Ethnic Minority States: Devolution, Occupation, and Coexistence*. Singapore: Institute of Southeast Asian Studies (ISEAS).

Chang, Wen-Chin. 1999. "Beyond the Military: The Complex Migration and Resettlement of the KMT Yunnanese Chinese in Northern Thailand." PhD diss., KU Leuven, Belgium.

———. 2004. "Guanxi and Regulation in Networks: The Yunnanese Jade Trade between Burma and Thailand, 1962–88." *Journal of Southeast Asian Studies* 35 (3): 479–501.

———. 2013. "The Everyday Politics of the Underground Trade in Burma by the Yunnanese Chinese since the Burmese Socialist Era." *Journal of Southeast Asian Studies* 44 (2): 292–314.

Chaofaa Saenwi เจ้าฟ้าแสนหวี. 2001. ประวัติศาสตร์ไทใหญ่ พื้นไทตอนกลาง เชียงใหม่ สำนัก พิมพ์ตรัสวิน.

Charnvit ชาญวิทย์ เกษตรศิริ. (1982) 2001. พม่า: ประวัติศาสตร์และการเมือง กรุงเทพ มูลนิธิ โครงการตำราสังคมศาสตร์และมนุษยศาสตร์.

Chatterjee, Partha. 1993. *The Nation and Its Fragments: Colonial and Postcolonial Histories.* Princeton, NJ: Princeton University Press.

Cheesman, Nick 2002. "Seeing 'Karen' in the Union of Myanmar." *Asian Ethnicity* 3:199–220.

Chit Hlaing, FKL. 2007. "Some Remarks upon Ethnicity Theory and Southeast Asia, with Special Reference to the Kayah and the Kachin." In *Exploring Ethnic Diversity in Burma*, edited by Mikael Gravers, 107–22. Malaysia: NIAS Press.

Cline, Lawrence E. 2009. "Insurgency in Amber: Ethnic Opposition Groups in Myanmar." *Small Wars and Insurgencies* 20 (3–4): 574–91.

Cochrane, Wilbur Willis. 1915. *Shans.* Vol. 1. Rangoon: Superintendent, Government Printing, Burma.

Cohen, Erik. 1996. *Thai Tourism: Hill Tribes, Islands, and Open-Ended Prostitution.* Bangkok: White Lotus.

Cohn, Bernard S. 1996. *Colonialism and Its Forms of Knowledge: The British in India.* Princeton, NJ: Princeton University Press.

Cohn, Bernard S., and Nicholas B. Dirks. 1988. "Beyond the Fringe: The Nation State, Colonialism, and the Technologies of Power." *Journal of Historical Sociology* 1 (2): 223–29.

Collis, Maurice. 1938. *Lords of the Sunset: A Tour in the Shan States.* New York: Dodd.

Condominas, Georges. 1990. *From Lawa to Mon, Saa' to Thai: Historical and Anthropological Studies of Southeast Asian Social Places.* Canberra: Research School of Pacific and Asian Studies, Australian National University.

Conway, Susan. 2006. *The Shan: Culture, Art and Crafts.* Bangkok: River Books.

Cowell, Adrian. 1997. "The Opium Kings." *Public Broadcasting Network: Frontline.*

———. 2005. "Opium Anarchy in the Shan State of Burma." In *Trouble in the Triangle: Opium and Conflict in Burma*, edited by Martin Jelsma, Tom Kramer, and Pietje Vervest, 1–21. Chiang Mai: Silkworm.

de Lacouperie, A. Terrien. 1885. *The Cradle of the Shan Race: By Terrien de Lacouperie.* New York: Scribner & Welford.

Denes, Alexandra. 2006. "Recovering Khmer Ethnic Identity from the Thai National Past: An Ethnography of the Localism Movement in Surin Province." PhD diss., Cornell University.

Department of Information, Shan State. 1986. *Historical Facts about the Shan State.* N.p.: Department of Information.

Douglass, William A. 1998. "A Western Perspective on an Eastern Interpretation of Where North Meets South: Pyrenean Borderland Cultures." In *Border Identities: Nation and State at International Frontiers,* edited by Thomas W. Wilson and Hastings Donnan, 62–95. Cambridge: Cambridge University Press.

Downing, John. 2001. *Radical Media: Rebellious Communications and Social Movements.* London: SAGE.

Draper, John, and Joel Sawat Selway. 2019. "A New Dataset on Horizontal Structural Ethnic Inequalities in Thailand in Order to Address Sustainable Development Goal 10." *Social Indicators Research* 141 (1): 275–97.

Duara, Prasenjit. 2003. *Sovereignty and Authenticity: Manchukuo and the East Asian Modern.* Lanham, MD: Rowman & Littlefield.

Dupont, Alan. 1999. "Transnational Crime, Drugs, and Security in East Asia." *Asian Survey* 39 (3): 433–55.

Eberhard, David M., Gary F. Simons, and Charles D. Fennig, eds. 2021. "Shan." *Ethnologue: Languages of the World.* 24th ed. Dallas, TX: SIL International. Online edition: https://www.ethnologue.com/language/shn.

Eberhardt, Nancy. 1988. Introduction to *Gender, Power, and the Construction of the Moral Order: Studies from the Thai Periphery,* edited by Nancy Eberhardt, 3–12. Madison: University of Wisconsin Press.

———. 2006. *Imagining the Course of Life: Self-Transformation in a Shan Buddhist Community.* Honolulu: University of Hawai'i Press.

———. 2007. "Negotiating Shan Identity in Northern Thailand." Presentation at the Shan Buddhism and Culture Conference, School of Oriental and African Studies, University of London, 8–9 December.

———. 2008. "Rite of Passage or Ethnic Festival? Shan Buddhist Novice Ordinations in Northern Thailand." *Contemporary Buddhism* 10 (1): 51–63.

Elliott, Patricia W. (1999) 2006. *The White Umbrella: A Woman's Struggle for Freedom in Burma.* Bangkok: Friends.

Eriksen, Thomas Hylland. 2010. *Ethnicity and Nationalism: Anthropological Perspectives.* London: Pluto.

Evans, Grant. 1999. "Introduction: What Is Lao Culture and Society?" In *Laos: Culture and Society,* edited by Grant Evans, 1–34. Chiang Mai: Silkworm.

———. 2014. "The Ai-Lao and Nan Chao/Tali Kingdom: A Re-orientation." *Journal of the Siam Society* 102:221–56.

Featherstone, Mike, ed. 1990. *Global Culture: Nationalism, Globalization, and Modernity.* London: SAGE.

Ferguson, Jane M. 2010. "Sovereignty in the Shan State." In *Ruling Myanmar in Transition*, edited by Nicholas Cheesman, Monique Skidmore, and Trevor Wilson, 52–62. Singapore: Institute of Southeast Asian Studies (ISEAS).

———. 2012. "From Contested Histories to Ethnic Tourism: Cinematic Representations of Shans and Shanland on the Burmese Silver Screen." In *Film in Contemporary Southeast Asia: Cultural Interpretation and Social Intervention*, edited by David Lim and Hiroyuki Yamamoto, 23–40. London: Routledge.

———. 2013. "Burmese Super Trouper: How Burmese Poets and Musicians Turn Global Popular Music into Copy Thachin." *Asia Pacific Journal of Anthropology* 14 (3): 221–39.

———. 2015. "Who's Counting? Ethnicity, Belonging, and the National Census in Burma/Myanmar." *Bijdragen tot de Taal-, Land- en Volkenkunde* 171:1–28.

———. 2016. "Yesterday Once More: Tracking Unpopular Music in Contemporary Myanmar" *Journal of Burma Studies* 20 (2): 229–57.

Fink, Christina. 2001. *Living Silence: Burma under Military Rule.* London: Zed.

———. 2008. "Militarization in Burma's Ethnic States: Causes and Consequences." *Contemporary Politics* 14 (4): 447–62.

Fiskesjö, Magnus. 2013. "Introduction to Wa Studies." *Journal of Burma Studies* 17 (1): 1–27.

———. 2017. "People First: The Wa World of Spirits and Other Enemies." *Anthropological Forum* 27 (4): 340–64.

Fujimura, Hitomi. 2020. "Disentangling the Colonial Narrative on the Karen National Association of 1881: The Motive of the Karen Baptist Intellectuals' Claim for a Nation." *Journal of Burma Studies* 24 (2): 273–312.

Gibson, Richard Michael, and Wen H. Chen. 2011. *The Secret Army: Chiang Kai-shek and the Drug Warlords of the Golden Triangle.* Singapore: John Wiley & Sons.

Gogoi, Padmeswar. 1968. *The Tai and the Tai Kingdoms: With a Fuller Treatment of the Tai-Ahom in the Brahmaputra Valley.* Gauhati: Lakshmi Printing Press.

Grabowsky, Volker, and Renoo Wichasin. 2008. *Chronicles of Chiang Khaeng: A Tai Lü Principality of the Upper Mekong.* Chiang Mai: Silkworm.

Gravers, Mikael. 1999. *Nationalism as Political Paranoia in Burma: An Essay on the Historical Practice of Power.* Surrey: Curzon.

———. 2007. "Introduction: Ethnicity against State—State against Ethnic Diversity?" In *Exploring Ethnic Diversity in Burma*, edited by Mikael Gravers, 1–33. Malaysia: NIAS Press.

Grundy-Warr, Carl, and Elaine Wong Siew Yin. 2002. "Geographies of Displacement: The Karenni and the Shan across the Myanmar-Thailand Border." *Singapore Journal of Tropical Geography* 23 (1): 93–122.

Gupta, Akhil, and James Ferguson. 1992. "Beyond 'Culture': Space, Identity, and the Politics of Difference." *Cultural Anthropology* 7:6–23.

Haberkorn, Tyrell. 2011. *Revolution Interrupted: Farmers, Students, Law, and Violence in Northern Thailand.* Madison: University of Wisconsin Press.

Hang Hseng Yawd ႁၢင်ႈသႅင်ယွတ်ႈ. 1995. ၶေႃႈပူင်ၵႂၢမ်းလွမ်ပွင်သိုၵ်းမွၵ်ႇလၢတ်ႈသၢင်ႇသွၼ် မၢႆ 2 တပ်ႉသိုၵ်းမိူင်းတႆး.

Haseman, John B. 1999. *The Thai Resistance Movement during the Second World War.* Bangkok: Chalemnit Press.

Hobsbawm, E. J. 1993. *Nations and Nationalism since 1780: Programme, Myth, Reality.* Cambridge: Cambridge University Press.

Hpu Twoi Hawk ပူႈတွႆႉႁွၵ်ႈ. 2000. လိူၼ်ၾၢပ်ႇပိတ်ႉရိူဝ်ၵ်းပိူၼ်း ႁွၼ်းၶေႃ [*Independence*] 17 (2).

Hseng Küng Möng သႅင်ၵိုင်ႇမိူင်း. 1987. ၼိူင်ႈမၢႆလိူဝ်ႉထၢတ်ႈ ၸိုင်းလိၵ်ႈ 4:19–22.

Hsöng Kham Haw သိူင်ႈၶမ်းႁေႃ. 2002. လွင်ႈၽႅင်းၵႂၢမ်းတႆးပၢၼ်မႂ်ႇ, ၸိုင်းလိၵ်ႈ 20:8–15.

Ikeya, Chie. 2011. *Refiguring Women, Colonialism, and Modernity in Burma.* Honolulu: University of Hawai'i Press.

Izikowitz, Karl Gustav. 1951. *Lamet; Hill Peasants in French Indochina.* Götenborg: Göteborgs etnografiska museum.

Jiraporn Witayasakpan. 1992. "Nationalism and the Transformation of Aesthetic Concepts: Theatre in Thailand during the Phibun Period." PhD diss., Cornell University.

Jonsson, Hjorleifur. (2002) 2006. *Mien Relations: Mountain People and State Control in Thailand.* Chiang Mai: Silkworm.

Kaise, Ryoko. 1999. "Tai Yai Migration in the Thai-Burma Border Area: The Settlement and Assimilation Process, 1962–1997." MA thesis, Chulalongkorn University.

Kanchana กาญจนะ ประกาศวุฒิสาร. 2004. ทหารจีนคณะชาติก๊กมินตั๋งตกค้างทางภาคเหนือประเทศไทย เชียงใหม่ สยามรัตน พริ้นติ้ง.

Kasian Tejapira. 2001. *Commodifying Marxism: The Formation of Modern Thai Radical Culture, 1927–1958.* Kyoto: Kyoto University Press.

Keyes, Charles F. 1977. *The Golden Peninsula: Culture and Adaptation in Mainland Southeast Asia.* New York: Macmillan.

———, ed. 1981. *Ethnic Change.* Seattle: University of Washington Press.

———. 1983. "Introduction: The Study of Popular Ideas of Karma." In *Karma*, edited by Charles Keyes and E. Valentine Daniel, 1–26. Berkeley: University of California Press.

———. 2002. "Presidential Address: 'The Peoples of Asia'—Science and Politics in the Classification of Ethnic Groups in Thailand, China, and Vietnam." *Journal of Asian Studies* 61 (4): 1163–93.

Khuensai Jaiyen ၶိုၼ်းသႂ်. 1999. သိုပ်ၶၢၼ်ႇၽႅၼ်ႇ ၶွမ်ႇမတီႇၼိုင်ပွင်ၵွၵ်ပပ်ႉၵိူၼ်းလိၵ်ႈတႆး.

Khun Loi Leng ၶုၼ်လွႆလႅင်း. 1991. ၵၢၼ်ၸွႆႈလွႆမေႃႇၵမ်ႇမီးယဝ်ႉ. ၸိုင်းလိၵ်ႈ 8. Pp. 163–67.

Khun Sa. ၸဝ်ႈၶုၼ်သႃႇ. 1989. ၶေႃႈပူင်ၵႂၢမ်းလွမ်ပွင်သိုၵ်းၸဝ်ႈၶုၼ်သႃႇ, ၸိုင်းလိၵ်ႈ 6. Pp. 8–10.

———. 1992. *Khun Sa: His Own Story and Thoughts.* N.p.: n.p.

Khur Hsen ၶိူဝ်းသႅၼ်. 1996. ပိူၼ်ႉၶိူဝ်းတႆးငလႈပိူၼ်းမိူင်းတႆး. Self-published.

———. 1999. ရ]့်လ]ဝါင်းဧလ့်သ္ဂိ၆့်ဖ္ဂိၵ်းတဲ့. Yangon: Mok Ko Soi Leng Printing Press.

Ko Htwe. 2009. "Blending In." *The Irrawaddy*, October.

Kramer, Tom. 2005. "Ethnic Conflict and Dilemmas for International Engagement." In *Trouble in the Triangle: Opium and Conflict in Burma*, edited by Martin Jelsma, Tom Kramer, and Pietje Vervest, 33–59. Chiang Mai: Silkworm.

Kumar, M. Satish. 2006. "The Census and Women's Work in Rangoon, 1872–1931." *Journal of Historical Geography* 32:377–97.

Kuroiwa, Yoko, and Maykel Verkuyten. 2008. "Narratives and the Constitution of a Common Identity: The Karen in Burma." *Identities* 15 (4): 391–412.

Leach, Edmund R. 1960. "The Frontiers of 'Burma.'" *Comparative Studies in Society and History* 3 (1): 49–68.

———. (1954) 2004. *Political Systems of Highland Burma: A Study of Kachin Social Structure.* Oxford: Berg.

Lee, Hock Guan. 2009. "Furnivall's Plural Society and Leach's Political Systems of Highland Burma." *SOJOURN: Journal of Social Issues in Southeast Asia* 24 (1): 32–46.

Lehman, F. K. 2003. "The Relevance of the Founder's Cult for Understanding the Political Systems of the Peoples of Northern Southeast Asia and Its Chinese Borderlands." In *Founders' Cults in Southeast Asia: Ancestors, Polity, and Identity*, edited by Nicola Tannenbaum and Cornelia Ann Kammerer, 15–39. New Haven, CT: Yale University Press.

Lieberman, Victor B. 1987. "Reinterpreting Burmese History." *Comparative Studies in Society and History* 29 (1): 162–94.

———. 2003. *Strange Parallels: Southeast Asia in Global Context, c. 800–1830.* Vol. 1, *Integration on the Mainland.* Cambridge: Cambridge University Press.

Ling, Trevor. 1979. *Buddhism, Imperialism and War: Burma and Thailand in Modern History.* London: George Allen & Unwin.

Lintner, Bertil. 1984. "The Shans and the Shan State of Burma." *Contemporary Southeast Asia* 5 (4): 403–50.

———. 1990. *The Rise and Fall of the Communist Party of Burma (CPB).* Ithaca, NY: Cornell Southeast Asia Program.

———. 1994. *Burma in Revolt: Opium and Insurgency since 1948.* Bangkok: White Lotus Press.

———. 2002. *Blood Brothers: Crime, Business and Politics in Asia.* Chiang Mai: Silkworm Press.

———. 2003. "Myanmar/Burma." In *Ethnicity in Asia*, edited by Colin Mackerras, 174–93. London: Routledge.

———. 2014. "Who Are the Wa?" *The Irrawaddy*, 2 June.

———. 2021. *The Wa of Myanmar and China's Quest for Global Dominance.* Chiang Mai: Silkworm Press.

Lowis, C. C. 1902. *Census of India, 1901. Volume XII. Burma. Part I. Report.* Rangoon: Office of the Superintendent of Government Printing, Burma.

Lung Kaet လုင်းဂိတ်,. 1987. ပိုခန်းတီးၵူးၶိုင်းၶိုင်း ပပ်.သွင်.

Lysa, Hong. 2003. "Does Popular History in Thailand Need Historians?" In สู่ วัฒนธรรมสมัยใหม่ คนไทยควรศึกษารัฐ vs ประชา-ชาติ ไทยคดีศึกษา 2 April–September, pp. 31–66.

Malkki, Liisa H. 2002. "News from Nowhere: Mass Displacement and Globalized 'Problems of Organization.'" *Ethnography* 3:351–62.

Man Poe Aye မန်ဖိုးအေး. 2016. ဗမာပြည်ကွန်မြူနစ်ပါတီခရီးကြမ်း ရန်ကုန် Journalist Publishing.

Massola, James. 2018. *The Great Cave Rescue: The Extraordinary Story of the Thai Boy Soccer Team Trapped in a Cave for 18 Days.* Sydney: Allen & Unwin.

Maule, Robert Bruce. 1993. "British Policy and Administration in the Federated Shan States, 1922–1942." PhD diss., University of Toronto.

Maung Pu So Chan မောင်ပုဆိုးကြမ်း. 2014. တိုင်းရင်းသားလူမျိုးများအဘိဓာန် ရန်ကုန် အလင်းသစ်စာပေ.

Mawn Sai Hsük မွန်ႏၸိုင်ꩬ်ꩬိုꩰ်ꩶ. 1992. ပေꩡ်ကမ်,မေꩡꩠမꩩ ယꩩ,ပေꩡꩡꩶ ꩳိုꩠ်လꩴ်ဝꩶ 9:63–66.

McCoy, Alfred W. 1991. *The Politics of Heroin: CIA Complicity in the Global Drug Trade.* Chicago: Lawrence Hill Books.

———. 1999a. "Lord of Drug Lords: One Life as a Lesson for US Drug Policy." *Crime, Law and Social Change* 30:301–31.

———. 1999b. "Requiem for a Drug Lord: State and Commodity in the Career of Khun Sa." In *States and Illegal Practices*, edited by Josiah McC. Heyman, 129–67. Oxford: Berg.

Ministry of Information. 1953. *Kuomintang Aggression against Burma.* Yangon: Ministry of Information.

Ministry of Tourism and Sports กระทรวงท่องเที่ยวและกีฬา. 2016. "สถิติด้านท่องเที่ยว ปี 2559." https://www.mots.go.th/more_news_new.php?cid=435.

Möng Kham Hkö Hsang မိုင်ꩴခမ်ꩶꩡိုꩴ်ꩬꩩင်. 2011. ပိုခန်းꩬိုꩴ်တီးမိုင်ꩴတꩶ. Taunggyi: Won Wan.

Mukhom Wongthes. 2003. *Intellectual Might and National Myth: A Forensic Investigation of the Ram Khamhaeng Controversy.* Bangkok: Matichon.

Munasinghe, Viranjini. 2009. "Foretelling Ethnicity in Trinidad: The Post-emancipation 'Labor Problem.'" In *Clio/Anthropos: Exploring the Boundaries between History and Anthropology*, edited by Andrew Willford and Eric Tagliacozzo, 139–86. Stanford: Stanford University Press.

Murakami, Tadayoshi. 2009. "Lik Long (Great Manuscripts) and Care: The Role of Lay Intellectuals in Shan Buddhism." *Senri Ethnological Studies* 74:79–96.

Murashima, Eiji. 2006. "The Commemorative Character of Thai Historiography: The 1942–1943 Thai Military Campaign in the Shan States." *Modern Asian Studies* 40 (4): 1053–96.

Mya Maung. 1994. "On the Road to Mandalay: A Case Study of the Sinonization of Upper Burma." *Asia Survey* 24 (5): 447–59.

Nang Lawn Tai ဆေင်းလွန်ႇတႆး. 1984. သိုပ်ႇပိုႆႇယိင်းတႆးၵွတ်းၵႃႇၶူင်ႇၵုႆး ထိုင်းလဳင် 1 January, 27–28.

Naw, Angelene. 2001. *Aung San and the Struggle for Burmese Independence*. Chiang Mai: Silkworm.

Ni Ni Myint. 1983. *Burma's Struggle against Imperialism*. Rangoon: Universities Press.

Nipatporn นิพัทธ์พร เพ็งแก้ว. 2006. ไทรบพม่า. Bangkok: Open Books.

Niti นิธิ เอียวศรีวงศ์. 2004. ชาติไทย เมืองไทย แบบเรียนและอนุสาวรีย์ ว่าด้วยวัฒนธรรม รัฐ และรูปการณ์จิตสำนึก กรุงเทพ มติชน.

Niti. 2004. "แปลงความทรงจำ ไต สร้างเป็น ไทย." In ความเป็นไทย/ความเป็นไท ศูนย์ มานุษยวิทยาสิรินธร กรุงเทพมหานคร pp. 2–54.

———. นิติ ภวัครพันธุ์. 2015. เรื่องเล่าเมืองไต: พลวัตของเมืองชายแดนไทย-พม่า เชียงใหม่ ศูนย์อาเซียนศึกษา มหาวิทยาลัยเชียงใหม่.

Niti Pawakapan. 2006. "'Once Were Burmese Shans': Reinventing Ethnic Identity in Northwestern Thailand." In *Centering the Margin: Agency and Narrative in Southeast Asian Borderlands*, edited by Alexander Horstmann and Reed L. Wadley, 27–52. New York: Berghahn Books.

Okamura, Jonathan Y. 1981. "Situational Ethnicity." *Ethnic and Racial Studies* 4 (4): 452–65.

Onanong Thippimol, Thanasak Saijampa, Dulyapak Preecharushh, Supalak Ganjanakhundee, and Akkharaphong Khamkhun อรอนงค์ ทิพย์พิมล ธนศักดิ์ สายจำปา คุลยภาค ปรีชารัชช สุภลักษณ์ กาญจนขุนดี อัครพงษ์ คำคูณ. 2011 (2554). เขตแดนสยาม ประเทศไทย–มาเลเซีย–พม่า–ลาว–กัมพูชา กรุงเทพ มูลนิธิโครงการชชตำราสังคมศาสตร์และ มนุษยศาสตร์.

Owen, Norman G., ed. 2005. *The Emergence of Modern Southeast Asia*. Honolulu: University of Hawai'i Press.

Pannida พรรณิดา ชันธพันธุ์. 2011. การคงอยู่ของประเพณีพิธีกรรมของชาวไทใหญ่ในตำบล เมืองนะ อำเภอเชียงดาว จังหวัดเชียงใหม่ in มนธิรา ราโท, ed. อัตลักษณ์ไทใหญ่ในกระแส ความเปลี่ยนแปลง กรุงเทพ โรงพิมพ์แห่งจุฬาลงกรณมหาวิทยาลัย pp. 113–58.

Paskorn Jumlongrach. 2018. "The Plight of the Stateless." *Bangkok Post*, 14 August.

Peabody, Norbert. 2001. "Cents, Sense, Census: Human Inventories in Late Precolonial and Early Colonial India." *Comparative Studies in Society and History* 43 (4): 819–50.

Peleggi, Maurizio. 2007. *Thailand: The Worldly Kingdom*. London: Reaktion Press.

Pinkaew Luangaramsri. 2003. "Ethnicity and the Politics of Ethnic Classification in Thailand." In *Ethnicity in Asia*, edited by Colin Mackerras, 157–73. London: Routledge.

Pornpimon พรพิมล ตรีโชติ. 2005. ไร้แผ่นดิน เส้นทางจากพม่าสู่ไทย กรุงเทพ สำนักงาน กองทุนสนับสนุนการวิจัย.

Pyanchayay Hnint Yinchehmu Tana ပြန်ကြားရေးနှင့်ယဉ်ကျေးမှုဌာန 1961. ရှမ်းပြည်နယ်-စာဆောင် ရန်ကုန် ပြန်ကြားရေးနှင့်ယဉ်ကျေးမှုဌာန.

Rajah, Ananda. 1998. "Ethnicity and Civil War in Burma: Where Is the Rationality?" In *Burma: Prospects for a Democratic Future*, edited by Robert I. Rotberg, 135–50. Washington, DC: Brookings Institute Press.

———. 2002. "A 'Nation of Intent' in Burma: Karen Ethno-nationalism, Nationalism and Narrations of Nation." *Pacific Review* 15 (4): 517–37.

Reid, Anthony. 1993. *Southeast Asia in the Age of Commerce, 1450–1680*. Vol. 2, *Expansion and Crisis*. New Haven, CT: Yale University Press.

Renard, Ronald D. 1980. "The Role of the Karens in Thai Society during the Early Bangkok Period, 1782–1873." *Contributions to Asian Studies* 15:15–28.

———. 1996. *The Burmese Connection: Illegal Drugs and the Making of the Golden Triangle*. Boulder, CO: Lynne Rienner.

———. 2000. "The Differential Integration of Hill People into the Thai State." In *Civility and Savagery*, edited by Andrew Turton, 63–83. Richmond: Curzon.

———. 2001. *Opium Reduction in Thailand, 1970–2000: A Thirty-Year Journey.* Chiang Mai: Silkworm.

Renu เรณู วิชาศิลป์. 1998. สังเขปภูมิหลังของชาวไทใหญ่ในรัฐฉาน in ฉลาดชาย รมิตานนท์ วิระดา สมสวัสดิ์ เรณู วิชาศิลป์, ed. ไท อ๋ะ:Tai เชียงใหม่: โรงพิมพ์มิ่งเมือง.

Reynolds, Craig J., ed. 1991. *National Identity and Its Defenders: Thailand, 1938–1989*. Chiang Mai: Silkworm.

———. 2003. "State versus Nation in Histories of Nation-Building with Special Reference to Thailand." In สู่วัฒนธรรมสมัยใหม่ คนไทยควรศึกษารัฐ vs ประชา-ชาติ ไทย ตถีศึกษา 2 April–September, pp. 1–30.

Risley, H. H. 1891. "The Study of Ethnology in India." *Journal of the Anthropological Institute of Great Britain and Ireland* 20:235–63.

Risley, Herbert. 1915. *The People of India*. 2nd ed. Edited by W. Crooke. Calcutta and Simla: Thacker, Spink.

Robinne, François. 2020. "Thinking through Heterogeneity: An Anthropological Look at Contemporary Myanmar." *Journal of Burma Studies* 23 (2): 285–322.

Rungwaree Chalermsripinyorat. 2004. "Monumental Warfare." *The Irrawaddy*, March.

Sadan, Mandy. 2013. *Being and Becoming Kachin: Histories beyond the State in the Borderworlds of Burma*. Oxford: Oxford University Press.

Sai Aung Tun. 2001. "Shan-Myanmar Relations as Found in the Hsipaw Chronicle." Paper presented at Texts and Contexts in Southeast Asia, Yangon, 12–13 December.

———. 2009. *History of the Shan State from Its Origins to 1962*. Chiang Mai: Silkworm.

Sai Htwe Maung. 2007. "History of Shan Churches in Burma (Myanmar)." Self-published.

Sai Kham Mong. 2004. *The History and Development of the Shan Scripts*. Chiang Mai: Silkworm.

Sai Kham Hti လၢႆးၶမ်းတီႇ,. 1991. သႅၵ်ဝတၢႆသႅၵ်ဝတ်ၶၢႆး လႅၶ်းတၢႆလႅၶ်းပုတ်း ႁိုင်းလႆဝ်း 8:110–15.

Saimong Mangrai. 1965. *The Shan States and the British Annexation*. Ithaca, NY: Southeast Asia Program, Cornell University.

Sao Fa Lang တဝ်းၽၵ်ႇလင်. 1991. လွင်းၽၢမ်ႇၵမ်းၑတာၚ ႁိုင်းလႆဝ်း 8:53.

Sao Hsai Möng တဝ်းသၢႆမိူင်း. 1962. ပၵ်ႇၵိၼ်းလိၵ်ႇတႆး Taunggyi.

Sao Khwan Möng တဝ်းၶႂၢၼ်မိူင်း. 1986. ပိုၶ်းမိူင်းတႆးၑလၑၵၢၼ်ပၢႆးမိူင်းတႆး ၶွမ်,မတီ,ၶိင်ပွင်ကွၵ်, ပၵ်ႇလိၵ်ႇတႆး.

Sao Sanda. 2008. *The Moon Princess: Memories of the Shan States*. Bangkok: River Books.

Scott, James. 1985. *Weapons of the Weak: Everyday Forms of Peasant Resistance*. New Haven, CT: Yale University Press.

———. 2009. *The Art of Not Being Governed: An Anarchist History of Upland Southeast Asia*. New Haven, CT: Yale University Press.

Seksan Prasertkul. 1989. "The Transformation of the Thai State and Economic Change (1855–1945)." PhD diss., Cornell University.

Shalardchai Ramitanondh. 1998. "Experience and Reflections from Coordinating a Cross Country Comparative Research on the Cultures and Societies of Tai-Speaking Groups in Northern Thailand, Shan State of Burma and Assam State of India." In ฉลาดชาย รมิตานนท์ วิระดา สมสวัสดิ์ เรณู วิชาศิลป์, ed. ไท ตัะ Tai เชียงใหม่: โรงพิมพ์มิ่งเมือง 1–21.

SHAN. 2009. "Wa Votes Count in 2010." *Shan Herald Agency for News*, 22 July.

———. 2012. "Songwriter: 'Panglong Agreement' Inspired by Cartoon." *Shan Herald Agency for News*, 28 November.

Shanklin, Eugenia. 1998. "The Profession of the Color Blind: Sociocultural Anthropology and Racism in the 21st Century." *American Anthropologist* 100 (3): 669–79.

The Shan States Manual: Corrected Up to the 31st January 1932. 1933. Rangoon: Superintendent Government Printing and Stationery.

Shukla, Kavita. 2004. "The Shan in Thailand: A Case of Protection and Assistance Failure." Refugees International. Accessed 28 November 2007. http://www.refu geesinternational.org.

Silverstein, Josef. 1977. *Burma: Military Rule and the Politics of Stagnation*. Ithaca, NY: Cornell University Press.

Simms, Sao Sanda. 2017. *Great Lords of the Sky: Burma's Shan Aristocracy*. Xining, China: Asian Highlands Perspectives.

Siraporn Nathalang. 2012. "Ethnic Identity and Buddhist Tradition: An Analysis on Ethnic Shan Festivals in Thailand." In *Buddhism without Borders: Proceedings of the International Conference on Globalized Buddhism*, edited by Dasho Karma Ura and Dendup Chophel, 148–59. Thimphu, Bhutan: Centre for Bhutan Studies.

Sjöberg, Katarina. 1993. *The Return of the Ainu: Cultural Mobilisation and the Practice of Ethnicity in Japan*. London: Routledge.

Skinner, G. William. 1957. *Chinese Society in Thailand: An Analytical History.* Ithaca, NY: Cornell University Press.

Smith, Charles B., Jr. 1984. *The Burmese Communist Party in the 1980s.* Singapore: Institute of Southeast Asian Studies (ISEAS).

Smith, Martin. 1994. *Ethnic Groups in Burma: Development, Democracy and Human Rights.* London: ASI.

———. 1999. *Burma: Insurgency and the Politics of Ethnicity.* Bangkok: White Lotus.

Sompong สมพงศ์ วิทยศักดิ์พันธุ์. 1998. "ถิ่นฐานของกลุ่มชาติพันธุ์ไทในผืนแผ่นดินใหญ่เอเชี-ยตะวันออกเฉียงใต้." In ฉลาดชาย รมิตานนท์ วิระดา สมสวัสดิ์ เรณู วิชาศิลป์, ed. ไท ๗: Tai เชียงใหม่: โรงพิมพ์มิ่งเมือง.

———. 2001. ประวัติศาสตร์ไทใหญ่ กรุงเทพ โรงพิมพ์แห่งจุฬาลงกรณมหาวิทยาลัย.

South, Ashley, and Maria Katsabanis. 2007. *Displacement and Dispossession: Forced Migration and Land Rights in Burma.* Geneva: Centre on Housing Rights and Evictions.

Spiro, Melford E. 1966. "Buddhism and Economic Action in Burma." *American Anthropologist* 68 (5): 1163–73.

———. 1992. *Anthropological Other or Burmese Brother? Studies in Cultural Analysis.* New Brunswick, NJ: Transaction.

Spring News. 2016. "สมเด็จพระนเรศวรมหาราช" กับความศรัทธาของชาวไทใหญ่ในรัฐฉาน. Accessed 13 January 2020. https://www.youtube.com/watch?v=ngMKwjotOCc.

Srivatsan, R. 2005. "Native Noses and Nationalist Zoos: Debates in Colonial and Early Nationalist Anthropology of Castes and Tribes." *Economic and Political Weekly* 40 (19): 1986–98.

Steinberg, David I. 2001. *Burma: The State of Myanmar.* Washington, DC: Georgetown University Press.

Steinberg, Michael K. 2000. "Generals, Guerrillas, Drugs and Third World War-Making." *Geographical Review* 90 (2): 260–67.

Streckfuss, David. 1993. "The Mixed Colonial Legacy in Siam: Origins of Thai Racialist Thought, 1890–1910." In *Autonomous Histories, Particular Truths: Essays in Honor of John R. W. Smail,* edited by Laurie Sears, 123–53. Madison: Center for Southeast Asian Studies, University of Wisconsin.

Stengs, Irene. 2012. "Sacred Singularities: Crafting Royal Images in Present-Day Thailand." *Journal of Modern Craft* 5 (1): 51–68.

Sunait Chutintaranond. 1992. "The Image of the Burmese Enemy in Thai Perceptions and Historical Writings." *Journal of the Siam Society* 80 (1): 89–103.

Takatani, Michio. 2007. "Who Are the Shan? An Ethnological Perspective." In *Exploring Ethnic Diversity in Burma,* edited by Mikael Gravers, 178–99. Malaysia: NIAS Press.

Tambiah, Stanley J. 1976. *World Conqueror and World Renouncer: A Study of Buddhism and Polity in Thailand against a Historical Background.* Cambridge: Cambridge University Press.

———. 2002. *Edmund Leach: An Anthropological Life.* Cambridge: Cambridge University Press.

Ta Mö Lek တၢမိူဝ်းလိၵ်. 1998. မႂ်ႇၼိူဝ်ႈလၢတ်ႈ ၸိူင်းလိၵ်း 3:4–6.

Tannenbaum, Nicola. 1987. "Tattoos: Invulnerability and Power in Shan Cosmology." *American Ethnologist* 14 (4): 693–711.

———. 1995. *Who Can Compete against the World? Power-Protection and Buddhism in Shan Worldview.* Ann Arbor, MI: Association for Asian Studies.

———. 2002. "Monuments and Memory." In *Cultural Crisis and Social Memory*, edited by Shigeharu Tanabe and Charles Keyes, 137–53. Honolulu: University of Hawai'i Press.

———. 2009. "The Changing Nature of Shan Political Ritual and Identity in Maehongson, Northwestern Thailand." *Contemporary Buddhism* 10 (1): 171–84.

Tao Pai Söng ထဝ်ႈပႂ်းၸိူင်း. 2000. တပ်ႉသိုၵ်းလိူင်ႈတႆးလုၵ်ႉတီႈလွႆမႃး ၽိူၼ်ၶၢဝ်ႇတပ်ႉသိုၵ်းလိူ-င်ႈတႆး 2 (2): 1–3.

Tapp, Nicholas. 2000. "A New State in Tai Regional Studies: The Challenge of Local Histories." In *Civility and Savagery: Social Identity in Tai States*, edited by Andrew Turton, 351–60. Richmond: Curzon.

TBBC. 2005. *Thailand Burma Border Consortium Programme Report: January to June 2005.*

Terwiel, Barend Jan. 1978. "The Origin of the Tai Peoples Reconsidered." *Oriens extremus* 25 (2): 239–58.

———. 2003. *Shan Manuscripts Part 1.* Stuttgart: Franz Steiner.

Tetkatho Khin Maung Zaw တက္ကသိုလ်ခင်မောင်ဇော်. 2012. မြန်မာရုပ်ရှင်ရေစီးကြောင်းနှင့် မြန်မာ့ဂန္ထဝင်ရုပ်ရှင် 20၊ ရန်ကုန် နေမျိုးစာပေ.

Thak Chaloemtiarana. 2007. *Thailand: The Politics of Despotic Paternalism.* Ithaca, NY: Cornell University Press.

Thaung We U သောင်းဝေဦး. 2009. ကျွန်တော်နှင့်ဘိန်းစစ်ဆင်ရေးများ ရန်ကုန် မြရတနာစာပေ.

Thirapap ธีรภาพ โลหิตกุล. 1995. คนไทในอษาคเนย์ กรุงเทพ: บริษัท สำนักพิมพ์ประพันธ์สาส์น จำกัด.

Thitiwut Boonyawongwiwat. 2018. *The Ethno-Narcotic Politics of the Shan People: Fighting with Drugs, Fighting for the Nation on the Thai-Burmese Border.* Lanham, MD: Lexington.

Thongchai Winichakul. 1994. *Siam Mapped: A History of the Geo-body of a Nation.* Chiang Mai: Silkworm.

———. 2000. "The Quest for *Siwilai*: A Geographical Discourse of Civilizational Thinking in the Late Nineteenth and Early Twentieth-Century Siam." *Journal of Asian Studies* 59 (3): 528–49.

Toyota, Mika. 2005. "Subjects of the Nation without Citizenship: The Case of 'Hill Tribes' in Thailand." In *Multiculturalism in Asia*, edited by Will Kymlicka and Baogan He, 109–35. Oxford: Oxford University Press.

TRC (Thailand Revolutionary Council) ၵွင်ႇသီႇလိူင်ႈတႆးလုၵ်ႉၽိူၼ်ႉ. 1990a. ပိူၼ်းတွဝ်ၵိပ်ႈ လၼႈၶဵူႈပွင်ႁၢမ်းလဝ်ႈၶုၼ်သႂ်ႇ TRC (Thailand Revolutionary Council) ၵွင်ႇသီႇလိူင်ႈ တႆးလုၵ်ႉၽိူၼ်ႉ.

———. 1990b. ပုံဆင်းတူ၀ဲကိုပ်းၔလ့ၔၐၢးၮုၒ်ၐၢမ်ၔလၵ်ၐွဆ်ႏၵိုၵ်ႏ TRC (Thailand Revolutionary Council) ၐၵ်ႏၔ၀ီ,ၵိုၵ်ႏၐံ်ႏလုၵ်ၰ်ပုံ၆ဆ်ၰ်ၐ.

Turner, Alicia. 2014. *Saving Buddhism: The Impermanence of Religion in Colonial Burma.* Honolulu: University of Hawaiʻi Press.

U Pe Kin. 1994. *Pinlon: An Inside Story.* Yangon: New Light of Myanmar Press.

United Nations High Commission on Refugees (UNHCR). 2020. "UNHCR ประเทศไทย." Accessed 3 January 2020. http://unhcr.or.th.

United States Congress, House Committee on International Relations. 1975. *Proposal to Control Opium from the Golden Triangle and Terminate the Shan Opium Trade: Hearings before the Subcommittee on Future Foreign Policy Research and Development of the Committee on International Relations, House of Representatives, Ninety-Fourth Congress, First Session, April 22 and 23, 1975.* Washington, DC: US Government Printing Office.

United States House of Representatives. 1978. *Study Mission on International Controls of Narcotics Trafficking and Production, January 2–22, 1978.* Washington, DC: US Government Printing Office.

U Ohn Pe ဦးၔအုၵ်ႏၔ၀. 1984. ပၚ်လုၵ်ံ၀စ်ၵ်တၐ်ႏ ရၵ်ၵ်ုၵ်ၰ် ၰပၰ်ႏၸိုႏ.

Van Schendel, Willem. 2002. "Geographies of Knowing, Geographies of Ignorance: Jumping Scale in Southeast Asia." *Environment and Planning* 20:647–68.

Walker, Andrew, ed. 2009. *Tai Lands and Thailand: Community and State in Southeast Asia.* Singapore: NUS Press.

Wandi วันดี สันติวุฒเมธี. 2002. กระบวนการสร้างอัตลักษณ์ทางชาติพันธุ์ของชาวไทใหญ่ ชายแดนไทย-พม่า กรณีศึกษา: หมู่บ้านเปียงหลวง อำเภอเวียงแหง จังหวัดเชียงใหม่ วิทยานิพนธ์ปริญญาโทคณะสังคมวิทยาและมานุษยวิทยา มหาวิทยาลัยธรรมศาสตร์.

Willford, Andrew. 2006. *Cage of Freedom: Tamil Identity and the Ethnic Fetish in Malaysia.* Ann Arbor: University of Michigan Press.

Winai Pongsripian. 1983. "Traditional Thai Historiography and Its Nineteenth-Century Decline." PhD diss., University of Bristol.

Wipan วิพันธุ์ ชมะโชติ. 2008. แผ่นดินที่เสียไปประวัติศาสตร์จารึกด้วยน้ำตาความสูญเสียที่คนทั้งชาติต้องขมขื่น กรุงเทพ อนิเมทกรุ๊ป.

Witun วิทูรย์ ลายอู่. 2005. "ความฝันที่ถูกกลืน" สาละวินโพสต์, 27 December, pp. 32–33.

Wolters, O. W. 1999. *History, Culture and Region in Southeast Asian Perspectives.* Ithaca, NY: Southeast Asia Program, Cornell University.

———. 2008. *Early Southeast Asia, Selected Essays.* Edited by Craig J. Reynolds. Ithaca, NY: Southeast Asia Program, Cornell University.

Wong, Ka Fai. 2000. "Visions of a Nation: Public Monuments in Twentieth-Century Thailand." MA thesis, Chulalongkorn University.

Wyatt, David K. 1984. *Thailand: A Short History.* New Haven, CT: Yale University Press.

———. 2001. "Relics, Oaths and Politics in Thirteenth-Century Siam." *Journal of Southeast Asian Studies* 32 (1): 3–66.

Yasuda, Sachiko. 2008. "Shan on the Move: Negotiating Identities through Spatial Practices among Shan Cross-Border Migrants in Northern Thailand." MA thesis, Chiang Mai University.

Yawnghwe, Chao Tzang. 1987. *The Shan of Burma: Memoirs of a Shan Exile.* Singapore: Institute of Southeast Asian Studies.

Yawnghwe, Samara. 2013. *Maintaining the Union of Burma, 1946–1962: The Role of the Ethnic Nationalities in a Shan Perspective.* Bangkok: Chulalongkorn University Press.

Yellen, Jeremy. 2020. *The Greater East Asia Co-Prosperity Sphere: When Total Empire Met Total War.* Ithaca, NY: Cornell University Press.

Yos ยศ สันตสมบัติ. 2008 (2551). อำนาจ พื้นที่ และอัตลักษณ์ทางชาติพันธุ์ การเมืองวัฒนธรรม ของรัฐชาติในสังคมไทย กรุงเทพ ศูนย์มานุษยวิทยาสิรินธร.

Yos Santasombat. 2001. *Lak Chang: A Reconstruction of Tai Identity in Daikong.* Canberra: Pandanus Books.

Young, Edward M. 1995. *Aerial Nationalism: A History of Aviation in Thailand.* Washington, DC: Smithsonian Institution Press.

Zeus, Barbara, ed. 2008. *Identities in Exile: De- and Reterritorialising Ethnic Identity and the Case of Burmese Forced Migrants in Thailand.* Südostasien Working Papers 34. Berlin: Humboldt University.

INDEX

Page numbers in italics indicate illustrations.

AIDS, 159, 222, 223

Akha, 9, 12, 37, 179, 180

ancient Shanland: armed activities and, 8, 10, 16, 26, 27; Buddhism and, 19, 39, 256n6; China and, 3; coral reef as metaphor for uplands, 33, 35, 41; cosmopolitanism, 34, 39; cultural similarities/differences, 37, 39–40; culture and, 19, 39–40, 256n6, 257n7; described, 28, 32, 33–34, 60; identity, Shan/Tai, 19, 24; Kao Hai Haw (nine kingdoms), 5, 7, 8, 60; "lost territories" in Thailand, 47–48, 49, 54, 257n9; Mandala state described, 36, 256n4; Möng Mao Long/Great Mao Kingdom, 3–5, *4*, 5, 8, 14, 255n4; Myanmar/ Burma and, 4, 135; non-Tai groups and, 37; Original United Tai States (Saharat Tai Duem), 55, 66, 197; politics, 33–36, 37–38, 60, 136, 256nn3–4; precolonial kingdoms, 38, 257n7; repossession (repo) project and, 31, 135; schools/school

curriculum, 85; state-building and, 38–40, 256nn6–7; Tai-ness, 8, 38, 40, 66. *See also* Shan State(s); Shan/ Tai *sao hpa*; Suerkhan Fa

Anderson, Benedict, 24, 86, 257n10

anti-communism: MTA and, 130; SURA and, 65, 80, 83–84; Thailand/ Siam, 66, 68, 82, 84, 127, 259*chap*4n3

Anti-Fascist People's Freedom League (AFPFL), 56, 57, 65, 74

ants and bees metaphor, 195, 260n7

armed activities, and ancient Shanland, 8, 10, 16, 26, 27

armed activities, and Cold War geopolitics: black market economy, 77–78; CPB and, 67, 73; described, 77, 119; KMT, 68–69, 77, 119, 120–21; Myanmar/Burma and, 72, 73; nationalism, Shan/Tai, 61, 62–63, 64, 70–71, 74, 76–77, 79. See also *specific armed forces*

armed activities, and Myanmar/ Burma: BIA, 53, 56; Cold War

NEW PERSPECTIVES IN SOUTHEAST ASIAN STUDIES

*The Burma Delta: Economic Development and
Social Change on an Asian Rice Frontier, 1852–1941*
MICHAEL ADAS

*Rise of the Brao: Ethnic Minorities in
Northeastern Cambodia during Vietnamese Occupation*
IAN G. BAIRD

*Of Beggars and Buddhas:
The Politics of Humor in the "Vessantara Jataka" in Thailand*
KATHERINE A. BOWIE

Voices from the Plain of Jars: Life under an Air War, second edition
Edited by FRED BRANFMAN with essays and drawings
by LAOTIAN VILLAGERS

A Reckoning: Philippine Trials of Japanese War Criminals
SHARON W. CHAMBERLAIN

From Rebellion to Riots: Collective Violence on Indonesian Borneo
JAMIE S. DAVIDSON

Feeding Manila in Peace and War, 1850–1945
DANIEL F. DOEPPERS

*Repossessing Shanland: Myanmar, Thailand,
and a Nation-State Deferred*
JANE M. FERGUSON

*The Floracrats: State-Sponsored Science and the
Failure of the Enlightenment in Indonesia*
ANDREW GOSS

In Plain Sight: Impunity and Human Rights in Thailand
TYRELL HABERKORN

Revolution Interrupted: Farmers, Students, Law, and
Violence in Northern Thailand
TYRELL HABERKORN

Philippine Sanctuary: A Holocaust Odyssey
BONNIE M. HARRIS

Amazons of the Huk Rebellion: Gender, Sex, and
Revolution in the Philippines
VINA A. LANZONA

Dreams of the Hmong Kingdom:
The Quest for Legitimation in French Indochina, 1850–1960
MAI NA M. LEE

The Government of Mistrust: Illegibility and
Bureaucratic Power in Socialist Vietnam
KEN MACLEAN

An Anarchy of Families: State and Family in the Philippines
Edited by ALFRED W. MCCOY

Policing America's Empire: The United States, the Philippines,
and the Rise of the Surveillance State
ALFRED W. MCCOY

Vietnam's Strategic Thinking during the Third Indochina War
KOSAL PATH

The Hispanization of the Philippines:
Spanish Aims and Filipino Responses, 1565–1700
JOHN LEDDY PHELAN

Pretext for Mass Murder: The September 30th Movement and
Suharto's Coup d'État in Indonesia
JOHN ROOSA

www.ingramcontent.com/pod-product-compliance
Lightning Source LLC
Chambersburg PA
CBHW071731270326
41928CB00013B/2639